The Firebrand

THE FIREBRAND

*J. V. Carew.
from F. G. C.
Xmas
1903*

THE FIREBRAND

BY

S. R. CROCKETT

London
MACMILLAN AND CO., Limited
NEW YORK: THE MACMILLAN COMPANY
1901

All rights reserved

PRINTED BY
WILLIAM CLOWES AND SONS, LIMITED,
LONDON AND BECCLES.

CONTENTS

THE FIREBRAND

CHAPTER I

THE MAKING OF AN OUTLAW

RAMON GARCIA, called El Sarria, lay crouched like a wild beast. And he was a wild beast. Yet he smiled as he blinked into the midnoon heat, under his shaggy brows, from his den beneath the great rock of limestone that shadowed him.

El Sarria was hunted, and there was on his hands the blood of a man—to be more particular, on his left hand. For El Sarria had smitten hard and eager, so soon as he had seen Rafael de Flores—Rafael, the pretty boy, the cousin of his young wife, between whom and her relative there was at least cousinly affection. So the neighbours said, all but Manuela, the priest's housekeeper.

So Ramon smote and wiped his Manchegan knife on his vest, in the place under the flap at the left side where he had often wiped it before. He used the same gesture as when he killed a sheep.

In his cave of limestone Ramon was going over the scene in his own mind. That is why he licked his lips slowly and smiled. A tiger does that when after a full meal he moves the loose skin over his

E   B

neck twitchy-ways and yawns with over-fed content.
And Ramon, even though hunted, did the same.

When he married little Dolóres, Ramon Garcia
had not dreamed that so many things would happen.
He was a rich man as men go ; had his house, his
garden, his vines, a quintaine of olive-trees, was
accounted quite a match by old Manuela, the village
go-between, the priest's housekeeper, in whose hands
were the hearts of many maids.

These things he, Don Ramon Garcia, had
possessed (he was called Don then) and now—he
had his knife and the long, well-balanced gun which
was placed across the rests in the dryest part of the
cavern.

*   *   *   *   *

He remembered the day well. He had been
from home, down by Porta in the Cerdagne, to buy
cattle, and returning home more swiftly than he had
expected, his cattle following after in the herdsman's
care, the thought of pretty Dolóres making his
horse's feet go quicker, a song upon his lips, he had
approached the village of Sarria de la Plana, and the
home that was his own—and hers.

A swift-falling Spanish twilight it was, he
remembered, the sky, broadly banded of orange and
rose, was seen behind the highly piled houses.
From the whiteness of the long frontage, dots and
flecks flashed out. Black oblongs of glassless
window-space splashed the white. Here and there
a hint of vivid colour flung itself out almost defiantly
—a woman's red petticoat drying on a cord, the
green slats of a well-to-do window-blind. There
came to the ears of Ramon Garcia the click of
castanets from the semi-dark of wide-arched doors,
and the soft tink-a-tank of lightly thrummed guitars.

He saw a lover or two " eating iron," his hands clasping the bars behind which was the listening ear of his mistress.

And throughout this village were peace and well-accustomed pleasance. Ramon smiled. It was his home.

But not as he smiled up among the rocks of the Montblanch on the borderlands betwixt Aragon and Catalunia.

He smiled well-pleased and minded him upon the nights not so long gone by, when he too had " eaten iron," and clung a-tip-toe to the window-bars of little Dolóres, who lent him such a shy attention, scuttling off like a mouse at the least stirring within the house where all her kinsfolk slept.

There was none like her, his little Dolóres ! God had given her to a rough old fellow like him, one who had endured the trampling of the threshing floor as the car oxen drave round.

Little Dolóres, how all the men had been wild to have her, but she had loved none but Ramon Garcia alone ! So said Manuela Durio, the go-between, the priest's housekeeper, and if any did, she knew. Indeed, there was little told at confession that she did not know. Ramon smiled again, a wicked, knowing smile. For if Manuela owned the legitimate fifty years which qualified her for a place in the Presbytery of Sarria de la Plana, eyes and lips belied her official age. Anyway, she kept the priest's conscience—and—what was more important, she swore that little Dolóres loved Ramon Garcia and Ramon Garcia alone.

" Caballero ! Don Ramon ! "

He started. He had been thinking of the woman at that very moment, and there was her voice calling him. He turned about. The broad rose-glow had deepened to the smoky ruby of a Spanish gloaming, as it lingered along the western hill-tops. These last shone, in spite of the glowing darkness, with a limpid and translucent turquoise like that of the distant landscape in a Siennese picture.

"Don Ramon! wait—I would speak with you!"

It was indeed the priest's Manuela who called him, and though his heart hasted forward to Dolóres, and overleaped boundaries as a dog leaps a wall, still he could not refuse Manuela. Had she not brought them together at the first?

"Ah, Manuela, you are kind—there is good news up at the house, is there not? No ill has befallen the little one?"

"What has brought you home so soon?" cried the woman, a touch of impatient eagerness in her tones. "You will frighten Dolóres if you blunder it upon her all unshaven and travel-stained like that. Have you no more sense, when you know—— ?"

"Know what? I know nothing!" Ramon slurred his speech in his eagerness. "What is there to know?"

Manuela laughed—a little strained sound, as if she had been recovering a shaken equanimity, and was not yet sure of her ground.

"You, so long married—five, six months, is it not so—and yet not to know! But a fool is always a fool, Don Ramon, even if he owns a vineyard and a charming young wife ten times too good for him!"

"Truth of God!" gasped Ramon, with his favourite oath, "but I did not know. I am the father of all donkeys. But what am I to do, tell me, Manuela? I will obey you!"

The woman's countenance suddenly cleared.

"No, Don Ramon, we will not call the promised one—the blessed one, a donkey. A father! Yes, Don Ramon, but no father of *borricos*. No, no! There will not be so brave a babe from Navarra to Catalunia as yours and Lola's. But we must go quietly, very quietly. He walks far who begins slowly. He who treads upon eggs does not dance the *bolero*. You will bide here and talk to the holy Father, and I myself will go to the house of Ramon of the Soft Heart and the Lumbering Hoofs, and warn the little one warily. For I know her—yes, Manuela knows her. I am a widow and have borne children—ay, borne them also to the grave, and who, if not I, should know the hearts of young wives that are not yet mothers!"

She patted his arm softly as she spoke, and the great rough-husked heart of Ramon of Sarria, the Aragonese peasant, glowed softly within him. He looked down into Manuela's black eyes that hid emotion as a stone is hidden at the bottom of a mountain tarn. Manuela smiled with thin flexible lips, her easy subtle smile. She saw her way now, and to do her justice she always did her best to earn her wages.

Lovers would be lovers, so she argued, God had made it so. Who was she, Manuela, the housekeeper of Padre Mateo of Sarria, to interfere for the prevention of the designs of Providence? And cousins too—the young cavalier so gallant, so handsome—and—so generous with his money. Had he not even kissed Manuela herself one night when he came coaxing her to contrive something? *Who* could resist him after that? And what was a hand thrust through the *rejas*? What a kiss if

the bars of the grille happened to be broken. A
glass that is drunk from, being washed, is clean
as before. And when Ramon Garcia, that great
Aragonese oaf, kissed little Dolóres, what knew he
of pretty Don Rafael de Flores, the *alcalde's* son?
They had been lovers since childhood, and there was
no harm. 'Twas pity surely, to part them before
the time. Rafael was to marry the rich Donna
Felesia, the daughter of the vine-grower of Montblanch, who farmed the revenues of the great abbey.
He could not marry pretty little Dolóres! It was
a pity—yes, but—she had a feeling heart, this
Manuela, the priest's housekeeper, and the trade
had been a paying one since the beginning of the
world.

"Padre—Padre Mateo!" she cried, raising her
voice to the pitch calculated by long experience
to reach the father in his study. "Come down
quickly. Here is Don Ramon to speak with
your reverence!"

"Don Ramon—what Don Ramon?" growled a
voice from the stair-head, a rich baritone organ,
unguented with daily dole of oil and wine, not
to speak of well-buttered trout in a lordly dish,
and with rappee coloured red with the umber of
Carthagena to give timbre and richness thereto. It
was the voice of Don Mateo Balin, most pious and
sacerdotal vicar of Christ in the township of Sarria.

"Don Ramon Garcia, most reverend father!"
said Manuela, somewhat impatiently. "If you will
tap your snuff-box a little less often, you will be
all the sooner able to hear what he has to say to
you!"

"*Don* Ramon, indeed!—here's advancement,"
grumbled the priest, good-humouredly descending

the staircase one step at a time. To do this he held
his body a little sideways and let himself down as if
uncertain of the strength of the Presbytery stairs,
which were of stone of Martorel, solid as the altar
steps of St. Peter's.

"Good, good!" he thought to himself, "Manuela
wants something of this chuckle-head that she goes
Don-ing him, and, I wager, battening him with com-
pliments as greasy as an old wife's cookery the first
day after Lent. 'Tis only eggs in the pan that are
buttered, and I wonder why she has been buttering
this oaf." Then he spoke aloud. "Ah, Ramon,
back already! We thought you had been buying
beeves in the Cerdagne. I suppose the little Dolóres
dragged you back. Ho, ho, you young married men !
Your hearts make fools of your feet. 'Tis only
celibacy, that most sacred and wise institution of
Holy Mother Church, that can preserve man his
liberty—certainly, Manuela, I will put away my
snuff-box, I was not aware that it was in my hand !
And I will *not* drop any more on my new soutane,
which indeed, as you say, I had no business to be
wearing on an ordinary day."

While Don Mateo thus spoke, and, talking all
the time, moved lightly for so gross a man to and
fro on his verandah, Manuela with a quick hitch of
her muffling mantilla about the lower part of her
face, took her way swiftly up the village street.

"This way, Ramon—this way ! A plague take
those spider-legged chairs. They are all set crosswise
in the way of an honest man's feet. Manuela keeps
all so precise, nothing is ever left where it would be
most convenient. Not that she is not the best of
souls, our good Manuela and a pearl of price—a very
Martha in the house, a woman altogether above

rubies! Is she quite gone? Sit you down then, Ramon, here is the wine-skin, under the seat to the left, and tell me of your journey, speaking at ease as man to man. This is no confessional, which reminds me, sirrah, that you have not come to your duty since Easter. Ah, again the married man! 'He minds the things of his wife,' saith the holy apostle, in my opinion very justly."

Ramon had seated himself on a chair at one corner of the priest's verandah—a deep screen of leaves was over them. The mosquitoes and gnats danced and lit, hummed and bit, but neither the priest nor yet Ramon minded them in the least. They were men of Sarria, bred of the reed-fenced villages of the Aragonese border, blooded by the grey-backed, white-bellied mosquitoes which took such sore toll alike of the stranger within the wall, and through the skin of the Proselyte of the Gate.

But as the priest boomed forth his good-humoured gossip in a voice monotonous and soothing as the *coo-rooing* of a rock pigeon, suddenly there rose out of the tangle of roses and vine leaves behind him, an evil thing against which Don Ramon's birthright gave him no immunity. It stung and fled.

"Go home, fool!" hissed a voice in his ear, as he sat silent and spellbound in the dusk, "go home, shamed one. Your wife is with her lover, and Manuela has gone to warn them!"

The good priest hummed on, plaiting and re-plaiting his fingers and pursing his lips.

"As I was saying, 'tis no use marrying a woman without money. That is the *olla* without bacon. But for pleasure to himself, neither should a man marry without love. 'Tis a lying proverb which

sayeth that all women are alike in the dark. A fair
maid is surely worth a farthing candle to kiss her by.
Not that I know aught about the matter, being a
clerk and a man of years and bodily substance. But
a wise man learns many things in spite of himself.
What is the use of being a priest and not knowing?
But believe me, if money be the bacon and beef,
love is the seasoning of the dish, the *pimientos* and
Ronda pippins of a wise man's *olla!*"

Through this sacerdotal meditation the hissing
whisper lifted itself again. Ramon had not moved.
His great hand lay along the stone balustrade. A
mosquito was gorging himself at a vein upon the
hairy wrist.

"There is a broken bar on the lower window,
Ramon the fool! They are kissing each other
thereat and calling sweet names—these two, the
cousin whom she loves—Rafael, the pretty boy,
and little Dolóres whom you have made your
wife——"

"God's blood, for this I will have your life!"
cried Ramon so suddenly that the worthy priest
tumbled backward before he had even time to cross
himself. And Ramon was over the parapet with his
long knife bare in his hand. It had gone ill with
the traitor if Ramon Garcia had caught him then.

But even as he had arisen, exhaled from the
undergrowth like an evil breath, so he vanished
into the night, blown away by Ramon's rush over
the edge of the balcony like a fly escaping before a
man's hand.

"I will follow the liar to the world's end!" said
Ramon between his teeth, furiously, and he threshed
through the tangle as an elephant charges through
young jungle.

But even as he went the words of the viper fermented in his brain till he went mad.

"There *is* a broken bar—what more likely! The house is old—my father's father's. There was a tale of my grandfather's sister—avenged truly, but still a tale told in whispers in the twilight. God's truth, could it be even thus with Dolóres, little Dolóres, whom I have held next in honour and purity to Mary the mother of God?"

So he meditated, dashing this way and that to find his enemy.

"Ah, fool! Three times fool to trust a woman! How true the proverb, 'Who sees his wife crane her neck through the jalousies, had better twist it and be done!'"

He would go! Yes, he would know. If this thing were false (as he prayed God), he would kneel and kiss her little white feet. They were pink—yes, pink on the instep as the heart of a sea-shell. And he, Ramon, would set the arched instep on his neck and bid her crush him for a faithless unbelieving hound to suspect his own—his purest—his only!

But, that cousin, Rafael de Flores—ah, the rich youth. He remembered how once upon a time when he was a young man going to market driving his father's oxen, he had seen Rafael rushing about the orchard playing with Dolóres. They had been together thus for years, more like brother and sister than cousins.

Was it not likely? How could it be otherwise? He knew it all now. His eyes were opened. Even the devil can speak truth sometimes. He knew a way, a quicker road than Manuela dreamed of—up the edge of the ravine, across by the pine tree which had fallen in the spring rains. He would go and

take them together in their infamy. That would be
his home-coming.

*   *   *   *   *

" *You dog of dogs !* "

In the darkness of the night Ramon saw a
window from whose grille, bent outward at the
bottom like so many hoops, one had been slipped
cunningly aside.

" Chica, dearest—my beloved ! "

The face of the speaker was within, his body
without.

Up rose behind him the great bulk of Ramon
Garcia, henceforward to be El Sarria, the outlaw.

The Albacete dagger was driven deep between
the shoulder-blades. The young lithe body drew
itself together convulsively as a clasp knife opens
and shuts again. There was a spurt of something
hot on Ramon's hand that ran slowly down his
sleeve, growing colder as it went. A shriek came
from within the *rejas* of bowed iron.

*   *   *   *   *

And after this fashion Ramon Garcia, the vine-
dresser, the man of means, became El Sarria, the
man without a home, without friends, an outlaw of
the hills.

CHAPTER II

THE MAN WITHOUT A FRIEND

YET on the side of Rafael and little Dolóres Garcia there was something to be said. Ramon, had he known all, need not have become "El Sarria," nor yet need young de Flores, the alcalde's son, have been carried home to the tall house with the court-yard and the one fig-tree, a stab under his right shoulder-blade, driven through from side to side of his white girlish body.

It was true enough that he went to the house of Ramon to "eat iron," to "pluck the turkey," to "hold the wall." But 'twas not Dolóres, the wife of Ramon, who knew of it, but pretty Andalucian Concha, the handmaiden and companion Ramon had given his wife when they were first married. Concha was niece to the priest's Manuela, a slim sloe-eyed witty thing, light of heart and foot as a goose feather that blows over a common on a northerly breeze. She had had more sweethearts than she could count on the fingers of both hands, this pleasantly accom-modative maiden, and there was little of the teaching of the happy guileful province in which Concha needed instruction, when for health and change of scene she came to the house of Ramon and Dolóres Garcia in the upland village of Sarria.

These were the two fairest women in all Sarria—nay, in all that border country where, watered by the pure mountain streams, fertile Catalunia meets stern and desolate Aragon, and the foot-hills of the Eastern Pyrenees spurn them both farther from the snows.

Well might her lovers say there was none like her—this Concha Cabezos, who had passed her youth in a basket at her mother's feet in the tobacco manufactories of Sevilla, and never known a father. Tall as the tower of Lebanon that looketh towards Damascus, well bosomed, with eyes that promised and threatened alternate, repelled and cajoled all in one measured heave of her white throat, Concha of the house of Ramon, called "little" by that Spanish fashion of speech which would have invented a diminutive for Minerva herself, brought fire and destruction into Sarria. As the wildfire flashes from the east to the west, so the fame of her beauty went abroad. Also the wit of her replies—how she had bidden Pedro Morales (who called himself, like Don Jaime, "El Conquistador") to bring her a passport signed at all his former houses of call; how she had "cast out the sticks" of half the youth of the village, till despised batons strewed the ground like potsherds. And so the fame of little Concha went ever farther afield.

Yet when Rafael, the alcalde's son, came to the window on moonless nights, Concha was there. Hers was the full blood, quick-running and generous of the south, that loves in mankind a daintiness and effeminacy which they would scorn in their own sex.

So, many were the rich golden twilights when the two lovers whispered together beneath the broad

leaves of the fig-trees, each dark leaf rimmed with
the red of the glowing sky.   And Rafael, who was
to marry the vine-dresser's daughter, and so must
not "eat the iron" to please any maid, obeyed the
word of Concha more than all Holy Writ, and let it
be supposed that he went to the Ramon's house for
the sake of his cousin Dolóres.

For this he paid Manuela to afford him certain
opportunities, by which he profited through the
cleverness of Concha and her aunt Manuela.   For
that innocent maid took her mistress into her confidence—that is, after her kind.   It was wonderfully
sad, she pleaded.   She had a lover—good, generous,
eager to wed her, but his family forbade, and if her
kind mistress did not afford her the opportunity she
would die.   Yes, Concha would die.   The maids of
Andalucia ofttimes died for love.   Then the tears ran
down her cheeks and little Dolóres wept for company,
and because she also was left alone.

Thus it chanced that this foolish Rafael, the
alcalde's son, marched whistling softly to his fate.
His broad sombrero was cocked to the left and
looped on the side.   His Cordovan gloves were
loosely held in his right hand along with his tasselled
cane.   He had an eye to the pavemented street, lest
he should defile his lacquered shoes with the points
carved like eagle's beaks.   He whistled the *jota* of
Aragon as he went, and—he quite forgot Ramon,
the great good-humoured giant with whom he had
jested and at whom he had laughed.   He was
innocent of all intent against little Lola, his playmate.   He would as soon have thought of besieging
his sister's balcony, or "plucking the turkey" under
his own mother's window.

But he should not have forgotten that Ramon

Garcia was not a man to wait upon explanations, when he chanced on what seemed to touch the honour of his house. So Rafael de Flores, because he was to marry Felesia Grammunt and her wine-vats, and Concha the Andaluse, because to be known as Rafael's sweetheart might interfere with her other loves, took the name of Ramon Garcia's wife in vain with light reckless hearts. This was indeed valorously foolish, though Concha with her much wisdom ought to have known better. But a woman's experience, that of such a woman as Concha at least, refers exclusively to what a man will do in relation to herself. She never considered what Ramon Garcia might do in the matter of his wife Dolóres.

Concha thought that giant cold, stupid, inaccessible. When she first came into the clear air of the foot-hills from Barcelona (where a promising adventure had ended in premature disaster) she had tried her best wiles upon Ramon.

She had met him as he came wearied home, with a basin of water in her two hands, and the deference of eyelashes modestly abased. He passed her by, merely dipping his finger-tips in the water without so much as once looking at her. In the shade of the pomegranate trees in the corner, knowing herself alone, she had touched the guitar all unconscious, and danced the dance of her native Andalucia with a verve and abandon which she had never excelled. Then when Ramon discovered himself in an arbour near by and congratulated her upon her performance —in the very middle of her tearful protestations that if she had only known he was there, she would never, never have dared, never have ventured, and could he forgive her—he had tramped unconscious away. And instead of forgiving her in a fit and proper

manner, he had said he would go and bring down
his wife to see her dance the *bolero* in the Andalucian
manner.   It would afford Doña Dolóres much
pleasure.

With such a man who could do anything? It
was a blessing all men were not alike, said Concha
with a pout.   And indeed from Cadiz by the sea
to the mountains of the north she had found men
otherwise—always quite otherwise, this innocent
much experienced little Concha.

     *   *   *   *   *

Meanwhile the hunters closed in on Ramon the
brigand on the hills above Montblanch.   One
cannot kill (or as good as kill) an alcalde's son
without suffering for it, and it chanced that the
government, having been reproached on all sides for
lack of vigour, and being quite unable to capture
Don Carlos or Zumalacarregui, had resolved to
make an example of Ramon, called " El Sarria."

So to begin with, it had confiscated all that
Ramon possessed—house and farm, vineyard and
oliveyard, wine-presses and tiers of well-carpentered
vats with the wine of half a score of vintages
maturing therein.   These were duly expropriated in
the name of the government of the most Christian
regent Doña Maria Cristina.   But how much of
the produce stuck to the fingers of General Rodri-
guez, the military governor, and of Señor Amado
Gomez, administrator of so much of the province
as was at that time in the hands of the Cristinos,
who shall say?   It is to be feared that after these
gentlemen had been satisfied, there remained not a
great deal for the regencial treasure-chest at Madrid.

Meantime Ramon lay on his rock-ledge and
wondered—where little Dolóres was, chiefly, and to

this he often returned.   If he had had time that night would he have killed her ?   Sometimes he thought so, and then again—well, she was so small, so dainty, so full of all gentle ways and winsomenesses and— hell and furies, it was all deceit !   She had been deceiving him from the first !   Those upward glances, those shy, sweet confidences, sudden, irresistible re- vealings of her heart, he had thought they were all for him.   Fool !   Three times fool !   He knew better now.   They were practised on her husband that she might act them better before her lover.   God's truth, he would go down and kill her even now, as he had killed that other.   Why had he not waited ? He could easily have slain the soldiers who had rushed upon him, whom that hell-cat Manuela had brought—ah, he was glad he had marked her for life.

*   *   *   *   *

" *Ping !   Ping !* "   Two rifle bullets sang close past the brigand's head as he lay in his rocky fast- ness.   He heard them splash against the damp stone behind him, and the limestone fell away in flakes. A loose stone rumbled away down and finally leaped clear over the cliff into the mist.

El Sarria's cavern lay high up on the slopes of the Montblanch, the holy white mountain, or rather on an outlying spur of it called the Peak of Basella. Beneath him, as he looked out upon the plain, three thousand feet below, the mists were heaped into glistening white Sierras, on which the sun shone as upon the winter snows of the far away Pyrenees.

As the sun grew stronger Ramon knew well that his mountain fastness would be stormed and enveloped, by these delusive cloud-continents.   They would rise and dissipate themselves into the faint bluish haze of noonday heat.

Already there appeared far down the cleft called the Devil's Gulf, which yawned below the Peak of Basella, certain white jets of spray tossed upwards as from a fountain, which were the forerunners of that coming invasion of mist that would presently shut him out from the world.

But not a moment did Ramon waste. As quick as the grasshopper leaps from the flicked forefinger, so swift had been El Sarria's spring for his rifle. His cartouches lay ready to his hand in his belt of untanned leather. His eyes, deep sunken and wild, glanced everywhere with the instant apprehension of the hunted.

Ping! Ping!

Again the bullets came hissing past him. But Ramon was further back within his cave this time, and they whistled over his head. The chips of brittle limestone fell with a metallic clink on the hard stone floor.

El Sarria saw from whence one at least of his enemies had fired. A little drift of white reek was rising from the mouth of a cavern on the opposite escarpment of the Montblanch. He knew it well, but till now he had thought that but one other person did so, his friend Luis Fernandez of Sarria. But at the same moment he caught a glimpse of a blue jacket, edged with red, round the corner of a grey boulder up which the young ivy was climbing, green as April grass. The contrast of colour helped his sight, as presently it would assist his aim.

"The Lads of the Squadron!" he murmured grimly. And then he knew that it had come to the narrow and bitter pass with him.

For these men were no mere soldiers drafted from cities, or taken from the plough-tail with the furrow-clay heavy upon their feet. These were men like himself; young, trained to the life of the brigand and the contrabandista. Now they were "Migueletes"—"Mozos de la Escuadra"—"Lads of the Squadron," apt in all the craft of the smuggler, as good shots as himself, and probably knowing the country quite as well.

For all that El Sarria smiled with a certain knowledge that he had a friend fighting for him, that would render vain all their vaunted tracker's craft. Miguelete or red-breeched soldier, guerilla or contrabandista, none could follow him through that rising mist which boiled like a cauldron beneath. Ramon blew the first breath of its sour spume out through his nostrils like cigarette smoke, with a certain relish and appreciation.

"They have found me out, indeed, how, I know not. But they have yet to take Ramon Garcia!" he muttered, as he examined the lock of his gun.

He knew of a cleft, deep and secret, the track of an ancient watercourse, which led from his cave on the Puig, past the cliff at the foot of which was perched the great and famous Abbey of Montblanch, to another and a yet safer hold among the crags and precipices of Puymorens.

This none knew but his friend and brother, dearer to his soul than any other, save little Dolóres alone—Luis Fernandez, whose vineyard had neighboured his in the good days when—when he had a vineyard. He was the groomsman, who, even in those old days, had cared for Dolóres with more than a brother's care. The secret of the hidden passage was safe with him. Ramon held this thought to his soul amid the general wreck. This one friend at least was true. Meantime yonder was a

Miguelete behind a stone—a clumsy one withal.
He, El Sarria, would teach him the elements of his
trade. He drew a bead on the exposed limb. The
piece cracked, and with a yell the owner rolled
back behind his protecting boulder. For the next
hour not a cap-stem was seen, not a twig of juniper
waved.

El Sarria laughed grimly. His eye was still
true and his rifle good as ever. That was another
friend on whose fidelity he could rely. He patted
the brown polished stock almost as he used to do
little Lola's cheek in the evenings when they sat at
their door to watch José, the goatherd, bringing his
tinkling flock of brown skins and full udders up
from the scanty summer pasturage of the dried
watercourses.

Ah, there at last! The mist rose quite quickly
with a heave of huge shoulders, strong and yet unconscious, like a giant turning in his sleep. From
every direction at once the mist seemed to swirl upwards till the cave mouth was whelmed in a chaos of
grey tormented spume, like the gloom of a thunder-
cloud. Then again it appeared to thin out till the
forms of mountains very far away were seen as in a
dream. But Ramon knew how fallacious this mirage
was, and that the most distant of these seeming
mountain summits could be reached in a dozen
strides—that is, if you did not break your neck on
the way, much the most probable supposition of all.

Ramon waited till the mist was at its thickest,
rising in hissing spume-clouds out of the deeps.
Then with a long indrawing of breath into his lungs,
like a swimmer before the plunge, he struck out
straight for the cave on the face of the Montblanch
from which the bullets had come.

But long ere he reached it, the ground, which had been fairly level so far, though strewn with myriads of rocky fragments chipped off by winter frosts and loosened by spring rains, broke suddenly into a succession of precipices. There was only one way down, and El Sarria, making as if he would descend by it, sent instead a great boulder bounding and roaring down the pass.

He heard a shouting of men, a crash and scattering thunder of falling fragments far below. A gun went off. A chorus of angry voices apostrophised the owner, who had, according to them, just as much chance of shooting one of his comrades as El Sarria.

Ramon laughed when he heard this, and loosening a second huge stone ("to amuse the gentlemen in the blue and red," he said), he sent it after the first.

Then without waiting to ascertain the effect, Ramon plunged suddenly over an overhanging rock, apparently throwing himself bodily into space. He found his feet again on an unseen ledge, tip-toed along it, with his fingers hooked in a crack, and lo! the rock-face split duly in twain and there was his cleft, as smooth and true as if the mountain had been cut in half, like a bridescake, and moved a little apart.

There was the same glad defiance in the heart of El Sarria, which he had felt long ago, when as a boy he lay hidden in the rambling cellars of the old wine-barn, while his companions exhausted themselves in loud and unavailing research behind every cask and vat.

And indeed the game was in all points identically the same. For in no long space of time, Ramon could hear the shouting of his pursuers above him.

It was dark down there in the cleft, but once he caught a glimpse of blue sky high above him, and again the fragrance of a sprig of thyme was borne to his nostrils. The smell took him at an advantage, and something thickened painfully in his throat. Dolóres had loved that scent as she had loved all sweet things.

"It is the bee's flower,"she had argued one night, as he had stood with his arm under her mantilla, looking out at the wine-red hills under a fiery Spanish gloaming, "the bees make honey, *and I eat it!*"

Whereat he had called her a "greedy little pig," with a lover's fond abuse of the thing he most loves, and they had gone in together quickly ere the mosquitoes had time to follow them behind the nets which Ramon had held aside a moment for her to enter.

Thinking of this kept Ramon from considering the significance of the other fact he had ascertained. Above he saw the blue sky, deep blue as the Mediterranean when you see it lie land-bound between two promontories.

Then it struck him suddenly that the mist must have passed. If he went now he would emerge in the clear sunshine of even. Well, it mattered not, he would wait in the cleft for sunset and make his escape then. He knew that the "Lads of the Squadron" would be very hot and eager on the chase, after one of them had tasted El Sarria's bullet in his thigh. He would have a short shrift and no trial at all if he fell into their hands. For in those days neither Carlist nor Cristino either asked or gave quarter. And, indeed, it was more than doubtful if even the Carlists themselves would spare El Sarria, whose hand was against every man, be he King's man or Queen's man.

The evening darkened apace. Ramon made his way slowly to the bottom of the cleft. There was the wide *arroyo* beneath him, brick-red and hot, a valley of dry bones crossed here and there by rambling goat tracks, and strewn with boulders of all sizes, from that of a chick-pea to that of a cathedral.

It was very still there. An imperial eagle, serenely adrift across the heavens, let his shadow sail slowly across the wide marled trough of the glen. There could be no fear now.

" Well," thought Ramon, with philosophy, " we must wait—none knows of this place. Here I am secure as God in his Heaven. Let us roll a cigarette ! "

So, patiently, as only among Europeans a Spaniard can, El Sarria waited, stretching his fingers out to the sun and drawing them in, as a tiger does with his claws, and meanwhile the afternoon wore to evening.

At last it was time.

Very cautiously, for now it was life or death, yet with perfect assurance that none knew of his path of safety, Ramon stole onward. He was in the jaws now. He was out. He rushed swiftly for the first huge boulder, his head drawn in between his shoulders, his gun held in his left hand, his knife in his right.

But from the very mouth of the pass six men sprang after him, and as many more fronted him and turned him as he ran.

"Take him alive ! A hundred duros to the man who takes El Sarria alive ! "

He heard the voice of the officer of Migueletes. He saw the short, businesslike sword bayonets dance about him like flames. The uniforms mixed themselves with the rocks. It was all strange and weird as in a dream.

But only one face he saw crystal clear. One man alone inevitably barred his way. He dropped his gun. He could run better without it. They were too many for that, and it was not needed. He tore his way through a brace of fellows who had closed in upon him eager for the reward.

But through all the pother he still dashed full at the man whose face he knew. This time his knife made no mistake. For assuredly no enemy, but a friend, had done this—even Luis Fernandez, the brother of his heart.

And leaving the wounded strewn among the grey boulders and all the turmoil of shouting men, Ramon the hunted, broke away unscathed, and the desolate wilderness of Montblanch swallowed him up. Yet no wilderness was like this man's heart as he fled down and down with his knife still wet in his hand. He had no time to wipe it, and it dripped as he ran.

For this man had now neither wife nor friend.

CHAPTER III

COCK O' THE NORTH

"*CARAI! Caramba! Car*—— *!* This bantam will outface us on our own dunghill! Close in there, Pedro! Take down the iron spit to him, José! Heaven's curses on his long arm! A foreigner to challenge us to fight with the knife, or with the sword, or with the pistol!"

From the kitchen of the venta at San Vicencio, just where the track up the Montblanch takes its first spring into the air, came these and other similar cries. It was a long and narrowish apartment—the upper portion merely of a ground-floor chamber, which occupied the whole length of the building.

Part of the space was intended for horses and mules, and indeed was somewhat overcrowded by them that night. These being alarmed by the tumult and shoutings, were rearing so far as their short unsinkered head-stalls permitted them, and in especial making play with their feet at the various *machos* or he-mules scattered among them. These gladly retaliated, that being their form of relaxation, and through the resulting chaos of whinnying, stamping, neighing, and striking of sparks from pavement stones, skirmished a score of brown imps, more than half naked, each armed with a baton or stout wand

25

with which he struck and pushed the animals entrusted to their care out of the reach of harm, or
with equal goodwill gave a sly poke with the sharp
spur of the goad to a neighbour's beast, by way of
redressing any superiorities of heels or teeth.

But all the men had run together to the kitchen
end of the apartment. Where the stable ended
there was a step up, for all distinction between the
abode of beasts and of men. Over this step most of
those who had thus hasted to the fray incontinently
stumbled. And in the majority of instances their
stumble had been converted into a fall by a blow on
the sconce, or across the shoulders, from the flat of
a long sword wielded by the arm of a youth so tall
as almost to reach the low-beamed ceiling along
which the spiders were scuttling, in terror doubtless
of the sweeping bright thing on which the firelight
played as it waved this way and that.

First in the fray were a round dozen of
Migueletes, come in from an unsuccessful chase,
and eager to avenge on a stranger the failure and
disgrace they had suffered from one of their own
race. Next came a young butcher or two from the
killing-yards, each already a *toreador* in his own
estimation. The rest were chiefly *arrieros* or carriers,
with a stray gipsy from the south, dark as a Moor;
but every man as familiar with the use of his long
curved sheath-knife as a cathedral priest with his
breviary.

Meanwhile the tall young man with the long
sword was not silent. His Spanish was fluent if
inelegant, and as it had been acquired among the
majos of Sevilla and the mule-clippers of Aragon
rather than in more reputable quarters, his speech
to the critical ear was flavoured with a certain rich

allusiveness of personality and virility of adjective
which made ample amends (in the company in which
he found himself) for any want of grammatical
correctness.

With the Spanish anathemas that formed the
main portion of his address, he mingled certain
other words in a foreign tongue, which, being strong-
sounding and guttural, served him almost as well
in the Venta of San Vicencio as his *Carais* and
Carambas.

"*Dogs of dog-mothers without honour!* Come on,
and I will stap twal inches o' guid steel warranted
by Robin Fleming o' the Grassmarket doon your
throats! A set o' gabbling geese—tak' that! With
your virgins and saints! Ah, would you? There,
that will spoil your sitting down for a day or
two, my lad! Aye, scart, gin it does ye ony
guid?"

A knife in his left hand, and in his right the
long waving sword, bitter and sometimes unknown
and mysterious words in his mouth, this youth kept
his enemies very successfully at bay, meeting their
blades six at a time, and treading and turning so
lightly that as he lunged this way and that, there
was a constant disorganisation among the opposing
ranks, as one and the other sprang back to elude his
far-reaching point.

"He is of the devil—a devil of devils!" they
cried. "We shall all perish," wailed an old woman,
shrinking back further into the chimney-corner, and
wringing her hands.

Meanwhile the youth apostrophised his blade.

"My bonny Robin Fleemin'—as guid as ony
Toledan steel that ever was forged! What do
you think o' that for Leith Links? And they

wad hae made me either a minister or a cooper's
apprentice ! "

As he spoke he disarmed one of his chief opponents, who in furious anger snatched a pistol and
fired point-blank.   The shot would indubitably
have brought down the young hero of the unequal
combat, had not a stout ruddy-faced youth, who
had hitherto been leaning idly against the wall,
knocked up the owner's arm at the moment the
pistol went off.

"Ha' done ! " cried the new-comer in English ;
" twenty to one is bad enough, specially when that
one is a fool.   But pistols in a house-place are a
disgrace !   Stand back there, will ye ? "

And with no better weapon than a long-pronged
labourer's fork snatched from the chimney-corner,
he set himself shoulder to shoulder with the young
Scot and laid lustily about him.

That son of an unkindly soil, instead of being
grateful for this interference on his behalf, seemed at
first inclined to resent it.

" What call had ye to put your neck in danger
for an unkenned man's sake ? " he cried, crabbedly.
" Couldna ye hae letten me fill thae carles' skins as
fu' o' holes as a riddle ? "

" I am not the man to stand and see a countryman in danger ! " said the other, while the broad
sweeps of his companion's sword and the energetic
lunges of his own trident kept the enemy at a
respectful distance.

Suddenly a thought struck the Englishman.
Without dropping the fork, he rushed to the hearth,
where the *ollas* and *pucheros* of the entire company
bubbled and steamed, he caught the largest of the
pots in one hand and threatened to overturn the

entire contents among the ashes and *débris* on the floor.

"I speak their lingo but ill," he cried to his companion ; "but tell them from John Mortimer, that if they do not cease their racket, I will warrant that they shall not have an onion or a sprig of garlic to stink their breaths with this night. And if that does not fear them, nothing will—not Purgatory itself!"

The young man communicated this in his own way, and though every man among his assailants was to the full as brave as himself, the threat of the Englishman did not fail in its effect. The *arrieros* and Aragonese horse-clippers drew off and consulted, while the Scot who had caused all the disturbance, dropped his point to the floor, and contented himself with wrapping his cloak more tightly about his defensive arm. He had evidently been some time in the country, for he wore the dark *capa* and red *boina* of Navarra, and answered the deputation which now came forward with readiness and composure. Whoever gave in, it would certainly not be he. That, at least, was the impression given by his attitude.

"Certainly, most certainly," he said. "I will be glad to meet any one of you anywhere. I will stand to my words spoken in any language, or any field of honour, from the carpet of a prime minister to one of your infernal dusty *campos*, with any weapon, from pistol and sword to a tooth-pick— with any Spaniard, or Frenchman, or mongrel tyke that ever lifted wine pot."

"Is this a way to speak to gentlemen—I put it to you, caballeros?" cried one of the deputation, a huge rawboned Galician, angrily.

The Scot instantly detected the accent of the speaker and, dismissing him with the gesture one uses to a menial, called out, "Caballeros, indeed! What needs this son of the burden-bearing animal to speak of Caballeros? Is there any old Castilian here, of the right ancient stock? If so, let him arbitrate between us. I, for one, will abide by his decision. The sons of gentlemen and soldiers will not do wrong to a soldier and a stranger!"

Then from the darkest and most distant corner, where he had sat wrapped in his great striped mantle with the cape drawn close about his head, rose a man of a little past the middle years of life, his black beard showing only a few threads of grey, where the tell-tale wisdom tuft springs from the under lip.

"Young sir," he said courteously, "I am an Old Castilian from Valladolid. I will hear your cause of quarrel, and, if you so desire, advise my compatriots, if they in their turn will consent to put their case into my hands."

There was some demur at this among the rougher gipsies and muleteers, but every one was anxious for the evening meal, and the fragrant earthen pipkins and great iron central pot gave forth a good smell. Also a red-waistcoated man-servant ran hither and thither among them, whispering in the ear of each belligerent; and his communication, having presumably to do with the stranger's quality and condition, had a remarkable effect in casting oil upon the waters. Indeed, the Migueletes had withdrawn as soon as the Castilian came forward, and presently he of Galicia, having consulted with his fellows, answered that for his part he was quite prepared to submit the causes of strife to the noble cavalier from Valladolid, provided the stranger also would abide by the decision.

"I have said so," put in the Scot fiercely, "and *my* custom is not to make a promise at night for the purpose of breaking it in the morning!"

CHAPTER IV

A LITTLE COMB-CUTTING

By his accent of defiance, the Scot evidently considered that he had made a personal point here, but the Old Castilian gravely passed the insult over.

"Will the Señor state his case?" he said, bowing to the young man.

"I came to this venta, the proprietor of which, and all his relations, may God confound for liars and thieves! When I entered I paid for one week's good straw and barley in coined silver of Mexico. The unshorn villain stole the feed from under my horse's nose so soon as my back was turned, and then to-night, upon my complaining, set his rascal scullions on to vilify my country, or at least a country which, if not mine, is yet no concern of his or theirs. Whereupon I tendered to all the cleaner of them my cartel, offering to fight them with any weapon they might name, and in any place, for the honour of Scotland and the Presbyterian religion!"

Though he had never heard of either of these last, the grey-bearded umpire gravely wagged his head at the statement of the Scot, nodded in acknowledgment, and turned with equal gravity and distinction to the Gallegan as the representative of the opposite faction. He motioned him to proceed.

"This man," said the Galician, speaking in the

harsh stuttering whisper affected by these Iberian hewers of wood and drawers of water, "this man for these ten days past hath given all in the *Venta* bad money and worse talk. To-day he would have cheated *Dueño*, and we, like true men, took up the cudgels for the good patron."

"Hear the bog-trotting cowards lie!" cried the Scot, fiercely. "Save for the barley, I paid no money, good or bad. All I had remains here in my belt. If I gave bad money, let him produce it. And, save in the matter of his beast's provend, who gives money at the entering in of a hotel?"

"Least of all a Scot," put in the Englishman, who had been following with some difficulty the wordy warfare.

"Then because he would not exchange good money for the bad, and because of his words, which carried stings, we challenged him to fight, and he fought. That, worthy Señor, is the beginning of the matter, and the end."

"Sir," said the Scot to the Old Castilian, "there was no question of money. None brought my reckoning to me——"

"No," sighed the landlord, from beyond the bottle-encumbered counter where he had taken refuge, "because he threatened to let daylight into the vitals of the man who carried it to him."

"But as to the insults to his country?" asked the old Castilian, "you ought to have borne in mind that for that cause will a man fight quicker than for his sweetheart."

"So it is, Señor, we deny it not," answered the Gallegan; "yet this fellow, after abusing the English and their land till there were no more ill words in the language, turned upon us because we

D

chanced to agree with him, outs with his pocket-
book and deals round what he calls 'cartels of
defiance' as if he dealt a hand at ombre. Then,
after some give and take of ill words, as your honour
knows the custom is, he pulls his blade upon us,
and makes play as you saw. We are poor fellows,
and know no more than how to defend ourselves.
And if we fight, our custom is to do it with a
couple of Albacete knives before half the town, and
be done with it. But this stranger was all for duels,
and seconds, and codes of honour, after the mode of
Paris."

"And a very excellent thing too, sir," said the Old
Castilian, smiling at the Scot, "but in their due place,
and their place is hardly in the kitchen of the venta
of San Vicencio. Listen to me. My finding is this.
You will all shake hands, after an apology given and
received in the matter of the stranger's country, and
since he has paid no reckoning these ten days according to his own statement, the which I believe, he
shall defray his count so soon as it shall be presented
to him by the host. Are you agreed?"

"Agreed!" said the Gallegan, holding out his
hand to the Scot, "and I regret, on behalf of myself
and my companions, that we ever said aught to the
discredit of England, the very distinguished country
of which the Señor stranger is a native."

The Scot shrugged his shoulders in the French
manner, but nevertheless held out his hand with
some show of heartiness.

"I am no citizen of England, thank God," he
said, "I own no such pock-pudding land, but it
will be a heavy day when Rollo Blair of Castle Blair,
in the good shire of Fife, sits still with his hands in
his pockets and hears a garlic-eating Frenchman

abuse the English, with whom his forbears fought so many good fights."

"I thank you on behalf of my country for your championship, such as it is," said the stout Englishman, smiling ; "things that cut and thrust or go off with a bang, are not in my way. But if my knuckles are any good against the bridge of a man's nose, they shall henceforth be at your country's service. For the rest, bills of lading and exchanges at thirty days are more in my line."

"Ah," said the young Scot, twirling an almost invisible moustache, "commerce I know little of. I was bred to the profession of arms. My good father taught me the sword and the pistol, according to the practice of the best modern schools. Sergeant McPherson, his orderly, gave me instruction in the sabre and bayonet. I was intended for a commission in the 77th, my father's old regiment, when a pecuniary loss, the result of an unfortunate speculation, broke my poor father's heart and sent me out to seek my fortune with no more than Robin Fleeming's sword and my right arm."

"Poor capital to start on," said the Englishman, in his bluff manner, as he examined the article in question ; "now you do not happen to write a good round hand, do you ?"

The Scot started and laid his hand on his sword hilt.

"Sir," he cried, "your avocations do not permit you to understand how great an insult you offer to a gentleman !"

"Oh," said the other, "I don't know at all that you would have suited. Our manager down at Barcelona is a very particular man ; but then I would have said a good word for you, and being the owner's son——"

"Say no more of the matter, I beg of you," said the Scot, haughtily. "I have not yet been reduced to the necessity of choosing a mercantile career."

"And that is a most fortunate thing for you," quoth the Englishman, with the utmost gravity.

"Eh?" said the Scot, somewhat surprised, and, being occupied with his own thoughts and with keep-- ing an eye on the door, not exactly taking the Englishman's meaning, "Oh, you were speaking of a mercantile career. Yes, I am indeed fortunate in that my lines have been cast in pleasanter places than before a ream of foolscap on a desk."

"It pays well, though," said the other placidly.

"For me, I care nothing for money," said Rollo Blair. "Eh! what is this?"

He wheeled round quickly in response to a tap upon his arm, and the Englishman, looking at him keenly (though apparently intently regarding the opposite wall), saw him turn visibly paler.

The landlord was at Master Rollo Blair's elbow with the reckoning written out upon a long sheet of paper. A couple of serving men, who were probably privy to the extravagant total, stood sniggering and whispering in a neighbouring archway. The Gallegan and his companions sat crossing their legs and gossip- ing watchfully, darting inquisitive glances under their brows at their late adversary, to see how he would bear himself. Only that noble gentleman, the Old Castilian, sipped his chocolate unmoved, and, with the perfection of good manners, stared at the fire.

From red to white, and from white back again to a kind of greenish paleness, went and came the hues of the young man's complexion. The son of the house of Blair of Blair was manifestly unhappy. He put his hand in one pocket. He clapped another. His purse was not in either.

"Perchance 'tis in your honour's equipage," suggested the landlord wickedly ; "shall I call your body-servant to bring it ?"

It was a face of bitter chagrin that Rollo Blair of Blair lifted to the Englishman who had meantime never ceased from his study of a fly upon the wall. He beckoned him a little apart with a look of inimitable chagrin.

"Sir," he said, "will you buy from me a silver-hilted sword. It was my grandfather's, and he fought well with it at Killiecrankie. It is the sole article of value I possess—— "

Here a kind of a sob came into his voice. "God knows, I would rather sell my right hand !" he said brusquely.

"How came you to run up such a bill, having no effects ?" said the Englishman, looking at him coolly, and taking no notice of the young man's offer of his weapon, which he continued to hold by the scabbard.

"I can hardly tell," said the Scot, hanging his head, "but only two nights ago there was a young French lord here who out-faced me first at the cards and then at the drinking of wine. So I was compelled to order in more and better to be upsides with him !"

"There is no meaner ambition, especially on an empty purse," said the Englishman, not moving from the angle of wall upon which he leaned.

"Curse me that ever I troubled myself to appeal to a cold-livered Englishman !" cried the young man, "I will go to the Castilian over yonder. He looks as if he might have the bowels of a man. At

least he will not palm off a gentleman in distress
with moral precepts culled from last week's sermon!"

The Englishman leaped forward and clapped the
hot-headed Scot on the shoulder. With the other
hand he drew a well-filled wallet, with a mercantile
calendar slipped into the band, from his pocket.

"There," he said, heartily, "let me be your
banker. 'Tis worth a score of reckonings to hear
a Scotsman speak disrespectfully of sermons. My
name is John Mortimer——"

"Of the Mortimers of Plas Gwynedd in
Carnarvonshire? Why, my grandmother was of
that——" Rollo Blair was beginning a genealogical
disquisition with great eagerness when the Englishman stopped him.

"No," he said, "at least not that I know of.
My father made mouse-traps before he took to
cotton-spinning, and I never so much as heard
whether I had any grandfather. I am plain John
Mortimer of Chorley at your service. I think you
are an honest lad, sorely led astray by whimsies in
the brain, but you are honest, and in a far land. You
are welcome to my purse and, credit to any reasonable amount which will put you in the way of
repaying your obligation, as I am sure you desire
to do."

"I shall not sleep sound at night till I do,"
returned the youth, firmly. "But first I desire to
inform you that I have had an ill opinion of your
nation—an opinion to which, in spite of your great
personal kindness and the obligation under which
you place me, I am bound to adhere."

The Englishman nodded carelessly.

"There speaks an honest man, but also a foolish
one!" said Mortimer, shaking his head; "you

should try the foreign wine trade for a year or two. It is wonderfully curbing to a man's vocabulary!"

The Scot stood a moment at gaze, manifestly debating with himself.

"And you will not accept of my sword?" he said. "I assure you it is worth enough to discharge my small liabilities twice over."

"Swords are not legal tender in the wine business," said the other, smiling, "nor yet when I go home with a knowledge of languages to help sell my father's grey cloth! You are as welcome as my brother to the loan," he added, "and I promise you I will accept repayment as gladly from you as from him."

"You make the matter easier indeed," said Rollo Blair, recovering his spirits with a bound. "Here, landlord, can you change this gold ounce, or is the matter too great a one for your petty venta?"

The young men had been standing a little back, in the shadow of one of the arches, in which were empty mangers and the rings of head-stalls, so that the patron could not observe the passing of the Englishman's purse from hand to hand.

"Your servant, Señor!" said the innkeeper, no Spaniard, but a French Jew of Roussillon, "what can I have the honour of ordering for your excellencies' supper!"

"Order yourself out of my sight?" cried the Scot imperiously. "We are going up to the monastery to dine with my uncle the Abbot!"

The patron of the venta fell back a couple of steps, and the two serving men ceased to grin and instead bowed most obsequiously.

"He is a nephew of the Abbot, perhaps (who knows) his son! There will be fine doings out of this night's work, if he tells Don Baltasar all, as he doubtless will."

This was the whispered comment of one servitor in the ear of his master. Said the other—

"Speak him fair, patron, for the love of God! For if the monks are adverse, we are sped. Our pipe is as good as out. And perchance a yet worse thing may happen!"

And he leaned over till his lips almost touched mine host's ear.

"My God!" gasped the latter, "what a country! Would that I were safe back again in mine own house with green blinds in Roussillon!"

The Englishman and the Scot were now walking amicably arm in arm to and fro in front of the inn. The Scot had quite recovered his military demeanour, and again twirled his moustache with an air. The silver-hilted sword shone no brighter on the morn of Killiecrankie. The unused spurs tinkled melodiously.

The landlord stood with his hands deferentially folded. The young men took not the faintest notice of him, but continued to pace slowly to and fro.

Mine host of the venta of Montblanch cleared his throat. The Scot cast a single scornful glance at him, which he caught as a dog catches a bone.

"My most noble lords," he said, "I trust that the unfortunate occurrence of this evening will not prevent this house from having your honours' custom in the future, and that you too will say no word of all this to the most reverend Abbot Don Baltasar!"

"Make yourself easy on that score," said the Scot; "as soon as we are round the corner we will forget that such a refuge for fleabitten knaves anywhere exists out of Pandemonium ! "

Lower still bowed the obsequious patron, for this was his idea of the way a gentleman should speak to an innkeeper. Abuse showed his quality.

"Shall I order a carriage to convey your honours up to the Abbey?" said the landlord, preparing to take his leave. "I know a patron, who has a coach-and-six ! "

"We will walk on our feet," replied the Scot, no whit abashed, "ah—in pursuance of a vow made at Salamanca ! "

The landlord withdrew, making an obeisance that was almost an oriental salaam.

"But is the Abbot really your uncle?" inquired the Englishman, as they set out.

"As much as you are," said the Scot, "but all the same we shall dine with him, or my name is not Rollo Blair of Blair Castle in the shire of Fife ! "

"The Lord send it," said the Englishman devoutly ; "perhaps in that case he will part with his Priorato wine a farthing the gallon cheaper ! "

CHAPTER V

THE ABBEY OF MONTBLANCH

THE great monastery of Montblanch was of regal,
nay almost of imperial dignity. Though no emperor
(as at Yuste) had here laid aside the world and
assumed the cowl, yet mighty Kings of Aragon
and Navarra lay buried within its walls, and its long
line of mitred abbots included many in whose veins
ran the royal blood of all the Spains.

Almost completely encircled by wild sierras, it
was yet situated upon a plain, as it were let into the
very heart of the mountains. A clear trout stream,
which furnished many a Friday's breakfast to the
monks, ran through a rich vale. Of no place within
fifty leagues, could it be so truly said, that all about it
and above it there was heard a sound of many waters.

Of the various potencies and pre-eminences of
Montblanch, civil and ecclesiastical, there was no
end. A hundred villages owned its lordship. The
men were serfs, the women handmaids. Soul and
body they were bound to their masters of the
monastery of Montblanch. Without permission
they dared neither to wed nor to bury, neither to
increase nor to multiply, to lay the bride on the
bride-bed nor the corpse upon the bier.

Nor, to thrill the listener's blood, were darker
tales awanting, whispered with a quiver of the flesh,

as men crouched closer about the glowing charcoal pan, and women glanced fearfully out between the green lattice strips at the twinkling lights of the Abbey, set high above them under the silent stars.

It was said, not openly indeed, but rather with an awestruck lowering of the voice and fearful glances to right and left, that when the inquisition was done away with in the Spain of the cities and provinces, the chiefs of the Holy Office had found a last place of refuge beneath the grey rocks of Montblanch, and that whoso offended against the monks of the mountain, or refused to them flock or herd, son or daughter, sooner or later entered the doors of the monastery never to be visible again in the light of day.

So at least ran the tale, and as the two young men made their way upward from San Vicencio, by the mountain path beside which the stream brattled and sulked alternate, Rollo Blair told these things to the Englishman as one who half believed them.

"It is not possible," answered the latter scornfully ; "this is no century in which such things can be done. Has civilisation not reached as far as Aragon ? Who talks of the rack and the inquisition at this time of day ?"

The young Scot halted a sturdy peasant who came whistling down the path, a bundle of tough reed stems over his shoulder.

"Did you ever hear of the black room of the monastery of Montblanch ?" he said, pinching the man's blue overall between finger and thumb.

The sunburnt Aragonese crossed himself and was silent.

"Speak, have you heard ?"

The other nodded, and made with his digits that

" fig of Spain " which averts the evil eye ; but under his loose blouse half furtively as if ashamed of his precaution.

" I have heard ! " he said, and was silent.

" Do you wish to enter it ? " said Rollo.

" God forbid ! " quoth the man with conviction.

" And why ? " pursued the Scot, wishful to make his point.

" Because of those who go in thither, no one ever comes out."

The man, having thus spoken, hastened to betake himself out of sight, his feet, shod with sandals of esparto grass, pad-padding from side to side of the narrow mountain path.

" You see," said Rollo Blair, " mine uncle, reverend man, is no favourite in his own district."

It was now drawing towards evening, and the rich orange glow characteristic of northern Iberia deepened behind the hills, while the bushes of the wayside grew indistinct and took on mysterious shapes on either side.

" My object in coming to Spain is simple," said the Englishman, of whom his companion had asked a question. " Before my father retires and confides to me his spinning mills at Chorley, he stipulates that I shall make by my own exertions a clear profit of a thousand pounds. I, on my part, have agreed neither to marry nor to return till I can do so with a thousand pounds thus acquired in my hand. I thought I could make it as easily in the wine business as in any other of which I had no knowledge. And so, here I am ! " concluded the young man.

" Lord," cried Blair, " if my father had insisted on any such conditions with me, he would have made me a wandering Jew for life, and a perpetual bachelor to boot! A thousand pounds! Great Saint Andrew, I would as soon think of getting to heaven by my own merits!"

"Spoken like an excellent Calvinist!" cried the Englishman. "But how came you into this country, and can you in any way assist me in the buying of good vintages, out of which I may chance to make profit? Besides the firm's credit, I have a private capital of one hundred pounds, of which at present eight or nine are in a friend's hands!"

"Good Lord!" cried the Scot, "then I by my folly have put you by so much farther from your happiness. But of course you have a sweetheart waiting for you on your return?"

"I have yet to see the woman I would give a brass farthing to marry, or for whose mess of connubial pottage I would sell my good bachelor's birthright."

"Fegs," said Rollo Blair, gazing with admiration upon his shorter companion, and, as was his wont when excited, relapsing into dialect, "the shoe has aye pinched the ither foot wi' me, my lad. No to speak o' Peggy Ramsay, I think I hae been disappointed by as mony as a round dozen o' lasses since I shook off the dust o' the Lang Toon o' Kirkcaldy."

"Disappointed?" queried his companion, "how so, man? Did you not please the maids?"

"Oh, aye, it wasna that," returned the squire of Fife, taking his companion's arm confidentially; "the lasses, to do justice to their good taste, were maistly willing eneuch. There's something aboot a lang man like me that tak's them, the craiturs, and I hae a way o' my ain wi' them, though I never gat mair schooling than my father could thrash into me wi' a dog whip. But the fact is that aye afore the thing

gaed far eneuch, I cam to words wi' some brither or
faither o' the lass, and maybe put a knife into him,
or as it were an ounce o' lead, I wadna wonder—to
improve his logic."

"In other words you are quarrelsome?" said
Mortimer shortly.

The Scot removed his hand from the Englishman's arm and drew himself to his full height.

"There" he said, "I beg to take issue with you,
sir! Argumentative I may be, and it is my nature,
but to the man who flings it in my teeth that I am
of a quarrelsome disposition, I have but one answer.
Sir, receive my card!"

And with great gravity he pulled from his pocket
an ancient card-case of damaged silver, bulged
and dinted out of all shape, opened it, and burst
into a loud laugh.

"I declare I have not one left! I spent them
all on those Aragonese dogs down there, who
thought, I daresay, that they were soup tickets on
the *frailuchos'* kitchen up above. And anyway it is
heaven's own truth, I *am* a quarrelsome, ungrateful
dog! But forgive me, Mr. Mortimer, it is my
nature, and at any rate it does not last long. I am
not yet of those 'that age and sullens have,' as my
father used to say. A desperate wise man my father,
and well read! I would have learned more from
him if I had not preferred Sergeant McPherson and
the stables, to the study and my father's Malacca
cane about my shoulders each time I made a false
quantity."

"But you have not answered my question," said
the Englishman. "I am here to buy wines. I am
above all anxious to take over to England some
thousand hectolitres of the famous Priorato of

Montblanch, and any other vintages that will suit the English market."

"But how on a hundred pounds can you expect to do so much?" asked the Scot, with an unlooked-for exhibition of native caution.

"Oh, I have enough credit for anything that I may buy on account of the firm. The hundred is my own private venture, and it struck me that with your command of the language and my knowledge of business, we might be able to ship some Spanish wines to the Thames on very favourable terms. I should of course be glad to pay you the usual commission."

"Vintages and commissions and shipments are so much Greek to me," said Rollo Blair; "but if I can do anything to lessen the weight of obligement under which you have placed me, you can count on my services. I am scarce such a fool as my tongue and temper make me out sometimes! You are the only man alive I have tried to pick a quarrel with and failed."

"I think we shall do very well together yet," said Mortimer; "the usual commission is five per cent. on all transactions up to a hundred pounds—above that, seven and a half."

"Damn you and your commissions, sir," cried Blair, hotly. "Did I not tell you I would do my best, on the honour of a Scottish gentleman!"

"Very likely," returned the other, dryly; "but I have always found the benefit of a clear and early understanding between partners."

They had been gradually ascending the narrow path which wound through clumps of rosemary, broom, thyme, and bay-tree laurel to a sheltered little plain, much of it occupied by enclosed gardens and the vast white buildings of the monastery itself.

The moon, almost full but with a shaving off its right-hand side which kept it a full hour late, shone behind the two adventurers as they stood still a moment to take in the scene.

Pallid limestone pinnacles rose high into serene depths of indigo, in which the stars twinkled according to their size and pre-eminence, nearer and farther, gradually retiring into infinite space. In the clefts high up were black tufts of trees, that seemed from below like so many gooseberry bushes. A kind of three days' stubble of beard covered the plain itself right up to the monastery wall, while here and there was heard the continuous tinkle of many goat bells as the leaders alternately strayed and cropped the herbage between the boulders.

Stretching from side to side was the white abbey, not so much imposing for architectural beauty, but because of its vast size, its Titanic retaining walls and multitude of windows, now mere splashed oblongs of darkness irregularly scattered along the white walls. Only at one end the chapel was lit up, and from its windows of palest gold, and Madonna blue, and ruby red, came the sweet voices of children beginning to sing the evening hymn as it stands in the Breviary for the use of the faithful in the archdiocese of Tarragona—

> " Rosasque miscens liliis
> Aram vetustam contegit."

CHAPTER VI

BROTHER HILARIO

At the great entrance gate they paused, uncertain which way to turn, for from the windows of the chapel a bright light shone forth upon the grey waste without, whitening alike the dark green creepers of the juniper and the pale yellow spears of the restless broom. But a chance encounter decided the matter for them.

"Well, ah, my good sometime enemy," cried a shrill eager voice, "have you forgotten Étienne de Saint Pierre, and how we are to fight below the windmill at Montmartre the first time you come to Paris?"

"Lord, it is the hare-brained Frenchman!" cried Rollo, yet with some glow of pleasure in his face. The very talk of fighting stirred him.

"Then there are a pair of you!" said John Mortimer, quietly, like a man dropping his fly into a pool on a clear evening.

"Eh, what's that?" angrily cried the Scot, but was diverted from further inquiry by the sight of a figure that darted forward out of the darkness of the wall.

A smallish slender man, dressed in a costume which would have recalled the Barber of Seville, had it not been for the ecclesiastical robe that surmounted

and as it were extinguished its silken gorgeousness.
A great cross of gold set with jewels swung at the
young man's breast and was upheld by links as large
as those which sustain a lord mayor's badge of office.

"Ah, I have renounced the world, my dear
adversary," cried the newcomer enthusiastically, "as
you will also. I am no longer Etienne de Saint
Pierre, but Brother Hilario, an unworthy novice of
the Convent of the Virgin of Montblanch!"

"But, sir," cried Rollo Blair, "you cannot take
up the religious life without some small settlement
with me. You are trysted to meet me with the
smallsword at the Buttes of Montmartre—you to
fight for the honour of Señorita Concha of Sarria
and I to make a hole in your skin for the sweet sake
of little Peggy Ramsay, who broke my heart or ever
I left the bonny woods o' Alyth to wander on this
foreign shore!"

"Your claim I allow, my dear Sir Blair," cried
the Frenchman, "but the eternal concerns of the
soul come first, and I have been wicked—wicked—
so very wicked—or at least as wicked as my health
(which is indifferent) would allow. But the holy
Prior—the abbot—mine uncle, hath shown me the
error of my ways!"

John Mortimer turned directly round till he
faced the speaker.

"Odds bobs," he cried, "then after all there is
a pair of them. *He is this fellow's uncle too!*"

The Frenchman gazed at him amazed for a
moment. Then he clapped his hand fiercely on the
place where his sword-hilt should have been, crying,
"I would have you know, Monsieur, that the word
of a Saint Pierre is sacred. I carry in my veins the
blood of kings!"

And he grappled fiercely for the missing sword-hilt, but his fingers encountering only the great jewelled cross of gold filigree work, he raised it to his lips with a sudden revulsion of feeling.

"Torrentes iniquitatis conturbaverunt me.
Dolores inferni circumdederunt me."

He spoke these words solemnly, shaking his head as he did so.

"What! still harping on little Dolóres?" cried Blair; "I thought little Concha was your last—before Holy Church, I mean."

The little Frenchman was beneath the lamps and he looked up at the long lean Scot with a peculiarly sweet smile.

"Ah, you scoff," he said, "but you will learn—yes, you will learn. My uncle, the Prior, will teach you. He will show you the Way, as he has done for me!"

"It may be so," retorted the Scot, darkly; "I only wish I could have a chance at him. I think I could prove him all in the wrong about transubstantiation—that is, if I could keep my temper sufficiently long.

"But," he added, "if it be a fair question to put to a novice and a holy man, how about the divine right of kings that you talked so much of only a week ago, and especially what of Don Carlos, for whom you came to fight?"

"Ah, my good cousin Carlos, my dear cousin," cried Etienne Saint Pierre, waving his hands in the air vehemently, "his cause is as dear and sacred to this heart as ever. But now I will use in his behalf the sword of the Spirit instead of the carnal weapon I had meant to draw, in the cause of the Lord's

anointed. I will *pray* for the success of his arms
night and morning."

At this moment the colloquy at the abbey gate
was broken up by a somewhat stout man, also in the
garb of a novice, a long friar's robe being girt un-
comfortably tight about his waist. In his hand he
held a lantern.

"Monsieur—Brother Hilario, I mean—a thousand devils run away with me that ever I should
speak such a shake-stick name to my master—the
Holy Prior wishes to speak with you, and desires to
know whether you would prefer a capon of Zaragoza
or two Bordeaux pigeons in your *olla* to-night?"

"Come, that is more promising," cried the Scot;
"we will gladly accept of your invitation to dine with
you and your uncle, and give him all the chance he
wants to convert me to the religious life. We accept
with pleasure—pleased, I am sure, to meet either the
Saragossan capon or the two Bordeaux pigeons!"

"Invitation!" cried the astonished Brother
Hilario. "Did I invite you? If so, I fear I took
a liberty. I do not remember the circumstance."

"Do you doubt my word!" cried the Scot, with
instant frowning truculence. "I say the invitation
was implied if not expressed, and by the eyes of
Peggy Ramsay, if you do not get us a couple of
covers at your uncle's table to-night, I will go
straight to the Holy Prior and tell him all that
I know of little Concha of Sarria, and your plot
to carry her off—a deal more, I opine, than you
included in your last confession, most high-minded
friar!"

"That was before my renunciation of the flesh,"
cried Saint Pierre, manifestly agitated.

The Scot felt his elbow touched.

"I was under her balcony with a letter last Friday, no further gone, sir," whispered the novice in the cord-begirt robe ; "blessed angels help me to get this nonsense out of his head, or it will be the death of us, and we will never night-hawk it on the Palais Royal again ! "

"And on what pious principles do you explain the love-letter you sent last Friday ! " said Rollo, aloud. "What if I were to put it into the hands of your good uncle the Prior ? If that were to happen, I warrant you would never ride on one of the white abbey mules in the garb of the brothers of Mont-blanch ! "

The stout novice rubbed his hands behind his master's back, and grinned from ear to ear. But the effect upon Saint Pierre was not quite what Rollo intended.

Instead of being astonished and quailing at his acuteness, the young Frenchman suddenly fired up in the most carnal and unmonkish fashion.

"You have been making love to my little Concha yourself, you dirty Scots rogue ! I will have your life, monsieur ! Guard yourself ! "

"'*Your* Concha'—do you say, Master Friar ? " cried Blair ; "and pray who gave you a right to have Conchas on your hands with the possessive adjective before them ? Is that permit included in your monkish articles of association ? Is adoration of pretty little Conchas set down in black and red in your breviaries ? Answer me that, sir ! "

"No matter, monsieur," retorted the Frenchman ; "I was a man before I was a monk. Indeed, in the latter capacity I am not full-fledged yet. And I hold you answerable if in anything you have offended against the lady you have named, or used arts to wile her heart from me ! "

"l give you my word I never set eyes on the wench—but from what I hear—— "

"Stop there," cried the second novice ; "be good enough to settle that question later. For me, I must go back promptly with the answer about the capon of Zaragoza and the two Bordeaux pigeons ! "

The Scot looked at the Frenchman. The Frenchman looked at the Scot.

"As a compliment to the fair lady the Señorita Concha, say to my uncle the capon, François ! " said the lover.

"And as a compliment to yourself, my dear Brother Hilario, say to his lordship *also* the two Bordeaux pigeons ! "

"*And* the pigeons, François ! " quoth the latest addition to the brotherhood of Montblanch, with perfect seriousness.

CHAPTER VII

THE ABBOT'S DINNER

ROLLO BLAIR kept his gasconnading promise. He dined with "his uncle," the abbot, that most wise, learned, and Christian prelate, Don Baltasar Varela.

The abbot of Montblanch was glad to see Milord of Castle Blair in the land of the Scots. It was not a Christian country, he had been informed.

"Then your venerability has been misinformed," cried Rollo, who thirsted for argument with the high ecclesiastic upon transubstantiation, consubstantiation, and all the other "ations" of his creed. But the Abbot parried him neatly at the very first assault, by an inquiry as to what he thought of *transverberacion.*

At this Rollo gasped, and found immediate occasion to change the subject to the famous wine of the Abbey, *el Priorato,* while the little Frenchman beamed appreciation of his uncle's ecclesiastical learning, and that wise prelate twirled his thumbs about each other and discoursed at large, his shrewd unfathomable grey eyes now fixed on one and now on another of the company, as though he were fathoming them severally with some infallible mental gauge, by which he could calculate their measure of capacity to a hair.

Costly wines were on the table. Silver and cut

glass of Venice sparkled on spotless cloth. Silent-
sandalled lay brethren of the Order waited on the
Prior and his guests. Course after course was
brought in, discussed, and removed. The Abbot,
Don Baltasar Varela, himself ate little. He watched
his guests' appetites, however, with manifest interest,
and directed the servitors with almost imperceptible
movements of his hand. He appeared to favour
each one of the three equally.

Yet an observer as detached as Don Baltasar
himself would have detected that the chief part of his
attention was given to the young man, Rollo Blair,
and that the Prior, with a gently subtle smile, kept
murmuring to himself at each quick retort and flash
of repartee.

"'Fiery as a Scot' indeed! A true proverb!
This fellow is the man we want, if so we can pay his
price. The others——"

And Don Baltasar shrugged his shoulders slightly
and contemptuously, as he glanced from the broad
stolid features of John Mortimer of Chorley to the
bright volatile countenance of his nephew Etienne,
Count of Saint Pierre—though, as we know, in so
doing he did much injustice to two men very brave
after their kind, albeit their kind was not that for
which the Prior of Montblanch happened to be
presently on the outlook.

Rollo never emptied his glass (and he did so
frequently) but one of Abbot Baltasar's eyelids
quivered, and the glass was immediately filled again.

Thus supplied with inspiration the stream of the
youth's conversation flowed steadily. His tones rose
till they dominated the table. His vocabulary ex-
panded, and as he had learned his Castilian in strange
places, his occasional freedom of expression bore
somewhat heavily upon the lay brothers, who, fearful

of the watchful grey eye of their superior, dared
not so much as to smile behind their hands.

As Rollo's tongue loosened and his heart enlarged,
the Prior with a twitch of his thumb indicated that
the doors were to be closed, and turned again to give
yet graver and more courteous attention to the conversation of his guest.

Master Blair's muse was the historical—and, alas !
the autobiographical.

"Through his sword-arm I sent Killiecrankie,
which is a better blade than any ever forged at
Toledo—as I, Rollo Blair, stand ready to affirm and
make good upon any man every day of the week ! "

" I agree," said John Mortimer, " 'tis better than
my only razor, which is an infernally bad piece of
metal, and not fit to scrape a hog with ! "

"And *I* agree," sighed Etienne, " because the remainder of my life I have resolved to devote to contemplation upon holy things. *Vade retro me, Satana !* "

The Scot turned upon him like a flash.

" *You* have renounced the world "—he queried—
" did I hear you say ? "

The Frenchman nodded. "And its vanities ! "
he agreed with a twirl of his chain.

"Since Friday night, I presume ? " Again began
the fateful questioning, at which Mortimer kicked
Rollo severely under the table. The poor novice and
martyr to monarchial principles flushed visibly. He
was afraid of what the mad Scot might say next.
But at that very moment of danger Rollo curbed his
tongue. He would not let the name of little Concha
pass his lips. Still the novice in his uncle's presence
was game too excellent to let slip easily.

"Contemplation ! " he laughed aloud, " you will,
you say, pass your days in contemplation. The relics

of the saints will serve you from this day forth, most gentle penitent. Why, man, you should go straight to Cologne. They have the bones of eleven thousand virgins there, I am told. These might chance to serve you some while!"

"Speaking of relics," said the abbot, rising, to prevent further awkwardness of discourse, "there is a midnight celebration which it is my duty to attend, but do not let that disturb you from finishing your wine. Son Hilario, I absolve you from attendance, that you may keep these friends of yours in company. When you are weary, touch this bell, and Father Anselmo, my confessor, will show you the treasures and reliquaries of the Abbey—the former, alas! now scanty, since the visit of your compatriots, Messire Etienne, who came in the year eight, with their un-hallowed melting-pots. But there are as many relics as ever, praise be to the saints—mostly stones. There is never any lack of stones at Montblanch, though sometimes we poor anchorites of the Virgin may chance to lack bread."

As he spoke he looked about at the well-laden table, the bursting figs, the bunches of purple grapes, the shining silver and snowy linen.

"Benedicite, good gentlemen!" he said, and went out with bowed head and a rustle of flowing robe.

"But the wine—the wine! You have forgotten the wine!" cried John Mortimer, suddenly re-membering his purpose in coming to Montblanch.

"Ma foi!" exclaimed Brother Hilario, "has the Englishman not yet had enough! I have heard of how these islanders drink, but this passes credit."

"Ay, it cowes Kirkcaldy!" cried Rollo. "He is indeed a maisterfu' drinker, this Englishman!"

"What?" queried the Frenchman, still mystified, and moving towards the decanters. "Does he want more wine? How much would satisfy him, think you?"

"I could take somewhere about sixty thousand gallons at present, and as much more in a week or two!" said Mortimer, pulling out his pocket-book.

The Frenchman looked at Rollo for enlightenment. Our insular measures of capacity were naturally strange to him.

"About twenty thousand *arrobas* at present might satisfy him, he says, but he would like more in a week or two!"

Monsieur Etienne de Saint Pierre fell back, lax with astonishment.

"*Mon Dieu!*" he cried, "I never believed it before, but I see now it is true. An Englishman bathes himself, and drinks the contents of his bath when he is finished. It is that he may be ready for the twenty thousand *arrobas* of Priorato! But you are pleased to jest, gentlemen, is it not so?"

The matter was explained.

"I can arrange that with my uncle," said Etienne, as soon as he fully understood John Mortimer's purpose; "I understand something about wines, for I grow some square leagues of vines on my lands in France. Moreover, I will see to it that your friend does not pay too high a price for the Priorato! And now for the relics! We have already wasted too much time."

He rang the bell and called in the abbot's confessor. Father Anselmo was a gaunt, severe man, of more than the average height, with black hair streaked with grey, and fixed and stony eyes. With him there appeared a younger and more jovial monk,

with small eyes that perpetually twinkled, and a
smile that seemed to catch itself up as with a click
each time that the stern gaze of Father Anselmo
turned his way. This monk was evidently only a
novice, or a lay brother on his probation, for he wore
the lesser habit and carried in his hand a great bunch
of keys, which he tinkled freely, as if in that silent
place he took a certain pleasure in the sound.

Father Anselmo gazed with severe disapproval
upon the rich appointments of the abbot's table, and
austerely refused for himself and his companion any
refreshment beyond a glass of cold water.

But on the other hand the eyes of the keybearer perused with evident longing every salver
and decanter. Whereupon the wild Scot, being restrained by no scruples, religious or otherwise, passed
him first of all a glass of wine behind his superior's
back, which he drank at a gulp without a sound, his
eyes all the while on the lean rounded shoulders of
the father confessor.

A full bottle of wine followed and was instantly
concealed beneath the novice's long robe. A plate
of grapes, half a dozen pears, a loaf of wheaten bread,
all were passed to him one by one, and as swiftly and
silently disappeared, none being bold enough to guess
whither.

"By the Lord, I'll try him with a whole melon,"
muttered Rollo; "I believe that, swollen as he is,
he could stow away a keg of butter quite comfortably."

But before he could put this jovial son of Peter
the keybearer to the test, Father Anselmo had
gathered his robes ascetically about him, and signed
to the abbot's guests to follow him to the reliquary
chamber.

CHAPTER VIII

SANCTUARY

THE severe confessor solemnly preceded them, a candle in his hand. Rollo thought that Father Anselmo had the air of perpetually assisting at an excommunication, a burning of heretics, or other extreme disciplinary ceremony of Holy Church. His inferior, the bearer of the Petrine keys, dimpled behind him, rattling the wards vigorously to hide any tendency of the bottle of wine to make music of its own in his ample skirts.

The treasury of Montblanch had indeed been most grievously despoiled by the French, according to the immemorial custom of that most Christian nation upon its campaigns, and only the most used dishes were now of silver or silver gilt. All the rest were of homely pewter silvered over—which, as the confessor said, resembled most men's characters, in that they looked well enough from a distance, and on the whole served just as well. He surveyed the company of young men so meaningly as he said this, that the Scot was only restrained from challenging him on the spot, by the pressure of John Mortimer's arm upon one side, and an almost tearful expression of entreaty on Brother Hilario's face upon the other.

The Confessor selected two keys from the bunch

and inserted them into a couple of locks in a small iron door at the foot of certain gloomy steps.

The Scot who was imaginative, thought that he could discern some faint stirrings of life about his feet. Accordingly he stamped once or twice, having an instinctive hatred of little creeping vermin, which (with wasps) were the only things he feared in heaven or earth.

But the faint stirring ceasing, he grew interested in watching Father Anselmo and the novice bearing simultaneously on the keys, which turned together quite suddenly. Then the Confessor touched a spring concealed behind some drapery and the door opened.

A former visitor, Marshal Souchy, had obtained the same privilege by tying the late Abbot up by the thumbs till he gave the order for the treasury to be opened. In the despatches which he forwarded to his imperial master this fact appeared in the following form : "After half an hour's persuasion the Abbot of Montblanch decided to give up his treasures to your officers, and to celebrate a solemn service in thanksgiving for the arrival in Aragon of the delivering armies of his Majesty the Emperor."

The paucity of treasures of silver and gold in the treasury of Montblanch was, however, more than made up for by the extraordinary number of relics of saints which the monastery possessed. It was at this point that the novice, who appeared to act as a kind of showman in ordinary to the vaults, took up his tale.

"Brother Atanasio, do your duty!" the Confessor had said with a solemn voice, precisely as if he had been ordering the first turn of the great wheel of the garotte.

And in words that fairly tumbled over each other with haste the custodian began his enumeration.

"Here we have a bud from the rod of Aaron—also the body of Aaron himself; the clasp of the robe of Elijah, the prophet, which Elisha did not observe when he picked up the mantle—also the aforesaid Elijah and Elisha; the stone on which the angel sat in the holy sepulchre; the stone on which holy St. Peter stumbled when he let John outrun him; the words he said on that occasion, which are not included in Holy Writ, but were embroidered on a handkerchief by his mother-in-law, probably out of spite; the stone on which the Sainted Virgin was sitting when the angel saluted her, the stone on which she sat down to watch the crucifixion; the stone from Mount Sinai upon which St. Joseph prayed going down to Egypt; a stone from the house of St. Nicholas, and another from his sepulchre——"

Athanasius the rosy had only proceeded so far with his enumeration when a groan came as it were from the ground, and the Scot leaped violently aside.

"Good God!" he cried, "there is some one suffering down here—through that door, I think! Open it, you black-a-vised sweep of darkness! I am a true-blue Presbyterian, I tell you, and I will have no Torquemada business where Rollo Blair is."

But the dark monk only shook his head, and for the first time smiled.

"The exclamatory stranger is misled by a curious echo, which has given this place its name. It is called 'The Gate of the Groans,' and our wise predecessors chose the place for the entrance of their treasure-chamber, as giving ignorant men the idea that the properties of the Abbey were protected by demons! I had not, however, hoped that the ingenious little arrangement would deceive one so wise and experienced as the *caballero* with the long sword. Our novice, Brother Hilario, will inform his friend that what I have said is well known in the monastery to be the case!"

"I have heard it so stated," said Etienne, with some reluctance, and speaking not at all as his monastic name would import.

The groans came again and again, apparently from the earth, and Rollo, not yet fully convinced, stamped here and there with his foot and battered the walls with the basket of his sword, till he added a dint or two to the tasselled hilt of "Killie-crankie." All in vain, however, for the walls were solid, and the floor beneath his feet rang dull and true.

"Firm as the Rock of Peter," said the Confessor grimly, "on which Holy Church is built. *Tu es Petrus, et super hanc petram* —— !"

"I know that verse," cried the Scot, getting quickly in front of him; "but I can show you in a quarter of an hour that the Romanist argument from these words proceeds upon a misconception—if you will do me the honour to follow me—— !"

"Follow *me* !" said the sepulchral monk curtly, and pointing upwards as the sound of a bell was wafted down to them faintly. "That is the hour of midnight. Let us attend the call !"

So for that time Rollo's argument against the Romanist doctrine of the Rock of Peter was shut within him. It was not long, however, before he had other matters to think of.

They followed their guide through a maze of dark passages, till, with a sudden "Attention!" he halted them before a door, from the other side of which came a sound of voices.

The door opened and all the world seemed suddenly filled with clear singing and glorious light.

Without the least preparation or preface Father Anselmo ushered the three young men into the great chapel of the order of the Virgin of Montblanch.

To Rollo it seemed almost an indecency to be thus transported from stuffy cases of doubtful relics and the chill darkness of earth-smelling passages, to this place where unseen suppliant voices assailed the Deity with a perpetual song.

The three youths blinked at the sudden light as they stepped within, and each of them glanced at their dress, apprehending with the instinct common to those who find themselves unexpectedly in crowded places, that it must be disordered. They followed their guide mechanically to the Holy Water laver. Etienne made the necessary signs and a low reverence towards the altar. Rollo's devotion to the Presbyterian form of worship did not prevent his imitating his companion with the easy adaptability of youth to place and circumstance, but quite unexpectedly they ran upon a rock in the matter of John Mortimer.

"Do as I do, you obstinate ass!" hissed Rollo in his ear. "Take some of the water on one finger and make the sign of the cross—that is, if you want to sleep in an unpricked skin this night!"

"Be hanged if I do," muttered John Mortimer, between his teeth. "I am not much given to religion

F

myself, but my father is a Primitive Methodist, and built them a church in Chorley. And I never could look the old man in the face again if I dotted myself all over with their heathen holy water!"

"It's little of the Abbot's Priorato you'll ever ship then, my good friend," muttered Rollo; "but please yourself!"

The Englishman had rooted his heels to the pavement and squared his hands by his sides as one who would in nowise be dislodged from his resolve.

"I do not care if I never put a drop of wine into cask," he said, doggedly. "I won't go back to Chorley after having denied my father's brand of religion, even if my own vintage is of the poorest."

"There's more ways of killing a cat than choking her with cream!" growled Rollo; "take this, then, you stiff-necked English deevil!"

And bowing towards the altar, and again towards the Father Confessor, who had been regarding them with a sinister curiosity, with the utmost gravity Rollo made certain gestures with his hands, and dipping his fingers again in the laver, he made the sign of the cross on his friend's forehead and breast, before the Englishman had time to protest.

"In fulfilment of a vow!" he exclaimed in a whisper to Father Anselmo. "My companion has promised to St. Vicente Ferrer of Valencia that he will not make the sign of the cross upon his person till he can do it at the Basilica of holy St. Peter at Rome. He hath a mortal sin still upon his conscience."

"Then let him come to me," said the Confessor. "I will deal with him in a more summary fashion!"

*　　　*　　　*　　　*　　　*

It was the season of pilgrimage, and many were
the penitents who availed themselves of the monks'
three days statutory hospitality. These were seated
about the dark church on chairs and stools supplied
them by the sacristans, and on two of the latter John
Mortimer and Rollo presently found themselves,
while Brother Hilario went off to the gallery reserved
for novices of his standing. Now and then a
woman would steal forward and add a tall candle to
the many thousands which burned upon the altar,
or a man kneel at the screen of golden bars beyond
which were the officiating priests and their silently-
moving acolytes.

The church lay behind in deep shadow, only the
higher lights shining here on a man's head, and
there on a woman's golden ornament. The Abbot
sat to the right in his episcopal robes, with his mitre
on a cushion beside him. A priest stood by this
chair with the crozier in his hand.

The brethren of the Order could be seen in their
robes occupying the stalls allotted to them. There
was another organ and choir far down the church,
high to the right of the pillar by which the young
men sat. The presence of this second choir was
betrayed by a dim illumination proceeding from
behind the fretted balustrade of the loft.

With the quick sympathy of his nature, Rollo,
forgetting his sometime devotion to his native
Presbytery, which indeed was chiefly of the con-
troversial sort, permitted himself to be carried away
by the magnificent swing of the music, the resonance
of the twin organs, now pouring their thunder
forth so as to shake at once the hearers' diaphragms
and the fretted roof of blue and gold above them,
now sweet and lonesome as a bird warbling down in

Elie meadows in the noon silences. Anon Rollo shut
his eyes and the Chapel of the Virgin of Montblanch
incontinently vanished. He was among the great
Congregation of all the Faithful, he alone without a
wedding garment. The place where he stood seemed
filled with surges of aureate light, but the night lay
banked up without, eager and waiting to envelop
him, doomed to be for ever a faithless wandering son
of the great Father. Snatches of his early devotions
came ramblingly back to him, prayers his mother had
taught him, Psalms his old nurse had insisted on his
learning, or mayhap crooned about his cradle. Such
were the first words which came to him—

> "That man hath perfect blessedness,
> Who walketh not astray,
> In counsel of ungodly men,
> Nor stands in sinners' way."

The impressions, hitherto vivid, blurred themselves at this point. Rollo Blair was kneeling at his
mother's knee. He thought of his first sweetheart
who had nearly made him a minister, and, perchance,
a better man. The night that was waiting imminent
outside, silently overleapt the barriers of golden
light. Rollo Blair's head fell forward against a
pillar—and, while the music thundered and wailed
alternate, and the great service swept on its gorgeous
way, the wild unhaltered Scot, soothed by a lullaby
of sound, slept the sleep of the young, the tired, and
the heart-free.

How long he slumbered he could not tell, but
he was awakened by a violent thrust in the ribs from
the elbow of John Mortimer.

"Great jimminy! what's that? Look, man,
look!"

Rollo opened his eyes, bleared with insufficient

sleep, and for a long moment all things danced weirdly before them, as gnats dance in the light of the moon. He saw dimly without understanding the swinging altar lamps in a blur of purple haze, the richly-robed priests, the myriad candles, the dark forms of the worshippers. But now, instead of all eyes being turned towards the brilliance of the golden altar, it was towards the door at the dark end of the chapel that they looked.

He could distinguish a tumult of hoarse voices without, multitudinous angry cries of men, the clatter of feet, the sharp clash of arms. A shot or two went off quite near at hand.

" Seize him—take the murderer ! Hold him ! "

The shoutings came clear now to Rollo's brain, and rising to his feet he half drew his sword, as though he himself had been the hunted man. But with a smile he let the blade slide back, which it did as easily as a stone slips into water. For though Killiecrankie's hilt might be battered, without ribbon or bow-knot, Rollo saw to it that Robin Fleeming's blade played him no tricks. His life had depended too often upon it for that, and might again.

Within the chapel of the monastery the service went on almost unheeded, save by a few of the elders, faithful women whom piety and deafness kept to their reverence. The men crowded unanimously towards the door outside which the turmoil waxed wilder and wilder.

Then, shedding to either side a surge of men, as the bow of a swift ship casts a twin wave to right and left, a man with only scraps of rags clinging to him rushed up the aisle of the nave. His hair was red-wet and matted about his brow. There was a gash

on one shoulder. His right arm hung useless by his
side. He was barefooted, but still in his left hand
he held a long knife, of which the steel was dimmed
with blood.

"El Sarria! El Sarria!" cried the voices behind
him. "There are a hundred duros on his head!
Take him! Take him!"

And in a moment more the whole church was
filled with the clangour of armed men. Bright
uniforms filled the doorways. Sword bayonets
glinted from behind pillars, as eager pursuers
rushed this way and that after their prey, overturn-
ing the chairs and frightening the kneeling women.

Straight along the aisle, turning neither to right
nor left, rushed the hunted man. On the steps
which lead up to the gilded railing he threw down
his knife, which with a clang rebounded on the
marble floor of the church.

A priest came forward as if to bar the little wicket
door. But with a bound El Sarria was within, and
in another he had cast himself down on the uppermost steps of the high altar itself and laid his hands
upon the cloth which bore *Su Majestad*, the high
mystery of the Incarnation of God.

At this uprose the Abbot, and stepping from his
throne with a calm dignity he reached the little
golden gate through which the hunted man had
come one moment before the pursuers. These were
the regular Government troops, commanded by a
Cristino officer, who with a naked sword in his hand
pointed them on.

Blind with anger and the loss of many comrades,
they would have rushed after the fugitive and slain
him even on the holy place where he lay.

But the Abbot of the Order of the Virgin of

Montblanch stood in the breach. They must first pass over his body. He held aloft a cross of gold with a gesture of stern defiance. The crozier-bearer had moved automatically to his place behind him.

"Thus far, and no farther!" cried the Abbot; "bring not the strife of man into the presence of the Prince of Peace. This man hath laid his hands upon the horns of the altar, and by Our Lady and the Host of God, he shall be safe!"

CHAPTER IX

THE SHADOW OF THE DESTROYER

THE Abbot of Montblanch, Don Baltasar Varela, was supposed to be occupied in prayer and meditation. But in common with many of his abbatical brethren, he employed his leisure with quite other matters. Many have been the jests levelled at the higher clergy of the Church of Rome, rich, cloistered, and celibate, in their relations to the other sex.

But all such jests, good against even certain holy popes of Rome and their nephews, fell harmless against the triple brass of the reputation of Don Baltasar, present head of the great Monastery of Montblanch.

Things might be whispered against the practice of divers of the brethren of the Order. But out of the sphere of his immediate jurisdiction, Don Baltasar concerned himself not with other men's matters.

"To his own God he standeth or falleth," quoth Don Baltasar, and washed his hands of the responsibility.

But there were one or two offences which Don Baltasar did not treat in this manner, and of these anon.

Meantime the Abbot talked with his confessor, and in the security of his chamber was another man

to the genial host, the liberal and well-read church-
man, the courteous man of the world who had
listened so approvingly to the wild talk of Rollo the
Scot, and so condescendingly clinked glasses with
Brother Hilario, the rich young recruit who had
come from his native province to support the cause
of *el Rey Absoluto*, Don Carlos V. of Spain.

The chamber itself was different. It contained
one chair, plain and rude as that of any anchorite,
in which the Abbot sat, a stool for the father confessor, a pallet bed, a rough shelf with half a dozen
worn volumes above it, two great books with locked
clasps of metal—these composed the entire furniture
of the chamber of one of the most powerful princes
of Holy Church in the world.

"It is no use, Anselmo," said the Abbot, gravely
toying with the clasp of one of the open books, in
which a few lines of writing were still wet, "after
all, we are but playing with the matter here. The
cure lies elsewhere. We may indeed keep our petty
bounds intact, sheltering within a dozen of leagues
not one known unfaithful to the true King, and the
principles of the Catholic religion ; but we do not
hold even Aragon with any certainty. The cities
whelm us in spite of ourselves. Zaragoza itself
is riddled with sedition, rottenly Jacobin to the
core ! "

"An accursed den of thieves ! " said the gloomy
monk. "God will judge it in His time ! "

"Doubtless—doubtless. I most fully agree ! "
said the Abbot, softly, "but meantime it is His will
that we use such means as we have in our hands to
work out the divine ends. It is well known to you
that there is one man who is driving this estate of
Spain to the verge of a devil's precipice."

With a look of dark shrewdness the priest dropped his head closer to his superior's ear.

"Mendizábal," he said, "Mendizábal, the Jew of Madrid, the lover of heretic England, the overgrown cat's-paw of the money-brokers, the gabbler of the monkeys' chatter called 'liberal principles,' the evil councillor of a foolish queen."

"Even so," sighed the Abbot. "To such God for a time grants power to scourge His very elect. Great is their power—for a time. They flourish like a green bay tree—for a time. But doth not the Wise Man say in the Scripture, 'Better is wisdom than many battalions, and a prudent man than a man of war'? You and I, father, must be the prudent men."

"But will not our brave Don Carlos soon rid us of these dead dogs of Madrid?" said the Confessor. "What of his great generals Cabrera and El Serrador? They have gained great victories. God has surely been with their arms!"

The Prior shrugged his shoulders with a slight but inconceivably contemptuous movement, which indicated that he was weary of the father's line of argument.

"Another than yourself, Anselmo, might mistake me for a scoffer when I say that in this matter we must be our own Don Carlos, our own generals—nay, our own Providence. To be plain, Carlos V.—that blessed and truly legitimate sovereign, is a donkey; Cabrera, a brave but cruel *guerrillero* who will get a shot through him one fine day, as all these gluttons for fighting do!—The rest of the generals are even as Don Carlos, and as for Providence—well, believe me, reverend father, in these later days, even Providence has left poor Spain to fend for herself?"

"God will defend His Church," said the Confessor solemnly.

"But how?" purred the Abbot. "Will Providence send down three legions of angels to sweep the Nationals from sea-board to sea-board, from Alicante even to Pontevedra?"

"I, for one, place neither bounds nor limits upon the Divine power!" said the dark monk, sententiously.

"Well, then, I do," answered the Prior; "those of common sense, and of requiring us who are on earth to use the means, the commoner and the more earthly the better."

The monk bowed, but did not again contradict his superior. The latter went on—

"Now I have received from a sure hand in Madrid, one of us and devoted to our interests, an intimation that so soon as the present Cortes is dissolved, Mendizábal means to abolish all the convents in Spain, to seize their treasures and revenues, turn their occupants adrift, and with the proceeds to pay enough foreign mercenaries to drive Don Carlos beyond the Pyrenees and end the war!"

During this speech, which the Prior delivered calmly, tapping the lid of his golden snuff-box and glancing occasionally at the Father Confessor out of his unfathomable grey eyes, that gloomy son of the Church had gradually risen to his full height. At each slow-dropping phrase the expression of horror deepened on his countenance, and as the Abbot ended, he lifted his right arm and pronounced a curse upon Mendizábal, such as only the lips of an ex-inquisitor could have compassed, which might have excited the envy of Torquemada the austere,

and even caused a smile of satisfaction to sit upon
the grim lips of San Vicente Ferrer, scourge of the
Jews.

The Prior heard him to the end of the anathema.

"*And then ?*" he said, quietly.

The dark monk stared down at his chief, as he
set placidly fingering his episcopal ring and smiling.
Was it possible that in such an awful crisis he
remained unmoved ?

"The day of anathemas is over," he said ; "the
power of words to loose or to bind, so far as the
world is concerned, is departed. But steel can still
strike and lead kill. We must use means, Father
Anselmo, we must use means."

"*I* will be the means—*I*, Anselmo, unworthy
son of Holy Church—with this dagger I will strike
the destroyer down ! Body and soul I will send
him quick to the pit ! I alone will go ! Hereby
I devote myself ! Afterwards let them rend and
torture me as they will. I fear not ; I shall not
blench. I, Anselmo, who have seen so many . . . .
—shall know how to comport myself ! "

"Hush ! " said the Abbot, for the first time
seriously disturbed, and looking over his shoulder
at the curtained door, "moderate your voice
and command yourself, father. These things are
not to be spoken of even in secret. The Jew of
Madrid shall die, because he hath risen up against
the Lord's anointed ; but your hand shall not drive
the steel ! "

"And why, Baltasar Varela ?" said the dark
priest, "pray tell me why you claim the right to
keep me from performing my vow ? "

"Let that tell you why ! " said the Prior with
severity. And without rising, so circumscribed was

his chamber, he reached down the small wall-mirror, which he used when he shaved, and handed it to the Father Confessor. " Think you, would a countenance like that have any chance of being allowed into the ante-rooms of the Prime Minister ? "

" I would disguise myself," said the priest.

The Prior smiled. " Yes," he said, " and like a *sereno* in plain clothes, look three times the monk you are with your frock upon you ! No, no, Anselmo ; Holy Church has need of you, but she does not require that you should throw your life away uselessly."

He motioned the Confessor to a seat, and passed him his snuff-box open, from which the dark monk took a pinch mechanically, his lips still working, like the sea after a storm, in a low continuous mutter of Latin curses.

" I have found my instruments," said the Prior. " They are within the walls of the Abbey of Mont-blanch at this moment. And we have just two months in which to do our business."

The Father Confessor, obeying the beckoning eyebrow of his superior, inclined his ear closer, and the Prior whispered into it for some minutes. As he proceeded, doubt, hope, expectation, certainty, joy, flitted across the monk's face. He clasped his hands as the Abbot finished.

" God in His Heaven defend His poor children and punish the transgressor ! "

" Amen," said the Abbot, a little dryly ; " and we must do what we can to assist Him upon the earth,"

CHAPTER X

A MAN AND HIS PRICE

THESE were memorable days for all the three youths, who so unexpectedly found themselves within the Convent of Montblanch. The Cristino soldiery, having fraternised with the Abbey cooks, and having been treated well from the Abbey cellars, departed about their business, leaving guards behind them to watch the exits and entrances of the hill-set monastery.

Then a peace majestic, and apparently eternal as the circle of the mountains, settled down upon Montblanch. Of all the men who dwelt there, monk and novice, lay-brother and serving-man, only two, the Abbot Baltasar and the gloomy Confessor, knew that the Abbey of the Virgin, after existing six hundred years, and increasing in riches and dignity all the while, had but eight weeks more in which to live its sweet and cloistered life.

For the rest the Abbot was the most unconcerned of all, and as to the Confessor, even a sentence of immediate execution could not have added to the consistent funereal gloom of his countenance.

But to the three young men, altogether relieved from any cares of mind, body, or estate, these days of peace revealed new worlds. The sweet-tongued bells which called dreamily to morning prayer awoke

them in their cells.   The soft yet fresh mountain air
that came in through their open windows, the Psalms
chanted in a strange tongue, the walks to the caves
of the hermits, and the sanctuaries of the saints
scattered up and down the mountain steeps, had gone
far to convince John Mortimer that there had been
religion in the world before the coming of his father's
Primitive Methodism.   Even hare-brained Rollo
grew less argumentative, and it was remarked that
on several occasions he left his long sword Killiecrankie behind him when he pilgrimed to the
conventual chapel.

As for Brother Hilario, he became so saintly that
his man-servant, François (who regretted bitterly the
Palais Royal and its joys), haunted him with offers
to convey mission or missives to *la petite* Concha of
Sarria with the utmost discretion, only to be repulsed
with scorn.

To chant in the choir, to live laborious days, to
count the linen of the brotherhood, to ride a white
mule, and to sleep in a whitewashed cell, these were
in future to be the simple daily pleasures of Brother
Hilario, late Count of Saint Pierre.   Never more
would he sing a lusty serenade beneath a lady's
window, never more throw his cloak about his
mouth and follow a promising adventure at a carnival
masquerade.

These grey monastery walls were to contain his
life for ever.   Its simple range of duties and frugal
pleasures were to satisfy him till the day when, the
inhabitant of one of its rocky cells, he should be
found dead upon a stiff frosty morning, and the bones
of this new Saint Hilario (and eke the stone on
which he had sat), would be added to the others in
the reliquary chamber of the Abbey.

There were, however, at least two objections to this. Firstly, Brother Hilario was not yet twenty-five years of age and a Frenchman, with the blood of youth running very hotly in his veins; and, secondly, unless the unexpected happened, the monastery in two months more would cease to exist upon the face of the earth.

The Abbot cultivated the society of all the three youths. But as the Englishman spoke little French and no Spanish, as the manner of his nation is, their intercourse was, of course, restricted. Nevertheless, the affair of the Priorato wine went forward apace, and the bargain was struck with the almoner of the convent at a rate which satisfied all parties. John Mortimer paid £90 down in hard cash as earnest of the price, being the balance of the private venture with which he meant to purchase the right to return to Chorley and its paternal spindles.

But the preference of the Abbot for the headstrong Scot of Fife was too manifest to be ignored, and many were the speculations among the brethren as to what might be the purpose of Don Baltasar in thus spending so much of his time with a stripling heretic.

That he had such purpose none doubted, nor that the results would in due time be seen to the honour of the Holy House of Montblanch. For though the brethren used the dearest privilege of all brotherhoods—that of grumbling freely at the Superior—none questioned either Don Baltasar's capacity or his single-mindedness where the Order was concerned.

The Abbot sounded the depths of the young man. He met his Scottish caution with a frank confession of his purpose.

" I am putting my life and the lives of all these

good and holy men in your hands, Don Rollo," he said. "Any day there may be a Nationalist army here. Their outposts are watching us even now. A fugitive was pursued to the very altar of sanctuary the other night! What! You saw him? Ah, of course, it was the night when our pleasant acquaintanceship began. Frankly, then, we are all Carlists here, Don Rollo. We stand for the King, who alone will stand for us."

"Your secret, or any secret, is safe with me," said Rollo grandly, turning his quick frank eyes upon the Prior. "Not death—no, nor torture—could drag a word from me against my will."

The Abbot perused him with his eyes thoughtfully for a moment.

"No, I do not think they would," he said slowly, and without his usual smile.

"Further, I would desire to enlist you as a recruit," he went on, after a pause. "There are many English fighting in our ranks, but few of your brave northern nation. Don Rollo, we need such men as you are. We can give them a career. Indeed, I have at present a mission in hand such as might make the fortune of any brave man. It is worth a general's commission if rightly carried through. Not many young men have such a chance at twenty-two. Ah, rogue, rogue—I heard of your doings the other night down at the inn of San Vicente, and of how with your sole sword you held at bay a score of Migueletes and Aragonese gipsies —smart fellows with their knives all of them!"

"It was nothing," said Rollo modestly; "the cowards did not mean fighting. It was never in their eyes."

"Pardon me," said the Prior, "I know these

G

fellows a great deal better than you, and it was a very great deal indeed. Your life hung upon the turning of a hair!"

"Well, for that time the hair turned my way, at any rate," said Rollo, who honestly thought nothing of the affair, and did not wish the Abbot, if he had indeed serious business on hand, to measure him by a little public-house *fracas*.

"Ah," said he gently, "you follow your star! It is good policy for those who would go far. Also I think that your star will lead you shortly into some very good society."

The Abbot paused a little ere he made the plunge. Perhaps even his steadfast pulse felt the gravity of the occasion.

Then he began to speak—lightly, rapidly, almost nervously, with the sharp staccato utterance with which Don Baltasar concealed his intensest emotion.

"The commission is a great one," said the Abbot. "This great Order, and all the servants of God in Spain, depend for their lives on you. If you succeed, Don Carlos will assuredly sit on the throne of his fathers; if you fail, there is an end. But it is necessary that you should carry with you your two friends. I, on my part, will give you a guide who knows every pass and bridle-path, every cave and shelter-stone, betwixt here and Madrid."

"Then I am to go to Madrid?"

"Not, as I hope, to Madrid, but to La Granja, where your work will await you. It is, as you may know, a palace on the slopes of the Guadarrama mountains, much frequented by the court of the Queen-Regent at Madrid."

"There is to be no bloodshed among the prisoners?" said Rollo. "Fighting is very well, but I am not going to be heart or part in any shootings of unarmed men!"

"My friend," said the Abbot, with affectionate confidentiality, laying his arm on the young man's sleeve, "I give you my word of honour. All you have to do is to bring two amiable and Catholic ladies here—the Lady Cristina and her little maid. They are eager to be reconciled to mother Church, but are prevented by evil councillors. They will come gladly enough, I doubt not, so soon as they are informed of their destination."

"Well," said Rollo, "on these conditions I will undertake the task; but as to those who are there in the palace with her? How are they to fare?"

"Your instructions," said the Abbot, "are these. You will go first to the camp of General Cabrera, to whom I will give you a letter. He will furnish you with such escort as may be thought desirable. You will also receive from him detailed orders as to what you must do when you arrive at La Granja. And I will see to it that you go from this place with a colonel's commission in the service of Carlos V. of Spain. Does that satisfy you?"

It did, but for all that the Abbot gave Rollo no hint as to what was to be the fate of those who might be taken at La Granja in the company of the little queen and her mother, the Regent Maria Cristina.

There was no difficulty at all about Etienne Saint Pierre, but John Mortimer was all for devoting his energies to the task of getting his casks of Priorato down to Barcelona for shipment. It was only after he had seen the Nationalist guards stave in cask after cask of his beloved wine, on which he was depending to lay the foundation of his fortune, drinking as much as they could, and letting the rest run to waste on the hillside, that the sullen English anger arose, and burned hotly in the bosom of John Mortimer.

"Then I will help to clear them out of the country, if they will not let me ship the property I have bought and paid good earnest money upon! I can shoot a pistol as well as any one—if the man is only near enough!"

So presently, these three, and another behind them, were riding out of the gates of Montblanch, a colonel's commission in the army of Don Carlos in Rollo's breast-pocket, a monopoly promise of all the Priorato wine for six years in that of John Mortimer, and in Brother Hilario's a dispensation absolving him for the length of his military service from all conventual and other vows.

It is difficult to say which of the three was the happiest.

"That bit of paper is worth more than a thousand pounds any day at Barcelona!" said John Mortimer triumphantly, slapping the pocket which contained the Abbot's undertaking about the Priorato. "It is as good as done if only I can get those sixty hogs-heads down to the sea, as an earnest of what is to come!"

Ah, if only, indeed!

Rollo smiled quietly as he put his hand into his pocket, and touched the colonel's commission that nestled there.

"I must keep a tight rein on my command," he said. "I hear these Carlist fellows are the devil and all!"

But as for Brother Hilario, it is grievous to state that he stood up in his stirrups and hallooed with pure joy when he lost sight of the monastery towers, that he threw his pocket breviary into a ditch, and concealed carefully the jewelled crucifix in the breast of his blue velvet coat — with the intent, as he openly averred, of pawning it so soon as they got to Madrid.

He turned round upon the huge attendant—a simple Gallegan peasant by his dress—who followed them by order of the Abbot.

" By the way, sirrah," he cried, " we pass through the village of Sarria, do we not ? "

The Gallegan lifted a pair of eyes that burned slumberously, like red coals in a smith's furnace, and with a strange smile replied, " Yes, *caballero*, we do pass through Sarria."

As for the Prior, he stood at the gate where he had given the lads his benediction, and watched them out of sight.   Father Anselmo was at his elbow, but half a pace behind.

"There they go," said the Prior.   "God help them if the Nationalists overhaul them.   They carry enough to hang them all a dozen times over.   But praise to St. Vincent and all the saints, nothing to compromise us, nor yet the Abbey of Our Lady of Montblanch ! "

CHAPTER XI

It was indeed Ramon Garcia, who on a stout shaggy pony, a portmanteau slung before and behind him, followed his masters with the half-sullen, wholly downcast look of the true Gallegan servitor. He was well attired in the Galician manner, appearing indeed like one of those Highlanders returning from successful service in the Castillas or in Catalunia, all in rusty brown double-cloth, the *paño pardo* of his class, his wide-brimmed hat plumed, and his *alpargatas* of esparto grass exchanged for holiday shoes of brown Cordovan leather.

But in his eyes, whenever he raised them, there burned, morose and unquenchable, the anger of the outcast El Sarria against the world. He lifted them indeed but seldom, and no one of the cavaliers who rode so gallantly before him recognised in the decently clad, demure, well-shaven man-servant supplied to them by the Abbot, the wild El Sarria, whom with torn mantle and bleeding shoulder, they had seen fling himself upon the altar of the Abbey of Montblanch.

So when little Etienne de Saint Pierre, that Parisian exquisite and true Legitimist, finding himself emancipated alike from vows conventual and monkish attire, and having his head, for the time being, full of the small deceiver Concha, the

86

companion of Dolóres Garcia, inquired for the village of Sarria and whether they would chance to pass that way, he never for a moment thought that their honest dullish Jaime from far away Lugo, took any more interest in the matter than might serve him to speculate upon what sort of *anisete* they might chance to find at the village venta.

By favour of the Abbot the three voyagers into the unknown had most gallant steeds under them, and were in all things well appointed, with English and French passports in their own several names and styles as gentlemen travelling for pleasure, to see strange lands, and especially this ancient, restless, war-distracted country of Spain.

Their servant, Jaime de Lugo, was appropriately horsed on a little round-barrelled Asturian pony, able to carry any weight, which padded on its way with a quiet persistence that never left its master far behind the most gallant galloper of the cavalcade.

So these three rode on towards the camp of the most redoubted and redoubtable General Cabrera.

This chief of all the armies of Don Carlos was then at the height of his fame. His fear was on all the land. He was brave, cruel, perfectly unscrupulous, this "Killer of Aragon," this "Butcher of Tortosa." In a few months he had achieved a fame greater almost than that of Zumalacarregui, the prince of *guerrilleros*, himself.

At this time Cabrera was holding half a dozen of the Cristino generals at bay, including Minos himself, the chief of all. His tactics consisted in those immemorial rapid movements and unexpected appearances which have characterised Spanish guerilla warfare ever since the Carthagenians invaded the

land, and the aboriginal Celtiberians took to the
mountains of Morella and the wild passes of Aragon,
just as Cabrera and El Serrador were doing at
this date.

Meanwhile southward out of the pleasant hills of
Montblanch, our three lads were riding, each with
his own hopes and fears in his heart. Rollo of
course was the keenest of the party ; for not only
was the work to his liking, but he was the natural
as well as the actual leader. He alone knew the
Abbot's purposes, or at least as much of them as Don
Baltasar had thought it wise to reveal to his emissary
—which after all was not a great deal.

But John Mortimer had failed to rouse himself
to any enthusiasm even under the spur of Rollo's
defiant optimism.

They would return to Montblanch in a week or
two, the latter averred. By that time the passes
would be cleared. John's wine would be safe. The
Abbot's seven-year undertaking in his pocket was
good for the face of it at any wine-shipper's in Barcelona. In a month he (Rollo) would be a colonel—
perhaps a general, and he (John Mortimer) rich
beyond the dreams of avarice.

"Or both of us may be dead, more likely !"
suggested the latter, with gloomy succinctness.

"Dead—nonsense !" cried Rollo. "See here,
man, you believe in God, or at any rate your father
does. So, hang it, you must have at least a kind of
second-hand interest Above. Now, is there not a
time appointed for you to die ? Here, look at this
clock " (he took an ancient and very bulbous-faced
watch out of his pocket). "This minute hand has
to push that hour hand so many times round before
the moment comes for your ghost to mount and ride.

Till that time comes, let your heart sit care-free. You cannot hasten, or retard that event by one solitary tick—can you? No? Well then, keep the ball rolling meantime, and if it rolls to the camp of Cabrera, why, you will be just as safe there as in your bed at Chorley with the curtains drawn and your prayers said!"

"I have a notion I could hasten the event in my own case by some few ticks, with the assistance of this unaccustomed little plaything!" said John Mortimer, who had been listening to this harangue of Rollo's with manifest impatience. And as if to prove his words, he made a sweeping motion with his pistol in the air. Instantly Rollo showed great interest.

"Good heavens, man, do you know that weapon is fresh-primed, and the trigger at full cock? If you are anxious to get a ball through your head, I am not!"

John Mortimer laughed long and loud.

"What about the appointed ticks on the watch-dial now, Master Blair? Have you forgotten you can neither hasten nor retard the day of your death? When the minute hand approaches the inevitable moment, Fate's full stop—did you not call it, you must mount and ride to Hades! Till then, you know, you are perfectly safe."

Rollo looked disgusted.

"That is the worst of trying to argue with an Englishman," he said; "his head is like a cannon ball, impervious to all logic. He does not attend to your premisses, and he never has any of his own! Of course, *if* it were ordained by the powers Above that at this moment you should suddenly go mad and shoot us all, *that* would be our appointed time,

and you would no more hasten it by your tomfoolery
than if a star fell out of the firmament and knocked
this round world to everlasting potsherds!"

"*Umm!*" said John Mortimer, still unconvinced,
"very likely—but—if I saw my wine-barrels on the
ship '*Good Intent*' of Liverpool, and my thousand
pounds upon deposit receipt in honest William
Deacon's Bank in Chorley, it would be a hanged
sight more comfort to me than all the appointed
ticks on all the appointed watches in the world!"

And so saying, the Englishman rode on his way
very sullenly, muttering and shaking his head at
intervals, as if the journey and adventure they had
entered upon, were not at all to his liking.

During this fatalistic controversy between Rollo
and his friend, Etienne de Saint Pierre had dropped
somewhat behind. He had been interested in the
remark of the glum servitor who followed them
that they must of necessity pass through the village
of Sarria.

"Do you know that place well?" he said, speaking in Castilian, which, being of Spanish descent on
his mother's side, he knew as accurately as his native
language.

"What place?" queried the Gallegan without
raising his eyes. Etienne was not disturbed by the
apparent ill-humour of the fellow. It was, as he
knew, natural to these corner-men of Spain. But he
wondered at the rascal's quite remarkable size and
strength. The arm which showed below the velvet-
banded cuff of the rusty brown coat was knotted and
corded, like the roots of an oak where the water
wears away the bank in the spring rains. His chest,
where his embroidered shirt was open for a hand's-
breadth down, showed a perfect network of scars,

ridged white cuts, triangular purple stabs, as it were punched out and only half filled in, as well as cicatrices where wounds reluctant to heal had been treated by the hot iron of half the unskilful surgeons in Spain.

But after all these things are no novelty in Iberia, where the knife is still among the lower orders the only court of appeal, and Etienne made no remark upon them. He had indeed other affairs on his mind of a more engrossing nature.

"Mon Dieu," he communed with himself, " 'tis a full calendar month since I kissed a pretty girl. I wonder what on earth it feels like?"

The path to Sarria was steep and long, but their guide, now permanently in the van, threaded his way betwixt stone and stone, now down the narrow gorge of an *arroyo* littered with *débris* and then up the next talus of slate chips like a man familiar from infancy with the way.

From a commanding hill-top he pointed away to the southward and showed them where the bayonet of a Cristino outpost glinted every half minute as the sentinel stalked to and fro upon his beat.

The Gallegan chuckled a little when the Englishman remarked upon their danger, and tapped his long rifle significantly.

"The danger of the Cristino soldier, you mean," he said, "why, masters mine, I could lead you to a place from which you might shoot yonder lad so secretly that his comrades would never know from what quarter arrived his death."

It was evening ere they drew near the village of Sarria, which lay, a drift of rusty red roofs and white-washed walls beneath the tumbled Aragonese foot-hills. The river ran nearly dry in its channel and the mill had stopped. There was not enough water to drive the clacking under-shot wheel of Luis Fernandez the comfortable, propertied miller of Sarria, who had been so cruelly wounded by the outlaw Ramon on the night when he claimed shelter from the Carlist monks of Montblanch. Ah, well, all that would soon be at an end, so at least they whispered in Sarria! If all tales were true, monks, monastery tithes, and rights of sanctuary, they would all go together. The wise politicians at Madrid, eager for their country's good (and certain advantages upon the stock exchange), were about to pass the besom of destruction over the religious houses, sweeping away in a common ruin grey friar and white friar and black friar. Nay, the salaried parish priests would find themselves sadly docked, and even stout Father Mateo himself was beginning to quake in his shoes and draw his girdle tighter by a hole at a time to prepare for the event.

So at least the bruit went forth, and though none save the Prior of Montblanch and his confidant knew anything for certain, the air was full of rumours; while between the Carlist war and the report of the great coming changes, the minds of men were growing grievously unsettled. Honest folk and peaceful citizens now went about armed. The men sat longer at the *cafés*. They returned later home. They spoke more sharply to their wives when they asked of them why these things were so.

By the little village gate where Gaspar Perico, the chief representative of the town dues of Sarria, sat commonly at the receipt of custom, a group of men occupied a long bench, with their pints of wine and the sweet syrup of pomegranates before them, as is the custom of Aragon on summer evenings.

The venta of Sarria was kept by a nephew of Gaspar's, the octroi man, one recently come to the district. His name was Esteban, and like his uncle he had already got him the name of a "valiant," or of a man ready with his tongue and equally ready with his knife.

With the younger Perico's coming, the venta *El Corral* had promptly become the Café de Madrid, while the prices of all liquors rose to mark the change, even as in a like proportion their quality speedily diminished. Customers would doubtless have left at this juncture but for the fact that Esteban was his uncle's nephew, and that Perico the Elder sat at the receipt of custom.

So at this newly named Café de Madrid our travellers alighted, and the silent Gallegan, gathering the reins in his hands, disappeared into the stables, whose roofs rose over the low front of the venta like a cathedral behind its cloisters.

"Good evening to you, young cavaliers!" cried the gallant Gaspar, who commonly did the honours even in the presence of his nephew, the nominal host of the venta. The younger man had followed the Gallegan to the stables with a declared intent of seeing that the horses were properly provided for.

"You have come far to-day?" inquired Gaspar courteously.

"From the Abbey of——" (here Rollo kicked Etienne suddenly) "I mean we passed the Abbey of Montblanch, leaving behind us gladly such a nest of Carlist thieves! From the true nationalist city of Zaragoza we come," said the Count de Saint Pierre in a breath.

"You are all good men and true here, I observe," said Rollo, who had seen Cristino colours on the official coat of Gaspar Perico.

"Good men and good nationals!" cried Gaspar. "Indeed, I believe you! I should like to see any other show his face in Sarria. There never was one since Ramon Garcia became an outlaw, and he fled the village rather than face me, the champion of the province. Ah, he knew better than to encounter this noble and well-tried weapon!"

And as he spoke he tapped the brown stock of his blunderbuss, and took a wholly superfluous squint down the stock to be certain that the sights were properly adjusted, or perhaps to show the excellent terms he was on with his weapon.

At this very moment, Esteban the bully, Esteban the unconquered valiant, came running from the stables of the venta, holding his hands to his face, and behind him, towering up suddenly and filling the entire doorway, appeared the huge figure of the Gallegan. What had occurred between them no man could say. But the Gallegan with great coolness proceeded to cast out upon the rubbish heap before the door, armful after armful of chopped and partly rotten straw which exhaled a thin steam into the cool air of evening. He followed this up by emptying a huge leather-covered sieve full of bad barley several times upon the same vaporous mound. Then with the greatest composure and with a complete understanding of the premises, the Gallegan walked across to a smaller stable, where the landlord's own cattle were kept. He kicked the door open with two applications of his foot, and presently was lost to sight within.

"Shoot him—shoot him, uncle!" cried the half-tearful bully; "he hath smitten me upon the nose to the outpouring of my blood! Shall a Perico abide this? Shoot—for the honour of our name!"

But the valiant man of the receipt of customs was also a cautious one.

"Not so, dear Esteban," he said; "this man is the servant of three noble cavaliers of a foreign nation. If he has done wrong, their purses will make reparation. They are all rich, these foreigners! For all the spilt fodder they will also doubtless pay. Is it not so, *caballeros*?"

But Rollo, the readily furious, gripped his sword and said, "Not one groat or stiver, not a single maravedi, will I pay till I have spoken with our man-servant and know the cause of this disorder from himself."

And he laid his hand so determinedly on the hilt of Killiecrankie, whose basket had been endued with a new silk lining of red and tassels of the same colour, that the valiant men of Sarria thought better of any designs of attack they might have entertained, and preferred to await the event.

The Gallegan by this time had emerged from the smaller private stable with a good bushel measure of straw and barley, which he carried on his head towards the larger premises where his masters' three steeds and his own round-barrelled Aragonese pony had been settled for the night.

He waved his hand to the three at the venta door.

"There is now no fault! It is of good quality this time!" he cried.

And no one said a word more concerning the matter. Nor did Señor Esteban Perico again advert to the stout buffet his nose had received at the beginning of the affair. On the contrary, he was laboriously polite to the Gallegan, and put an extra piece of fresh-cut garlic in his soup when it came to supper-time. For after this fashion was the younger Perico made.

And while the three waited, they talked to all and sundry. For Etienne had questions to ask which bore no small relation to the present preoccupation of his mind.

Concha—oh yes, little Concha Cabezos from Andalucia, certainly they knew her. All the village knew her.

"A pretty girl and dances remarkably well," said Esteban Perico complacently, "but holds her head too high for one in her position."

"I do not call that a fault," said Etienne, moving along the wooden settle in front of the venta door to make room for the huge Gallegan, who at that moment strolled up. He did this quite naturally, for in Spain no distinctions of master or servant hold either upon church pavements or on venta benches.

"No, it is certainly no fault of Concha's that she keeps herself aloof," said a young fellow in a rustic galliard's dress—light stockings, knee breeches of black cloth, a short shell jacket, and a broad sash of red about his waist. He twirled his moustachios with the air of one who could tell sad tales of little Concha if only he had the mind.

"And why, sir?" cried Etienne, bristling in a moment like a turkeycock; "pray, has the young lady vouchsafed you any token of her regard?"

"Nay, not to me," said the local Don Juan, cautiously; "but if you are anxious upon the question, I advise you to apply to Don Rafael de Flores, our alcalde's son."

"What," cried the Frenchman, "is he her lover?"

"Her lover of many months," answered Don Juan, "truly you say right. And the strange thing is that he got himself stabbed for it too, by that great oaf Ramon Garcia, whom they now call 'El Sarria.' Ha! ha! and he was as innocent as yourself all the time."

"I will presently interview the Don Rafael de Flores," muttered Etienne. "This is some slander. 'Tis not possible Concha has been deceiving me— and she so young, so innocent. Oh, it would be bitter indeed if it were so!"

He meditated a moment, flicking his polished boot with a riding-whip.

"And all the more bitter, that up to this moment I thought it was I who was deceiving her."

But the young Don Juan of the Sarrian *café* liked to hold the floor, and with three distinguished cavaliers for listeners, it was something to find a subject of common interest. Besides, who knew whether he might not hear a tale or two to the disadvantage of little Concha Cabezos, who had flouted him so sadly at last carnival and made a score of girls laugh at him upon the open Rambla.

"It happened thus," he said, "you have heard of El Sarria the outlaw, on whose head both parties have set a price?"

"He was of our village," cried half a dozen at once. It was their one title to respect, indisputable in any company. They began all conversations when they went from home with Ramon Garcia's name, and the statement of the fact that they had known his father.

"And a fine old man he was; very gracious and formal and of much dignity."

"It happened thus," the youthful dandy went

H

on. " El Sarria came home late one night, and when he arrived at his own gable-end, lo, there by the *reja*, where the inside stairway mounts, was a youth 'plucking the turkey' with his sweetheart through a broken bar, and that apparently with great success. And the fool Ramon, his head being filled with his Dolóres, never bethought himself for a moment that there might be another pretty girl in the house besides his wife, and so without waiting either ' *Buenos !* ' or *Hola !* '—*click* went Ramon's knife into the lover's back ! Such a pair of fools as they were ! "

" And did this—this Rafael de Flores die ? " asked Etienne, divided between a hope that he had, and a fear that if so he might be balked of his revenge.

" Die ? No—he was about again before many weeks. But this foolish Ramon took straightway to the hills, because he thought that his wife was false and that he had killed her cousin and lover."

And even as Don Juan was speaking these words a young man of a slender form and particularly lithe carriage, dressed in the height of Madrid fashion, walked into the *café* with a smiling flourish of his hat to the company.

" A glass of vermuth, Esteban," he said, " and if any of these gentlemen will join me I shall feel honoured. Be good enough to tell them who I am, Gaspar, my friend."

" Señor cavalier," said the valiant man of Sarria, planting the butt of his blunderbuss firmly on the ground that he might lean upon it, and as it were more officially make the important introduction, " this is no other than the only son of our rich and dis-tinguished alcalde, Señor Don Rafael de Flores, concerning whom you have already heard some speech."

And Gaspar, who knew his place, stood back for the impressive civilities which followed. The jaws of the villagers dropped as they saw the three foreigners with one accord raise their hats from their heads and make each a reverence after his kind. Rollo, the tragical Scot, swept back his sombrero-brim in a grand curve as if it bore a drooping plume. John Mortimer jerked his beaver vertically off and clapped it down again as if he had a spite at the crown, while M. Etienne turned out his toes and in his elbows, as he bowed sharply at the waist with a severe and haughty expression, without, however, taking his hat from his head.

"I must do the honours, I see," said Rollo, laughing, "since we have no local trumpeter to do them for us. (Where in the world is that sullen dog, our most faithful Galician ?) This to the left is Monsieur de Saint Pierre, count of that name. Then next Mr. John Mortimer of Chorley in England, and as for me I am Rollo Blair of Blair Castle in the county of Fife, at your service."

At this point the aforesaid M. de Saint Pierre stepped forward. He had drawn out his card-case and selected a pasteboard with the care and deliberation with which a connoisseur may choose a cigar.

"I have the honour to present Señor Don Rafael with my cartel of defiance," he said simply.

The young man thus addressed stood a long moment dumb and fixed in the middle of the floor, gazing at the engraved lines on the card, which he had mechanically accepted, without comprehending their meaning.

"A cartel !" he stammered at last ; "impossible.

I can have no cause of quarrel with this gentleman from France. I do not even know him ! "

But Etienne had all the science of the affair of honour at his finger-ends.

"I have nothing to say, sir," he replied, frigidly ; "I refer you to my second ! "

And he turned to his nearest companion, who happened to be John Mortimer. The Englishman, however, had but imperfectly understood.

"Well," he said in his best Spanish, "I am prepared to treat for any quantity, provided the quality be to my satisfaction. But mind, the terms are, 'delivered on the quay at Barcelona.' *No more Priorato pigs in pokes for John Mortimer of Chorley.*"

He relapsed into English with the last clause, and sticking his thumbs into the pockets of his waistcoat, he waited Don Rafael's reply to his ultimatum.

"Holy Virgin, are they all mad ?" that young gentleman was crying in a passion of despair when Rollo stepped forward and bowed courteously.

"The matter is briefly this, as I understand it," he said. " My friend, M. Etienne de Saint Pierre, has been in terms of considerable amity with a certain young lady—whose name I need not repeat in a public place. He has been given to understand that you claim a similar high position in her favour. If this be so, Señor, my principal wishes to end the difficulty by a duel to the death, so that the young lady may not be put to the painful necessity of making a choice between two such gallant men. I make it *quite* clear, do I not ? Two of you love one lady. The lady cannot accept both. You fight. There remains but one. The lady is in no difficulty ! Do you both agree ? "

"I agree most heartily," said Etienne, rubbing his hands cheerfully, and practising feints in the air with his forefinger.

"But not I—not I!" cried Don Rafael, with sudden frenzy; "I do not agree—far from it, indeed. I would have you know that I am a married man. My wife is waiting for me at home at this moment. I must go. I must, indeed. Besides, I am under age, and it is murder in the first degree to shoot an unarmed man. I am not in love with any person. I make claims to no lady's affection. I am a married man, I tell you, gentlemen—I was never in love with anybody else. I told my wife so only this morning!"

"Not with Doña Concha Cabezos of this village?" said Etienne, sternly. "I am advised that you have been in the habit of making that claim."

"Never, never," cried the gallant, wringing his hands. "Saints, angels, and martyrs—if this should come to my wife's ears! I swear to you I do not know any Concha—I never heard of her. I will have nothing to do with her! Gentlemen, you must excuse me. I have an engagement!"

And with this hurried adieu the little man in the Madrid suit fairly bolted out of the *café*, and ran down the street at full speed.

And in the dusk of the gable arches the Gallegan sat with his head sunk low in his hands.

"What a fool, Ramon Garcia! What a mortal fool you were—to have thought for a moment that your little Dolóres could have loved a thing like that!"

CHAPTER XII

THE CRYING OF A YOUNG CHILD

"And now, gentlemen," said Monsieur Etienne grandly, "where is the young gentleman who traduced in my hearing the fair fame of Doña Concha Cabezos ? *Ma foi*, I will transfer my cartel to him ! "

Then, with great dignity, uprose the ancient valiant man of the octroi of Sarria, for he felt that some one must vindicate the municipality.

"Cavalier," he said, with a sweeping bow which did honour at once to himself and to the place in which they were assembled, "there may be those amongst us who have spoken too freely, and on their behalf and my own I convey to you an apology if we have unwittingly offended. In a venta—I beg my nephew's pardon—in a *café*, like the Café de Madrid, men's tongues wag fast without harm being intended to any man, much less to any honourable lady. So it was in this case, and in the name of the loyal town of Sarria, I express my regret. If these words be sufficient, here is my hand. The Café de Madrid, sir, begs your acceptance of a bottle of the best within its cellars. But if your lordship be still offended, there are twenty men here who are ready to meet you on the field of honour. For I would have you know, gentlemen, that we are also *Caballeros*. But it must be with the weapons in the use of which we have some skill—the cloak wrapped about the left arm, the Manchegan knife in the right hand. Or, if our Aragonese custom please not your honours, I make myself personally responsible for any words that may have been spoken ; aye, and will be proud to stand out upon the hillside and exchange shots with you till you are fully satisfied—standing up, man to man, at one hundred yards. This I do because the offence was given in my nephew's *café*, and because for forty years I have been called the Valiant Man of Sarria !"

The ancient Gaspar stood before them, alternately patting the stock of his blunderbuss and pulling the ragged ends of his long white moustachios, till Rollo, who could recognise true courage when he saw it, stepped up to him, and making a low bow held out a hand, which the other immediately grasped amid plaudits from the assembled company.

"You are a brave man, a valiant man, indeed, Señor——" he was beginning.

"Gaspar Perico, at your service—of the wars of the Independence !" interrupted the old man, proudly.

"You have not forgotten the use of your weapons, *Señor Valiente !*" said the young Scot. "Take off your hat, Etienne," he added in French, "and accept the old fellow's apology as graciously as you can. I am your second, and have arranged the matter for you already !"

With a little grumbling Etienne complied, and was graciously pleased to allow himself to be appeased. Rollo felt for him, for he himself knew well what it is to itch to fight somebody and yet have to put up one's sword with the point untried. But a new

feeling had come into his soul. A steadying-rein
was thrown over his shoulder—the best that can be
set to diminish the ardours of a firebrand like this
hot-headed Scot. This was responsibility. He was
upon a mission of vast importance, and though he
cared about the rights and wrongs of the affair not at
all, and would just as soon have taken service with
the red and yellow of the nationals as with the white
boinas of Don Carlos, once committed to the
adventure he resolved that no follies that he could
prevent should damage a successful issue.

So, having settled the quarrel, and partaken of
the excellent smuggled vermuth de Torino, in which,
by his uncle's order, Esteban the host and his guests
washed away all traces of ill-feeling, the three sat
down to enjoy the *puchero*, which all this while had
been quietly simmering in the kitchen of the inn.
At their request the repast was shared by Gaspar
Perico, while the nephew, in obedience to a sign
from his uncle, waited at table. It was not difficult
to perceive that Señor Gaspar was the true patron
of the Café de Madrid in the village of Sarria.

    *   *   *   *   *

So soon as he knew that the cause for which he
had stabbed his wife's cousin had been one that in
no wise concerned little Dolóres the disguised
Ramon Garcia went out to seek his wife, a great
pity and a great remorse tearing like hungry
Murcian vultures at his heart. He was not worthy
even to speak to that pure creature. His hasty
jealousy had ruined their lives. He it was who had
squandered his chances, lost his patrimony, broken
up their little home behind the whispering reeds of
the Cerde. Yes, he had done all that, but—*he loved
her.* So he went forth to seek her, and the night

closed about him, grey and solemn with a touch of chill in the air. It was not hot and stifling like that other when he had come home to meet his doom and crept up through a kind of blood-red haze to strike that one blow by the latticed *reja* of his house.

Ramon did not hide and skulk now. He walked down the street with his long locks shorn, his beard clean shaven, his Gallegan dress and plumed hat, secure that none of his fellow townsmen would recognise him. And, at least in the semi-darkness, he was entirely safe.

There he could see the little white shed on the roof where Dolóres used to feed her pigeons, and he smiled as he remembered how before he married he had been wont to keep various breeds, such as Valencia tumblers, pouters, and fast-flying carriers upon which he used to wager a few reals with his friends.

But that was in his bachelor days. He smiled again as he thought that when Dolóres came it was a different story. Never was such a little house-wife. She was all for the pot. She would have him part with his fine sorts, save and except one or two tumblers that she used to feed from her balcony. She loved to see them from her window circling, wheeling, and as it were, play-acting in the air. For the rest, the commonest kinds that laid the most eggs, brought up the largest broods, and took on the plumpest breasts when fed with ground maize and Indian corn, green from the patch which he grew on purpose for her behind the willows—these were his wife's especial delight.

Ramon opened the little wicket to which she had so often run to meet him, under the three great fig trees. The gate creaked on unaccustomed hinges.

The white square of a placard on the post caught his eye. It was too dark to see clearly, or else El Sarria would have seen that it was a bill of sale of the house and effects of a certain Ramon Garcia, outlaw. As he stepped within his foot slipped among the rotten figs which lay almost ankle-deep on the path he had once kept so clean. A buzz of angry wasps arose. They were drunken, however, with the fermenting fruit, and blundered this way and that like men tipsy with new wine.

The path before him was tangled across and across with bindweed and runners of untended vine. The neglected artichokes had shot, and their glary seed-balls rose as high as his chin like gigantic thistles.

The house that had been so full of light and loving welcome lay all dark before him, blank and unlovely as a funeral vault.

Yet for all these signs of desolation Ramon only reproached himself the more.

"The little Dolóres," he thought, "she has felt herself forsaken. Like a wounded doe she shrinks from sight. Doubtless she comes and goes by the back of the house. The sweet little Dolóres——" And he smiled. It did not occur to him that she would ever be turned out of the house that was his and hers. She would go on living there and waiting for him. And now how surprised she would be. But he would tell her all, and she would forgive him. And it is typical of the man and of his nation that he never for a moment dreamed that his being "El Sarria," a penniless outlaw with a price on his head, would make one whit of difference to Dolóres.

After all what was it to be outlawed? If he did this service for the Abbot and Don Carlos—a hard

one, surely——he would be received into the army of
Navarra, and he might at once become an officer.
Or he might escape across the seas and make a home
for Dolóres in a new country.   Meantime he would
see her once more, for that night at least hold her
safe in his arms.

But by this time he had gone round the gable
by the little narrow path over which the reeds continually rustled.   He passed the window with the
broken *reja*, and he smiled when he thought of the
ignominious flight of Don Rafael down the village
street.   With a quickened step and his heart thud-
ding in his ears he went about the little reed-built
hut in which he had kept Concha's firewood, and
stood at the back-door.

It was closed and impervious.   No ray of light
penetrated.   "Perhaps Concha has gone out, and
the little one, being afraid, is sitting alone in the
dark, or has drawn the clothes over her head in bed."

He had always loved the delightful terrors with
which Dolóres was wont to cling to him, or flee to
throw herself on his bosom from some imaginary
peril—a centipede that scuttled out of the shutter-
crack or a he-goat that had stamped his foot at her
down on the rocks by the river.   And like a healing
balm the thought came to him.   For all that talk in
the venta—of Concha this and Concha that, of lovers
and aspirants, no single word had been uttered of his
Dolóres.

"What a fool, Ramon !   What an inconceivable
fool !" he murmured to himself.   "*You* doubted
her, but the common village voice, so insolently
free-spoken, never did so for a moment !"

He knocked and called, his old love name for
her, "Lola—dear Lola—open !   It is I—Ramon !"

He called softly, for after all he was the outlaw, and the Migueletes might be waiting for him in case he should return to his first home.

But, call he loud or call he soft, there was no answer from the little house where he had been so happy with Dolóres. He struck a light with his tinder-box and lit the dark lantern he carried.

There was another bill on the back-door, and now with the lantern in his hand he read it from top to bottom. It was dated some months previously and was under the authority of the *alcalde* of Sarria and by order of General Nogueras, the Cristino officer commanding the district.

"This house, belonging to the well-known rebel, outlaw and murderer, Ramon Garcia, called El Sarria, is to be sold for the benefit of the government of the Queen-Regent with all its contents——" And here followed a list, among which his heart stood still to recognise the great chair he had bought at Lerida for Dolóres to rest in when she was delicate, the bed they twain had slept in, the very work-table at which she had sewn the household linen, and sat gossiping with Concha over their embroidery.

But there was no doubt about the matter. Dolóres was gone, and the eye of El Sarria fell upon a notice rudely printed with a pen and inserted in a corner of the little square trap-door by which it was possible to survey a visitor without opening the door.

"Any who have letters, packages, or other communications for persons lately residing in this house, are honourably requested to give themselves the trouble of carrying them to the Mill of Sarria, where they will receive the sincere thanks and gratitude of the undersigned

"LUIS FERNANDEZ."

Ramon saw it all.   He knew now why his friend had arranged for his death at the mouth of the secret hiding-place.   He understood why there was no talk about Dolóres at the inn.   She was under the protection of the most powerful man in the village, save the alcalde alone.   Not that Ramon doubted little Dolóres.   He would not make that mistake a second time.

But they would work upon her, he knew well how, tell her that he was dead, that Luis Fernandez has been his only friend.   He recollected, with a hot feeling of shame and anger, certain speeches of his own in which he had spoken to her of the traitor as his "twin brother," the "friend of his heart," and how even on one occasion he had commended Dolóres to the good offices of Luis when he was to be for some weeks absent from Sarria upon business.

He turned the lamp once more on the little announcement so rudely traced upon the blue paper.   A spider had spun its web across it.   Many flies had left their wings there.   So, though undated, Ramon judged that it was by no means recent.

"Ah, yes, Don Luis," he thought grimly, "here is one who has a message to leave at the mill-house of Sarria."

But before setting out Ramon Garcia went into the little fagot-house, and sitting down upon a pile of kindling-wood which he himself had cut, he drew the charges of his pistols and reloaded them with quite extraordinary care.

Then he blew out his lantern and stepped forth into the night.

*   *   *   *   *

At the venta the three adventurers supped by themselves. Their Gallegan retainer did not put in an appearance, to the sorrow of Mons. Etienne who wished to employ him in finding out the abiding-place of the faithless but indubitably charming Doña Concha.

However, the Gallegan did not return all night. He had, in fact, gone to deliver a message at the house of his sometime friend Don Luis Fernandez.

When he arrived at the bottom of the valley through which the waters of the Cerde had almost ceased to flow, being so drained for irrigation and bled for village fountains that there remained hardly enough of them to be blued by the washerwomen at their clothes, or for the drink of the brown goats pattering down to the stray pools, their hard little hoofs clicking like castanets on the hot and slippery stones of the river-bed. Meanwhile El Sarria thought several things.

First, that Luis Fernandez had recovered from his wound and was so sure of his own security that he could afford to take over his friend's wife and all her responsibilities. Ramon gritted his teeth, as he stole like a shadow down the dry river-bed. He had learned many a lesson during these months, and the kite's shadow flitted not more silently over the un-peopled moor than did El Sarria the outlaw down to the old mill-house. He knew the place, too, stone by stone, pool by pool, for in old days Luis and he had often played there from dawn to dark.

The mill-house of Sarria was in particularly sharp contrast to the abode he had left. Luis had always been a rich man, especially since his uncle died ; he, Ramon, never more than well-to-do. But here were magazines and granaries, barns and drying-lofts. Besides, in the pleasant angle where the windows looked down on the river, there was a dwelling-house with green window-shutters and white curtains, the like of which for whiteness and greenness were not to be seen even within the magnificent courtyard of Señor de Flores, the rich alcalde of Sarria.

This was illuminated as Ramon came near, and, from the darkness of the river gully, he looked up at its lighted windows from behind one of the great boulders, which are the teeth of the Cerde when the floods come down from the mountains. How they rolled and growled and groaned and crunched upon each other ! Ramon, in all the turmoil of his thoughts, remembered one night when to see Dolóres and to stand all dripping beneath her window, he had dared even that peril of great waters.

But all was now clear and bright and still. The stars shone above and in nearly every window of the mill-house there burned a larger, a mellower star. It might have been a *festa* night, save that the windows were curtained and the lights shone through a white drapery of lace, subdued and tender.

He crept nearer to the house. He heard a noise of voices within. An equipage drove up rapidly to the front. What could bring a carriage to the house of Luis Fernandez ?

A wild idea sprang into Ramon's brain. He had been so long in solitude that he drew conclusions rapidly. So he followed the train of thought upon which he had fallen, even as the flame runs along a train of gunpowder laid on the floor.

They had been long persuading her—all these months he had been on the mountain, and now they had married her to his false friend, to Luis Fernandez. It was the eve of the wedding-feast, and the guests were arriving. His knife had deceived him a second time. He had not struck true. Where was his old skill? There—surely his eyesight did not deceive him—was Luis Fernandez walking to and fro within his own house, arm in arm with a friend. They had lied to Dolóres and told her he was dead, even as the Migueletes would certainly do to claim the reward. There upon the balcony was a stranger dressed in black; he and Luis came to an open window, leaned out, and talked confidentially together. The stranger was peeling an orange, and he flung the peel almost upon the head of El Sarria.

Ramon, fingering his pistol butt, wondered if he should shoot now or wait. The two men went in again, and solved the difficulty for that time. Moreover, the outlaw did not yet know for certain that his wife was within the mill-house.

He would reconnoitre and find out. So he hid his gun carefully in a dry place under a stone, and stole up to the house through the garden, finding his way by instinct, for all the lighted windows were now on the other side.

Yet El Sarria never halted, never stumbled, was never at a loss. Now he stepped over the little stream which ran in an artificial channel to reinforce the undershot wheel from above, when the Cerde was low. Another pace forward and he turned sharply to the left, parted a tangle of oleanders, and looked out upon the broad space in front of the house.

It was a doctor's carriage all the way from La

Bisbal that stood there. It was not a wedding then; some one was ill, very ill, or the *Sangrador* would not have come from so far, nor at such an expense to Don Luis, who in all things was a careful man. Moreover, to Ramon's simple Spanish mind the *Sangrador* and the undertaker arrived in one coach. Could he have struck some one else instead of Don Luis that night at the chasm? Surely no!

And then a great keen pain ran through his soul. He heard Dolóres call his name! High, keen, clear—as it were out of an eternity of pain, it came to him. "*Ramon, Ramon—help me, Ramon!*"

He stood a moment clutching at his breast. The cry was not repeated. But all the same, there could be no mistake. It was her voice or that of an angel from heaven. She had summoned him, and alive or dead he would find her. He drew his knife and with a spring was in the road. Along the wall he sped towards the door of the dwelling-place: it stood open and the wide hall stretched before him empty, vague, and dark.

Ramon listened, his upper lip lifted and his white teeth showing a little. He held his knife, yet clean and razor-sharp in his hand. There was a babel of confused sounds above; he could distinguish the tones of Luis Fernandez. But the voice of his Dolóres he did not hear again. No matter, he had heard it once and he would go—yes, into the midst of his foes. Escape or capture, Carlist or Cristino did not matter now. She was innocent; she loved him; she had called his name. Neither God nor devil should stop him now. He was already on the staircase. He went noiselessly, for he was bare of foot, having stripped in the river-bed, and left his brown cordovans beside his

I

gun. But before his bare sole touched the hollow of the second step, the one sound in the universe which could have stopped him reached his ear—and that foot was never set down.

El Sarria heard the first cry of a new-born child.

CHAPTER XIII

DON TOMAS DIGS A GRAVE

No Cristino bullet that ever was moulded could have stopped the man more completely. He stood again on the floor of the paven hall, pale, shaking like an aspen leaf, his whole live soul upturned and aghast within him.

And above the youngling blared like a trumpet.

El Sarria was outside now. His knife was hidden in his breast. There was no need of it, at least for the present. He looked out of the gate upon the white and dusty highway. Like the hall, it was vague and empty, ankle-deep too in yet warm dust, that felt grateful to his feet after the sharp stones of the *arroyo* out of which he had climbed.

Under the barn a woman crouched by a fire near a little tent pitched in a corner, evidently taking care of the *tan* in the absence of her companions. Gipsies they were, as he could see, and strangers to the place. Perhaps she could tell him something. She called aloud to him, and he went and sat down beside her, nothing loth.

"You are a Gallegan, I see!" said the woman, while she continued to stir something savoury in a pot without appearing to pay Ramon much attention.

"A Gallician from Lugo—yes—but I have been long in these parts," answered El Sarria, mindful of his accent.

"And we of Granada—as you may both see and hear!" said the old gipsy, tossing her head with the scorn of the Romany for the outlander.

"What is going on up there?" he said, indicating the mill-house with his thumb. And as he spoke, for the first time the woman ceased stirring the pot and turned her eyes upon him.

"What is that to thee?" she inquired with a sudden fiery thrill in her speech.

As fierce and strong beat the passion in the heart of El Sarria, but nevertheless he commanded himself and answered, "Naught!"

"Thou liest!" she said; "think not to hide a heart secret from a hax, a witch woman. Either thou lovest to the death or thou hatest to the death. In either case, *pay!* Pay, and I will tell thee all thy desire, according to the crossing of my hand!"

El Sarria drew a gold double *duro* from his pouch and gave it into her withered clutch.

"Good," she said, "'tis a good crossing! I will tell you truth that you may take oath upon, whether kissing or slaying be in your thought. A woman is sick to the death or near by. A babe little desired is born. The Tia Elvira is with her. Whether the woman live or die, the Tia will decide according to the crossing of *her* hand. And the babe—well, when the mother is soon to be a bride, its life is not like to be long! A rough crossing for so short a sojourn, I wot. Good morning, brave man's son! And to you, sir, a safe journey till the knife strikes or the lips meet!"

The cryptic utterance of the witch woman sitting crooning over her pot affected El Sarria greatly. He did not doubt for a moment that Dolóres lay within the house of Luis Fernandez, and that he had heard the crying of his own firstborn son. He arose uncertainly, as if the solid earth were swaying beneath him.

Leaving her pot simmering on the wood-ashes, the gipsy woman came after Ramon to the corner of the garden. The broad-leaved fig-trees made a dense green gloom there. The pale grey undersides of the olive whipped like feathers in the light chill breeze of night.

"There—go in there!"

She pointed with her hand to a little pillared summer-house in the garden. It was overgrown with creepers, and Luis had placed a fountain in it, which, however, only played when the waters were high in the Cerde.

"Whether you hate the old or love the young, bide there," she whispered; "there is no need that Tia Elvira should have all the gold. Cross my hand again, and I am your servant for ever."

Ramon gave her a gold *duro*.

"I am not a rich man," he said, "but for your goodwill you are welcome!"

"You run eager-hearted in the dust with bare and bleeding feet," she said. "You carry a knife naked in your bosom. Therefore you are rich enough for me. And I will spite Tia Elvira if I can. She would not give me so much as an *ochavo* of all her gettings. Why should I consider her?"

And she gripped Ramon by the arm with claws like eagles' talons and stood leaning against him, breathing into his ear.

"Ah, Gallego, you are strong to lean against. I love a man so," she said. "Once you had not stood so slack and careless if La Giralda had leaned her breast against your shoulder—ah me, all withered now is it and hard as the rim of a sieve. But you love this young widow, you also. She is El Sarria's widow, they tell me, he whom the Migueletes slew at the entering in of the Devil's Cañon. A fine man that, *Caramba!* And so you too wish to marry her now he is dead. If I were a widow and young I would choose you, for you are of stature and thickness, yes— a proper man through and through. Scarce can I meet my old arms about your chest. Yet woman never knows woman, and she may chance to prefer Don Luis. But the babe is in their way—the babe that cried to-night. Luis does not wish it well. He longs for children of his own by this woman, and El Sarria's brat would spoil his inheritance. The Tia let the secret out in her cups!"

She stopped and unclasped her arms.

"Ah," she said, "you love not Don Luis. I felt it when I spoke of his having issue by that woman. I wot well the thing will never happen. Your knife or your pistol (of these you have two) will have conference with him before that. But, if you wish this child to live—though I see not why you should, save that its father was like you a proper man and the slayer of many—stand yonder in the shadow of the summer-house, and if any come out with the babe, smite! If it be a man, smite hard, but if it be Aunt Elvira, the *hax*, smite ten times harder. For she is the devil in petticoats and hath sworn away many a life, as she would do mine if she could. I, who have never wished her any harm all the days of my life! There, put your arm about me yet a moment—so. Now here is your gold back. I wish it not. The other is better. Tighter! Hold me yet closer a moment. Ay-ah, dearie, it is sweet to feel once more the grip of a strong man's

arms about one—yes—though he love another—and
she a little puling woman who cannot even deliver herself of her first-born son without a *Sangrador*. Go—
go, they are coming to the door. I see the lights disappear from the chamber above. Remember to strike
the Tia low—in the groin is best. She wears amulets
and charms above, and you might miss your mark !"

So, much astonished, and with his gold pieces in
his hand, Ramon found him in the little roughly
finished lath-and-plaster temple. He sat on the dry
basin of the fountain and parted the vine leaves with
his hands. He was scarce a dozen yards from a door
in the wall—a door recently broken, which by two
stone steps gave direct access to the garden.

Behind him were the wall and the fig-tree where
he had spoken with the gipsy. As he looked he
fancied a figure still there, dark against the sky,
doubtless the woman La Giralda waiting to see if his
knife struck the Tia in the proper place.

Ramon listened, and through the darkness he
could discern the keen, insistent, yet to his ear sweet
crying of the babe, presently broken by a series of
pats on the back into a staccato bleat, and finally
stilling itself little by little into an uncertain silence.

Then the door into the garden was cautiously
opened, and a man clumsily descended. He shut
the door softly behind him and stood a while gazing
up at the lighted room. Then shaking his fist at the
illuminated panes, he moved towards the summer-
house. El Sarria thought himself discovered, and
with a filling of his lungs which swept his breast up
in a grand curve, he drew his knife and stood erect
in the darkest corner.

Stumbling and grumbling the man came to the
aperture. He did not descend the step which led to

the interior, but instead groped through one of the
open windows for something behind the door.

"May holy San Isidro strike my brother with his
lightnings!" he muttered. "He gives me all the
ill jobs, and when I have done them but scant thanks
for my pains!"

His hand went groping blindly this way and that,
unwitting of what lurked in the further gloom.

"From Ramon Garcia's knife at the Devil's
Gorge to this young one's undoing, all comes to
poor Tomas. And now, when he might have left me
the mill-house he must needs marry this widow
Garcia and set to work forthwith to chouse me out
of my inheritance! A foul pest on him and on
his seed!"

This mutter of discontent he interspersed with
yet more potent anathemas, as he groped here and
there in the darkness for what he sought. By-and-by
he extracted a spade, a mattock, and a skin-covered
corn measure holding about the quarter of an *arroba*.

With these he went grumbling off towards the
deep shade of the fig-tree where Ramon had talked
with the gipsy woman. With great impartiality he
cursed his brother Luis, El Sarria and his knife, the
widow Dolóres and her child.

Ramon heard him laugh as he stumbled among
the vine roots.

"It is a blessing that such puling brats need no
iron collar when sentenced to the garotte. It will
not be pleasant, I suppose—a nasty thing enough to
do. But after all, this little trench under the fig-tree
will be an excellent hold over my good brother Luis.
Many a stout 'ounce' of gold shall he bleed because
of the small squalling bundle that shall be hushed to
sleep under this garden mould!"

Nothing was heard for the next ten minutes but the measured stroke of the mattock, and the deep breathing of the night workman.   But a broad shadow had drifted silently out from the corner of the little temple summer-house, and stood only a yard or two from the hole Don Tomas was making in the ground under the fig-tree.

El Sarria knew his man by this time, though he had not seen him for many years.   The grave-digger was Don Tomas, Luis Fernandez's ne'er-do-well brother, who had been compelled to flee the country the year of Angoulême's French invasion, for giving information to the enemy.   He it was whom he had seen at his old tricks by the Devil's Cañon.   Not but what Luis must all the same have set him on, for he alone knew of the secret way of retreat.

Presently with many puffs and pants Tomas finished the work to his satisfaction.   Then he shook a handful of grass and leaves into the bottom of the excavation.

"There," he muttered with a cackle of laughter, "there is your cradle-bed cosily made, young Don Ramon !   Would that your father were lying cheek by jowl with you !   Would not I cover you both up snugly.   Holy Coat of Treves, but I am in a lather ! This it is to labour for others' good !   I wonder how soon that hell-hog Tia Elvira will be ready to do her part.   The *Sangrador* must have gone home hours ago.   She is to bring the youngling out and then go back to tell her story to the mother how sweetly it passed away—ah, ah—how heavenly was its smile.   So it will be—so it will !   Tomas Fernandez knows the trick.   He has quieted many a leveret the same way ! "

The garden door opened again, this time very

slightly, a mere slit of light lying across the tangled green and yellowish grey of the garden. It just missed El Sarria and kindled to dusky purple a blossom of oleander that touched his cheek as he stooped. The whites of his eyes gleamed a moment, but the digger saw him not. His gaze was fixed on his brother in the doorway.

"The signal," he muttered, "I am to go and wait outside for the Tia. Of course, as usual, my good and respectable brother will not put a finger to the job himself. Well, *toma!* he shall pay the more sweetly when all is done—oh yes, Luis shall pay for all!"

He was standing leaning upon his mattock at the head of the little grave which he had destined for the child of Dolóres Garcia. He had been whistling a gay Andalucian lilt of tune he had learned on his long travels. A devil of a fellow this Tomas in his day, and whistled marvellously between his teeth—so low that (they said) he could make love to a Señorita in church by means of it, and yet her own mother at her elbow never hear.

"Well, better get it over!" he said, dropping his mattock and starting out towards the door. "Here comes the Tia!"

But at that moment the heavens fell. Upon the head of the midnight workman descended the flat of his own spade. El Sarria had intended the edge, but Tomas's good angel turned the weapon at the last moment or else he had been cloven to the shoulder-blade. For it was a father's arm that wielded the weapon. Down fell the digger of infant graves, right athwart the excavation he himself had made. His mouth was filled with the dirt he had thrown out, and the arm that threw it swung like a pendulum to and fro in the hole.

CHAPTER XIV

THE HOLY INNOCENTS

With small compunction El Sarria turned Don Tomas over with his foot and coolly appropriated the cloak he had discarded, as also his headgear, which was banded with gay colours, and of the shape affected by the dandies of Seville.

Then swinging the cloak about him, and setting the hat upon his head jauntily, he strode to the garden door.

Above he could hear the angry voice of a woman, with intervals of silence as if for a low-toned inaudible reply. Then came a wail of despair and grief—that nearly sent him up the stairs at a tiger's rush, which would have scattered his enemies before him like chaff. For it was the voice of his Dolóres he heard for the second time. But of late El Sarria had learned some of the wisdom of caution. He knew not the force Luis might have within the house, and he might only lose his own life without benefiting either Dolóres or his son.

Then there was a slow foot on the stairs, coming down. The light went out above, and he heard a heavy breathing behind the closed door by which he stood.

" Tomas—Tomas ! " said a voice, " here is the brat. It is asleep ; do it quietly, so that the mother may not be alarmed. I cannot stir without her hearing me and asking the reason."

And in the arms of Ramon Garcia was placed the breathing body of his first-born son. The door was shut before he could move, so astonished he was by the curious softness of that light burden, and Tia Elvira's unamuleted groin escaped safe for that time —which, indeed, afterwards turned out to be just as well.

So at the door of his enemy El Sarria stood dumb and stricken, the babe in his arms. For the fact that this child was the son of his little Dolóres, annihilated for the moment even revenge in his soul.

But a hand was laid on his shoulder.

"Haste thee, haste," hissed the witch-wife, La Giralda, Elvira's friend and rival, " hast thou smitten strongly ? She lies behind the door. I cannot hear her breath, so all must be well. I saw thee stoop to the blow. Well done, well done ! And the brain-pan of the ill-disposed and factious Señor Tomas is comfortably cracked, too. He had but sevenpence in his pockets, together with a bad peseta with a hole in it. Such fellows have no true moral worth. But come away, come away ! Presently Don Luis will miss the Tia and give the alarm. Give me the babe ! "

But this Ramon would not do, holding jealously to his own.

"What can you, a man, do with a babe ?" she persisted. " Can you stop its mouth from crying ? Is there milk in your breasts to feed its little blind mouth ? Give it to me, I say ! "

"Nay," said El Sarria, shaking her off, " not to you. Did not this murderous woman come from your waggons ? Is not her place under your canvas ? "

"It shall be so no more, if your stroke prove true," said the gipsy. " I shall be the queen and bring up this youngling to be the boldest horse-thief betwixt this filthy Aragon and the Gipsy-barrio of Granada, where La Giralda's cave dives deepest into the rock."

"No, I will not!" said the man, grasping the babe so tightly that it whimpered, and stretched its little body tense as a bowstring over his arm. " I will take him to the hills and suckle him with goat's milk! He shall be no horse-thief, but a fighter of men!"

"Ah, then you are an outlaw—a lad of the hills? I thought so," chuckled the woman. " Come away quickly, then, brave manslayer; I know a better way than either. The sisters, the good women of the convent, will take him at a word from me. I know the night watch—a countrywoman of mine, little Concha. She will receive him through the wicket and guard him well—being well paid, that is, as doubtless your honour can pay!"

"What, little Concha Cabezos?" said Ramon with instant suspicion. " Was she not a traitress to her mistress? Was it not through her treachery that her mistress came hither?"

"Little Concha—a traitress," laughed the old woman. " Nay—nay! you know her not, evidently. She may, indeed, be almost everything else that a woman can be, as her enemies say. No cloistered Santa Teresa is our little Concha, but, for all that, she is of a stock true to her salt, and only proves fickle to her wooers. Come quickly and speak with her. She is clever, the little Concha, and her advice is good."

They passed rapidly along the road, deep in white dust, but slaked now with the dew, and cool underfoot. The babe lifted up his voice and wept.

"Here, give him me. I cannot run away with him if I would," said the gipsy. "You may keep your hand on my arm, if only you will but give him me!"

And the gipsy woman lifted the little puckered features to her cheek, and crooned and clucked till the child gradually soothed itself to sleep face-down on her shoulder.

"How came Concha at the house of the nuns?" said Ramon.

"That you must ask herself," answered the woman; "some quarrel it was. Luis Fernandez never loved her. He wished her out of the house from the first. But here we are!"

First came a great whitewashed forehead of blind wall, then in the midst a small circular tower where at one side was a door, heavily guarded with great iron plates and bolts, and on the other a deep square aperture in which was an iron turnstile—the House of the Blessed Innocents at last.

The gipsy woman went directly up to the wicket, and whispered through the turnstile. There was a dim light within, which presently brightened as if a lamp had been turned up.

The woman stepped back to El Sarria's side.

"The little Concha is on duty," she whispered. "Go thou up and speak with her! Nay, take the child if thou art so jealous of him. I would not have stolen the boy. Had the nationals not killed El Sarria at the Devil's Gorge, I had said that thou wert the man himself!"

Ramon took the babe awkwardly.

"At any event thou art a brave fighter," she murmured, "and cracked that evil-doing Tomas's

skull for him to a marvel. Thou shalt have all the
help La Giralda can give thee ! "

Ramon, with the babe in his arms, put his head
within, and spoke to Concha. A little cry, swiftly
checked, came forth from the whitewashed portress'
lodge of the House of the Innocents. Then after
five minutes Ramon kissed the little puckered face
of his son, and each of the dimpled fat red hands he
held so tightly clenched, and laid him on the revolving iron plate of the conventual turnstile. Without
a creek the axle turned, and in a moment more the
child was in the arms of Holy Church, pleasantly
represented for the nonce by the very secular charms
of little Concha Cabezos.

Then a word or two were spoken. Concha told
the outlaw how, by a letter purporting to come from
himself, forged by Don Luis or his brother, Dolóres
had been advised to put herself under the protection
of his beloved friend Don Luis Fernandez " until
the happier days." Concha also told how the miller
had found an excuse to send her from the house in
disgrace, and how for her needlework and skill in fine
broidery she had been received at the Convent of the
Holy Innocents, how Manuela from the priest's
house and this gipsy wise-woman " Tia Elvira " had
watched over Dolóres ever since, not allowing her to
hold any communication with the outside world, and
especially with her former waiting-maid.

" Then came the news of your death," she continued, " and after that the guard upon Dolóres was
redoubled, and till to-night I have heard nothing.
But the babe shall be safe and unknown here among
the sisters. Yet for the future's sake give me some
token that you may claim him by. All such things
are entered in a book as being brought with a child."

El Sarria passed within the turnstile a golden wristlet his mother had given him at his first communion, when he was the best and most dutiful boy in all Sarria, and held by the priest to be a pattern communicant.

"Can you not stay yet other twenty-four hours in Sarria?" asked Concha. "If so, we must try to bring your Dolóres where she will be as safe as the child."

"I would stay a year to preserve from harm a hair of her head—I who have wronged her!"

"Ah," sighed Concha through the wicket, as if she knew all about unworthy suspicion on the part of lovers, "men are like that. They are ready to suspect the most loving and the most innocent, but we women forgive them!"

Then pouting her pretty red lips the little Concha spoke low in the ear of El Sarria a while. After five minutes of this whispered colloquy, she added aloud—

"Then we will proceed. Go, do your part. You may trust La Giralda. Go quickly. You have much to do."

And little Concha snapped to the shutter of the wicket in his face.

Much to do. Yes, it was true. What with Dolóres in the power of his false friend Luis and the evil hag Tia Elvira, his gentlemen to attend upon at their inn, and the grave-digger lying with a broken head in the garden, El Sarria might be said to have had some private business upon his hands. And this, too, in addition to his affairs of state—the Abbot's commission, his own outlawry, and the equal certainty of his being shot whether he fell into the hands of the Carlists or of the national soldiers.

Yet in spite of all these, never since the evil night of his first home-coming to Sarria had he been so happy as when he retraced his way in company with La Giralda in the direction of the mill-house.

And as he went, thinking no thought save of Dolóres and his love, suddenly the only man who would have dared to cross his path stood before him.

" Ah, sirrah," cried Rollo the Scot, " is this your service ? To run the country with women— and not even to have the sense to choose a pretty one. What mean you by this negligence, dog of Galicia ? "

" I attend to my own affairs," answered Ramon, with a sullen and boding quiet ; " do me the favour to go about yours." ·

Hot-blood Rollo leaped upon him without a word, taking the older and stronger man at un- awares with his young litheness. He saw Ramon's fingers moving to the knife in its sheath by his side. But ere they could reach it, his hand was on the giant's wrist and his pistol at his ear.

" A finger upon your Albacetan and you die ! " cried Rollo. " I would have you Gallegans learn that the servant is not greater than his lord."

Now Ramon knew that not his life, but that of Rollo, hung on a hair. For he was conscious that La Giralda's knife was bare and that that determined lady was simply choosing her opportunity. If Rollo had been older most likely Ramon would have waited motionless for Giralda's thrust, and then turned the young man under his heel, precisely as he had done to the grave-digger earlier in the evening. But as they rode from the abbey he had admired the young fellow's gallant bearing and perhaps heard also of his

K

flouting of his own Miguelete enemies at the inn of San Vicente. So for this time he had pity upon him.

"Stand back, Giralda," he commanded. Then to Rollo he said, "Forgive my seeming negligence, Señor. It was only seeming. The honour of my wife and the life of my child are at stake. I am Ramon Garcia the outlaw, whom you saw fall upon the altar of the Abbey of Montblanch. This is my home. My wife is here and near to death in the house of mine enemy. Let these things be my excuse!"

Rollo dropped his pistol, like a good sportsman mechanically uncocking it as he did so. His generous impulses were as fierce and swift as his other passions.

"Tell me all," he said, "'fore God I will help you—ay, before any king or monk on earth. A brave man in such trouble has the first claim of all upon Rollo Blair!"

"And your companions?" said El Sarria.

"I give myself no trouble about them," cried Rollo. "Señor Mortimer will visit the vineyards and wine cellars to-morrow and be happy. And as for gay Master Etienne, has he not the little Concha to search for? Besides, even if he had not, he would not be six hours in the place without starting a new love affair."

Then, as they turned backwards along the road, El Sarria told Rollo all his tale, and the young Scot found himself, for the first time, deep among the crude mother-stuff of life and passion.

"And I thought that I had lived!" he said, and looked long at the huge form of the outlaw by his side, to whom deadly peril was as meat and drink, whom any man might slay, and gain a reward for the deed.

"I see it!" cried Rollo, whose quick brain caught the conditions of the problem even as Ramon was speaking. "And if I help, my companions will help also. I answer for them!"

For this young man was in the habit, not only of undertaking remarkable adventures himself, but, out of mere generosity, of engaging his friends in them as well. Yet never for a moment did Rollo doubt that he was acting, not only for the best, but positively in a manner so reasonable as to be almost humdrum.

So upon this occasion, finding El Sarria in difficulties, he pledged himself to the hilt to assist that picturesque outlaw. Yet, doubtless, had he first come across a captain of Migueletes in trouble about Ramon's capture, he would have taken a hand in bringing about that event with a truly admirable and engaging impartiality. This was perhaps the quality which most of all endeared Rollo to his friends.

"Concha—Concha," Rollo was thinking deeply and quickly; "tell me what kind of girl is this Concha?"

"She is as other girls," said El Sarria, indifferently enough, who had not till that night troubled his head much about her, "a good enough girl—a little light-hearted, perhaps, but then—she is an Andaluse, and what can you expect? Also well-looking——"

"And has been told so as often as I was in my youth!" said the old woman La Giralda, breaking in. "Of Concha Cabezos this man knows nothing, even if he be El Sarria risen from the dead (as indeed I suspected from the first). And if, as he says, she is somewhat light of heart and heel, the little Concha has a wise head and a heart loyal to all except her would-be lovers. Being a Sevillana, and with more than a drop of Romany blood in her veins, she hath never gotten the knack of that. But you may trust her with your life, young stranger, aye, or (what is harder) with another woman's secret. Only, meantime, do not make love to her. That is a game at which the Señorita Concha always wins!"

Rollo twirled his moustache, and thought. He was not so sure. At twenty-five, to put a woman on such a pedestal is rather a whet to the appetite of a spirited young man.

"And what do you intend to do with the grave-digging Fernandez?" asked Rollo.

"Why," said Ramon, simply, "to tell truth, I intended to cover him up in the grave he had made, all but his head, and let him get out as best he could!"

"Appropriate," agreed Rollo, "but crude, and in the circumstances not feasible. We must take this Fernandez indoors after we have arranged the garrison of the house. We will make his brother nurse him. Fraternal affection was never better employed, and it will keep them both out of mischief. And how soon, think you, could your wife be moved?" asked Rollo.

Ramon shrugged his shoulders helplessly, and turned to La Giralda.

"When I had my second," she said ("he that was hanged at Gibraltar by the English because the man he stabbed died in order to spite him), it was at the time of the vintage. And, lo! all unexpectedly I was overtaken even among the very clusters. So I went aside behind the watcher's *caña* huts. . . . And after I had washed the boy I went back and finished my row. There are no such women in these days, El Sarria. This of thine——"

"Peace, Giralda," said Ramon, sternly; "Dolóres is as a dove, and weak from long trouble of heart. On your head, I ask of you, could we move her in twenty-four hours and yet risk nothing of the life?"

"Yes, as the Virgin sees me," asserted La Giralda, holding up her hands, "if so be I have the firming of the bands about her—of linen wide and strong they must be made—to be mine own afterwards. And then she must be carried between four stout men, as I will show you how."

"It shall be done," cried Rollo. "I will find the men, do you provide the linen, El Sarria. I will hie me to the convent early to-morrow morning and talk with this little Concha!"

"You will not be admitted," said La Giralda, somewhat scornfully; "the Mother Superior is most strict with all within the walls."

"But I shall ask for the Mother Superior," said the modest youth, "and, gad! if I get only six quiet minutes of the old lady, I warrant she will refuse me nothing—even to the half of her kingdom. Meantime, here we are! Is it not so?"

The huge black circle of the mill-wheel rose before them against the whitewash of the unwindowed wall. They could not see the millhouse itself from this point, and they halted before going further, in order to make their dispositions.

"What we are going to do is not strictly within the letter of the law," explained Rollo, cheerfully, "but it is the best I can think of, and containing as it does the elements of justice, may commend itself as a solution to all parties. If these Fernandez gentlemen kidnap other men's wives, devise the murder of their children, and strive to have the men themselves shot, they cannot very well complain of a little illegality. This is the house. Well, it must be ours for twenty-four hours—no more, no less. Then, if no accidents happen, we will return it to Señor Luis Fernandez. All set? *Adelante,* then!"

And with Rollo in the van, El Sarria following a little behind and La Giralda bolting the doors and generally protecting the rear, the party of possession went upwards into the mill-house to argue the matter at length with Señor Luis and his friend the Tia Elvira.

These worthy people, however, were not in the sick-chamber of Dolóres Garcia, which, on the whole, was just as well. At an earlier part of the night the Tia had administered to Dolóres a potion which caused her to sleep soundly for several hours. For the Tia was skilled in simples, as well as in a good many things of a nature far from simple. A faint clinking sound, as of counting money, guided Rollo to the spot.

The master of the house and his faithful " Tia " sat bending over a table in the upper hall, or general meeting-place of the family. The door which opened off the stairway up which the visitors came, gave a slight creak, but Luis Fernandez and his associate were so engrossed in their work that neither of them lifted their eyes.

A considerable number of trinkets of gold and silver, articles of attire, crucifixes, and ornaments were spread out upon the table. As soon as Ramon's eyes fell upon these, Rollo felt him grip his arm convulsively, but the young man resolutely kept the outlaw behind him. The time was not yet.

Tia Elvira was not for the moment on good terms with her companion.

"Listen, Luis Fernandez," she said, extending a pair of withered claws across the table like the talons of some unclean bird; "if you think that I am going to do your business and run hot chances of the iron necklace that has no beads, and then when all is done allow your father's son to cheat me out of my dues, you are much mistaken. If you do not deliver me all the ornaments her husband gave this woman Dolóres, according to your agreement, by the chief of the devils that inhabit the four hells I will go to the *Corregidor* to-morrow at daybreak and lodge information against you and your brother for the crime of child murder!"

"And where, think you, would you find yourself in such a case?" quoth Luis Fernandez, a cold-eyed, dark-haired man of forty years of age. He sat leaning well over the table, the more precious of the objects gathered between his arms. "You were the nurse in attendance, my Tia — to that the *Sangrador* would bear witness. He left you in charge of the infant, my dear aunt. And though times are hard and men in office unbelieving, I still think that I, Luis Fernandez, could command enough testimony in this town to bring the guilt (if guilt there be) home to a certain Elvira the Gipsy, whose record, at any rate, is none of the best!"

He laughed a little chuckling laugh as the hag exploded into a swarm of crabbed gipsy oaths.

"But enough of this, Tia," he said; "be reasonable, and you will find me generous. Only I must be the judge of what is mine own, that is all, my bitter-sweet Ronda pippin."

"Curses upon you and all that you may bring

forth, on your burying, on your children and your children's children ! " cried the woman.

"Come—come—that will do, Tia," cried Luis, striking the table with his hand. "I value not your curses this single fig of Spain." (Here he made towards her the gesture with finger and thumb which averts the evil eye.) "But if I hear any more of this I will put you to the door without so much as a single silver spoon. Whereupon you will be welcome to do your worst."

"I do not see why you want both the woman and the goods," whined the Tia, altering her tone. "Did you not say that you desired to keep nothing which would remind her of her old life ? And have not I, by my decoctions and distillations, kept this silly Dolóres in a dream like that of a child all these weeks since we got rid of that imp of Satan, Concha Cabezos of Seville ? "

"You have—you have indeed done well, my Tia," said the man soothingly, "and you will find me by no means ungrateful. But come, let us get this matter settled, and then I must go and look for my drunken good-for-nothing of a brother, who has doubtless stolen the key of the wine-cellar, and is at his old tricks again."

"Well, at any rate, I insist upon that string of silver beads," said the old woman, greedily. "I have been thinking of it all these days, and do not forget that it was I who wormed out of the widow the hiding-place where that cunning little Concha had placed Ramon Garcia's strong box."

"There—take it, then," said the man impatiently, and a heavy string of beads was slid across the table with a clanking noise. "I had not thought you so good a Christian, Tia ! "

"Oh, it is not that," chuckled the hag, clutching the necklace fiercely, as a starving dog might fall on a bone, and concealing it instantly beneath her skirts. "But each link hath the stamp upon it—the mint stamp of Seville—and will pass current for a good duro wherever one may chance to be. With such a necklace one can never be in want."

"Well," said Luis, "the devil fly away with you and it, Tia! I keep all the ornaments of gold—let that be understood. My wife might, upon an occasion, take a yearning for them, and if I had them not to give her, it might be to the danger of my house and succession. So this gold cross——"

("My mother's!" breathed Ramon hotly in Rollo's ear.)

"This knife with the hilt top set with brilliants——"

("My father's—he had it from the great Lor' Wellington for a message he brought to him at Vitoria.")

"These trifles—a pair of ear-rings, a ring of pearls, a comb for the hair in gold—all these I reserve for myself."

As he spoke, he tossed them, one after the other, into a heavy iron-bound box which, with chains and padlocks displayed, stood open upon the floor.

As each article tinkled among the others, the Tia gave a little wince of bodily pain, and her skinny talons scratched the wood of the table with a sound distinctly audible at the door behind which the intruders stood.

Then a quick loud cackle of laughter came from Fernandez. He had found something among the parchments.

"'Hereby I plight thee my troth,'" he read

from a paper in his hand, "'for ever and for ever, as
a true heart and a true lover, signed, Ramon.' This
she has kept in a case in her bosom, I suppose, with
the picture of the oaf," he added, "and is as like him
as it is like St. Nicholas, the patron saint of all thieves.
And, holy Michael in the seventh heavens! here is their
marriage certificate all complete—a very treasure-
house of connubial happiness. But these need not
go into the strong box. I, Luis Fernandez, have
made an end of them. The woman is mine, and
so will I also make an end of these relics of folly."

He took the papers to tear them across, but the
stout parchment resisted a moment. His brow
darkened, and he clutched them more securely to
rend them with an effort.

But a slight noise in the apartment and a cry
from the Tia caused him to look up.

A knife was at his throat, and a figure stood
before him, one huge hand pinning him to his seat.

"Ramon," he cried, his voice, which had been
full of chuckling laughter, rising suddenly to a thin
shriek. "God in heaven, Ramon Garcia!"

And with a trembling hand he tried to cross
himself.

"Give!" said Ramon, in a hollow voice, and
mechanically the miller placed the papers in his
hands.

"'Fore God, Ramon, I thought you were dead!"
gasped the man.

"No, friend, not dead," came the answer, "but
Ramon Garcia come back in the flesh to settle
certain accounts with his well-beloved comrade and
brother of many years, Luis Fernandez, of the mill-
house of Sarria."

CHAPTER XV

ROLLO INTERVENES

WITH eyes injected, wide open mouth, and dropped jaw the man sat all fallen together in his seat, the gold ornaments still strewed about him, the pencil with which he had been checking them fallen from his nerveless grasp.

"I have accounted for the old lady," said Rollo, who with the eager professional assistance of La Giralda had been gagging and securing the Tia. La Giralda with a wicked glee also undertook the office of searcher of her rival's person, into the details of which process the unlearned historian may not enter—suffice to say that it was whole-hearted and thorough, and that it resulted in a vast series of objects being slung upon the table, many of them plundered from Don Luis's own house and others doubtless secreted during the process of overhauling Ramon's strong box.

"Ah-ah, most excellent Tia, you will not refuse me a peseta as my share next time you go out a-caudle-ing!" said La Giralda, all in a grinning triumph when she had finished, and to fill the cup yet fuller, was adjusting her friend's gag to a more excellent advantage.

"Stay where you are, Luis Fernandez," said El Sarria, sternly, as he sat down with his pistols on either side of him. "I advise you not to move hand or foot, if you set any value upon your life. I shall have much to say to you before—before the morning!"

And the doomed man, recognising the accents of deadly intent in his late friend's voice, let his head sink into his hands with a hopeless moan.

"Meantime I will put these things in order," said the Scot, in whose military blood ran the instinct of loot, and he was beginning to throw all the objects of value indiscriminately into the open chest when El Sarria checked him.

"I will take only what is mine own—and hers," he said, "but meantime abide. There is much to be said and done first!"

Then he turned his broad deeply lined brow upon Fernandez, who looked into his eyes as the trembling criminal, hopeless of mercy, waits the black cap and the sentence.

Rollo had settled the Tia on the floor with her head on a roll of household stuffs which she herself had rolled up in her cloak for transport.

La Giralda asked her friend if she felt herself as comfortable as might be, and the Tia looked up at her with the eyes of a trapped wild-cat. Then the Scot stood on guard by the door which led to the staircase, his sword drawn in his hand. The picturesqueness of the scene at the table appealed to the play-actor in him.

El Sarria held the documents in his hand which Fernandez had been about to destroy, and waved them gently in his enemy's face as a king's advocate might a written indictment in a speech of accusation.

"You betrayed me to the death, friend Luis, did

you not? You revealed my hiding-place. That is count the first!" he began.

And the wretched man, his lips dry and scarce obeying his will, strove to give utterance to the words, "It was all my brother's doing. I swear it was my brother!"

"Bah," said El Sarria, "do not trouble to lie, Luis, being so near the Other Bar where all must speak truth. You knew. You were the trusted friend. Your brother was not, and even if you were not upon the spot, as I thought, the blood-hounds were set on the trail by you and by no other."

Fernandez made no reply, but sank his head deeper between his hands as if to shut out his judge and probable executioner from his sight.

"Pass, then," said the outlaw, "there is so much else that it matters not whether you were at the Devil's Cañon or no. At any rate, you decoyed my wife here, by a letter purporting to be written to Dolóres Garcia by her husband—— "

"Concha Cabezos lies. She was a liar from the beginning. That also was my brother. I swear to you!" cried the wretched man, in so pitiful an accent that for the first time Rollo felt a little sorry for him.

But there was no gleam of pity in the eyes of Ramon. Instead, he lifted a pistol and toyed with it a moment thoughtfully.

"Luis," he said, "your brother has his own sins to answer for. Beneath the fig-tree in the corner an hour or two ago, his sins ran him to earth. Whether at this moment he is alive or dead I know not—neither care. But you cannot saddle him, in the flesh or out of it, with your peccadilloes. Be a

man, Luis. You used not to be a coward as well
as a thief and a murderer."

But neither insults nor appeals could alter the
fixed cloud of doom that overspread the face of Don
Luis. He did not again interrupt, but heard the
recital of El Sarria in silence, without contradiction
and apparently without hope.

"You brought my wife here by this forged letter
while you knew I was alive and while you were
plotting your best to kill me. You procured my
outlawry, and the confiscation of my property—
which I doubt not you and the worthy Alcalde de
Flores shared between you. You have kept my wife
drugged by that hell-cat these many days, lest she
should find out your deceit. You plotted to slay
the child of her womb—*my son*, Luis, do you hear,
my only son ! "

The outlaw's voice mounted into a solemn and
awful tone of accusation, like a man in hell calling
the roll of his own past happinesses.

"Now, Luis Fernandez," thundered Ramon,
after a period of silence, "what have you to say to
all this ? Have you any reasons to advance why
you should not die by my hand ? "

"Ramon, Ramon, do not kill me in my sins,"
cried the wretched man. "By the memory of our
boyhood together let me at least receive absolution
and go clean ! "

"Even as you would have made me go unshriven
by the mouth of the Devil's Cañon—even as this very
night you sent forth to the holy ministry of the
worm, and the consolations of the clod the young
child, unblessed and unbenisoned, without touch of
priestly hand or sprinkling drop of holy water !
Even so, Luis, friend of my youth, according to the

measure ye mete it shall be measured to you again.
The barley bushel is good measure also for the
rye!"

Rollo, standing by the door and looking over the
heads of accuser and accused, saw through a window
the first green streaks of a doubtful dawn drawn
livid and chill athwart a black sky. He went across
to El Sarria and whispered in his ear. Fernandez
lifted up his head and eyed the Scot with a kind of
dull curiosity as if he wondered what his part in the
affair might be. And the keen and restless eyes of
the Tia watched him also, from where she lay pillowed
on her stolen bundle like a bound and helpless
Fury.

In quick whispers Rollo urged a plan of action
upon El Sarria, by which he hoped to obtain a
reprieve and perhaps his life for the wretched man.
But he did not advert to this, only to the necessity
of haste, and to the perilous state of Dolóres. This
was indeed his great argument. Whatever happened
she must be cared for. The matter of the traitors
could be arranged later. While Ramon sat considering, the active eyes of the young Scot discovered
a small iron-faced door open at one corner of the
chamber. He went across and pulled aside the
curtain which half concealed the entrance.

"A regular strong room, by Jove!" he cried;
"here is everything comfortable for our friends
while we settle our other affairs. We shall need our
good Señor Don Luis, from time to time during the
morning, but I doubt not he will oblige us."

Rollo sounded all over the strong room of the
mill-house for any signs of another possible exit, but
all was solid masonry. Besides which, the chests of
valuables and papers, the casks of fine liquors and

smuggled cigars proved that this was intended for a secret wall chamber in which to conceal the valuables of the house in case of alarm. Such hiding-places are not uncommon in the old houses of Spain, as Rollo knew, though this was the first he had seen.

"Give yourself the pain of entering, Señor," he said to Fernandez, and without waiting for any overt permission from Ramon, he caught up the old hag Tia Elvira in his arms and carried her, bundle and all, into the room.

"Here I am compelled to leave you for the time being in the dark, Don Luis," he said courteously. "But I think you will agree that your state is not the less gracious for that. I shall return immediately and present certain propositions for your consideration."

"You are an Englishman," cried Fernandez, "you will not stand by and see a man murdered in cold blood."

"The blood is none so cold that I can see," said Rollo, shrugging his shoulders. "I will do the best I can for you, Señor; only do not try any tricks with us. The least sign of further treachery will be fatal, and we have many friends about us."

CHAPTER XVI

DON LUIS IS WILLING

So saying, Rollo went out and locked the door behind him, leaving La Giralda with a loaded pistol seated beside it to prevent any egress, in case Fernandez had some way of opening the bolts from the inside known only to himself.

When Rollo returned from arranging these matters he found El Sarria's place vacant. But the young man following the direction of La Giralda's nod went out, and in a chamber about which hung a peculiar atmosphere of drugs, he found the outlaw on his knees by a woman's bedside.

Rollo stole forward on tiptoe, and in the pale glimmer of dawn he saw for the first time the features of Dolóres, the wife of Ramon the outlaw.

He could discern eyelashes that lay very broad and dark upon colourless cheeks, a white-wrapped form under snowy coverlets, straight as the dead arrayed for burial, but nevertheless evidently alive, and sleeping peacefully with gently heaving breast.

The giant's head was sunk on the coverlet and his lips touched the damp fingers of the hand which lay without the sheet.

With true reverence Rollo touched Ramon on the shoulder and pointed to the window. The pale unearthly green of the sky spaces between the dark purple bars of cloud was fast changing to orange tinged with a smoky scarlet. The sun would not long delay, and there was a little matter out in the garden which must be arranged.

As Rollo anticipated, Tomas the scapegrace did not look handsome as he lay on the upturned soil. The blood had hardened upon the bruise on his crown where his own spade in El Sarria's hands had beaten him down, much as a gardener might level a rank stinging nettle.

" Carry him within," he ordered ; " we will attend to his case better indoors ! "

Already with spade and mattock Rollo was filling up the grave, stamping down the soil with his foot as he proceeded. Then after having laid away the tools in the little temple, he followed El Sarria upstairs. Tomas was lying very limp and still on the table from which the trinkets had been gathered into the box, and El Sarria, who gave himself no concern about his handiwork, was bending over the box of jewellery, rapidly throwing out all articles which he did not recognise as belonging to his wife or himself.

Rollo reminded him of his gun which he had left in the dry river-bed, and El Sarria set off to fetch it lest it should be recognised.

Then Rollo, who was now thoroughly enjoying himself "in the belly of an adventure" as he expressed it, called out, " Lay down that pistol, mother, we shall not need it for a while, and do you give me a hand with this rascal's sore head. What think you of it ? "

" The stroke was dealt with a strong arm," said La Giralda, critically. " I saw it done—also heard it. It sounded like the driving in of a gate-post. But yet, most unfortunately, I do not think the man will die

—unless—unless"—she fingered the keen little knife she carried lovingly—" unless indeed matters are a little assisted."

"Stop, mother; we cannot afford to have any *Barranco de los Martires* business this time! We are not in Granada within the gipsy barrio, remember, nor yet within hearing of the bells of Sevilla. Do as I bid you, and help me to bathe and bind up the scoundrel's pate."

The old woman did so with an air of protest, finally, however, consenting to make a plaster of certain herbs which she found in the household cabinet of simples, and having boiled them, applied the result like a turban to Don Tomas's unconscious crown.

All the while she murmured bitterly at intervals, "It is a pity! A pity! I do not believe he will die—unless, in spite of the Englishman, La Giralda has the nursing of him!"

Presently Ramon returned with his gun, which he would have set himself down to clean with the utmost nonchalance, if Rollo had not summoned him away to more important business.

"It is the accursed night-dew!" he said in explanation; "much depends on never putting off the drying and oiling of one's weapons."

"Now," said Rollo, "if you are ready, I in my turn should like to have my little interview with Don Luis!"

"You?" cried the outlaw, astonished.

Rollo nodded.

"Why not?" he said cheerfully; "we shall need his assistance very often to-day! Open the door, La Giralda."

The door clicked open, and there sat Luis Fernandez blinking upon a smuggled keg of French spirits, and in the corner the Tia's little black eyes twinkled like restless stars from her uneasy pillow.

Ramon carried in the limp body of Tomas, at sight of which Luis Fernandez flung up his hands with a shrill cry.

"You have killed him, then—as you will kill me!" he moaned, and ran towards the door of the strong room.

"Not so," said Rollo, stopping him with composure; "your brother is, as I think, as comfortable as the circumstances will permit, and more likely to recover than he deserves. Be good enough to tell La Giralda where to find a lamp or candle-box, so that in taking care of him you may not be hindered by darkness."

As he spoke Rollo had been arranging a couch of boxes and pillows, on which without the slightest regard to his enemy's comfort El Sarria flung his burden down.

But Rollo did his best for the unconscious man, and then when La Giralda had returned with a lamp, he turned sharply upon Don Luis.

"Sir," he said, "you know the causes of quarrel between yourself and Don Ramon Garcia, for whom I am acting. You know also what chances you have, if I do not use the influence I possess to counsel other and milder methods. Are you then willing to be guided entirely by me or do you prefer to be dealt with by my principal upon his own account, and without regard to my advice?"

Luis Fernandez clasped Rollo's hand.

"By the Virgin and all the saints," he cried, "I will do to the line and letter all that you desire of me in every particular. I know well that I have no other hope."

"Good," said Rollo; "then you will to-day show yourself about the Casa as usual. You will give any necessary orders to your foreman when he comes at the accustomed hour. This you will do in your own chamber and in my presence, urging a slight *calentura* as a reason for not venturing out. You will speak to La Giralda as to your servant, and in fine—you will comport yourself as if nothing had occurred, and as if no such man as Ramon Garcia were within a thousand leagues of the mill-house of Sarria! Do you agree?"

"I agree to anything, to everything!" said Fernandez, eagerly.

"But remember," continued Rollo, "in order to compass this I am stretching a good many points. I saw your eye brighten just now when I spoke of giving orders. Now, remember, if there is the slightest attempt at foul play, we may indeed lose our game, and with it our lives, but first of all and quite suddenly, one man shall die, and that man is —Luis Fernandez."

He added this asseveration—

"And this, I, Rollo Blair, of Blair Castle in the Shire of Fife, swear by Almighty God and the honour of a Scottish gentleman."

CHAPTER XVII

A GRAVE IRREGULARITY

The day wore in the mill-house of Sarria precisely as many thousands of days had done before. The foreman came for the keys from his master's bed-room at six of the clock. He wondered at the unwonted sight of his patron up and fully dressed at that hour, and still more at the tall young foreigner who sat with his book so studiously silent at the table opposite his master. The old gipsy woman Elvira, too, was gone and another in her place. But after all it was none of his business, and the mill must go on. For the dam had filled up and there was much corn to grind. Old withered Elisa, the goatherd " patrona," led her tinkling flock past the door a score of yards and then returned with her pail as was her wont. She saw Señor Fernandez at his window, and he made a strange appealing motion with his hands to her, then glanced over his shoulder.

Perhaps (so she thought) the poor man had taken to drinking at night as that wicked brother of his used to do down at the *venta*. But the true nature of the Señor's complaint did not dawn upon her till later.

From nine till half-past eleven none outside of the mill-house saw Señor Luis. The stranger also was absent upon his occasions, and the doctor, coming early to see his patient, found only the gipsy woman, who did not appear to have understood the directions he had given her the day before. The Señor himself was out of the way, but the doctor, glad to find his patient so quiescent and apparently in such good condition, soon took his leave, and in the mill-house La Giralda ruled alone.

*   *   *   *   *

With Rollo now for a time the tale runs more briskly. He set off for the *venta*, where he found Etienne and John Mortimer sitting at meat. Etienne was breaking his fast sparely upon a cup of chocolate and a glass of water, while John Mortimer had by hook or crook evolved something resembling a frying-pan, in which he had achieved the cooking of some bacon and eggs together with a couple of mutton chops. He was browning some bread before the fire to serve for English toast as Rollo entered, looking as fresh as if he had been newly roused from a twelve hour's sleep.

"Good morning, friends of mine," he cried; "you are in excellent case, I see. John, I have made arrangements for you to go and visit some vineyards to-day. Old Gaspar will guide you with his gun over his valiant shoulder. You can pick up points about wine-buying, without doubt. As to you, Etienne, *mon vieux*, I have found your Concha, and I am going to see her myself in half an hour. Shall I give her your love?"

"What!" cried Saint Pierre; "you jest. It cannot be my cruel, cruel little Conchita, she who fled from me and would not take the smallest notice of all my letters and messages? Where is she?"

"She is at the nunnery of the Sisters of Mercy

outside the village.   Poor Etienne! I am indeed
sorry for you.   With your religious views, it will
be impossible for you to make love to a nun!"

"Would I not?" cried Etienne, eagerly; "*mon
Dieu*, only procure me a chance, and I will let you
see!   But a nunnery is a hard nut to crack.   How
do you propose to manage it?"

"I intend to make friends with the Lady
Superior," said Rollo, confidently.

"You have a letter of introduction to her,
doubtless?" said Etienne.

"I do not at present even know her name; but
all in good time!" said the youth, coolly.

"For stark assurance commend me to a Scot,"
cried Etienne, with enthusiasm.   "You take to
adventure as if it were chess.   We poor French
take the most ordinary affairs as if they were dram-
drinking, and so are old and *ennuyés* at thirty."

"And the English?" asked Rollo.

"Oh," laughed Etienne, "the English take to
adventure as our friend there takes to his breakfast,
and that perhaps is the best way of all."

He pointed with a smile to where, at the table's
end, John Mortimer of Chorley, having made all
preparations with the utmost seriousness for his
repast, was on the point of turning on the operating
mill.   The cook of the *venta*, who had been much
interested in John's culinary operations, had come
up to see how he would deal with the result when
completed.

John had brewed himself some tea from a small
parcel he carried in his saddle-bags.   This, made in
a coffee-pot, was arranged at a certain distance from
his dexter elbow.   The bacon and eggs were on
a platter exactly in front, flanked on the left by the

smoking mutton chops, while the toast was stuck erect in an empty cruet-stand. In fact a Chorley breakfast-table was reproduced as exactly as circumstances would admit.

Then John Mortimer bent his head a moment over his plate, murmured something in memory of his father, the Primitive Methodist, in lieu of a blessing, said "Hem" in a loud gruff tone, hitched his chair forward a little, squared his shoulders, and fell to.

"That is why we French have no colonies!" said Etienne, admiringly. "In this little Spanish village he has found all the materials of an English breakfast."

"And that is why *I* shall never make any money," said Rollo, and proceeded to break his fast on a couple of eggs dropped into white wine, before setting out for the convent.

"Etienne," said Rollo, suddenly checking his glass in mid-air as an idea occurred to him, "lend me that ring of your sainted uncle's, the one with the picture of Don Carlos."

The young Frenchman indolently drew it from his hand, laid it on the polished marble top of the table, and with his forefinger flipped it across to Rollo.

"Who is the girl?" he said simply.

But Rollo with equal simplicity ignored his question, and did not even pause to thank him for the loan. It was a way these young men had with one another. Like the early Christians, they had all things in common. It was their single point of resemblance to the primitive Church.

"What shall I say to your Concha—that is, if I chance to see her?" said Rollo, as he brushed his clothes and saw to the neatness of his neck ribbon.

Etienne held down his head.

"Indeed," he said a little reluctantly, "I am not so anxious that you should say anything at all about me. The little minx did not treat me so very well when I came this way on my last visit to my uncle. And to tell the truth, there is an exceedingly pretty girl living only three doors from the *venta*. I have already spoken to her, and she has smiled at me thrice over the fence."

"Take my advice, and stick to the little Andaluse," said Rollo, laughing. "They do not understand that kind of thing here, dear Etienne. Remember Master Rafael, who got a knife somewhere between his shoulder-blades in this same village."

"I shall bear in mind what you say, my good Rollo," said Etienne ; "meantime I shall dress myself afresh and walk in the gardens. They are, as it seems to me, contiguous. Perhaps it may chance that I shall see—*her !*"

"That leaves me a freer hand with Concha, then," murmured Rollo to himself, as he stuck his hat on the back of his head, and strode out into the stable yard smiling to himself.

He had his horse brought out and saddled. Then he mounted and rode down the village street towards the convent of the pious Sisters of Mercy. The plan he meant to adopt had entered his mind, as it were, with the eggs and white wine. He had not given the matter a thought before. He smiled to himself as he rode, for he wondered how he would succeed with this good Mother Superior, and what manner of girl he would find that wicked, tricksome Concha to be, whose name was in all men's mouths with a certain approving flavour, as of a pleasant naughtiness to be alternately scolded and cajoled. One thing this Master Rollo was as sure of as that he was a Scot. And that was—he never could, would, or should fall in love with such a girl.

So Rollo rode with a clatter of spurs and accoutrement up to the gate of the convent. Dismounting, he advanced briskly to the gate and knocked loudly upon it with his riding-whip.

In a few moments a sour-faced portress opened the little square wicket and looked through at him. The diamond-shaped lattice bars, which cut her features into minute lozenges, did not improve her good looks.

"I must see the Mother Superior immediately on important business!" quoth the brisk youth, slapping his waistcoat and settling the hilt of his sword in a business-like manner, as if he had all his life been in the habit of making early morning calls upon Mothers Superior.

The portress laughed.

"A likely story," she said, "that I am to trail across the yard and leave my business here, to fetch the Lady Superior from her devotions to see a young man at the outer gate."

"If you do not admit me," Rollo went on, unabashed, "not only the Lady Superior will suffer, but the cause which all good Christians have at heart."

He suddenly thrust his bare hand close to the wicket and showed the ring which Etienne had given him.

"Do you know this?" he said.

At his first threatening motion the woman had mechanically withdrawn, but now curiosity brought

her again closer to the grating, on perceiving that
Rollo made no attempt to intrude his hand within.

"These are the royal arms of Spain, are they
not?" she said, and dropped an involuntary courtesy.

Then Rollo played his trump card. The ring
was made with a certain secret spring beneath the
stone, which when touched sprang up like the lid of
a box, and a beautiful little miniature was revealed,
encircled with hair of a dark brown colour.

"Do you know who that is?" he said.

"His absolute Majesty Carlos Quinto!" said
the portress with a deep reverence.

"Well, then," Rollo went on, "take this ring,
and with it the hair of the anointed and Christian
King. It is a great trust, but I give it into your
hands. Carry it reverently as a token to the Lady
Superior that a messenger from the King waits to
speak a word with her!"

The head of the portress disappeared from the
young man's sight with the profundity and compass
of the reverence with which she received the image
of the sovereign of all true Catholic hearts. She went
off immediately, and by standing on tiptoe in the
white dust, Rollo could see her heavy black skirts
playing bo-peep with a pair of very thick ankles.

As the young man stood drumming his fingers
upon the window-sill, with his nail he detached flake
after flake of plaster, and filliped each as it fell into
the courtyard. He had only occupied himself with
this amusement for five minutes, when suddenly the
most piquant face in the world appeared at the wicket.

"Better that you should look to your horse," a
pair of red lips said in the soft Southland speech of
Andalucia, "he is chafing himself to pieces on a too
tight curb!"

"Thank you, Señorita!" said Rollo, his heart instantly disturbed within him, for he was a merciful man by nature and consistently kind to his beast. Then he turned about, loosened the curb, and, looking over his horse, noticed that the tail strap also lathered the animal, whereupon he eased that. Then with a smiling countenance he turned for approval to the face at the wicket, but he was too late. His mentor had vanished.

He waited full ten minutes in the glaring sunshine, till indeed he well-nigh staggered as he felt the hot beams reflected full upon him from the whitewashed brick and painted door. There was not a handbreadth of shade anywhere, and the iron handles and girds of the barred windows were nearly red-hot.

Presently, however, through the breathless noonday he heard heavy footsteps approaching, accompanied by a most raucous and asthmatical breathing. The door of the porter's lodge was opened, and he caught again the heavy rustle of cloth clogging itself about unwontedly hasty ankles.

"The Mother Superior waits!" gasped the portress, opening the great door suddenly, and the young man found himself forthwith within the Convent of the Holy Innocents.

The Lady Superior proved to be a woman of about fifty-five or sixty years of age, in person stout and rubicund, a smile of good humour habitually repressed upon her lips, and a mouth slightly pulled down at the corners, contradicting the first impression of her jovial countenance.

"You are young, Colonel," she said, frowning upon Rollo's good looks with a certain affectation of gloom quite foreign to her nature, "very young to be the messenger of a King!"

"I can, indeed, hardly claim that honour," said Rollo, smiling and bowing, "but I have the honour to belong to the army of Carlos Quinto, and to be entrusted with a most serious mission on his behalf. My good friend Don Baltasar Varela, Prior of the Abbey of Montblanch, a name probably known to you——"

"He is my cousin germane—my good and honoured friend," said the Lady Superior.

Rollo bowed.

"He has given me a general introduction to all religious houses where the name of the true King is held in reverence. You will observe that the mandate bears the seal of the Propaganda of the Faith and is dated from Rome itself!"

The Lady Superior looked again at the great and pious names upon Rollo's commission, and marvelled yet more.

"So young," she said, "so boyish almost—yet so highly honoured! It is wonderful!"

Then she handed the parchment back to him.

"How can I assist you?" she said. "Command me. There is nothing consistent with the order and discipline of this house that I will not grant to you!"

Rollo bowed grandly.

"I thank you in the name of my master," he said; "the King will not forget fitly to reward his faithful servants. I ask what is indeed somewhat irregular, but is nevertheless necessary. There is a man of this place, who for the King's cause has become an outlaw, one Ramon Garcia——"

The Prioress rose from her seat indignantly.

"He is a murderer—in intent, if not in act," she said. "He is no true man, but a villain——"

"Many men have been called so," said Rollo, gravely, "who for the King's sake have borne reproach gladly—of whom this Ramon, called El Sarria, is one. What he has done has been by order of our Don Carlos——"

"Indeed, that is true, my lady," interjected a very pretty and unconventual young person, rising suddenly from behind certain frames of embroidery where she had been at work unseen, "the gentleman refers to that same Ramon Garcia, whose letters recommendatory I had the honour of submitting to you this morning. To kill in the King's name is surely no sin, else were soldiering a sin, and your reverend worthiness knows that, shriven or unshriven, the soldiers of Carlos Quinto go straight to heaven. And none can deny that, while on earth, a handsome uniform covers a multitude of sins!"

"Hush, child, hush!" cried the Abbess, holding up her hands in horror; "your talk savours of the world. And indeed, that reminds me—how in the world came you here?"

"I was seated at the embroidery," said the girl, demurely; "you set me the task yourself to be ready for our Lady of the Pillar's festival on Tuesday next."

"Well, child, well—you can go now," said the Abbess, with a nod of dismission; "I would speak with this young man alone!"

The girl cast a look at Rollo which remained with him long. It seemed to say, "I would gladly talk more with you, for your person is somewhat to my mind, and I do not think that further converse with me would prove entirely disagreeable to you!"

This message was conveyed in a single glance, and Rollo, not the most impressionable of youths, read it every syllable without the slightest difficulty.

He held up his hand almost involuntarily.

" If this damosel is by any chance the Señorita Concha Cabezos, as I have some reason to suppose, though I have never before seen the young lady, it might be advantageous if she remained. She was formerly, as I am informed, in the family of Don Ramon Garcia, and can assist my mission very materially."

Then Rollo opened out his plans in so far as they concerned Dolóres, showing the Prioress how important it was, for the success of the arduous mission on which they had been despatched, that El Sarria should leave no anxieties behind him, and beseeching her for the sake of the King's cause, to receive Dolóres within the convent as she had already received her child.

The Prioress considered a while, and after many dubious shakings of the head, finally agreed.

" It is indeed gravely irregular," she said, " but in these untoward circumstances the King's service overrides all. I will receive Dolóres Garcia."

" And if it be your will I will arrange the details with the Señorita Concha," said Rollo, promptly. " I need not, in that case, further detain the noble and reverend Prioress ! "

The Lady Superior bent a quick sharp look upon the pair, but Rollo was grave and high of demeanour as became the envoy of a King, while Concha sat at her embroidery as demure as a mouse. She had gone back to her frame and was engaged in elaborating the wings of a cherub of exceedingly celestial aspect, in whom all the parts below the shoulder-blades had been suppressed by order of

the Lady Superior of the Convent of the Holy
Innocents.

"You will do your best, Concha," she said
gravely, admonishing that maiden with her forefinger, "to further the objects of this young man.
And, above all, be sure to show him the deference
due to his rank and mission!"

"Yes, my Lady Superior!" said little Concha
Cabezos, "I will treat him as if he were the King's
own high majesty in person!"

"A very proper spirit!" said the Prioress,
nodding and going out; "cultivate it, my young
friend!"

"I will!" said little Concha, and dropped a
curtsey behind her back, which, alas! was not without a certain wicked suggestion of contempt for
kings and dignitaries and their emissaries.

M

CHAPTER XVIII

A FLUTTER OF RED AND WHITE

"At your ambassadorial service !" said the Señorita
Concha, bowing still lower and holding out her
skirts at either side with a prettyish exaggeration
of deference ; "what commands has your Scottish
Excellency for poor little Concha ?"

"Ahem !" said Rollo, more than a little puzzled,
"they were not so much commands as—as—I thought
you might be able to help me."

"Now we are getting at it," said Concha Cabezos,
nodding with a wise air.

("I must be on my guard with this girl,"
thought Rollo, "I can almost bring myself to
believe that—yet it seems impossible—that—the
girl is chaffing me—me ! ")

"I wished to see you," he went on.

The girl curtsied again, bringing her hands
together in a little appeal almost childish. It looked
natural, yet Rollo was not sure. But at any rate the
sensation was a new one. He began to think of
what he had heard in the venta. But no, the girl
looked so sweet and demure, such babyish smiles
flickered and dimpled about the mouth—all scented
of fresh youth like a June hayfield. No, she—she
must have been traduced. Not that it mattered in
the least to him. He was cased in triple steel. His

heart was adamant. Or at least as much of it as he had not left in the possession of Peggy Ramsay, and, when he came to think of it, of several others.

"You were wishful to see me, sir?" murmured little Concha, "a great gentleman wanting to see me —wonderful—impossible."

"Neither one nor yet the other," said Rollo, a trifle sharply, looking at the girl with a glance intended to suppress any lurking tendency to levity; "if I desired to see you, it was not on my own account, but upon the King's service." He raised his voice at the last words.

"That explains it," said the girl, with her eyes cast down. She raised the lids sharply once and then dropped them again. Penitence and a certain fear could not have been better expressed. Rollo was more satisfied.

("After all," he thought, "the little thing does not mean any harm. It is only her simplicity!")

And he twirled his moustachios self-confidently.

"It is not often," he said to himself, "that she has the opportunity of talking to a man like me— here in this village! I suppose it is natural." It was—to Concha.

But the girl's expression altered so soon as she heard the service that was required of her, and she followed with rapt attention the tale of the garrisoning of the mill-house of Sarria, and the dire need of her former mistress and friend, Dolóres Garcia.

Little Concha's coquetry, her trick of experimenting upon all and sundry who came near her, her moods and whimsies, transient as the flaws that ruffle and ripple, breathe upon and again set sparkling the surface of a mountain tarn—all these dropped from the Andalucian maiden at the thought of another's need. A moment before, this young foreign soldier, with the handsome face and the excellent opinion of himself, had been but fair game to Concha ; a prey marked down, not from any fell intent, but for the due humbling of pride. For Concha was interested in bringing young men to a sense of their position, and mostly, it may be confessed, it did them a vast deal of good.

But in that moment she became, instead, the eager listener, the ready self-sacrificing comrade, the friend as faithful and reliable as any brother. It was enough for her that El Sarria was there in danger of his life, that Doña Dolóres must be delivered and brought into the safe shelter of the sisterhood, and— this with a glistening of little savage teeth, small and white as mother-of-pearl — that Luis Fernandez should be humbled.

"Let me see—let me see," she murmured, thoughtfully. "Wait, I will come with you." She took a glance at the young cavalier, armed *cap-à-pie*, and thought doubtless of the horse chafing and shaking its accoutrements in the shade of the porter's lodge. "No, I will not come with you. I will follow immediately, and do you, sir, return as swiftly as possible to the mill-house of Sarria."

And without the slightest attempt at coquetry Concha showed Rollo to the door, and that arrogant youth, slightly bewildered and uncertain of the march of events, found himself presently riding away from the white gate of the monastery with Etienne's ring upon his finger, and a belief crystallising in his heart that of all the maligned and misrepresented beings on the earth, the most maligned and the most innocent was little Concha Cabezos.

And instinctively his fingers itched to clasp his

sword-hilt, and prove this thesis upon Pedro Morales
or any venta rascal who might in future disparage her
good name.

Indeed, it was only by checking of his horse in
time that he kept himself in the right line for the
mill-house. His instinct was to ride to the venta
straightway and have it out with all the blind mouths
of the village in parliament assembled.

But luckily Rollo remembered the giant Ramon
Garcia, reckless and simple of heart, Dolóres his wife
and her instant needs, and the imprisoned Fernandez
family in the strong-room of the mill-house. It
was clear even to his warped judgment that these
constituted a first charge upon his endeavours, and
that the good name of Mistress Concha, despite the
dimples on her chin, must be considered so far a
side issue.

The mill-house remained as he had left it when
he rode away. The sunshine fell broad and strong
on its whitewashed walls and green shutters, most
of them closed hermetically along the front as was
the custom of Sarria, till the power of the sun was
on the wane. A workman or two busy down among
the vents, and feeding the mouths of the grinding
stones, looked up curiously at this unwonted visitor.
But these had been too frequent of late, and their
master's behaviour too strange for them to suspect
anything amiss.

It was now the hottest time of the forenoon, and
the heat made Rollo long for some of Don Luis's
red wine, which he would drain in the Catalonian
manner by holding the vessel well out and pouring a
narrow stream in a graceful arch into his mouth.
But for this he must wait. A captive quail on the
balcony said *check-check*, and rattled on the bars of

his cage to indicate that his water was finished, and that if somebody did not attend to him speedily he would die.

As Rollo went down the little slope, past the corner of the garden where Ramon had spoken first with La Giralda, it seemed to him that over the broiling roofs of the mill-house he caught the glimmer of something cool and white. He halted his horse and stood momentarily up in his stirrups, whereupon the glimmer upon the roof seemed to change suddenly to red and then as swiftly vanished.

Certainly there was something wrong. Rollo hurried on, giving the three knocks which had been agreed upon at the closed outer door of the house. It was opened by La Giralda.

"Who is signalling from the roof?" he asked hurriedly.

The old gipsy stared at him, and then glanced apprehensively at his face. It had grown white with sudden anxiety.

"A touch of sun—you are not accustomed—you are not of the country to ride about at this time of day. No one has been signalling. Don Ramon is with his wife, waiting for you; and, as I think, not finding the time long. I will bring you a drink of wine and water with a *tisane* in it, very judicious in cases of sun-touch!"

The latter was much in the line of the young man's desires, yet being still unsatisfied, he could not help saying, "But, La Giralda, I saw the thing plainly, a signal, first of white and then of red, waved from the roof, as it seemed, over the mill-wheel."

La Giralda shook her head.

"Eyes," she said, "only eyes and the touch of

the sun. But tell me, what of Concha, and how you sped with the Lady Superior ? "

But Rollo was not to be appeased till he had summoned El Sarria, and with him examined the strong-room where the prisoners were kept ; as before, Don Luis sat listlessly by the table, his brow upon his hand. He did not look up or speak when they entered. But his brother moaned on about his wounded head, and complained that La Tia had drunk all the water. This being replenished, Don Tomas wandered off into muttered confidences concerning his early travels, how he had made love to the Alcalde's daughter of Granada, how he had fought with a *contrabandista* at Ronda fair—with other things too intimate to be here set down, ever returning, however, to his plea that the Tia Elvira had defrauded him of his fair share of the water-jug.

"Nay, not so," said the Tia, soothingly ; "every drop of the water you have drunk, Don Tomas. But it is your head, your poor head. I turned the poultice, and with the water he speaks of moistened the leaves afresh. And how, worthy Señors, is the dear lady ? I trust, well. Ah ! had she been left in my care, all had gone right with her ! "

"In *your* care ! In *your* care, hell-hag ! " cried El Sarria, fiercely, taking a step threateningly towards her, "aye, the kind of safety my child would have experienced had that gentleman, your brother there, been allowed to finish his grave-digging business. Let me not hear another word out of your mouth, lest I do the world a service by cutting short a long life so ill-spent ! "

The Tia took the hint and said nothing. But her eyes, cast up to the roof, and her hands spread abroad palm outwards, expressed her conviction that

ever thus do the truly good and charitable suffer for
their good deeds, their best acts being mistaken and
misinterpreted, and their very lives brought into
danger by the benevolence of their intentions.

Had Rollo but followed the direction of her gaze
he might have had his doubts of La Giralda's theory
of sunstroke to explain the signalling from the roof.
For there, clearly to be seen out of the half-open
trapdoor, was a little scarlet strip of cloth stirred by
the wind, and doubtless conspicuous from all the
neighbouring hills about the village of Sarria.

But Rollo, eager to get to his task of arranging
the transport for the evening, so that Dolóres might
be taken in safety and comfort to the Convent of the
Holy Innocents, was already turning to be gone,
while Ramon Garcia, afraid to trust himself long in
the same apartment with the traitor, stood outside
fingering the key.

"Bring wine and water!" cried Rollo to La
Giralda, "and, Don Luis, in an hour I will trouble
you to take a little tour of the premises with me,
just to show your men that all is right."

Luis Fernandez bowed slightly but said nothing,
while the invalid from his couch whined feebly that
all the water was for him. The others might have
the wine or at least some of it, but he must have all
the water.

So Rollo Blair and his companion withdrew into
the cool guest-chamber of the mill-house without
having seen the little waving strip of red upon the roof.
As soon as they were gone, however, Don Luis leaped
up, and with a long fishing-pole he flaunted a strip of
white beside the red, waving it this way and that for
a long time, till in the close atmosphere of the strong-
room the sweat rained from him in great drops.

Then he leaped down at last, muttering, " If the General is within twenty miles, as I think he is, that ought to bring him to Sarria. The angels grant that he arrive in time" (here he paused a moment, and then added with a bitter smile), "or the devils either. I am not particular, so be that he come !"

CHAPTER XIX

SIGNALS OF STORM

A LONG strip of Moorish-looking wall and certain towers that glittered white in the sun, advertised to Rollo that he approached the venta of Sarria. Without, that building might have passed for the palace of a grandee ; within—but we know already what it was like within.

Rollo was impatient to find his companions. He had just discovered that he had most scurvily neglected them, and now he was all eagerness to make amends. But the house-place of the Café de Madrid was tenanted only by the Valiant and a clean silently-moving maid, who solved the problem of perpetual motion by finding something to do simultaneously in the kitchen, out in the shady *patio* among the copper water-vessels, and up in the sleeping chambers above.

Rollo's questioning produced nothing but a sleepy grunt from Don Gaspar Perico.

"Gone — no ! They had better not," he muttered, "better not—without paying their score— bread and ham and eggs, to say nothing of the noise and disturbance they had occasioned. The tallest was a spitfire, a dare-devil—ah, your excellency, I did not know——"

Here Don Gaspar the Valiant, who had been muttering in his beard more than half asleep, awoke

170

suddenly to the fact that the dare-devil aforesaid stood before him, fingering his sword-hilt and twisting his moustache.

But he was a stout old soldier, this Gaspar Perico, and had a moustache of his own which he could finger with anybody.

"I crave your pardon, Señor," he said, rising and saluting, "I think I must have been asleep. Until this moment I was not aware of your honourable presence."

"My companions—where are they?" said Rollo, hastily. He had much on his mind, and wished to despatch business. Patience he had none. If a girl refused him he sprang into the first ship and betook himself to other skies and kinder maidens. If a battle went wrong, he would fight on to the death, or at least till he was beaten into unconsciousness. But of the cautious generalship which draws off in safety and lives to fight another day, Rollo had not a trace.

"Your companions—nay, I know nothing of them," said the veteran: "true it is he of the stoutness desired to buy my wine, and when I gave him a sample, fine as iced Manzanilla, strong as the straw-wine of Jerez, he spat it forth upon the ground and vowed that as to price he preferred the ordinary robbers of the highway!"

Rollo laughed a little at this description of John Mortimer's method of doing business, but he was eager to find his comrades, so he hastily excused himself, apologised for his companion's rudeness, setting it down to the Señor Mortimer's ignorance of the language, and turned to go out.

But as he passed into the arcaded *patio* of the inn, the silent maidservant passed him with a flash of white cotton gown. Her grass shoes made no noise on the pavement. As she passed, Rollo glanced at her quickly and carelessly, as it was his nature to look at every woman. She was beckoning to him to follow her. There could be no doubt of that. She turned abruptly through a low doorway upon the top of which Rollo nearly knocked out his brains.

The Scot followed down a flight of steps, beneath blossoming oleander bushes, and found himself presently upon a narrow terrace-walk, divided from a neighbouring garden by a lattice of green-painted wood.

The silent maidservant jerked her thumb a little contemptuously over her shoulder, elevated her chin, and turning on her heel disappeared again into her own domains.

Rollo stood a moment uncertain whether to advance or retreat. He was in a narrow path which skirted a garden in which fuchsias, geraniums, and dwarf palms grew abundantly. Roses also clambered among the lattice-work, peered through the chinks, and drooped invitingly over the top.

A little to the right the path bent somewhat, and round the corner Rollo could hear a hum of voices. It was in this direction also that the silent handmaid of Gaspar Perico's kitchen had jerked her thumb.

Rollo moved slowly along the path, and presently he came in sight of a pretty damsel on the farther side of the trellis paling, deeply engaged in a most interesting conversation. So far as he could see she was tall and dark, with the fully formed Spanish features, a little heavy perhaps to Rollo's taste, but charming now with the witchery of youth and conscious beauty.

Her hand had been drawn through one of the diamond-shaped apertures of the green trellis-work,

which proved how small a hand it was. And, so far
as the young Scot could judge from various con-
tributory movements on the lady's part, it was
at that moment being passionately kissed by some
person unseen.

The low voice he had heard also proceeded from
this fervent lover, and the whole performance made
Rollo most unreasonably angry.

"What fools!" he muttered, turning on his heel,
adding as an afterthought, "and especially at this
time of day."

He was walking off in high dudgeon, prepared
to give the silent maid a piece of his mind—indeed,
a sample most unpleasing, when something in the
tone of the lover's voice attracted him.

"Fairest Maria, never have I loved before," the
voice was saying. "I have wandered the world
heretofore, careless and heart-free, that I might have
the more to offer to you, the pearl of girls, the all
incomparable Maria of Sarria!"

The fair hand thrust through the lattices was
violently agitated at this point. Its owner had
caught sight of Rollo standing on the pathway, but
the lover's grasp was too firm. As Rollo looked
a head was thrust forward and downwards—as it
were into the picture. And there, kneeling on the
path, was Monsieur Etienne, lately Brother Hilario
of Montblanch, fervidly kissing the hand of reluctant
beauty.

As Rollo, unwilling to intrude, but secretly
resolving to give Master Lovelace no peace for some
time, was turning away, a sharp exclamation from
the girl caused the kneeling lover to look up. She
snatched her hand through the interstices of the
palisades on the instant, fled upward through the

rose and fuchsia bushes with a swift rustle of skirts, and disappeared into a neighbouring house.

Etienne de Saint Pierre rose in a leisurely manner, dusted the knees of his riding-breeches, twirled his moustache, and looked at Rollo, who stood on the path regarding him.

"Well, what in the devil's name brings you here?" he demanded.

The mirthful mood in which he had watched his comrade kneel was already past with Rollo.

"Come outside, and I will tell you," he said, and without making any further explanation or asking for any from Etienne, he strode back through the courtyard of the venta and out into the sunlit road.

A muleteer was passing, sitting sideways on his beast's back as on an easy-chair, and as he went by he offered the two young men to drink out of a leathern goatskin of wine with a courteous wave of the hand. Rollo declined equally courteously.

Then turning to his friend, who still continued to scowl, he said abruptly, "Where is Mortimer?"

"Nay, that I know not—looking for another meal, I suppose," answered the little Frenchman, shrugging his shoulders, one higher than the other.

Rollo glanced at him from under his gloomy brows.

"Nay," he said, "this is serious. I need your help. Do not fail me to-night, and help me to find Mortimer. I had not the smallest intention of intruding upon you. Indeed, but for that maid at the inn, I should never have found you."

"Ah," commented Etienne, half to himself, "so I owe it to that minx, do I? Yes, it is a mistake—so close as that. But no matter; what can I do for you?"

"It is not for myself," Rollo answered, and forthwith in a low voice told his tale, the Frenchman assenting with a nod of the head as each point was made clear to him.

Unconsciously they had strolled out of the village in the direction of the Convent of the Holy Innocents, and they were almost under its walls when the little Frenchman, looking up suddenly, recognised with a start whither he was being led.

"Let us turn back," he said hastily; "I have forgotten an engagement!"

"What, another?" cried Rollo. "If we stay here three days you will have the whole village on your hands, and at least half a dozen knives in your back. But if you are afraid of the Señorita Concha, I think I can promise you that she is not breaking her heart on your account!"

In spite of this assurance, however, Etienne was not easy in his mind till they had turned about and were returning towards the village. But they had not left the white walls of the Convent behind, before they were hailed in English by a stentorian voice.

"Here, you fellows," it said, "here's a whole storehouse of onions as big as a factory—strings and strings of 'em. I wanted to go inside to make an offer for the lot, and the old witch at the gate slammed it in my face.

Looking round, they saw John Mortimer standing on one leg to eke out his stature, and squinting through a hole in the whitewashed wall. One hand was beckoning them frantically forward, while with the other he was trying to render his position on a sun-dried brick less precarious.

"I suppose we must go back," said Etienne,

with a sigh; "imagine standing on a brick and getting so hot and excited—in the blazing sun, too— all for a few strings of onions. I declare I would not do it for the prettiest girl in Spain!"

But there could be no doubt whatever that the Englishman was in earnest. Indeed, he did not move from his position till they were close upon him, and then only because the much-enduring brick resolved itself into its component sand and sun-dried clay.

"Just look there!" he cried eagerly; "did you ever see the like of that—a hundred double strings hung from the ceiling to the floor right across! And the factory nearly a hundred and fifty yards long. There's a ship-load of onions there, a solid cargo, I tell you, and I want to trade. I believe I could make my thousand pounds quicker that way, and onions are as good as wine any day! Look in, look in!"

To satisfy his friend, Rollo applied his eye to the aperture, and saw that one of the Convent buildings was indeed filled with onions, as John Mortimer had said. It was a kind of cloister open at one side, and with rows of pillars. The wind rustling through the pendant strings filled the place with a pleasant noise, distinctly audible even outside the wall.

"A thousand pounds, Rollo," moaned John Mortimer, "and that old wretch at the wicket only laughed at me, and snapped the catch in my face. They don't understand business here. I wish I had them apprenticed to my father at Chorley for six months, only for six months. They'd know the difference!"

Rollo took his friend's arm and drew him away.

"This is not the time for it," he said soothingly, "wait. We are going to the Convent to-night. The Mother Superior has permitted the lady on whose account we are here to be removed there after dark, and we want your help."

"Can I speak to the old woman about the onions then?"

"Certainly, if there is an opportunity," said Rollo, smiling.

"Which I take leave to doubt," thought Etienne to himself, as he meditated on his own troubles in the matter of little Concha and the maiden of the green lattice.

"Very well, then," said Mortimer, "I'm your man; I don't mind doing a little cloak-and-dagger considered as trimmings—but business is business."

The three friends proceeded venta-wards, and just as they passed the *octroi* gate the same muleteer who had passed them outward bound, went in before them with the same leathern bottle in his hand. And as he entered he tossed his hand casually towards Gaspar Perico, who sat in the receipt of custom calmly reading an old newspaper.

"Now that's curious," said John Mortimer, "that fellow had a red and white cloth in his hand. And all the time when I was skirmishing about after those onions in the nuns' warehouse, they were waving red and white flags up on the hills over there—*wig wag* like that!"

And with his hand he illustrated the irregular and arbitrary behaviour of the flags upon the hills which overlooked the village of Sarria to the south.

And at the sound of his words Rollo started, and his countenance changed. It was then no mere delusion of the eye and brain that he had seen when

N

he entered the precincts of the mill-house of Sarria,
as La Giralda would fain have persuaded him.   The
thought started a doubt in his mind.

Who after all was that old woman?   And what
cause had El Sarria for trusting her?   None at all,
so far as Rollo knew, save that she hated the Tia
Elvira.   Then that flicker of red and white on the
hillside to the south among the scattered boulders and
juniper bushes, and the favour of the same colour in
the muleteer's hand as he went through the gate!

Verily Rollo had some matter for reflection, as,
with his comrades, one on either hand of him, he
strolled slowly back to the venta.

·   "I wonder," said John Mortimer, as if to himself, "if that young woman who walks like a pussy-
cat will have luncheon ready for us.   I told her to
roast the legs of the lamb I bought at the market
this morning, and make an *olla* of the rest.   But
I don't believe she understands her own language—
a very ignorant young woman indeed."

"I, on the other hand, think she knows too
much," murmured Etienne to himself.

But Rollo, the red and white flutter of the
mysterious signal flags before his eyes, seen between
him and the white-hot sky of day, only sighed, and
wished that the night would anticipate itself by
a few hours.

And so, dinner being over, and even John
Mortimer satisfied, the drowsy afternoon of Sarria
wore on, the clack of the mill-wheel down at the
mill, and the clink of the anvil where Jaime
Casanovas, the smith, was shoeing a horse, being
the only sounds without; while in the venta itself
the whisk of the skirts of the silent handmaid, who
with a perfectly grave face went about her work,

alone broke the silence. But Monsieur Etienne's ears tingled red, for he was conscious that as often as she passed behind his chair, she smiled a subtle smile.

He thought on the green lattices and the path so near and so cool. But with all his courage he could not go out under the observant eyes of Rollo and with that abandoned Abigail smiling her ironic smile. So, perforce, he had to sit uneasily with his elbows on the table and watch the dreary game of dominoes which his companions were playing with the chipped and greasy cubes belonging to the venta of Gaspar and Esteban Perico.

And outside, though they knew it not, the red and white pennon was still flying from the roof of the mill-house of Sarria, and on the hills to the south, through the white sun-glare, flickered at intervals an answering signal.

Meanwhile in a hushed chamber the outlaw sat with his wife's hand in his, and thought on nothing, save that for him the new day had come.

CHAPTER XX

Upon the village of Sarria and upon its circling mountains night descended with Oriental swiftness. The white houses grew blurred and indistinct. Red roofs, green shutters, dark window squares, took on the same shade of indistinguishable purple.

But in the west the rich orange lingered long, the typical Spanish after-glow of day edging the black hills with dusky scarlet, and extending upwards to the zenith sombre and mysterious, like her own banner of gold and red strangely steeped in blood.

In the mill-house of Sarria they were not idle. Ramon Garcia and Rollo had constructed a carrying couch for Dolóres, where, on a light and pliant framework of the great bulrush *cañas* that grew along the canal edges, her mattress might be laid.

It was arranged that, after Dolóres had been conveyed with Concha and La Giralda in attendance to the Convent of the Holy Innocents, the three young men and El Sarria should return in order to release and warn the brothers Fernandez of the consequences of treachery. Thereafter they were to ride out upon their mission.

Crisp and clear the night was. The air clean-tasting like spring water, yet stimulating as a draught of wine long-cooled in cellar darkness.

Very gently, and as it were in one piece like a swaddled infant, Dolóres was lifted by El Sarria in his arms and laid upon the hastily-arranged ambulance. The four bearers fell in. La Giralda locked the doors of the mill-house, and by a circuitous route, which avoided the village and its barking curs, they proceeded in the direction of the convent buildings.

As often as the foot of any of the bearers slipped upon a stone, Ramon grew sick with apprehension, and in a whisper over his shoulder he would inquire of Dolóres if all was well.

"All is well, beloved," the voice, weak and feeble, would reply. "You are here—you are not angry with me. Yes, all is well."

They moved slowly through the darkness, La Giralda, with many crooning encouragements, waiting upon Dolóres, now lifting up the corner of a coverlid and now anxiously adjusting a pillow.

It was done at last, and with no more adventure than that once when they were resting the carrying couch under a wall, a muleteer passed, and cried, "Good-night to you, folk of peace!" To which El Sarria grunted a reply, and the man passed on, humming a gay Aragonese ditty, and puffing his cigarette, the red point of which glowed like a firefly long after both man and beast had been merged in the general darkness of the valley.

They were soon passing under the eastern side of the convent.

"Ah, I can smell them," murmured John Mortimer, exstatically, "a hundred tons, if not more. I wonder if I could not tackle the old lady to-night about them?"

He spoke meditatively, but no one of the party

took the least notice. For Rollo was busy with the future conduct of the expedition. Etienne was thinking of the girl behind the green lattices, while the others did not understand a word of what he said.

John Mortimer sighed a deep and genuine sigh.

"Spain is very well," he muttered; "but give me Chorley for doing business in!"

At last they were at the little white cowl of the porter's lodge, out of which the black bars of the wicket grinned with a semblance of ghastly mirth.

Rollo knocked gently. The panel slid back noiselessly, and there was the face of Concha Cabezos dimly revealed. No longer mischievous or even piquant, but drawn and pale with anxiety.

"There are bad people here," she whispered, "who have persuaded the Lady Superior that you are impostors. She will not receive or keep Dolóres Garcia unless she is satisfied——"

"What?" came from the rear in a thunderous growl.

"Hush, I bid you!" commanded Rollo, sternly, "remember you have put this in my hands." And the outlaw fell back silenced for the moment—his heart, however, revolving death and burnings.

"Trust me with your papers—your credentials," said Concha, quickly. "These will convince her. I will bring them to you at the mill-house to-morrow morning!"

Rollo ran his knife round the stitching of his coat where he carried these sacredest possessions.

"There," he said, "remember—do not let them out of your sight a moment. I am putting far more than my own life into your hands."

"I will cherish them as the most precious thing

in the world. And now, I will go and show them
to the Lady Superior."

"Not till you have taken in my Dolóres as you
promised," came the voice of El Sarria, "or by
Heaven I will burn your convent to the ground.
She shall not be left here in the damp dews of the
night."

"No, no," whispered Concha, "she shall be laid
in the lodge of the portress, and La Giralda shall
watch her till her own chamber is prepared, and I
have eased the mind of the Lady Superior."

The great bars were drawn. The bolts gave
back with many creakings, and through the black
gap of the main gate they carried Dolóres into
the warm flower-scented darkness of the portress's
lodge.

She was laid on a bed, and the moment after
Concha turned earnestly upon the four men.

"Now go," she said, "this instant! I also
have risked more than you know. Go back!"

"Can I not stay with her to-night?" pleaded
El Sarria, keeping the limp hand wet with chill
perspiration close in his.

"Go—go, I say!" said Concha. "Go, or it
may be too late. See yonder."

And on a hill away to the west a red light
burned for a long moment and then vanished.

The three young men went out, but El Sarria
lingered, kneeling by his wife's bedside. Rollo went
back and touched him on the shoulder.

"You must come with us—for *her* sake!" he
said. And he pointed with his finger. And
obediently at his word the giant arose and went out.
Rollo followed quickly, but as he went a little palm
fell on his arm and a low voice whispered in his ear—

"You trust me, do you not?"

Rollo lifted Concha's hand from his sleeve and kissed it.

"With my life—and more!" he said.

"What more?" queried Concha.

"With my friends' lives!" he answered.

And as he went out with no other word Concha breathed a sigh very softly and turned towards Dolóres. She felt somehow as if the tables were being turned upon her.

*   *   *   *   *   *

Outside there was a kind of waiting hush in the air, an electric tension of expectation, or so at least it seemed to Rollo.

As they marched along the road towards the mill-house, they saw a ruddy glow towards the south.

"Something is on fire there!" said John Mortimer. "I mind when Graidly's mills were burnt in Bowton, we saw a glimmer in the sky just like yon! And we were at Chorley, mind you, miles and miles away!"

"They are more like camp-fires behind the hills," commented Etienne, from his larger experience. "I think we had better clear out of Sarria to-night."

"That," said Rollo, firmly, "is impossible so far as I am concerned. I must wait at the mill-house for the papers. But do you three go on, and I will rejoin you to-morrow."

"I will stay," said El Sarria, as soon as Rollo's words had been interpreted to him.

"And I," cried Etienne. "Shall it be said that a Saint Pierre ever forsook a friend?"

"And I," said John Mortimer, "to look after the onions!"

The mill-house was silent and dark as they had

left it. They could hear the drip-drip of the water from the motionless wheel. An owl called at intervals down in the valley. Rollo, to whom La Giralda had given the key, stooped to fit it into the keyhole. The door was opened and the four stepped swiftly within. Then Rollo locked the door again inside.

They heard nothing through all the silent, empty house but the sound of their own breathing. Yet here, also, there was the same sense of strain lying vague and uneasy upon them.

"Let us go on and see that all is right," said Rollo, and led the way into the large room where they had found Luis Fernandez. He walked up to the window, a dim oblong of blackness, only less Egyptian than the chamber itself. He stooped to strike his flint and steel together into his tinder-box, and even as the small glittering point winked, Rollo felt his throat grasped back and front by different pairs of hands, while others clung to his knees and brought him to the ground.

"Treachery! Out with you, lads—into the open!" he cried to his companions, as well as he could for the throttling fingers.

But behind him there arose the sound of a mighty combat. Furniture was overset, or broke with a sharp crashing noise as it was trampled underfoot.

"Show a light, there," cried a quick voice, in a tone of command.

A lantern was brought from an inner room, and there, on the floor, in the grasp of their captors, were Ramon Garcia, still heaving with his mighty exertions, and Rollo the Scot, who lay very quiet so soon as he had assured himself that present resistance would do no good.

"Bring in the others," commanded the voice again, "and let us see what the dogs look like."

Mortimer and Etienne, having been captured in the hall, while trying to unlock the outer door, were roughly haled into the room. Rollo was permitted to rise, but the giant was kept on his back while they fastened him up securely with ropes and halters.

Then Luis Fernandez came in, an evil smile on his dark handsome face, and behind him a little thick-set active man in some military dress of light material. The uniform was unfamiliar to Rollo, who, for a moment, was in doubt whether he was in the hands of the Cristinos or in those of the partisans of Don Carlos.

But a glance about the chamber eased his mind. The white *boinas* of the Basque provinces, mingled with the red of Navarra, told him that he had been captured by the Carlists.

"Well," said a little dark man with the curly hair, black and kinked like a negro's, "give an account of yourselves and of your proceedings in this village."

"We are soldiers in the service of His Excellency Don Carlos," said Rollo, fearlessly; "we are on our way to the camp of General Cabrera on a mission of importance."

Luis Fernandez looked across at his companion, who had seated himself carelessly in a large chair by the window.

"Did I not tell you he would say that?" he said. The other nodded. "On a mission to General Cabrera," repeated the chief of Rollo's captors; "well, then, doubtless you can prove your statement by papers and documents. Let me see your credentials."

"I must know, first, to whom I have the honour of speaking," said Rollo, firmly.

"You shall," said the man in the chair.   "I am General Cabrera, in the service of His Absolute Majesty, Carlos, Fifth of Spain.   I shall be glad to receive your credentials, sir."

Then it flashed upon Rollo that all his papers were in the hands of Concha Cabezos. He had given them to her that she might show them to the Lady Superior, and so insure a welcome for poor little Dolóres, whom they had left lying on the bed in the portress's lodge at the Convent of the Holy Innocents.

"I can indeed give you the message, and that instantly," said Rollo; "but I am unfortunately prevented from showing you my credentials till the morning.   They are at present at the—in the hands of a friend——"

Here Rollo stammered and came to a full stop. Luis Fernandez laughed scornfully.

"Of course," he said: "what did I tell you, General?   He has no credentials."

Cabrera struck his clenched fist on the table.

"Sir," he said, "you are a strange messenger. You pretend a mission to me, and when asked for your credentials you tell us that they are in the hands of a friend.   Tell us your friend's name, and how you came to permit documents of value to me and to the cause for which you say that you are fighting, to fall into any hands but your own."

Rollo saw that to refer to the Convent of the Holy Innocents, or to mention Concha's name, would infallibly betray the hiding-place of Dolóres to her enemies, so he could only reiterate his former answer.

" I am unfortunately prevented by my honour from revealing the name of my friend, or why the documents were so entrusted. But if your excellency will only wait till the morning, I promise that you shall be abundantly satisfied."

" I am not accustomed to wait for the morning," said Cabrera. " There is no slackening of rein on the King's service. But I have certain information as to who you are, which may prove more pertinent to the occasion, and may, perhaps, prevent any delay whatsoever."

Cabrera leisurely rolled and lighted a cigarette, giving great attention to the closing of the paper in which it was enwrapped.

" I am informed," he said, when he had successfully achieved this, " that you are three members of the English Foreign Legion which has been fighting for the Cristino traitors. What have you to say to that ? "

" That it is a lie," shouted Etienne, thrusting himself forward. " I a Cristino ! I would have you know that I am the Count of Saint Pierre, a cousin in the second degree of Don Carlos himself, and that I came to Spain to fight for the only true and constitutional King, Carlos the Fifth."

Cabrera turned his head and scrutinised the little Frenchman.

" Ah, then," he said dryly, " if that be so, perhaps you have taken better care of your papers than this tall gentleman, who has such trust in his friends."

" A Saint Pierre does not need papers to prove his identity," said Etienne, proudly.

" They are sometimes convenient, nevertheless, even to a Saint Pierre," said Cabrera, with irony :

"they may prevent certain little mistakes which are more easily made than remedied."

There was a long pause at this point.

"What is your business here, Monsieur de Saint Pierre?" continued the Carlist General suavely, throwing away his cigarette end after inhaling the "breast" to the last puff with infinite satisfaction.

"I was sent on a mission, along with these two gentlemen, at the instance of my uncle, Don Baltasar Varela, the Abbot of Montblanch, and one of the most trusted councillors of Don Carlos!"

"Doubtless—doubtless," said Cabrera; "but have you the papers to prove it? Or any letter in your uncle's handwriting authorising you to commit the lawless acts you have committed on the person and property of this faithful servant of the King?"

"All the papers in connection with the mission were in the care of my friend Monsieur Rollo Blair, of Blair Castle," said Etienne. "He was appointed chief of the expedition by my uncle, Don Baltasar, and if he has parted temporarily with them, it is doubtless for good and sufficient reasons."

"Search them," commanded Cabrera, suddenly, in a sharp tone of anger, in which for the first time the latent cruelty of his nature came out.

Their captors, with no great delicacy of handling, began to overhaul the contents of the pockets of the four. They examined their boots, the lining of their coats, and ripped up the seams of their waistcoats.

Upon Ramon, nothing at all was found, except the fragment of a handbill issued by the Nationalist general offering a reward for his capture; at which more than one of the men wearing the white *boinas* began to look upon him with more favour, though they did not offer to ease the sharply-cutting ropes with which they had bound him.

Upon John Mortimer was found a pocket-book full of calculations, and a little pocket Testament with an inscription in English, which made John Mortimer blush.

" Tell them my mother gave me that, and made me promise to carry it. I don't want them to take it away ! "

Rollo translated, and Cabrera, after turning over the pages, handed it back with a bow.

" A *gage d'amour ?* " he said, smiling.

" Yes, from my mother ! " said John Mortimer, blushing yet more.

The search through the pockets of Etienne produced nothing except a number of brief notes, daintily folded but indifferently written, and signed by various Lolas, Felesias, and Magdalenas. Most of these were brief, and to the point. " Meet me at the gate by the rose-tree at seven. My father has gone to the city ! " or only " I am waiting for you ! Come."

But in the outer pocket of Rollo Blair was found a far more compromising document. When the searcher drew it forth from his coat, the eyes of Luis Fernandez gleamed with triumph.

Cabrera took the paper and glanced it over carelessly, but as soon as his eye fell upon the signature the fashion of his countenance changed. He leaped to his feet.

" Nogueras ! " he cried; " you are in correspondence with Nogueras, the villain who, in cold blood, shot my poor old mother, for no crime but that of having borne me. Have the fellow out instantly, and shoot him ! "

Rollo stood a moment dumfounded, then he recovered himself and spoke.

"General Cabrera," he said, "this is a trick. I have had no correspondence with Nogueras. I had not even heard his name. This has been dropped into my pocket by some traitor. I hold a commission in the service of Don Carlos, and have had no communication with his enemies."

"But in this place you gave yourselves out as Nationalists, is it not so?" queried Cabrera.

"Certainly," answered Rollo; "we were on a secret mission, and we were given to understand that this was a hostile village."

Cabrera took up the letter again and read aloud—

"*To the young Englishman of the Foreign Legion, pretending service with Don Carlos.*

"You are ordered to obtain any information as to the movements of the brigand Cabrera and his men, by penetrating into their district, and, if possible, joining their organisation. You will report the same to me, and this pass will hold you safe with all servants and well-wishers of the government of the Queen-Regent.

"NOGUERAS."

The Carlist commander, whose voice had been rising as he read, shouted rather than uttered the name of the murderer of his mother. He did not again sit down, but strode up and down, his cavalry sword clanging and battering against the furniture of the little room as if expressing the angry perturbation of his mind.

"General," said Rollo, as calmly as if arguing

a point in theology, "if I had been guilty of this treachery, would I have kept a paper like that loose in an outer pocket? Is it not evident that it has been placed there by some enemy—probably by that archtraitor there, the miller Fernandez?"

Luis Fernandez smiled benignly upon Rollo, but did not speak. He believed that the poison had done its work.

Cabrera took not the slightest notice of Rollo's words, but continued to pace the floor frowning and muttering.

More than one Carlist soldier glanced at his neighbour with a look which said, plain as a printed proclamation, "It is all over with the foreigners!"

At last Cabrera stopped his promenade. He folded his arms and stood looking up at Rollo.

"The morning—I think you said. Well, I will give your friend till the morning to be ready with the proofs of your innocence. But if not, so soon as the sun rises over the hills out there, you four shall all be shot for spies and traitors. Take them away!"

CHAPTER XXI

TO BE SHOT AT SUNRISE !

THE Carlist soldiers conducted Rollo and his three friends to the granary of the mill-house, where in the mean time they were permitted to recline as best they might upon the various piles of grain heaped here and there in preparation for the work of the morrow.

The Carlists were mostly quite young, Basques and Navarrese, whose jokes and horseplay, even after a long day's marching, were boyish and natural.

Rollo and El Sarria were placed at one side of the granary, and at the other Etienne and John Mortimer lay at full length upon a heap of corn. Between paced a sentry with musket and bayonet.

The kindly lads had, with characteristic generosity, brought their prisoners a portion of their scanty rations—sausages and dried fish with onions and cheese, all washed down with copious draughts of red wine.

As before, owing to the position of Sarria among its mountains, the night fell keen and chill. The Carlists slept and snored, all save the double guards placed over the prisoners.

" Shall we try a rush ? Is it any use ? " whispered Rollo to El Sarria.

The outlaw silently shook his head. He had long ago considered the position, and knew that it was impossible. The windows were mere slits. There was only one trap-door in the floor, and that was closed. Moreover, there were fifty Carlists asleep in the loft, and the floor below was the bed-chamber of as many more.

Cast back upon his own thoughts, Rollo reviewed many things—his short life, the reckless ups-and-downs in which he had spent it—but all without remorse or regret.

"I might have been a lawyer, and lived to a hundred!" he said to himself. "It is better as it is. If I have done little good, perhaps I have not had time to do a great deal of harm."

Then very contentedly he curled himself up to sleep as best he might, only dreamily wondering if little Concha would be sorry when she heard.

Ramon Garcia sat with his eyes fixed on the sentry who had ceased his to-and-fro tramp up the centre, and now leaned gloomily against the wall, his hands crossed about the cross-bar of his sword-bayonet.

Across the granary John Mortimer reclined with his head in his hands, making vows never to enter Spain or trust himself under the leadership of a mad Scot, if this once he should get clear off.

"It isn't the being shot," he moaned; "it's not being able to tell them that I'm not a fool, but a respectable merchant able to pay my way and with a balance at William Deacon's Bank. But it serves me right!" Then a little inconsequently he added, "By gum, if I get out of this I'll have a Spanish clerk in the works and learn the language!"

Which was John Mortimer's way of making a vow to the gods.

Etienne, having his hands comparatively free,

and finding himself sleepless, looked enviously at Rollo's untroubled repose, and began to twist cigarettes for himself and the sentry who guarded his side of the granary.

Without, the owls circled and cried. A dog barked in the village above, provoking a far-reaching chorus of his kind. Then blows fell, and he fled yelping out of earshot.

Rollo was not wholly comfortable on his couch of grain. The bonds about his feet galled him, having been more tightly drawn than those of his companions in virtue of his chiefship. Nevertheless he got a good deal of sleep, and each time that he awoke it seemed to him that El Sarria was staring harder at the sentry and that the man had moved a little nearer.

At last, turning his head a little to one side, he heard distinctly the low murmur of voices.

"Do you remember Pancorbo?" said Ramon Garcia.

Rollo could not hear the answer, but he caught the outlaw's next question.

"And have you forgotten El Sarria, who, having a certain Miguelete under the point of his knife, let him go for his sweetheart's sake, because she was waiting for him down in the valley?"

The sentry's reply was again inaudible, but Rollo was fully awake now. Ramon Garcia had not abandoned hope, and why should he? When there was anything to be done, none could be so alert as Rollo Blair.

"I am El Sarria the outlaw," Ramon went on, "and these are my companions. We are no traitors, but good Carlists to a man. Our papers are——"

Here the words were spoken so low that Rollo

could not hear more, but the next moment he was
nudged by Ramon on the leg.

"Write a note to Concha Cabezos, telling her to
bring the papers here at once if she would save our
lives. You are sure she is faithful?"

"I am sure!" said Rollo, who really had no
reason for his confidence except the expression in her
eyes.

He had no paper, but catching the sentry's eye,
he nodded across to where Etienne was still dili-
gently rolling cigarettes.

"Alcoy?" he whispered.

The sentry shouldered his piece and took a turn
or two across the floor, keeping his eye vigilantly on
his fellow guard, who, having seated himself in the
window-sill, had dozed off to sleep, the cigarette still
drooping from the corner of his mouth. Yes, he
was certainly asleep.

He held out his hand to Etienne, who readily
gave him the last he had rolled. The sentry thanked
him with a quick martial salute, and after a turn or
two more, deftly dropped the crumbled tobacco upon
the floor and let the leaf drop on Rollo's knees with
a stump of pencil rolled up in it.

Then the young man, turning his back upon the
dozing guard in the stone window-sill, wrote with
some difficulty the following note, lying on his breast
and using the uneven floor of the granary for a desk.

"Little Concha" (it ran), "we are General
Cabrera's prisoners. Bring the papers as soon as
you receive this. Otherwise we are to be shot at
daybreak.—Rollo Blair."

There was still a little space left upon the leaf of

Alcoy paper, and with a half shamefaced glance at El Sarria, he added, "*And in any case do not wholly forget R. B.*"

He passed the note to the outlaw, who folded it to the size of a postage stamp and apparently gave directions where and to whom it was to be delivered.

"In half an hour we shall be relieved and I will go," said the Carlist ex-Miguelete, and resumed his steady tramp. Presently he awoke his comrade so that he might not be found asleep at the change of guard.

*　　*　　*　　*　　*

There was nothing more to be done till daybreak. They had played their last card, and now they must wait to see what cards were out against them, and who should win the final trick at the hour of sunrise.

Rollo fell asleep again. And so soundly this time, that he only woke to consciousness when a soldier in a white *boina* pulled roughly at his elbow, and ordered him to get up.

All about the granary the Carlists were stamping feet, pulling on boots, and flapping arms.

"It's a cold morning to be shot in," said the man, with rough kindliness ; "but I will get you some hot chocolate in a moment. That will warm your blood for you, and in any case you will have a quick passage. I will pick you a firing party of the best shots in the three provinces. The general will be here in a quarter of an hour, and the sun will rise in another quarter. One is just as punctual as the other. A cigarette ?—thank you. Well, you are a cool hand ! I'm off to see about the chocolate !"

And Rollo Blair, with a slight singing in his ears, and a chill emptiness about the pit of his stomach, stood on his feet critically rolling a cigarette in a leaf of Etienne's Alcoy paper.

John Mortimer said nothing, but looked after the man who had gone for the chocolate.

"I wish it had been coffee," he said; "chocolate is always bad for my digestion!"

Then he smiled a little grimly. His sufferings from indigestion produced by indulgence in this particular chocolate would in all probability not be prolonged, seeing that the glow of the sunrising was already reddening the sky to the east.

Etienne was secretly fingering his beads. And El Sarria thought with satisfaction of the safety of Dolóres; he had given up hope of Concha a full hour ago. The ex-Miguelete had doubtless again played the traitor. He took a cigarette from Rollo without speaking and followed him across the uneven floor between the heaps of trodden grain.

They were led down the stairway one by one, and as they passed through the ground floor, with its thick woolly coating of grey flour dust, a trumpet blew without, and they heard the trampling of horses in the courtyard.

"Quick!" said a voice at Rollo's elbow, "here is your chocolate. Nothing like it for strengthening the knee-joints at a time like this. I've seen men die on wine and on rum and on brandy; but for me, give me a cup of chocolate as good as that, when my time comes!"

Rollo drank the thick sweet strength-giving stuff to the accompaniment of clattering hoofs and jingling accoutrements.

"Come!" said a voice again, "give me the cup. Do not keep the general waiting. He is in no good temper this morning, and we are to march immediately."

The young man stepped out of the mill-door into the crisp chill of the dawn. All the east was a glory of blood-red cloud, and for the second time Rollo and his companions stood face to face with General Cabrera.

It was within a quarter of an hour of the sunrising.

CHAPTER XXII

HIS MOTHER'S ROSARY

IT was, as the soldier had said most truly, a cold morning to be shot in. But the Carlists, accustomed to Cabrera's summary methods, appeared to think but little of the matter, and jested as the firing parties were selected and drawn out. Ragged and desolate they looked as they stood on a slight slope between the foreigners and the red dawn, biting their cartridges and fingering the pulls of their rifles with hands numbed with cold. At elbow and knee their rags of uniforms flapped like bunches of ribbons at a fair.

"In the garden !" whispered Luis Fernandez to Cabrera.

"To the garden !" commanded the general, lighting a new cigarette and puffing vigorously, "and at this point I may as well bid you good-bye. I wish our acquaintance had been pleasanter. But the fortune of war, gentlemen ! My mother had not so long time to say her prayers at the hands of your friend Nogueras—and she was a woman and old, gentlemen. I doubt not you know as well how to die as she ?"

And they did. Not one of them uttered a word. John Mortimer, seeing there was now no chance of making his thousand pounds, set an example of unbending dignity. He comported himself, indeed, exactly as he would have done on his marriage day. That is, he knew that the eyes of many were upon him, and he resolved not to shame the performance. So he went through his part with the exact English mixture of awkward shyness and sulky self-respect which would have carried him creditably to the altar in any English church.

Etienne faced his death like the son of an ancient race, and a good Catholic. He could not have a confessor, but he said his prayers, committed his soul to God and the Virgin, and faced the black muzzles not greatly abashed.

As for El Sarria, death was his *métier*, his familiar friend. He had lived with him for years, as a man with a wife, rising up and lying down, eating and breathing in his company. "The fortune of war," as Cabrera said. El Sarria was ready. Dolóres and her babe were safe. He asked no more.

And not less readily fell into line Rollo Blair. A little apart he stood as they made ready to march out of the presence of the Carlist general. John Mortimer was already on his way, carefully and conscientiously ordering his going, that he might not in these last things disgrace his nation and his upbringing. Etienne and Ramon were following him. Still the young Scot lingered. Cabrera, nervously fingering his accoutrement and signing papers at a folding table, found time to eye him with curiosity.

"Did he mean to make a last plea for mercy?" he thought.

Cabrera smiled contemptuously. A friend of Nogueras might know Ramon Cabrera of Tortosa better. But Rollo had no such thought. He had in his fingers Etienne's last slip of Alcoy paper, in

which the cigarette of Spain, unfailing comforter, is
wrapped.   To fill it he had crumbled his last leaf of
tobacco.   Now it was rolled accurately and with
lingering particularity, because it was to be the last.
It lay in his palm featly made, a cigarette worthy to
be smoked by Don Carlos himself.

Almost unconsciously Rollo put it to his lips.
It was a cold morning, and it is small wonder that
his hand shook a little.   He was just twenty-three,
and his main regret was that he had not kissed little
Concha Cabezos—with her will, or against it—all
would have been one now.   Meantime he looked
about him for a light.   The general noticed his
hesitation, rose from the table, and with a low bow
offered his own, as one gentleman to another.
Rollo thanked him.   The two men approached as
if to embrace.   Each drew a puff of his cigarette,
till the points glowed red.   Rollo, retreating a little,
swept a proud acknowledgment of thanks with his
sombrero.   Cabrera bowed with his hand on his
heart.   The young Scot clicked his heels together
as if on parade, and strode out with head erect
and squared shoulders in the rear of his companions.

"By God's bread, a man!" said Cabrera, as he
resumed his writing, "'tis a thousand pities I must
shoot him!"

They stood all four of them in the garden of the
mill-house, underneath the fig trees in whose shade
El Sarria had once hidden himself to watch the midnight operations of Don Tomas.

The sun was just rising.   His beams red, low,
and level shot across the mill-wheel, turning the
water of the unused overshot into a myriad pearls
and diamonds as it splashed through a side culvert

into the gorge beneath, in which the gloom of night lingered.

The four men still stood in order. Mortimer and Etienne in the middle, with slim Rollo and the giant Ramon towering on either flank.

"*Load with ball—at six paces—make ready!*"

The officer's commands rang out with a certain haste, for he could already hear the clattering of the horses of the general's cavalcade, and he knew that if upon his arrival he had not carried out his orders, he might expect a severe reprimand.

But it was not the general's suite that rode so furiously. The sound came from a contrary direction. Two horses were being ridden at speed, and at sight of the four men set in order against the wall the foremost rider sank both spurs into her white mare and dashed forward with a wild cry.

The officer already had his sword raised in the air, the falling of which was to be the signal for the volley of death. But it did not fall. Something in the aspect of the girl-rider as she swept up parallel with the low garden wall, her hair floating disordered about her shoulders—her eyes black and shining like stars—the sheaf of papers she waved in her hand, all compelled the Carlist to suspend that last irrevocable order.

It was Concha Cabezos who arrived when the eleventh hour was long past, and leaped from her reeking horse opposite the place of execution. With her, wild-haired as a Mænad, rode La Giralda, cross-saddled like a man.

"General Cabrera! Where is General Cabrera?" cried Concha. "I must see him instantly. These are no traitors. They are true men, and in the service of Don Carlos. Here are their papers!"

"Where is Ramon Cabrera? Tell me quickly!" cried La Giralda. "I have news for him. I was with his mother when she died. They whipped me at the cross of Tortosa to tell what I knew—stripping me to the waist they whipped me, being old and the mother of many. Cabrera will avenge me. Let me but see Ramon Cabrera whom of old I suckled at my breasts!"

The officer hesitated. In such circumstances one might easily do wrong. He might shoot these men, and after all find that they were innocent. He preferred to wait. The living are more easily deprived of life than the dead restored to it. Such was his thought.

In any case he had not long to wait.

Round the angle of the mill-house swept the general and his staff, brilliant in scarlet and white, heightened by the glitter of abundant gold-lace. For the ex-butcher of Tortosa was a kind of military dandy, and loved to surround himself with the foppery of the *matador* and the brigand. At heart, indeed, he was still the *guerrillero* of Morella, riding home through the streets of that little rebel city after a successful foray.

As his eyes fell on the row of men dark against the dusty *adobe* of the garden wall, and on the two pale women, a dark frown overspread his face.

"What is the meaning of this?" he cried. "Why have you not obeyed your instructions? Why are these men not yet dead?"

The officer trembled, and began an explanation, pointing to Concha and La Giralda, both of whom stood for a moment motionless. Then flinging herself over the low wall of the garden as if her years had more nearly approached seventeen than

seventy, La Giralda caught the great man by the
stirrup.

"Little Ramon, Ramon Cabrera," she cried,
"have you forgotten your old nurse, La Giralda of
Sevilla, your mother's gossip, your own playmate?"

The general turned full upon her, with the
quick indignant threat of one who considers himself
duped, in his countenance. It had gone ill with La
Giralda if she had not been able to prove her case.
But she held something in her hand, the sight of
which brought the butcher of Tortosa down from
his saddle as quickly as if a Cristino bullet had
pierced him to the heart.

La Giralda was holding out to him an old string
of beads, simply carved out of some brown oriental
nut, but so worn away by use that the stringing had
almost cut through the hard and polished shell.

"My mother's rosary!" he cried, and sinking
on his knees, he devoutly received and kissed it.
He abode thus a moment looking up to the sky—
he, the man who had waded in blood during six
years of bitter warfare. He kissed the worn beads
one by one and wept. They were his mother's way
to heaven. And he did not know a better. In
which perchance he was right.

"Whence gat you this?" cried Cabrera, rising
sharply as a thought struck him; "my mother
never would have parted with these in her life—you
plundered it from her body after her death! Quick,
out with your story, or you die!"

"Nay, little foster-son," said La Giralda, "I was
indeed with your mother at the last—when she was
shot by Nogueras, and five minutes before she died
she gave her rosary into my hands to convey to you.
'Take this to my son,' she said, 'and bid him never

forget his mother, nor to say his prayers night and
morn. Bid him swear it on these sacred beads!'
So I have brought them to you. She kissed them
before she died. At the risk of my life have I
brought it."

"And these," said Cabrera—"do you know these
dogs, La Giralda?"

He pointed to the four men who still stood by
the wall, the firing party at attention before them,
and the eyes of all on the next wave of the general's
hand which would mean life or death.

La Giralda drew a quick breath. Would the
hold she had over him be sufficient for what she was
about to ask? He was a fierce man and a cruel, this
Ramon Cabrera, who loved naught in the world
except his mother, and had gained his present
ascendency in the councils of Don Carlos by the
unbending and consistent ferocity of his conduct.

"These are no traitors, General," she said; "they
are true men, and deep in the councils of the cause."

She bent and whispered in his ear words which
others could not hear. The face of the Carlist
general darkened from a dull pink to purple, and
then his colour ebbed away to a ghastly ashen white
as he listened.

Twice he sprang up from the stone bench where
he had seated himself, ground his heel into the
gravel brought from the river-bed beneath, and
muttered a characteristic imprecation, "Ten for
one of their women I have slain already—by
San Vicente after this it shall be a hundred!"

For La Giralda was telling him the tale of his
mother's shooting by Nogueras.

Then all suddenly he reseated himself, and
beckoned to Concha.

"Come hither," he said; "let me see these fellows' papers, and tell me how they came into your hands!"

Concha was ready.

"The Señor, the tall stranger, had a mission to the Lady Superior of the Convent," she began. "From Don Baltasar Varela it was, Prior of the great Carlist Monastery of Montblanch. He trusted his papers into her hands as a guarantee of his loyalty and good faith, and here they are!"

Concha flashed them from her bosom and laid them in the general's hands. Usually Cabrera was blind to female charms, but upon this occasion his eye rested with pleasure on the quick and subtle grace of the Andaluse.

"Then you are a nun?" he queried, looking sharply at her figure and dress.

"Ah, no," replied Concha, thinking with some hopefulness that she was to have at least a hearing, "I am not even a lay sister. The good Lady Superior had need of a housekeeper—one who should be free of the convent and yet able to transact business without the walls. It is a serious thing (as your honour knows) to provision even a hundred men who can live rough and eat sparely—how much harder to please a convent-school filled from end to end with the best blood in Spain! And good blood needs good feeding——"

"As I well knew when I was a butcher in Tortosa!" quoth Cabrera, smiling. "There were a couple of ducal families within the range of my custom, and they consumed more beef and mutton than a whole *barrio* of poor pottage-eaters!"

To make Cabrera smile was more than half the battle.

"You are sure they had nothing to do with the slayers of my mother?" He was fierce again in a moment, and pulled the left flange of his moustache into his mouth with a quick nervous movement of the fingers.

"I will undertake that no one of them hath ever been further south than this village of Sarria," said Concha, somewhat hastily, and without sufficient authority.

Cabrera looked at the papers. There was a Carlist commission in the name of Don Rollo Blair duly made out, a letter from General Elio, chief of the staff, commending all the four by name and description to all good servants of Don Carlos, as trustworthy persons engaged on a dangerous and secret mission. Most of all, however, he seemed to be impressed with the ring belonging to Etienne, with its revolving gem and concealed portrait of Carlos the Fifth.

He placed it on his finger and gazing intently, asked to whom it belonged. As soon as he understood, he summoned the little Frenchman to his presence. Etienne came at the word, calm as usual, and twirling his moustache in the manner of Rollo.

"This is your ring?" he demanded of the prisoner. Concha tried to catch Etienne's eye to signal to him that he must give Cabrera that upon which his fancy had lighted. But her former lover stubbornly avoided her eye.

"That is my ring," he answered dryly, after a cursory inspection of the article in question as it lay in the palm of the *guerillero's* hand.

"It is very precious to you?" asked the butcher of Tortosa, suggestively.

"It was given to me by my cousin, the king," answered Etienne, briefly.

"Then I presume you do not care to part with it?" said Cabrera, turning it about on his finger, and holding it this way and that to the light.

"No," said Etienne, coolly. "You see, my cousin might not give me another!"

But the butcher of Tortosa could be as simple and direct in his methods as even Rollo himself.

"Will you give it to me?" he said, still admiring it as it flashed upon his finger.

Etienne looked at the general calmly from head to foot, Concha all the time frowning upon him to warn him of his danger. But the young man was preening himself like a little bantam-cock of vanity, glad to be reckless under the fire of such eyes. He would not have missed the chance for worlds, so he replied serenely, "Do you still intend to shoot us?"

"What has that to do with the matter?" growled Cabrera, who was losing his temper.

"Because if you do," said Etienne, who had been waiting his opportunity, "you are welcome to the jewel—*after* I am dead. But if I am to live, I shall require it for myself!"

CHAPTER XXIII

THE BURNING OF THE MILL-HOUSE

CABRERA bit his lip for a moment, frowned still more darkly, and then burst into a roar of laughter. For the moment the *gamin* in him was uppermost—the same curly-pated rascal who had climbed walls and stolen apples from the market-women's stalls of Tortosa thirty years ago.

"You are a brave fellow," cried the general, "and I would to Heaven that your royal cousin had more of your spirit. Are all of your company of the same warlike kidney?"

"I trust I am afraid of no man on the field of honour," answered the loyal little Frenchman, throwing out his chest. "Yet I speak but the truth when I aver that there is not one of my companions who could not say grace and eat me up afterwards!"

Among the letters which had formed part of Rollo's credentials there was one superscribed "*To be opened in the camp of General Cabrera.*"

Cabrera now dismissed the firing party with a wave of his hand, the officer in command exchanging an encouraging nod with Rollo. Then he summoned that young man to approach. Rollo threw away the last inch of his cigarette, and going up easily, saluted the general with his usual self-possession.

" Well, colonel," said the latter, " I little thought to exchange civilities with you again ; but for that you have to thank this young lady. The fortune of war once more ! But if young men will entrust precious papers to pretty girls, they must have a fund of gratitude upon which to draw—that is, when the ladies arrive in time. On this occasion it was most exactly done. Yet you must have lived through some very crowded moments while you faced the muzzles of yonder rifles ! "

And he pointed to the lane down which the firing party was defiling.

Rollo bowed, but did not reply, awaiting the general's pleasure. Presently Cabrera, recollecting the sealed letter in his hand, gave it unopened to the youth.

" There," he said, " that, I see, is to be opened in the camp of General Cabrera. Well—where Cabrera is, there is his camp. Open it, and let us see what it contains."

" I will, general," said the young Scot, " in so far, that is, as it concerns your Excellency."

The Carlist general sat watching Rollo keenly as he broke the seal and discovered a couple of enclosures. One was sealed and the other open. The first he presented to Cabrera, who, observing the handwriting of the superscription, changed colour. Meanwhile, without paying any attention to him, Rollo read his own communication from beginning to end. It had evidently been passed on to him from a higher authority than the Abbot, for only the address was in the handwriting of that learned ecclesiast.

It ran as follows :

"To the Man who shall be chosen by our
trusted Councillor for the Mission Extraordinary in
the service of Carlos Quinto—These :

"You will receive from General Cabrera such
succour and assistance as may seem to you needful
in pursuance of the project you have in hand, namely
the capturing of the young Princess Isabel together
with her mother, the so-called Regent Cristina.
Thereafter you will bring them with diligence within
our lines, observing all the respect and courtesy due
to their exalted rank and to the sex to which they
belong.

"At the same time you are held indemnified for
all killings of such persons as may stand in your
way in the execution of the duty laid upon you,
and by order of the King himself you hereby take
rank as a full Colonel in his service."

Meanwhile Cabrera had been bending his brows
over the note which had been directed to him
personally. He rose and paced the length of the
garden-wall with the letter in his hand, while Rollo
stood his ground with an unmoved countenance.
Presently he stopped opposite the young man and
stood regarding him intently.

"I am, I understand, to furnish you with men
for this venture," he said ; "good—but I am at
liberty to prove you first. That you are cool and
brave I know. We must find out whether you are
loyal as well."

"I am as loyal as any Spaniard who ever drew
breath," retorted Rollo, hotly, "and in this matter
I will answer for my companions as well."

"And pray in what way, Sir Spitfire ?" said
Cabrera, smiling.

"Why, as a man should," said Rollo, "with his

sword or his pistol, or—as is our island custom—
with his fists—it is all the same to me ; yes, even
with your abominable Spanish knife, which is no
true gentleman's weapon ! "

"I am no unfriend to plainness, sir, either in
speech or action," said Cabrera ; " I see you are
indeed a brave fellow, and will not lessen the king's
chances of coming to his own by letting you loose
on the men under my command. Still for one day
you will not object to ride with us ! "

Rollo coloured high.

" General," he said, " I will not conceal it from
you that I have wasted too much time already ; but
if you wish for our assistance in your designs for
twenty-four hours, I am not the man to deny you."

" I thought not," cried Cabrera, much pleased.
" And now have you any business to despatch before
we leave this place ? If so, let it be seen to at
once ! "

" None, Excellency," said Rollo, " save that if
you are satisfied of our good faith I should like to
see Luis Fernandez the miller dealt with according
to his deserts ! "

" I will have him shot instantly," cried Cabrera ;
" he hath given false tidings to his Majesty's
generals. He hath belied his honest servants.
Guard, bring Luis Fernandez hither ! "

This was rather more than Rollo had bargained
for. He was not yet accustomed to the summary
methods of Cabrera, even though the butcher's hand
had hardly yet unclosed from himself. He was
already meditating an appeal in favour of milder
measures, when the guard returned with the news
that Luis Fernandez was nowhere to be found.
Dwelling-house, strong-room, mill, garden, and gorge

beneath—all had been searched. In vain—they were empty and void. The tumbled beds where the general and his staff had slept, the granary with its trampled heaps of corn ready for grinding, the mill-wheel with the pool beneath where the lights and shadows played at bo-peep, where the trout lurked and the water-boxes seemed to descend into an infinity of blackness—all were deserted and lonesome as if no man had been near them for a hundred years.

" The rascal has escaped ! " cried Cabrera, full of rage ; " have I not told you a thousand times you keep no watch ? I have a great mind to stand half a dozen of you up against that wall. Escaped with my entire command about the rogue's home-nest ! Well, set a torch to it and see if he is lurking anywhere about the crevices like a centipede in a crack ! "

Cabrera felt that he had wasted a great deal of time on a fine morning without shooting somebody, and it would certainly have gone ill with Don Luis or his brother if either of them had been compelled by the flames to issue forth from the burning mill-house of Sarria.

But they were not there. The cur dogs of the village and a few half-starved mongrels that followed the troops had great sport worrying the rats which darted continually from the burning granaries. But of the more important human rats, no sign.

All the inhabitants of the village were there likewise, held back from plundering by the bayonets of the Carlist troops. They stood recounting to each other, wistfully, the stores of clothes, the silk curtains, the uncut pieces of broadcloth, the household linen, the great eight-day clocks in their gilt ormolu cases. Every woman had something to add to the catalogue. Every householder felt keenly the injustice of permitting so much wealth to be given to the crackling flames.

"Yes, it was very well," they said ; "doubtless the Fernandez family were vermin to be burned up —smoked out. But they possessed much good gear, the gathering of many years. These things have committed no treason against either Don Carlos or the Regent Cristina. Why then are we not permitted to enter and remove the valuables ? It is monstrous. We will represent the matter to General Cabrera—to Don Carlos himself ! "

But one glance at the former, as he sat his horse, nervously twisting the reins and watching the destruction from under his black brows, made their hearts as water within them. Their pet Valiant, old Gaspar Perico, too, had judiciously hidden himself. Esteban the supple had accompanied him, and the venta of Sarria was in the hands of the silent, swift-footed, but exceedingly capable maid-servant who had played the trick upon Etienne.

The Sarrians therefore watched the mill-house blaze up, and thanked God that it stood some way from the other dwellings of the place.

Suddenly Cabrera turned upon them.

"Hearken ye, villagers of Sarria," he cried, " I have burned the home of a traitor. If I hear of any shelter being granted to Luis Fernandez or his brother within your bounds, I swear by the martyred honour of my mother that on my return I will burn every house within your walls and shoot every man of you capable of bearing arms. You have heard of Ramon Cabrera. Let that be enough."

The villagers got apprehensively behind each other, and none answered, each waiting for the other, till with mighty bass thunder the voice rang out again:

"Have you no answer?" he cried, "no promise? Must I set a dozen of you with your backs against the wall, as I did at Espluga in Francoli, to stimulate those dull country wits of yours?"

Then a young man gaily dressed was thrust to the front. Very unwilling he was to show himself, and at his appearance, with his knees knocking together, a merry laugh rang out from behind Cabrera.

That chieftain turned quickly with wrath in his eye. For it was a sound of a woman's mirth that was heard, and all such were strictly forbidden within his lines.

But at the sight of little Concha, her dark eyes full of light, her hands clapping together in innocent delight, her white teeth disclosed in gay and dainty laughter, a certain *maja* note of daring unconvention in her costume, she was so exactly all that would have sent him into raptures twenty years before when he was an apprentice in Tortosa, that the grim man only smiled and turned again to the unwilling spokesman of the municipality of Sarria.

A voice from the press before the burning house announced the delegate's quality.

"Don Raphael de Flores, son of our *alcalde*."

"Speak on, Don Raphael," cried Cabrera; "I will not shoot you unless it should be necessary."

Thus encouraged the trembling youth began.

"Your Excellency," he quavered, "we of Sarria have nothing to do with the family of Fernandez. We would not give any one of them a handful of maize or a plate of lentil broth if he were starving. We are loyal men and women—well-wishers to the cause of the only true and absolute King Carlos Quinto."

"I am credibly informed that it is otherwise," said Cabrera, "and that you are a den of red-hot nationals. I therefore impose a fine of two thousand *duros* on the municipality, and as you are the alcalde's son, we will keep you in durance till they be paid."

Don Raphael fell on his knees. His pale face was reddened by the flames from the mill-house, the fate of which must have afforded a striking object-lesson to a costive magistracy in trouble about a forced loan.

"We are undone," he cried; "I am a married man, your Excellency, and have not a *maravedi* to call my own. You had better shoot me out of hand, and be done with it. Indeed, we cannot possibly pay."

"Go and find your father," cried Cabrera; "he pocketed half of the price of Don Ramon Garcia's house. I cannot see my namesake suffer. Tell him that two thousand *duros* is the price up till noon. After that it will have risen to four thousand, and by three of the afternoon, if the money be not paid into the treasury of the only absolute and Catholic sovereign (in the present instance my breeches pocket), I shall be reluctantly compelled to shoot one dozen of the leading citizens of the township of Sarria. Let a strong guard accompany this young man till he returns from carrying his message."

In this wise did Cabrera replenish the treasury of his master Don Carlos, and with such pleasant argument did he induce reluctant *alcaldes* to discover the whereabouts of their strong boxes.

For a remarkably shrewd man was General Ramon Cabrera, the butcher of Tortosa.

CHAPTER XXIV

HOW TO BECOME A SOLDIER

THE change in the aspect of affairs would have
made a greater difference to most companies of
adventurers than it did to that of which Master
Rollo Blair of Blair Castle in the shire of Fife was
the leader. In the morning they had all risen with
the expectation of being shot with the sun-rising.
At ten of the clock they were speeding southward
on good horses, holding acknowledged rank and
position in the army of the only Catholic and
religious sovereign.

But they were a philosophic quartette. Rollo
drew in the morning air and blew it back again
through his nostrils without thinking much of how
nearly he had come to kissing the brown earth of
Luis Fernandez's garden with a dozen bullets
through his heart. Mortimer meditated somewhat
sulkily upon his lost onions, rustling pleasantly back
there in the cool *patio* of the nunnery. Etienne
sorrowed for his latest love idyll ruthlessly cut short,
and as to El Sarria, he thought of nothing save that
Dolóres had come back to him and that he had yet
to reckon with the Fernandez family. The next
time he would attend to the whole matter himself,
and there would be no mistakes.

It was not without sadness that Rollo looked his

last on the white walls of the convent of the Holy Innocents. He was glad indeed to have placed Dolóres in safety—glad that she and her child were together, and that the good sisters were responsible for them. Between them the four had made up a purse to be sent by Concha to the Mother Superior, to be applied for the behoof of her guests till the better days should come, and Ramon Garcia be able to claim his wife and first-born son.

But Concha had refused point-blank.

"The babe came through the wicket. The mother arrived by night, a fugitive asking pity, like the Virgin fleeing down to Egypt in the pictures," said Concha. "The convent needs no alms, nor does the Lady Superior sell her help. Keep the money, lads. If I am not a fool you will need it more than the sisterhood of the Holy Innocents before you come to your journey's end."

And with that she blew them each a dainty kiss, distinguishing no one above the other, dropped a curtsey to the general, whose eyes followed her with more than usual interest, leaped on her white mare and rode off, attended by La Giralda riding astride like a man, in the same fashion in which she had arrived.

So little Concha was gone from his sight, and duty loomed up suddenly gaunt and void of interest before Rollo. To risk his life was nothing. When he got nearer to the goal, his blood would rise, that he knew. To capture a queen and a regent at one coup, to upset a government, to bring a desolating war to an end—these were all in the day's work. But why, in the name of all that was sanest and most practical, did his heart feel like lead within him and his new dignity turn to Dead Sea ashes in his mouth?

It was not long before Cabrera dropped back, that he might talk over ways and means with the young colonel. It was clear that the *guerrilla* chieftain did not believe greatly in the project.

"I do not understand all this," he said; "it is not my way. What have we to do with taking women and children prisoners? Let us have no truck, barter, or exchange with the government at Madrid except at the point of the bayonet. That is my way of it, and if my advice had been taken before, my master would at this moment have been in the royal palace of his ancestors. But these secret embassies in the hands of foreigners—what good can come of them?"

Rollo explained such things as the Abbot of Montblanch had made clear to him—namely, that the Regent and her daughter were by no means averse to Holy Church, nor yet eager to keep the true King out of his own. But, they were in the power of unscrupulous men—Mendizabal, Linares, and others, who for their own ends published edicts and compelled the ladies to sign them. If they were captured and sequestered for their own good, the ministry would break down and Don Carlos would reign undisturbed.

Rollo thought the exposition a marvel of clearness and point. It was somewhat disappointing, therefore, when he had finished to hear from Cabrera the unmoved declaration : " A Cristino is a Cristino whether in the palace of Madrid or on the mountains of Morella. And the quickest way is the best way with such an one, wherever met with ! "

" But you do not mean to say that you would shoot the girl-Queen or the mother-Regent if they fell into your hands?" cried Rollo, aghast at the horror.

The deep underlying anger leaped up fiery red into the eyes of the *guerrilla* chief.

"Aye, that would I," he cried, "as quickly as they slew my own old mother in the barrack yard of Tortosa!"

And thinking of that tragedy and the guilt of Nogueras, Rollo felt there was something to be said for the indomitable, implacable little butcher-general of Don Carlos.

Cabrera was silent for a while after making this speech, and then abruptly demanded of Rollo how many men he would require for his undertaking.

"I am bidden to place my entire command at your service," he said with obvious reluctance, glancing out of his little oblique eyes at the young colonel.

Rollo considered a while before answering.

"It is my opinion that the fewer men concerned in such a venture the greater the chances of success," he said at last; "furnish me with one petty officer intimately acquainted with the country between Zaragoza and San Ildefonso, and I will ask no more."

Cabrera drew a long breath and looked at the young man with infinitely more approval than he had before manifested.

"You are right," he said, "three times right! If you fail, there are fewer to go to the gallows. In prison fewer ill-sewn wine-skins to leak information. If you succeed, there are also fewer to divide the credit and the reward. For my own part, I do not think you will succeed, but I will provide you with the best man in my command for your purpose and in addition heartily wish you well out of your adventure!"

Cabrera was indeed immensely relieved to find
the desires of our hero so moderate.   He had been
directed to supply him with whatever force he
required, and he expected to be deprived of a
regiment at least, at a most critical time in the
affairs of the Absolute King.

"Young man," he said, "you will certainly be shot
or hanged before you are a month older.   Nevertheless in the mean time I would desire to have the
honour of shaking you by the hand.   If you were
not to die so soon, undoubtedly you would go far!
It is a pity.   And the Cristinos are bad shots.   They
will not do the job half as creditably as my fellows
would have done it for you this morning!"

The man who was chosen by Cabrera to accompany them on their mission was of a most remarkable appearance.   Tall, almost as tall as El Sarria,
he was yet distinguished from his fellows by a
notable gauntness and angularity of figure.

"A step-ladder with the bottom bars missing!"
was Rollo's mental description of him, as he stood
before them in a uniform jacket much too tight for
him, through which his ribs showed not unlike the
spars of a ladder.

But in other respects Sergeant Cardono was a remarkable man.   The iron gravity of his countenance,
seamed on the right-hand side by a deep scar, took
no new expression when he found himself detailed
by his general for this new and dangerous mission.

With a single salute he fell out and instantly
attached himself to Rollo, whom he relieved of his
knapsack and waterbottle on the spot.   Sergeant
Cardono paid no attention whatever to the other
three, whom he evidently regarded as very subordi-
nate members of the expedition.

As soon as they arrived at the village where they were to part from the command of Cabrera, Sergeant Cardono promptly disappeared. He was not seen for several hours, during which Rollo and El Sarria wandered here and there endeavouring in that poor place to pick up some sustenance which would serve them in lieu of a dinner. They had but poor success. A round of black bread, a fowl of amazing age, vitality, and muscular development, with a few snails, were all that they could obtain by their best persuasions, aided by the money with which Rollo was plentifully supplied. John Mortimer looked disconsolately on. He had added a little ham on his own account, which last he had brought in his saddle-bags from the venta of Sarria. But everything pointed to a sparse meal, and even the philosophic Etienne shrugged his shoulders and departed to prospect at a certain house half a mile up the road where, as they had ridden rapidly by, a couple of pretty girls had looked out curiously at the tossing Carlist *boinas*.

Rollo and El Sarria were carrying their scanty provend to a house where a decent-looking woman had agreed to cook it for them, when their gloomy reveries were interrupted by a sudden apparition which burst upon them as they stood on the crest of a deep hollow.

The limestone hills had been rent asunder at the place, and from the bare faces of the rocks the neighbouring farmers and villagers had quarried and carried away such of the overhanging blocks as could easily be trimmed to suit their purposes.

Part of what remained had been shaped into a *hornito*, or stone oven, under which a fire had been kindled, and a strange figure moved about, stirring

the glowing charcoal with a long bar of iron. On
a smaller hearth nearer at hand a second fire blazed,
and the smell of fragrant cookery rose to the
expectant and envious nostrils of the four.

It was Sergeant Cardono, who moved about
whistling softly, now attending to the steaming *olla*,
now watching the rising bread in the *hornito*.

Perceiving Rollo, he saluted gravely and remarked, " Dinner will be served in half an hour."
The others, as before, he simply ignored. But in
deference to his new commander he stopped whistling
and moved about with his lean shoulders squared as
if on parade.

When the bread and the skinny chicken were
placed in his hands, he glanced at them with somewhat of superciliousness.

" The bread will serve for crumbs," he said, and
immediately began to grate the baton-like loaf with
a farrier's hoof-rasp which he used in his culinary
operations. " But this," he added, as he turned
over the bird, " is well stricken in years, and had
better be given to the recruits. They have young
teeth and have had practice upon dead artillery
mules ! "

So saying, he went casually to the edge of the
little quarry, whistled a peculiar note and tossed the
bird downward to some person unseen, who appeared
from nowhere in particular for the purpose of
receiving it.

When the dinner was ready Sergeant Cardono
announced it to Rollo as if he had been serving
a prince. And what was the young man's astonishment to find a table, covered with a decent white
cloth, under the shelter of a limestone rock, spread
for three, and complete even to table napkins,

which the sergeant had tied into various curious shapes.

As they filed down the slope the sergeant stood at attention, but when El Sarria passed he quickly beckoned him aside with a private gesture.

"You and I will eat after the foreigners," he explained.

El Sarria drew himself up somewhat proudly, but Sergeant Cardono whispered in his ear two or three words which appeared to astonish him so much that he did as he was bid, and stood aside while John Mortimer and Etienne de Saint Pierre seated themselves.

But Rollo, who had no great love for eating, and considered one man just as much entitled to respect as another, would not sit down till El Sarria was accommodated also.

"May it please your Excellency, Don Ramon and I have much to say to each other," quoth the Sergeant, with great respect, "besides your honour is aware—the garlic—the onions—we of this country love them ? "

"But so do I," cried Rollo, "and I will not have distinctions made on this expedition. We are all to risk our lives equally and we shall all fare equally, and if we are caught our dose of lead or halter-hemp will be just the same.

Here El Sarria interrupted.

"With respect," he said, "it is true that this gentleman hath some private matters to communicate to me which have nothing to do with the object of our mission. I crave your permission that for to-day I may dine apart with him ! "

After this there was no more to be said. El Sarria helped the sergeant to serve the meal, which

Q

was at once the proof of his foraging ability and his consummate genius as a cook. For though the day was Friday, the soup was very far from *maigre*. The stew contained both lamb and fresh pork cut into generous cubes with a sufficiency of savoury fat included. A sausage had been sliced small for seasoning and the whole had been so smothered in *garbanzos*, haricot beans, rice, mixed with strips of toothsome salt fish, that John Mortimer bent and said a well-deserved blessing over the viands.

"I don't usually in this country," he explained, "but really this is what my good old father would call a manifest providence. That fellow of ours will prove a treasure."

"It seems so," said Rollo, a little grimly, "that is, if he can scout and fight as well as he can cater and cook."

For himself the young Scot cared little what he ate, and would have dined quite cheerfully on dry bread and water, if any one would have listened to his stories of the wonders of his past life or the yet more wonderful achievements of his future. He would have sat and spun yarns concerning the notches on Killiecrankie at a dyke-back, though he had not tasted food for twenty-four hours, with the utmost composure and relish. But his companions were of another kidney, being all valiant trencher-men—John Mortimer desiring chiefly quantity in his eating, while Etienne, no mean cook himself, desiderated rather variety and delicacy in the dishes which were set before him.

At all events the dinner was a great success, though the Sergeant, who evinced the greatest partiality for Rollo, often reproached him with eating little, or inquired anxiously if the sauce of

a certain dish were not to his taste. Rollo, in the
height of his argument, would hastily affirm that it
was delicious, and be off again in chase of some deed
of arms or daring, leaving the Sergeant's *chef-d'œuvre*
untasted on his plate.

At this the Sergeant shook his head in private to
El Sarria.

" It will stand in his way, I fear me," he said
sententiously ; " was there ever a notable general
yet who had not a fine belly to wag before him upon
horseback ? 'Tis as necessary as the cock's feathers
in his hat. Now there is your cut-and-thrust officer
who is good for nothing but to be first in charges
and to lead forlorn hopes—this colonel of yours is
just the figure for him. I have seen many a dozen
of them get the lead between their ribs and never
regretted it before. But it is a devil's pity that this
young cockerel is not fonder of his dinner. How
regardeth he the women ? "

This last question was asked anxiously, yet with
some hope. But this also El Sarria promptly
scattered to the winds.

" I do not think that he regards them at all !
He has scarcely looked at one of them ever since
I first knew him."

Sergeant Cardono groaned, seemingly greatly
perturbed in spirit.

" I feared as much," he said, shaking his head ;
" he hath not the right wandering eye. Now, that
young Frenchman is a devil untamed ! And the
Englishman—well, though he is deeper, he also hath
it in him. But the colonel is all for fighting and his
duty. It is easy to see that he will rise but little
higher. When was there ever a great soldier without a weakness for a pretty woman and a good

dinner? Why, the thing is against nature. Now, my father fought in the War of the Independence, and the tales that he told of El Gran' Lor'—he was a soldier if you like, worthy of the white plumes! A cook all to himself closer at his elbow than an aide-de-camp—and as to the women—ah———!"

Sergeant Cardono nodded as one who could tell tales an he would. Yet the Sergeant Cardono found some reason to change his mind as to Rollo's qualifications for field-officership before the end of their first day apart from Cabrera.

It was indeed with a feeling of intense relief that the little company of five men separated from the white and red *boinas* of the butcher-general's cavalcade. Well-affected to them as Cabrera might be for the time being, his favour was so brief and uncertain, his affection so tiger-like, that even Sergeant Cardono sighed a sigh of satisfaction when they turned their horses' heads towards the far-away Guadarrama beyond which lay the goal of their adventuring.

Presently the tongues of the little cavalcade were unloosed. El Sarria and Sergeant Cardono having found subjects of common interest, communed together apart like old friends. John Mortimer and Etienne, who generally had little to say to each other, conversed freely upon wine-growing and the possibility of introducing cotton-spinning into the South of France. For Etienne was not destitute of a certain Gascon eye to the main chance.

Rollo alone rode gloomily apart. He was turning over the terms of his commission in his mind, and the more he thought, the less was he satisfied. It was not alone the desperateness of the venture that daunted Rollo, but the difficulty of providing for

the Queen-Regent and little princess when captured.
There were a couple of hundred miles to ride back
to those northern fastnesses where they would be
safe ; for the most part without cover and through
country swarming with Nationals and Cristino
partisans.

Riding thus in deep meditation, Rollo, whose
gaze was usually so alert, did not observe away to
the right a couple of horses ridden at speed and
rapidly overtaking their more tired beasts.

El Sarria, however, did not fail to note them,
but, fearing a belated message of recall from General
Cabrera, he did not communicate his discovery to his
companions, contenting himself with keeping his eye
upon the approaching riders.

Rollo was therefore still advancing, his reins flung
loosely upon his beast's neck and his whole attitude
betokening a melancholy resignation, a couple of
lengths before his companions, when a sudden
clattering of hoofs startled him. He looked up,
and there, on her white mare, well-lathered at girth
and bridle, was little Concha Cabezos, sitting her
panting beast with the grace of the true Andaluse.

Her hair was a little ruffled by the wind. Her
cheeks and lips were adorably red. There was a
new and brilliant light in her eye ; and after one
curiously comprehensive glance at the company, she
turned about to look for her companion, La Giralda,
who presently cantered up on a lumbering Estramenian gelding. La Giralda sat astride as before,
her lower limbs, so far as these were apparent, being
closely clad in leather, a loose skirt over them preserving in part the appearance of sex.

Rollo was dumb with sheer astonishment. He
could only gaze at the flushed cheek, the tingling

electric glances, the air completely unconscious and innocent of the girl before him.

"Concha!" he cried aloud. "Concha—what do you here? I thought—I imagined you were safe at the Convent of the Holy Innocents!"

And from behind Sergeant Cardono marked his cheek, alternately paling and reddening, his stammering tongue and altered demeanour, with the utmost satisfaction.

"Good—good," he muttered under his breath to El Sarria; "he will make a true general yet. The saints be praised for this weakness! If only he were fonder of his dinner all might yet be well!"

CHAPTER XXV

THE MISSION OF THE SEÑORITA CONCHA

"I too have a mission, I would have you know," said Concha, a dangerous coquetry showing through her grave demeanour, "a secret mission from the Mother Superior of the Convent of the Holy Innocents. Do not attempt to penetrate the secret. I assure you it will be quite useless. And pray do not suppose that only you can adventure forth on perilous quests!"

"I assure you," began Rollo, eagerly, "that I suppose no such thing. At the moment when you came up I was wishing with all my heart that the responsibility of the present undertaking had been laid on any other shoulders than mine!"

Yet in spite of his modesty, certain it is that from that moment Rollo rode no longer with his head hanging down like a willow blown by the wind. The reins lay no more lax and abandoned on his horse's neck. On the contrary, he sat erect and looked abroad with the air of a commander, and his hand rested oftener on the hilt of Killiecrankie, with the air of pride which Concha privately thought most becoming.

"And in what case left you my wife and babe?" suddenly demanded El Sarria, riding up, and inquiring somewhat imperiously of the new recruit concerning the matter which touched him most nearly.

"The Señora Dolóres is safe with the good sisters, and as in former times I was known to have been her companion, it was judged safest that I should not longer be seen in the neighbourhood. Likewise I was charged with the tidings that Luis Fernandez with a company of Cristino Migueletes has been seen riding southward to cut you off from Madrid, whither it is supposed you are bound!"

Rollo turned quickly upon her with some anger in his eye.

"Why did you not tell me that at first?" he said.

Concha smiled a subtle smile and turned her eyes upon the ground.

"If you will remember, I had other matters to communicate to your Excellency," she said meekly —almost too meekly, Rollo thought. "This matter of Luis Fernandez slipped my memory, till it was my good fortune to be reminded of it by Don Ramon!"

And all the while the long lean Sergeant Cardono, his elbows glued to his sides, sat his horse as if spiked to the saddle, and chuckled with quiet glee at the scene.

"He will do yet," he muttered; "'twas ever thus that my father told me of the Gran' Lor' before Salamanca. Be he as stiff as a ramrod and as frigid as his own North Pole, the little one will thaw him —bend him—make a fool of him for his soul's good. She is not an Andaluse of the gipsy blood for nothing! He will make him a soldier yet, this young man, by the especial grace of San Vicente de Paul, only I do not think that either of them will deserve readmission to the Convent of the Holy Innocents!"

More than once Rollo endeavoured to extract from Concha to what place her self-assumed mission was taking her, and at what point she would leave them. It was in vain. The lady baffled all his endeavours with the most consummate ease.

"You have not communicated to me," she said, "the purport of your own adventures. How then can I tell at what place our ways divide?"

"I am forbidden to reveal to any save General Cabrera alone my secret instructions!" said Rollo, with such dignity as he could muster at short notice.

"And I," retorted Concha, "am as strictly forbidden to reveal mine to General Cabrera or even to that notable young officer, Colonel Don Rollo of the surname which resembles so much a *borrico's* serenade!"

That speech would have been undoubtedly rude save for the glance which accompanied it, given softly yet daringly from beneath a jetty fringe of eyelash.

Nevertheless all Rollo Blair's pride of ancestry rose insurgent within him. Who was this Andalucian waiting-maid that she should speak lightly of the descendant of that Blair of Blair Castle who had stood for Bruce and freedom on the field of Bannockburn? It was unbearable—and yet, well, there was something uncommon about this girl. And after all, was it not the mark of a gentleman to pay no heed to the babbling of women's tongues? If they did not say one thing, they would another. Besides, he cared nothing what this girl might say. A parrot prattling in a cage would affect him as much.

So they rode on together over the great tawny

brick-dusty wastes of Old Castile, silent mostly, but the silence occasionally broken by speech, friendly enough on either side. Behind them pounded La Giralda, gaunt as the sergeant himself, leather-legginged, booted and spurred, watching them keenly out of her ancient, unfathomable gipsy eyes.

And ever as they rode the Guadarrama mountains rose higher and whiter out of the vast and hideous plain, the only interruption to the circling horizon of brown and parched corn lands. But at this season scrub-oak and juniper were the only shrubs to be seen, and had there been a Cristino outpost anywhere within miles, the party must have been discerned riding steadily towards the northern slopes of the mountains. But neither man nor beast took notice of them, and a certain large uncanny silence brooded over the plain.

At one point, indeed, they passed near enough to distinguish in the far north the snow-flecked buttresses of the Sierra de Moncayo. But these, they knew, were the haunts of their Carlist allies. The towns and villages of the plain, however, were invariably held by Nationals, and it had often gone hard with them, had not Sergeant Cardono detached himself from the cavalcade, and, venturing alone into the midst of the enemy, by methods of his own produced the materials for many an excellent meal. At last, one day the Sergeant came back to the party with an added gloom on his long, lean, leathern-textured face. He had brought with him an Estramaduran ham, a loaf of wheaten bread, and a double string of sausages. But upon his descending into the temporary camp which sheltered the party in the bottom of a *barranco*, or deep crack in the parched plateau overgrown with scented thyme and dwarf oak, it became obvious that he had news of the most serious import to communicate.

He called Rollo aside, and told him how he had made his way into a village, as was his custom, and found all quiet—the shops open, but none to attend to them, the customs superintendent in his den by the gate, seated on his easy chair, but dead—the presbytery empty of the priest, the river bank dotted with its array of worn scrubbing boards, but not a washerwoman to be seen. Only a lame lad, furtively plundering, had leaped backward upon his crutch with a swift drawing of his knife and a wolfish gleam of teeth. He had first of all warned the Sergeant to keep off at his peril, but had afterwards changed his tone and confessed to him that the plague was abroad in the valley of the Duero, and that he was the only being left alive in the village save the vulture and the prowling dog.

"The plague!" Sergeant Cardono had gasped, like every Spaniard stricken sick at the very sound of the word.

"Yes, and I own everything in the village," asserted the imp. "If you want anything here you must pay me for it!"

The Sergeant found it even as the cripple had said. There was not a single living inhabitant in the village. Here and there a shut door and a sickening smell betrayed the fact that some unfortunates had been left to die untended. Etienne and John Mortimer were for different reasons unwilling to taste of the ham and bread he had brought back, thinking that these might convey the contagion, but La Giralda and the Sergeant laughed their fears to scorn, and together retired to prepare the evening meal.

As the others made their preparations for the
night, watering their beasts and grooming them with
the utmost care, the little crook-backed imp from
the village appeared on the brink of the *barranco*, his
sallow, weazened face peeping suspiciously out of the
underbrush, and his crutch performing the most
curious evolutions in the air.

There was something unspeakably eerie in the
aspect of the solitary survivor of so many living
people, left behind to prey like a ghoul on the
abandoned possessions of the fear-stricken living
and the untestamented property of the dead.

Concha shrank instinctively from his approach,
and the boy, perceiving his power over her, came
scuttling like a weasel through the brushwood, till
little more than a couple of paces interposed between
him and the girl. Frozen stiff with loathing and
terror, it was not for some time that Concha could
cry out and look round hastily for Rollo, who
(doubtless in his capacity of leader of the expedition)
was not slow in hastening to her assistance.

"That boy—there!" she gasped, "he frightens
me—oh hateful! make him go away!" And she
clutched the young man's arm with such a quick
nervous grasp, that a crimson flush rose quickly to
Rollo's cheek.

"No," muttered Etienne to himself as he watched
the performance critically, "she was never in love
with you, sir! She never did as much for you
as that. But on the whole, with a temper like
Mistress Concha's, I think you are well out of it,
Monsieur Etienne!" Which wise dictum might or
might not be based on the fox's opinion as to sour
grapes.

All unconsciously Rollo reached a protecting hand

across to the little white fingers which gripped his arm so tightly.

"Go away, boy," he commanded ; "do you not see that you terrify the Señorita ?"

"I see—that is why I stay !" cried the amiable youth gleefully, flourishing his crutch about his head as if on the point of launching it at the party.

Rollo laid his hand on the hilt of Killiecrankie with a threatening gesture.

"If you come an inch nearer, I will give you plague !" cried the boy, showing his teeth wickedly, "and your wench also.   You will grow black—yes, and swell !   Then you will die, both of you.   And there will be no one to bury you, like those in the houses back there.   Then all you possess shall be mine, ha, ha !"

And he laughed and danced till a fit of coughing came upon him so that he actually crowed in a kind of fiendish exaltation.   But Rollo Blair was not a man to be jested with, either by devil or devil's imp. He drew a pistol from his belt, looked carefully to the priming, and with the greatest coolness in the world pointed it at the misshapen brat.

"Now listen," he said, "you are old enough to know the meaning of words ; I give you one minute to betake yourself to your own place and leave us alone !   There is no contagion in a pistol bullet, my fine lad, but it is quite as deadly as any plague.   So be off before a charge of powder catches you up !"

The sound of the angry voices had attracted La Giralda, who, looking up hastily from her task of building the fire beneath the gipsy tripod at which she and the Sergeant were cooking, advanced hastily with a long wand in her hand.

The imp wheeled about as on a pivot, and positively appeared to shrink into his clothing at the sight of her. He stood motionless, however, while La Giralda advanced threateningly towards him with the wand in her hand as if for the purpose of castigation. As she approached he emitted a cry of purely animal terror, and hastily whipping his crutch under his arm, betook himself, in a series of long hops, to a spot twenty yards higher up the bank. But La Giralda stopped him by a word or two spoken in an unknown tongue, harsh-sounding as Catalan, but curt and brief as a military order.

The boy stood still and answered in the same speech, at first gruffly and unwillingly, with downcast looks and his bare great toe scrabbling in the dust of the hillside.

The dialogue lasted for some time, till at last with a scornful gesture La Giralda released him, pointing to the upper edge of the *barranco* as the place by which he was to disappear : the which he was now as eager to do, as he had formerly been insolently determined to remain.

During this interview Rollo had stood absent-mindedly with his hand pressed on Concha's, as he listened to the strange speech of La Giralda. Even his acquaintance with the language of the gipsies of Granada had only enabled him to understand a word here and there. The girl's colour slowly returned, but the fear of the plague still ran like ice in her veins. She who feared nothing else on earth, was shaken as with a palsy by the terror of the Black Death, so paralysing was the fear that the very name of cholera laid upon insanitary Spain.

"Well ?" said Rollo, turning to La Giralda, who

stood considering with her eyes upon the ground, after her interview with the crookbacked dwarf.

"You must give me time to think," she said; "this boy is one of our people—a Gitano of Baza. He is not of this place, and he tells me strange things. He swears that the Queen and the court are plague-stayed at La Granja by fear of the cholera. They dare not return to Madrid. They cannot supply themselves with victuals where they are. The very guards forsake them. And the Gitanos of the hills—but I have no right to tell that to the foreigner—the Gorgio. For am not I also a Gitana?"

* * * * *

The village where Rollo's command first stumbled upon this dreadful fact was called Frias, in the district of La Perla, and lies upon the eastern spurs of the Guadarrama. It was, therefore, likely enough then that the boy spoke truth, and that within a few miles of them the Court of Spain was enduring privations in its aerial palace of La Granja.

But even when interrogated by El Sarria the old woman remained obstinately silent as to the news concerning her kinsfolk which she had heard from the crippled dwarf.

"It has nothing to do with you," she repeated; "it is a matter of the Gitanos!"

But there came up from the bottom of the ravine, the lantern-jawed Sergeant, long, silent, lean, parched as a Manchegan cow whose pasture has been burnt up by a summer sun. With one beckoning finger he summoned La Giralda apart, and she obeyed him as readily as the boy had obeyed her. They communed a long time together, the old gipsy speaking, the coffee-coloured Sergeant listening with his head a little to the side.

At the end of the colloquy Sergeant Cardono went directly up to Rollo and saluted.

"Is it permitted for me to speak a word to your Excellency concerning the objects of the expedition?" he said, with his usual deference.

"Certainly!" answered Rollo; "for me, my mission is a secret one, but I have no instructions against listening."

The Sergeant bowed his head.

"Whatever be our mission you will find me do my duty," he said; "and since this cursed plague may interfere with all your plans, it is well that you should know what has befallen and what is designed. You will pardon me for saying that it takes no great prophet to discover that our purposes have to do with the movements of the court."

Rollo glanced at him keenly.

"Did General Cabrera reveal anything to you before your departure?" he asked.

"Nay," said Sergeant Cardono; "but when I am required to guide a party secretly to San Ildefonso, where the court of the Queen-Regent is sojourning, it does not require great penetration to see the general nature of the service upon which I am engaged!"

Rollo recovered himself.

"You have not yet told me what you have discovered," he said, expectantly.

"No," replied the Sergeant with great composure—"that can wait."

For little Concha was approaching; and though he had limitless expectations of the good influence of that young lady upon the military career of his officer, he did not judge it prudent to communicate intelligence of moment in her presence. Wherein for once he was wrong, since that pretty head of the Andalucian beauty, for all its clustering curls, was full of the wisest and most far-seeing counsel — indeed, more to be trusted in a pinch than the *juntas* of half-a-dozen provinces.

But the Sergeant considered that when a girl was pretty and aware of it, she had fulfilled her destiny —save as it might be in the making of military geniuses. Therefore he remained silent as the grave so long as Concha stayed. Observing this, the girl asked a simple question and then moved off a little scornfully, only remarking to herself: "As if I could not make him tell me whenever I get him by himself!"

She referred (it is needless to state) not to Sergeant Cardono, but to his commanding officer, Señor Don Rollo Blair of Blair Castle in the self-sufficient shire of Fife.

CHAPTER XXVI

DEEP ROMANY

THE news which Sergeant Cardono had to communicate was indeed fitted to shake the strongest nerves. If true, it took away from Rollo at once all hope of the success of his mission. He saw himself returning disgraced and impotent to the camp of Cabrera, either to be shot out of hand, or worse still, to be sent over the frontier as something too useless and feeble to be further employed.

Briefly, the boy's news as repeated by La Giralda to the Sergeant, informed Rollo that though the court was presently at La Granja and many courtiers in the village of San Ildefonso, the royal guards through fear and hunger had mutinied and marched back to Madrid, and that the gipsies were gathering among the mountains in order to make a night attack upon the stranded and forsaken court of Spain.

In the sergeant's opinion not a moment was to be lost. The object of the hill Gitanos was pure plunder, but they would think nothing of bloodshed, and would doubtless give the whole palace and town over to rapine and pillage. Themselves desperate with hunger and isolation, they had resolved to strike a blow which would ring from one end of Spain to the other.

It was their intention (so the imp said) to kill the Queen-Regent and her daughter, to slaughter the ministers and courtiers in attendance, to plunder the palace from top to bottom and to give all within the neighbouring town of San Ildefonso to the sword.

The programme, as thus baldly announced, was indeed one to strike all men with horror, even those who had been hardened by years of fratricidal warfare in which quarter was neither given nor expected.

Besides the plunder of the palace and its occupants, the leaders of the gipsies expected that they would obtain great rewards from Don Carlos for thus removing the only obstacles to his undisputed possession of the throne of Spain.

The heart of Rollo beat violently. His Scottish birth and training gave him a natural reverence for the sanctity of sickness and death, and the idea of these men plotting ghoulishly to utilise "the onlaying of the hand of Providence" (as his father would have phrased it) for the purposes of plunder and rapine, unspeakably revolted him.

Immediately he called a council of war, at which, in spite of the frowns of Sergeant Cardono, little Concha Cabezos had her place.

La Giralda was summoned also, but excused herself saying, "It is better that I should not know what you intend to do. I am, after all, a black-blooded Gitana, and might be tempted to reveal your secrets if I knew them. It is better therefore that I should not. Let me keep my own place as a servitor in your company, to cut the brushwood for your fire and to bring the water from the spring. In those things you will find me faithful. Trust the gipsy no further!"

Rollo, remembering her loyalty in the matter of Dolóres at the village of El Sarria, was about to make an objection, but a significant gesture from the Sergeant restrained him in time.

Whereupon Rollo addressed himself to the others, setting clearly before them the gravity of the situation.

John Mortimer shook his head gravely. He could not approve.

"How often has my father told me that the first loss is the least! This all comes of trying to make up my disappointment about the Abbot's Priorato!"

Étienne shrugged his shoulders and philosophically quoted a Gascon proverb to the effect that who buys the flock must take the black sheep also.

El Sarria simply recollected that his gun and pistols were in good order, and waited for orders.

The conference therefore resolved itself into a trio of consultants—Rollo because he was the leader, Sergeant Cardono because he knew the country, and Concha—because she was Concha!

They were within an hour or two's rapid march of La Granja over a pass in the Guadarrama. The sergeant volunteered to lead them down into the gardens in that time. He knew a path often travelled by smugglers on their way to Segovia.

"It is clear that if we are to carry away the Queen-Regent and her daughter, we must forestall the gipsies," said Rollo.

Concha clasped her hands pitifully.

"Ah, the poor young Queen!" she cried. "Praise to the saints that I was not born a princess! It goes to my heart to make her a prisoner!"

The Sergeant uttered a guttural grunt which

intimated that in his opinion the influence of the petticoat on the career of a soldier might be overdone. Otherwise he maintained his gravity, speaking only when he was directly appealed to and giving his judgment with due submission to his superiors.

Finally it was judged that they should make a night march over the mountains, find some suitable place to lie up in during the day, and in the morning send in La Giralda and the Sergeant to San Ildefonso in the guise of fagot sellers to find out if the gipsy boy of Baza had spoken the truth.

*　　　*　　　*　　　*　　　*

San Ildefonso and La Granja are two of the most strangely situated places in Spain. A high and generally snow-clad Sierra divides them from Madrid and the south. The palace is one of the most highlying upon earth, having originally been one of the mountain granges of the monks of Segovia to which a king of Spain took a fancy, and, what is more remarkable, for which he was willing to pay good money.

Upon the site a palace has been erected, a miniature Versailles, infinitely more charming than the original, with walks, fountains, waterfalls all fed by the cold snow water of the Guadarrama, and fanned by the pure airs of the mountains. This Grange has been for centuries a favourite resort of the Court of Spain, and specially during these last years of the Regent Cristina, who, when tired with the precision and etiquette of the Court of Madrid, retired hither that she might do as she pleased for at least two or three months of the year.

Generally the great park-gates stood hospitably open, and the little town of San Ildefonso, with its lodgings and hostels, was at this season crowded with courtiers and hangers-on of the court. Guards circulated here and there, or clattered after the Queen-Regent as she drove out on the magnificent King's highway which stretched upwards over the Guadarrama towards Madrid, or whirled down towards Segovia and the plains of Old Castile. Bugles were never long silent in *plaza* or barrack yard. Drums beat, fifes shrilled, and there was a continuous trampling of horses as this ambassador or that was escorted to the presence of Queen Cristina, widow of Fernando VII., mother of Isabel the Second, and Regent of Spain.

A word of historical introduction is here necessary, and it shall be but a word. For nearly a quarter of a century Fernando, since he had been restored to a forfeited throne by British bayonets, had acted on the ancient Bourbon principle of learning nothing and forgetting nothing. His tyrannies became ever more tyrannical, his exactions more shameless, his indolent arrogance more oppressive. Twice he had to invoke the aid of foreign troops, and once indeed a French army marched from one end of Spain to the other.

But with the coming of his third wife, young Maria Cristina of Naples, all this was changed. Under her influence Fernando promptly became meek and uxorious. Then he revoked the ordinance of a former King which ordained that no woman should reign in Spain. He recalled his revocation, and again promulgated it according as his hope of offspring waxed or waned.

Finally a daughter was born to the ill-mated pair, and Don Carlos, the King's brother and former heir-apparent, left the country. Immediately upon the King's death civil war divided the state.

The stricter legitimists who stood for Don Carlos included the church generally and the religious orders. To these were joined the northern parts of Navarra and the Basque countries whose privileges had been threatened, together with large districts of the ever-turbulent provinces of Aragon and Catalunia.

Round the Queen-Regent and her little daughter collected all the liberal opinion of the peninsula, most of the foreign sympathy, the influence of the great towns and sea-ports, of the capital and the government officials, the regular army and police with their officers—indeed all the organised and stated machinery of government.

But up to the time of our history these advantages had been to some extent neutralised by the ill-success of the governmental generalship and by the brilliant successes of two great Carlist leaders—Tomas Zumalacarregui and Ramon Cabrera.

These men perfectly understood the conditions of warfare among their native mountains, and had inflicted defeat upon defeat on every Cristino general sent against them.

But a cloud had of late overspread the fair prospects of the party. Their great general, Tomas Zumalacarregui, had been killed by a cannon ball at the siege of Bilbao, and Cabrera, though unsurpassed as a guerrilla leader, had not the swift Napoleonic judgment and breadth of view of his predecessor. Add to this that a new premier, Mendizábal, and a new general, Espartero, were directing operations from Madrid. The former, already half English, had begun to carry out his great scheme of filling the pockets of the civil and military authorities by conveying to the government all the property belonging to the religious orders throughout Spain,

who, like our friend the Abbot of Montblanch, had
resolutely and universally espoused the cause of Don
Carlos.

It was an early rumour of this intention which
had so stirred the resentment of Don Baltasar Varela,
and caused him to look about for some instrument
of vengeance to prevent the accomplishment of the
designs of "that *burro* of the English Stock Exchange," as his enemies freely named Mendizábal.

But Cristina of Naples was a typical woman of
the Latin races, and, however strongly she might be
determined to establish her daughter on the throne
of Spain, she was also a good Catholic, and any oppres-
sion of Holy Church was abhorrent to her nature.

Upon this probability, which amounted to certainty in his mind, the Abbot of Montblanch
resolved to proceed.

Moreover, it was an open secret that a few
months after the death of her husband Fernando,
Cristina had married Muñoz, one of the handsomest
officers of her bodyguard. For this and other
Bourbon delinquencies, conceived in the good old
Neapolitan manner, the Spaniards generally had the
greatest respect—not even being scandalized when
the Queen created her new partner Duke of Rianzares, or when, in her *rôle* of honorary colonel of
dragoons, she appeared in a uniform of blue and
white, because these were the colours of the
" Immaculate Conception."

But enough has been said to indicate the nature
of the adventure which our hero had before him,
when after a toilsome march the party halted in the
grey of the dawn in a tiny dell among the wild
mountains of Guadarrama.

The air was still bleak and cold, though luckily

there was no wind. Concha, the child of the south, shivered a little as Rollo aided her to dismount, and this must be the young man's excuse for taking his blue military cloak from its coil across his saddle-bow, and wrapping it carefully and tenderly about her.

Concha raised her eyes once to his as he fastened its chain-catch beneath her chin, and Rollo, though the starlight dimmed the brilliance of the glance, felt more than repaid. In the background Étienne smiled bitterly. The damsel of the green lattice being now left far behind at Sarria, he would have had no scruples about returning to his allegiance to Concha. But the chill indifference with which his advances were received, joined to something softer and more appealing in her eyes when she looked at Rollo, warned the much-experienced youth that he had better for the future confine his gallantries to the most common and ordinary offices of courtesy.

Yet it was certainly a restraint upon the young Frenchman, who, almost from the day he had been rid of his Jesuit tutor, had made it a maxim to make love to the prettiest girl of any company in which he happened to find himself.

When, therefore, he found himself reduced to a choice between an inaccessible Concha and La Giralda, riding astride in her leathern leg-gear and sack-like smock, the youth bethought himself of his religious duties which he had latterly somewhat neglected; and, being debarred from earthly love by Concha's insensibility and La Giralda's ineligibility, it did not cost him a great effort to become for the nonce the same Brother Hilario who had left the monastery of Montblanch.

So, much to the astonishment of John Mortimer,

who moved a little farther from him, as being a kind
of second cousin of the scarlet woman of the Seven
Hills, Etienne pulled out his rosary and, falling on
his knees, betook him to his prayers with vigour
and a single mind.

Sergeant Cardono had long ago abandoned all
distinctive marks of his Carlist partisanship and
military rank.   Moreover, he had acquired, in some
unexplained way, a leathern Montera cap, a short
many-buttoned jacket, a flapped waistcoat of red
plush, and leathern small-clothes of the same sort as
those worn by La Giralda. Yet withal there remained something very remarkable about him.   His
great height, his angular build, the grim humour of
his mouth, the beady blackness of eyes which
twinkled with a fleck of fire in each, as a star might
be reflected in a deep well on a moonless night—
these all gave him a certain distinction in a country
of brick-dusty men of solemn exterior and rare
speech.

Also there was something indescribably daring
about the man, his air and carriage.   There was the
swagger as of a famous *matador* about the way he
carried himself. He gave a cock to his plain
countryman's cap which betokened one of a race at
once quicker and more gay—more passionate and
more dangerous than the grave and dignified inhabitants of Old Castile through whose country they
were presently journeying.

As Cardono and La Giralda departed out of the
camp, the Sergeant driving before him a donkey which
he had picked up the night before wandering by the
wayside, El Sarria looked after them with a sardonic
smile which slowly melted from his face, leaving
only the giant's usual placid good nature apparent

on the surface. The mere knowledge that Dolóres was alive and true to him seemed to have changed the hunted and desperate outlaw almost beyond recognition.

"Why do you smile, El Sarria?" said Concha, who stood near by, as the outlaw slowly rolled and lighted a *cigarrillo*. "You do not love this Sergeant. You do not think he is a man to be trusted?"

El Sarria shrugged his shoulders, and slowly exhaled the first long breathing of smoke through his nostrils.

"Nay," he said deliberately, "I have been both judged and misjudged myself, and it would ill become me in like manner to judge others. But if that man is not of your country and my trade, Ramon Garcia has lived in vain. That is all."

Concha nodded a little uncertainly.

"Yes," she said slowly, "yes—of my country. I believe you. He has the Andalucian manner of wearing his clothes. If he were a girl he would know how to tie a ribbon irregularly and how to place a bow-knot a little to the side in the right place—things which only Andalucians know. But what in the world do you mean by 'of your profession'?"

El Sarria smoked a while in silence, inhaling the blue cigarette smoke luxuriously, and causing it to issue from his nostrils white and moisture-laden with his breath. Then he spoke.

"I mean of my late profession," he explained, smiling on Concha; "it will not do for a man on the high-road to a commission to commit himself to the statement that he has practised as a bandit, or stopped a coach on the highway in the name of King Carlos Quinto that he might examine more at his ease the governmental mail bags. But our Sergeant—well, I am man-sworn and without honour if he hath not many a time taken blackmail without any such excuse !"

Concha seemed to be considering deeply. Her pretty mouth was pursed up like a ripe strawberry, and her brows were knitted so fiercely that a deep line divided the delicately arched eyebrows.

"And to this I can add somewhat," she began presently ; "they say (I know not with what truth) that I have some left-handed gipsy blood in me— and if that man be not a Gitano—why, then I have never seen one. Besides, he speaks with La Giralda in a tongue which neither I nor Don Rollo under-stand."

"But I thought," said El Sarria, astonished for the first time, "that both you and Don Rollo under-stood the crabbed gipsy tongue ! Have I not heard you speak it together ?"

"As it is commonly spoken—yes," she replied, "we have talked many a time for sport. But this which is spoken by the Sergeant and La Giralda is deep Romany, the like of which not half a dozen in Spain understand. It is the old-world speech of the Rom, before it became contaminated by the jargon of fairs and the slang of the travelling horse-clipper."

"Then," said El Sarria, slowly, "it comes to this—'tis you and not I who mistrust these two ?"

"No, that I do not," cried Concha, emphatically ; "I have tried La Giralda for many years and at all times found her faithful, so that her bread be well buttered and a draught of good wine placed along-side it. But the Sergeant is a strong man and a secret man——"

"Well worth the watching, then?" said El Sarria, looking her full in the face.

Concha nodded.

"Carlist or no, he works for his own hand," she said simply.

"Shall ye mention the matter to Don Rollo?" asked El Sarria.

"Nay—what good?" said Concha, quickly; "Don Rollo is brave as a bull of Jaen, but as rash. You and I will keep our eyes open and say nothing. Perhaps—perhaps we may have doubted the man somewhat over-hastily. But as for me, I will answer for La Giralda."

"For me," said El Sarria, sententiously, "I will answer for no woman—save only Dolóres Garcia!"

Concha looked up quickly.

"I also am a woman," she said, smiling.

"And quite well able to answer for yourself, Señorita!" returned El Sarria, grimly.

For the answers of Ramon Garcia were not at all after the pattern set by Rollo the Scot.

CHAPTER XXVII

THE SERGEANT AND LA GIRALDA

THE dust-heat of the desolate plains of Old Castile was red on the horizon when the Sergeant and his companion started together on their strange and perilous mission. Would they ever return, and when? What might they not find? A Court deserted and forlorn, courtiers fleeing, or eager to flee if only they knew whither, from the dread and terrible plague? A Queen and a princess without guards, a palace open to the plunder of any chance band of robbers? For something like this the imp of the deserted village had prepared them.

At all events, the Sergeant and La Giralda went off calmly enough in the direction of the town of San Ildefonso, driving their donkey before them. For a minute, as they gained the crest, their figures stood out black and clear against the coppery sunrise. The next they had disappeared down the slope, the flapping peak of Cardono's Montera cap being the last thing to be lost sight of.

The long, dragging, idle day was before the party in the dry ravine.

Etienne went to his saddle-bags, and drawing his breviary from the leathern flap, began to peruse the lessons for the day with an attentive piety which was not lessened by the fact that he had forgotten most

of the Latin he had learned at school. John Mortimer, on the other hand, took out his pocket-book,
and was soon absorbed by calculations in which wine
and onions shared the page with schemes for import-
ing into Spain Manchester goods woven and dyed to
suit the taste of the country housewives.

El Sarria sat down with a long sigh to his never-
failing resort of cleaning and ordering his rifle and
pistols. He had a phial of oil, a feather, and a fine
linen rag which he carried about with him for the
purpose. Afterwards he undertook the same office
for the weapons of Rollo. Those of the other
members of the expedition might take care of themselves. Ramon Garcia had small belief in their
ability to make much use of them, at any rate—the
sergeant being alone excepted.

These three being accounted for, there remained
only Rollo and Concha. Now there was a double
shelf a little way from the horses, from which the
chief of the expedition could keep an eye on the
whole encampment. The pair slowly and, as it
were, unconsciously gravitated thither, and in a
moment Rollo found himself telling "the story of
his life" to a sympathetic listener, whose bright eyes
stimulated all his capacities as narrator, and whose
bright smile welcomed every hairbreadth escape with
a joy which Rollo could not but feel must somehow
be heartfelt and personal. Besides, adventures
sound so well when told in Spanish and to a Spanish
girl.

Yet, strange as it may seem, the young man
missed several opportunities of arousing the com-
passion of his companion.

He said not a word about Peggy Ramsay, nor
did he mention the broken heart which he had come

so far afield to cure. And as for Concha, nothing could have been more nunlike and conventual than the expression with which she listened. It was as if one of the Lady Superior's "Holiest Innocents" had flown over the nunnery wall and settled down to listen to Rollo's tale in that wild gorge among the mountains of Guadarrama.

*   *   *   ⁱ   *

Meantime the Sergeant and his gipsy companion pursued their way with little regard to the occupations or sentiments of those they had left behind them. Cardono's keen black eyes, twinkling hither and thither, a myriad crows' feet reticulating out from their corners like spiders' webs, took in the landscape, and every object in it.

The morning was well advanced when, right across their path, a well-to-do farmhouse lay before them, white on the hillside, its walls long-drawn like fortifications, and the small slit-like windows counterfeiting loopholes for musketry. But instead of the hum of work and friendly gossip, the crying of ox-drivers yoking their teams, or adjusting the long blue wool over the patient eyes of their beasts, there reigned about the place, both dwelling and office-houses, a complete and solemn silence. Only in front of the door several she-goats, with bunching, over-full udders, waited to be milked with plaintive whimperings and tokens of unrest.

La Giralda looked at her companion. The Sergeant looked at La Giralda. The same thought was in the heart of each.

La Giralda went up quickly to the door, and knocked loudly. At farmhouses in Old Castile it is necessary to knock loudly, for the family lives on the second floor, while the first is given up to bundles of fuel, trusses of hay, household provender of the more indestructible sort, and one large dog which invariably answers the door first and expresses in an unmistakable manner his intention of making his breakfast off the stranger's calves.

But not even the dog responded to the clang of La Giralda's oaken cudgel on the stout door panels. Accordingly she stepped within, and without ceremony ascended the stairs. In the house-place, extended on a bed, lay a woman of her own age, dead, her face wearing an expression of the utmost agony.

In a low trundle-bed by the side of the other was a little girl of four. Her hands clasped a doll of wood tightly to her bosom. But her eyes, though open, were sightless. She also was dead.

La Giralda turned and came down the stairs, shaking her head mournfully.

"These at least are ours," she said, when she came out into the hot summer air, pointing to the little flock of goats. "There is none to hinder us."

"Have the owners fled?" asked the Sergeant, quickly.

"There are some of them upstairs now," she replied, "but, alas, none who will ever reclaim them from us! The excuse is the best that can be devised to introduce us into San Ildefonso, and, perhaps, if we have luck, inside the palisades of La Granja also."

So without further parley the Sergeant proceeded, in the most matter-of-fact way possible, to load the ass with huge fagots of kindling wood till the animal showed only four feet paddling along under its burden, and a pair of patient orbs, black and beady like those of the Sergeant himself, peering out of a hay-coloured matting of hair.

This done, the Sergeant turned his sharp eyes

s

every way about the dim smoky horizon. He could note, as easily as on a map, the precise notch in the many purple-tinted gorges where they had left their party. It was exactly like all the others which slit and dimple the slopes of the Guadarrama, but in this matter it was as impossible for the Sergeant to make a mistake as for a town-dweller to err as to the street in which he has lived for years.

But no one was watching them. No clump of juniper held a spy, and the Sergeant was at liberty to develop his plans. He turned quickly upon the old gipsy woman.

"La Giralda," he said, "there is small use in discovering the disposition of the courtiers in San Ildefonso—ay, or even the defences of the palace, if we know nothing of the Romany who are to march to-night upon the place."

La Giralda, who had been drawing a little milk from the udders of each she-goat, to ease them for their travel, suddenly sprang erect.

"I do not interfere in the councils of the Gitano," she cried; "I am old, but not old enough to desire death!"

But more grim and lack-lustre than ever, the face of Sergeant Cardono was turned upon her, and more starrily twinkled the sloe-like eyes (diamonds set in Cordovan leather) as he replied :—"The councils of the Rom are as an open book to me. If they are life, they are life because I will it; if death, then I will the death!"

The old gipsy stared incredulously.

"Long have I lived," she said, staring hard at the sergeant, "much have I seen, both of gipsy and Gorgio; but never have I seen or heard of the man who could both make that boast, and make it good!"

She appeared to consider a moment.

"Save one," she added, "and he is dead!"

"How did he die?" said the Sergeant, his tanned visage like a mask, but never removing his eyes from her face.

"By the *garrote*," she answered, in a hushed whisper. "I saw him die."

"Where?"

"In the great *plaza* of Salamanca," she said, her eyes fixed in a stare of regretful remembrance. "It was filled from side to side, and the balconies were peopled as for a bull-fight. Ah, he was a man!"

"His name?"

"José Maria, the Gitano, the prince of brigands!" murmured La Giralda.

"Ah," said the Sergeant, coolly, "I have heard of him.

CHAPTER XXVIII

THE DEAD AND THE LIVING

NOT a word more was uttered between the two. La Giralda, for no reason that she would acknowledge even to herself, had conceived an infinite respect for Sergeant Cardono, and was ready to obey him implicitly—a fact which shows that our sweet Concha was over-hasty in supposing that one woman in any circumstances can ever answer for another when there is a man in the case.

But on this occasion La Giralda's submission was productive of no more than a command to go down into the town of San Ildefonso, the white houses of which could clearly be seen a mile or two below, while the sergeant betook himself to certain haunts of the gipsy and the brigand known to him in the fastnesses of the Guadarrama.

Like a dog La Giralda complied. She sharpened a stick with a knife which she took from a little concealed sheath in her leathern leggings, and with it she proceeded to quicken the donkey's extremely deliberate pace.

Then with the characteristic cry of the goatherd, she gathered her flock together and drove them before her down the deeply-rutted road which led from the farm-house. She had not proceeded far, however, when she suddenly turned back, with a

quick warning cry to her cavalcade. The donkey
instantly stood still, patient amid its fagots as an
image in a church. The goats scattered like water
poured on flat ground, and began to crop stray blades
of grass, invisible to any eyes but their own, amid
wastes of cracked earth and deserts of grey water-
worn pebbles.

As she looked back, Sergeant Cardono was dis-
appearing up among the tumbled foothills and dry
beds of winter torrents, which render the lower spurs
of the Guadarrama such a puzzle to the stranger, and
such a paradise for the smuggler and *guerrillero*. In
another moment he had disappeared. With a long
quiet sigh La Giralda stole back to the farm-house.
In spite of her race, and heathenish lack of creed, the
spark of humanity was far from dead in her bosom.
The thought of the open eyes of the little girl, which
gazed even in death with fixed rapture upon her
wooden treasure, remained with her.

"The woman is as old as I—she can bide her
time!" she muttered to herself. "But the child—
these arms are not yet so shrunken that they cannot
dig up a little earth to lay the babe thereunder."

And at the chamber door La Giralda paused.
Like her people, she was neither a good nor yet a
bad Catholic. Consciously or unconsciously she held
a more ancient faith, though she worshipped at no
shrine, told no beads, and uttered no prayers.

"They have not been long dead," she said to
herself, as she entered; "the window is open and the
air is sweet. Yet the plague, which snatches away
the young and strong, may look askance at old
Giralda's hold on life, which at the best is no
stronger than the strength of a basting-thread!"

Having said these words she advanced to the

low trundle-bed, and, softly crooning in an unknown tongue over the poor dead babe, she lovingly closed its eyes, and taking a sheet from a wall-press that stood partially open, she began to enwrap the little girl in its crisp white folds. The Spaniards are like the Scottish folk in this, that they have universally stores of the best and finest linen.

La Giralda was about to lay the wooden puppet aside as a thing of little worth, but something in the clutch of the small dead hands touched and troubled her. She altered her intention.

" No, you shall not be parted ! " she said, " and if there be a resurrection as the priests prate of— why, you shall e'en wake with the doll in your arms ! "

So the pair, in death not divided, were wrapt up together, and the gipsy woman prepared to carry her light burden afield. But before doing so she went to the bed. It was an ancient woman who lay thereon, clutching the bed-clothes, and drawn together with the last agony. La Giralda gazed at her a moment.

" You I cannot carry—it is impossible," she muttered ; " you must take your chance—even as I, if so be that the plague comes to me from this innocent ! "

Nevertheless, she cast another coverlet over the dead woman's face, and went down the broad stairs of red brick, carrying her burden like a precious thing. La Giralda might be no good Catholic, no fervent Protestant, but I doubt not the First Martyr of the faith, the Preacher of the Mount, would have admitted her to be a very fair Christian. On the whole I cannot think her chances in the life to come inferior to those of the astute Don Baltasar Varela,

Prior of the Abbey of Montblanch, or those of many
a shining light of orthodoxy in a world given to
wickedness.

Down in the shady angle of the little orchard the
old gipsy found a little garden of flowers, geranium
and white jasmine, perhaps planted to cast into the
rude coffin of a neighbour, *Yerba Luisa*, or lemon
verbena for the decoctions of a simple pharmacopœia,
on the outskirts of these a yet smaller plot had been
set aside. It was edged with white stones from the
hillside, and many coloured bits of broken crockery
decorated it. A rose-bush in the midst had been
broken down by some hasty human foot, or perhaps
by a bullock or other large trespassing animal.
There were nigh a score of rose-buds upon it—all
now parched and dead, and the whole had taken on
the colour of the soil.

La Giralda stood a moment before laying her
burden down. She had the strong heart of her
ancient people. The weakness of tears had not
visited her eyes for years—indeed, not since she was
a girl, and had cried at parting from her first sweetheart, whom she never saw again. So she looked
apparently unmoved at the pitiful little square of
cracked earth, edged with its fragments of brown
and blue pottery, and at the broken rose-bush lying
as if also plague-stricken across it, dusty, desolate,
and utterly forlorn. Yet, as we have said, was her
heart by no means impervious to feeling. She had
wonderful impulses, this parched mahogany-visaged
Giralda.

"It is the little one's own garden—I will lay her
here!" she said to herself.

So without another word she departed in search
of mattock and spade. She found them easily and

shortly, for the hireling servants of the house had fled in haste, taking nothing with them. In a quarter of an hour the hole was dug. The rose-tree, being in the way, was dragged out and thrown to one side. La Giralda, who began to think of her donkey and goats, hastily deposited the babe within, and upon the white linen the red earth fell first like thin rain, and afterwards, when the sheet was covered, in lumps and mattock-clods. For La Giralda desired to be gone, suddenly becoming mindful of the precepts of the Sergeant.

"No priest has blessed the grave," she said ; " I can say no prayers over her ! Who is La Giralda that she should mutter the simplest prayer ? But when the Master of Life awakes the little one, and when He sees the look she will cast on her poor puppet of wood, He will take her to His bosom even as La Giralda, the mother of many, would have taken her ! God, the Good One, cannot be more cruel than a woman of the heathen ! "

And so with the broken pottery for a monument, and the clasp of infant hands about the wooden doll for a prayer to God, the dead babe was left alone, unblessed and unconfessed—but safe.

*　　*　　*　　*　　*

Meanwhile we must go over the hill with Sergeant Cardono. Whatever his thoughts may have been as he trudged up the barren glens, seamed and torn with the winter rains, no sign of them appeared upon his sunburnt weather-beaten face. Steadily and swiftly, yet without haste, he held his way, his eyes fixed on the ground, as though perfectly sure of his road, like a man on a well-beaten track which he has trod a thousand times.

For more than an hour he went on, up and ever

up, till his feet crisped upon the first snows of
Peñalara, and the hill ramparts closed in.   But when
he had reached the narrows of a certain gorge, he
looked keenly to either side, marking the entrance.
A pile of stones roughly heaped one upon the other
fixed his attention.   He went up to them and
attentively perused their structure and arrangement,
though they appeared to have been thrown together
at random.   Then he nodded sagely twice and passed
on his way.

The glen continued to narrow overhead.   The
sunshine was entirely shut out.   The jaws of the
precipice closed in upon the wayfarer as if to crush
him, but Sergeant Cardono advanced with the steady
stride of a mountaineer, and the aplomb of one who
is entirely sure of his reception.

The mountain silence grew stiller all about.
None had passed that way (so it seemed) since the
beginning of time.   None would repass till time
should be no more.

Suddenly through the utter quiet there rang out,
repeated and reduplicated, the loud report of a rifle.
The hills gave back the challenge.   A moment
before the dingy bedrabbled snow at Cardono's feet
had been puffed upwards in a white jet, yet he
neither stopped for this nor took the least notice.
Loyal or disloyal, true or false, he was a brave man
this Sergeant Cardono.   I dare say that any one
close to him might have discerned his beady eyes
glitter and glance quickly from side to side, but his
countenance was turned steadfastly as ever upon the
snow at his feet.

Again came the same startling challenge out of
the vague emptiness of space, the bullet apparently
bursting like a bomb among the snow.   And again

Cardono took as much notice as if some half-dozen of village loungers had been playing ball among the trees.

Only when a third time the *whisk* of the bullet in the snow a yard or two to the right preceded the sound of the shot, Cardono shook his head and muttered, "Too long range! The fools ought to be better taught than that!" Then he continued his tramp steadily, neither looking to the right nor to the left. The constancy of his demeanour had its effect upon the unseen enemy. The Sergeant was not further molested; and though it was obvious that he advanced each step in about as great danger of death as a man who is marched manacled to the garrote, he might simply have been going to his evening billet in some quiet Castilian village, for all the difference it made in his appearance.

Up to this point Cardono had walked directly up the torrent bed, the rounded and water-worn stones rattling and slipping under his iron-shod half-boots, but at a certain point where was another rough cairn of stones, he suddenly diverged to the right, and mounted straight up the fell over the scented thyme and dwarf juniper of the mountain slopes.

Whatever of uncertainty as to his fate the Sergeant felt was rigidly concealed, and even when a dozen men dropped suddenly upon him from various rocky hiding-places, he only shook them off with a quick gesture of contempt, and said something in a loud voice which brought them all to a halt as if turned to stone by an enchanter's spell.

The men paused and looked at each other. They were all well armed, and every man had an open knife in his hand. They had been momentarily

checked by the words of the Sergeant, but now they
came on again as threateningly as before. Their
dark long hair was encircled by red handkerchiefs
knotted about their brows, and in general they
possessed teeth extraordinarily white gleaming from
the duskiest of skins. The beady sloe-black eyes
of the Sergeant were repeated in almost every face,
as well as that indefinable something which in all
lands marks the gipsy race.

The Sergeant spoke again in a language apparently more intelligible than the deep Romany
password with which he had first checked their
deadly intentions.

"You have need of better marksmen," he said ;
"even the Migueletes could not do worse than
that !"

"Who are you ?" demanded a tall grey-headed
gipsy, who like the Sergeant had remained apparently
unarmed ; "what is your right to be here ?"

The Sergeant had by this time seated himself on
a detached boulder and was rolling a cigarette. He
did not trouble to look up as he answered carelessly, "To the Gitano my name is José Maria of
Ronda !"

The effect of his words was instantaneous. The
men who had been ready to kill him a moment
before almost fell at his feet, though here and there
some remained apparently unconvinced.

Prominent among these was the elderly man
who had put the question to the Sergeant. Without
taking his eyes from those of the Carlist soldier he
exclaimed, "Our great José Maria you cannot be.
For with these eyes I saw him garrotted in the Plaza
Mayor of Salamanca !"

The Sergeant undid his stock and pointed to

a blood-red band about his neck, indented deeply into the skin, and more apparent at the back and sides than in front.

"Garrotted in good faith I was in the Plaza of Salamanca, as this gentleman says," he remarked with great coolness. "But not to death. The executioner was as good a *Gitano* as myself, and removed the spike which strikes inward from the back. So you see I am still José Maria of Ronda in the flesh, and able to strike a blow for myself!"

The gipsies set up a wild yell. The name of the most celebrated and most lawless of their race stirred them to their souls.

"Come with us," they cried; "we are here for the greatest plunder ever taken or dreamed of among the Romany——"

"Hush, I command you," cried the elder man. "José Maria of Ronda this man may be, but we are *Gitanos* of the North, and need not a man from Andalucia to lead us, even if he carry a scarlet cravat about his neck for a credential!"

The Sergeant nodded approval of this sentiment and addressed the old gipsy in deep Romany, to which he listened with respect, and answered in a milder tone, shaking his head meanwhile.

"I have indeed heard such sayings from my mother," he said, "and I gather your meaning; but we *Gitanos* of the North have mingled too much with the outlander and the foreigner to have preserved the ancient purity of speech. But in craft and deed I wot well we are to the full as good Roms as ever."

By this time it was clear to the Sergeant that the old man was jealous of his leadership; and as he himself was by no means desirous of taking part in a midnight raid against a plague-stricken town, he

proceeded to make it clear that, being on his way to
his own country of Andalucia and had been led
aside by the gipsy cryptograms he had observed by
the wayside and the casual greeting of the crook-
backed imp of the village.

Upon this the old man sat down beside Sergeant
Cardono, or, as his new friends knew him to be,
José Maria the brigand.   He did not talk about the
intended attack as the Sergeant hoped he would.
Being impressed by the greatness of his guest, he
entered into a minute catalogue of the captures he
had made, the men he had slain as recorded on
the butt of his gun or the haft of his knife, and the
cargoes he had successfully " run " across the mountains or beached on the desolate sands of Catalunia.

" I am no inlander," he said, " I am of the sea-
coast of Tarragona.   I have never been south of
Tortosa in my life ; but there does not live a man
who has conducted more good cigars and brandy
to their destination than old Pépe of the Eleven
Wounds ! "

The sergeant with grave courtesy reached him
a well-rolled cigarette.

" I have heard of your fame, brother," he said ;
" even at Ronda and on the Madrid-Seville road
your deeds are not unknown.   But what of this
venture to-night ?   Have you enough men, think
you, to overpower the town watchmen and the
palace-guards ? "

The old gipsy tossed his bony hands into the
air with a gesture of incomparable contempt.

" The palace guards are fled back to Madrid," he
cried, "and as to the town watch they are either
drunk or in their dotage ! "

Meantime the main body of the gipsies waited

patiently in the background, and every few minutes
their numbers were augmented by the arrival of
others over the various passes of the mountains.
These took their places without salutation, like men
expected, and fell promptly to listening to the conversation of the two great men, who sat smoking
their cigarettes each on his own stone in the wide
wild corrie among the rocks of the Guadarrama
which had been chosen as an appropriate rendezvous.

Singularly enough, after the sergeant had shown
the scarlet mark of the strangling ring about his
neck, no one of all that company doubted for a
moment that he was indeed the thrice-famous José
Maria of Ronda. None asked a question as to his
whence or whither. He was José Maria, and therefore entitled not only to be taken at once into the
secrets of Egypt, but also, an it pleased him, to
keep his own.

And very desperate and bloody some of 'his own'
were. In the present instance, plunder and bloodshed were to proceed hand in hand. No quarter
was to be given to old or young. The plague-
stricken sick man and the watcher by the bed, the
woman feeding her fire of sticks under her *puchero,*
the child asleep on its pillow, the Queen in the
palace, the Princess in her nursery—all were to die,
quickly and suddenly. These men had sworn it.
The dead were no tale-tellers. That was the way of
Egypt—the ancient way of safety. Were they not
few and feeble in the midst of innumerable hordes of
the *Busne?* Had they not been driven like cattle,
abused like dogs, sent guiltless to the scaffold, shot
in batches by both warring parties? Now in this
one place at least, they would do a deed of vengeance
at which the ears of the world would tingle.

The Sergeant sat and smoked and listened. He
was no stranger to such talk. It was the way of his
double profession of Andalucian bandit and Carlist
guerrillero, to devise and execute deeds of terror and
death. But nothing so cold-blooded as this had
José Maria ever imagined. He had indeed appropriated the governmental mails till the post-bags
almost seemed his own property, and the guards
handed them down without question as to a recognised official. He had, in his great days, captured
towns and held them for either party according to
the good the matter was likely to do himself. But
there was something revolting in this whole business
which puzzled him.

"Whose idea was all this?" he asked at last. "I
would give much to see the *Gitano* who could devise
such a stroke."

The grim smile on the countenance of old Pépe
of the Eleven Wounds grew yet more grim.

"No gipsy planned it and no man!" he said
sententiously. "Come hither, Chica!"

And out from among the listening throng came
a girl of thirteen or fourteen, dressed neatly and
simply in a grey linen blouse belted at the waist
with a leather belt. A gay plaid, striped of orange
and crimson, hung neatly folded over her shoulder,
and she rested her small sunburnt hand on the
silver hilt of a pistol. Black elf-locks escaped from
beneath a red silk kerchief knotted saucily after the
fashion of her companions. But her eyes, instead
of being beady and black with that far-away con-
templative look which characterises the children of
Egypt, were bright and sunny and blue as the
Mediterranean itself in the front of spring.

"Come hither, Chica—be not afraid," repeated

old Pépe of the Eleven Wounds, "this is a great
man—the greatest of all our race. You have heard
of him—as who, indeed, has not!"

Chica nodded with a quick elfish grin of intense
pleasure and appreciation. "I was listening," she said,
"I heard all. And I saw—would that I could see it
again. Oh, if only the like would happen to me!"

"Tell the noble Don José who you are, my
pretty Chica," said Pépe, soothingly.

But the child stamped her sandalled foot. It
was still white at the instep, and the sergeant could
see by the blue veins that she had not gone long
barefoot. The marks of a child either stolen for
ransom or run away from home owing to some wild
strain in the blood were too obvious to be mistaken.
Her liberty of movement among the gipsies made
the latter supposition the more probable.

"I am *not* pretty Chica, and I am not little," she
cried angrily. "I would have you remember, Pépe,
that *I* made this plan, which the folk of Egypt are
to execute to-night. But since this is the great
brigand Don José of Ronda, who was executed at
Salamanca, I will tell him all about it."

She looked round at the dark faces with which
they were surrounded.

"There are new folk among these," she said,
"men I do not know. Bid them go away. Else I
will not speak of myself, and I have much to say to
Don José!"

Pépe of the Eleven Wounds looked about him,
and shook his head. Gipsydom is a commonwealth
when it comes to a venture like this, and save in the
presence of some undoubted leader, all Egypt has
an equal right to hear and to speak. Pépe's
authority was not sufficient for this thing.

But that of the Sergeant was.

He lifted his Montera cap and said, "I would converse a while with this maid on the affairs of Egypt. 'Tis doubtless no more than you know already, and then, having heard her story my advice is at your service. But she will not speak with so many ears about. It is a woman's whim, and such the wisest of us must sometimes humour."

The gipsies smiled at the gay wave of his hand with which Cardono uttered this truism and quickly betook themselves out of earshot in groups of ten and a dozen. Cards were produced, and in a few minutes half a score of games were in progress at different points of the quarry-like cauldron which formed the outlaws' rendezvous.

At once the humour of the child changed.

"They obeyed you," she said; "I like you for that. I mean to have many men obey me when I grow up. Then I will kill many—thousands and thousands. Now I can do nothing—only I have it in my head—here!"

The elf tapped her forehead immediately underneath the red sash which was tied about it. The Sergeant, though eager to hear her story and marvelling at such sentiments from the lips of a child, successfully concealed his curiosity, and said gently, "Tell me how you came to think of to-night——"

"Of what to-night?" asked the girl quickly and suspiciously.

"The deed which is to be done to-night," replied the Sergeant simply, as though he were acquainted with the whole.

She leaped forward and caught him by the arm.

"You will stay and go with us? You will lead us?" she hissed, her blue eyes aflame and with

T

trembling accents, "then indeed will I be sure of
my revenge. Then the Italian woman and her
devil's brat shall not escape. Then I shall be sure
—sure !"

She repeated the last words with concentrated
fury, apparently impossible to one of her age. The
Sergeant smoked quietly and observed her. She
seemed absolutely transfigured.

"Tell me that you will," she cried, low and
fierce, so that her voice should not reach the men
around ; "these, when they get there, will think of
nothing but plunder. As if rags and diamonds and
gold were worth venturing one's life for. But I
desire death—death—death, do you hear ? To see
the Italian woman and her paramour pleading for
their lives, one wailing over against the other, on
their knees. Oh, I know them and the brat they
call the little Queen ! To-night they shall lie dead
under my hands—with this—with this !"

And the girl flashed a razor-keen blade out of
her red waistband. She thrust the hilt forward into
the Sergeant's hands as if in token of fealty.

"See," she said, touching the edge lovingly, "is
it not sharp ? Will it not kill surely and swiftly ?
For months I have sharpened it—ah, and to-night
it will give me my desire !"

It was the Sergeant's belief that the girl was mad,
nevertheless he watched her with his usual quiet
scrutiny, the power of which she evidently felt. For
she avoided his eyes and hastened on with her story
before he had time to cross-question her.

"Why do I hate them ? I see the question on
your lips. Because the Italian woman hath taken
away my father and slain my mother—slain her as
truly and with far sharper agony than she herself shall

know when I set this knife to her throat. I am
the daughter of Muñoz, and I swore revenge on
the man and on the woman both when I closed
my mother's eyes. My mother's heart was broken.
Ah, you see, she was weak—not like me ! It would
take a hundred like the Neapolitan to break my
heart ; and as for the man, though he were thrice
my father, he should beg his life in vain."

She snatched her knife jealously out of his hand,
tried its edge on the back of her hand with a most
unchildlike gesture, and forthwith concealed it in her
silken *faja*. Then she laid her hand once more on
the Sergeant's arm.

"You will lead us, will you not, José Maria ?"
she said pleadingly. "I can trust you. You have
done many great deeds. My nurse was a woman of
Ronda and told me of your exploits on the road from
Madrid to Sevilla. You will lead us to-night. Only
you must leave these three in the palace to me. If
you will, you shall have also my share of the plunder.
But what do I say, I know you are too noble to
think only of that—as these wolves do !"

She cast a haughty glance around upon the gipsies
at their card-play.

"I, that am of Old Castile and noble by four
descents, have demeaned myself to mix with *Gitanos*,"
she said, "but it has only been that I might work
out my revenge. I told Pépe there of my plan. I
showed him the way. He was afraid. He told ten
men, and they were afraid. Fifty, and they were
afraid. Now there are a hundred and more, and
were it not that they know that all lies open and
unguarded, even I could not lead them thither. But
they will follow you, because you are José Maria of
Ronda."

The Sergeant took the girl's hand in his. She was shaking as with an ague fit, but her eyes, blue and mild as a summer sky, had that within them which was deadlier than the tricksome slippery demon that lurks in all black orbs, whether masculine or feminine.

"Chica," he said, "your wrongs are indeed bitter. I would give much to help you to set the balance right. Perhaps I may do so yet. But I cannot be the commander of these men. They are not of my folk or country. They have not even asked me to lead them. They are jealous of me! You see it as well as I!"

"Ah!" cried the girl, laying her hand again on his cuff, "that is because they do not wish you to share their plunder. But tell them that you care nothing for that and they will welcome you readily enough. The place is plague-stricken, I tell you. The palace lies open. Little crook-backed Chepe brought me word. He says he adores me. He is of the village of Frias, back there behind the hills. I do not love him, even though he has a bitter heart and can hate well. Therefore I suffer him."

The Sergeant rose to his feet and looked compassionately down at the vivid little figure before him. The hair, dense and black, the blue eyes, the red-knotted handkerchief, the white teeth that showed between the parted lips clean and sharp as those of a wild animal. Cardono had seen many things on his travels, but never anything like this. His soul was moved within him. In the deeps of his heart, the heart of a Spanish gipsy, there was an infinite sympathy for any one who takes up the blood feud, who, in the face of all difficulties, swears the *vendetta*. But the slim arms, the spare willowy body, the little white sandalled feet of the little girl—these overcame him with a pitifully amused sense of the disproportion of means to end.

"Have you no brother, Señorita?" he said, using by instinct the title of respect which the little girl loved the most. She saw his point in a moment.

"A brother—yes, Don José! But my brother is a cur, a dog that eats offal. Pah! I spit upon him. He hath taken favours from the woman. He hath handled her money. He would clean the shoes they twain leave at their chamber door. A brother —yes; the back of my hand to such brothers! But after to-night he shall have no offal to eat—no bones thrown under the table to pick. For in one slaying I will kill the Italian woman Cristina, the man Muñoz who broke my mother's heart, and the foisted changeling brat whom they miscall the daughter of Fernando and the little Queen of Spain!"

She subsided on a stone, dropped her head into her hands, and took no further notice of the Sergeant, who stood awhile with his hand resting on her shoulder in deep meditation. There was, he thought, no more to be said or done. He knew all there was to know. The men had not asked him to join them, so he would venture no further questions as to the time and the manner of attack. They were still jealous of him with that easily aroused jealousy of south and north which in Spain divides even the clannish gipsy.

Nevertheless he went the round of the men. They were mostly busy with their games, and some of them even snatched the stakes in to them, lest he should demand a percentage of the winnings after the manner of Sevilla. The Sergeant smiled at the reputation which distance and many tongues had

given him.   Then, with a few words of good fellow-
ship and the expression of a wish for success and
abundant plunder, he bade them farewell.   It was a
great deed which they designed and one worthy of
his best days.   He was now old, he said, and must
needs choose easier courses.   He did not desire twice
to feel the grip of the collar of iron.   But young
blood—oh, it would have its way and run its risks !

Here the Sergeant smiled and raised his Montera
cap.   The men as courteously bade him good-day,
preserving, however, a certain respectful distance,
and adding nothing to the information he had already
obtained.

But Chica, seated on her stone, with her scarlet-
bound head on her hand, neither looked up nor gave
him any greeting as his feet went slowly down the
rocky glen and crunched over the begrimed patches
of last year's snow, now wide-pored and heavy with
the heat of noonday.

CHAPTER XXIX

A LITTLE QUEEN AT HOME

MEANWHILE, leaving the grave in the shaded corner of the farm garden, La Giralda went out with many strange things moving in her heart. More than once she had seen her own children laid in the dust, with far less of emotion than this nameless little girl clutching her wooden puppet and smiling, well-pleased, in the face of the Last Terror.

She found the donkey standing still and patient between his fagot bundles. The she-goats, on the other hand, had scattered a little this way or that as this blade of grass or that spray of *encina* had allured them. But a sharp cry or two called them together. For it was many hours since any of them had been milked, and the full teats standing out every way ached for the pressing fingers.

The Sergeant had, of course, long since completely disappeared up the hillside, so La Giralda, with one comprehensive look back at the desolate farm-house, drove her little flock before her towards the town gates of San Ildefonso. Like a picture, the dustily red roofs lay beneath in the sunshine, spire and roof-garden, pigeon-house and terrace walk. Parts of the white palace of La Granja also were to be seen, but indistinctly, since it lay amid a pleasant distraction of greenery, and the woods waved and

279

the falling waters glimmered about it like the landscape of a dream.

From the *Colegiata* came the tolling of a bell, slow and irregular. All else was silent. Presently, with her little flock before her, La Giralda found herself skirting the high-paled ironwork which confines the palace. She pursued her way towards the town, taking care, however, to look sharply about her so that she might miss nothing.

The palace grounds seemed utterly deserted. The fountains slept; "Fame" drove no longer her waters fifty yards into the air ; the Frogs rested from their ungrateful labours open-mouthed and gasping for breath. Not even a gardener was to be seen scratching weeds on a path, or in the dimmest distance passing at random across one of the deep-shaded avenues. An unholy quiet seemed to have settled upon the place, the marvel of Castile, the most elevated of earthly palaces, broken only by the sombre tolling of the chapel bell, which would cease for five minutes without apparent reason, and then, equally without cause, begin all over again its lugubrious chime.

Down the zigzags towards the town went La Giralda, the goats taking advantage of the wider paths to stray further afield, and needing more frequently the touch of the wand, which the old woman had taken from the donkey's load in order to induce them to proceed.

As the gipsy passed along, a small shrill voice called upon her to stop, and from a side walk, concealed by roses and oleander bushes, late flowering because of the great elevation, a richly-dressed little girl came running. She ran at the top of her speed towards the gilt railings which towered high above her head. Her age appeared to be about that of the little girl whom La Giralda had buried among the pottery shards in that other meaner garden up on the mountain side.

"Stop," she cried imperiously, "I bid you stop! I am the Queen, and you must obey me. I have not seen any one for five days except stupid old Susana, who will be after me in a moment. Stop, I tell you! I want to see your goats milked. I love milk, and they will not give me enough, pretending that there is none within the palace. As if a Queen of Spain could not have all the milk she wanted! Ridiculous!"

By this time the little girl had mounted the parapet and was clinging with all her might to the iron railings, while a fat motherly person had waddled out of the underbrush in search of her, and with many exclamations of pretended anger and indignation was endeavouring to entice her away.

But the more the nurse scolded and pulled, the more firmly did the little maid cling to the golden bars. At last the elderly woman, quite out of breath, sat down on the stone ledge and addressed to her charge the argument which in such cases betokens unconditional surrender.

"My lady Isabel, what would your noble and royal mother say," she gasped, "thus to forget all the counsels and commands of those put in authority over you and run to the railings to chatter with a gipsy wife? Go away, goatherdess, or I will call the attendants and have you put in prison!"

La Giralda had stopped her flock, obedient to the wishes of the little maid, but now, with a low curtsey to both, she gathered them together with her peculiar whistling cry, and prepared to continue her way down into the village.

But this the little girl would in nowise permit. She let go the iron rail, and with both hands clenched fell upon her attendant with concentrated fury.

"Bad, wicked Susana," she cried, "I will have you whipped and sent about your business. Nay, I myself will beat you. I will kill you, do you hear? I have had nothing to eat and no one to play with for a week—not a gardener, not a dog, not even a soldier on guard to salute me or let me examine his sword-bayonet. And now when this dear, this sweet old Señora comes by with her lovely, lovely goats, you must perforce try to pull me off as if I were a village child that had played truant from the monks' school and must be birched for its fault!"

All the while she was speaking, the young Princess directed a shower of harmless blows at the skirts of her attendant, which Doña Susana laughingly warded off, begging all the while for pity, and instancing the direct commands of the little girl's mother, apparently a very exalted personage indeed, as a reason for her interference.

But Isabel of Spain was not to be appeased, and presently she had recourse to tears in the midst of her fury.

"You hate me—I know you do—that is what it means," she cried, "you would not have me happy even for a moment. But one day I shall be Queen, and do as I like! Yes, and drink as much warm goat's milk as I want, in spite of all the stupid, wicked, cruel Susanas in the world. And I shall throw you into a dungeon with nothing but mice and rats and serpents and centipedes—yes, and snails that leave a white slimy trail over you when they crawl! Ugh! And I will have your hands tied, so that you shall not be able to brush them off when they tickle your neck. Yes, I will, Susana! I swear it, and I am growing big—so big! And soon I shall be old enough to have you put in prison with the mice and snails, bad Susana! Oh, wicked Susana!"

Now, whether these childish threats actually had some effect, or whether the old lady was so soft-hearted as her comfortable appearance denoted, certain it is that she took a key from her pocket and passed it through the tall gilt railings to La Giralda.

"Go down a hundred yards or so," she said, "and there you will find a gate. Open it with that key and bring over your animals to the little pavilion among the trees by the fountain."

Upon hearing this the Princess instantly changed her tune. She had got her own way, and now it was "Beautiful Doña Susana! Precious and loveliest companion, when I am Queen you shall have the greatest and handsomest grandee in the kingdom to be your husband, and walk in diamonds and rubies at our court balls! Yes, you shall. I promise it by my royal oath. And now I will run to the house kitchen for basins to catch the goats' milk in, and my little churn to churn the butter in—and—and——"

But before she had catalogued half the things that she meant to find and bring she departed at the top of her speed, making the air ring with her shouts of delight.

Slowly, and with the meekest dignity, La Giralda did as she was bidden. She found the little gate, which, indeed, proved so narrow that she could not get her donkey to pass through with his great side-burdens of fagots. But as these were not at all heavy, La Giralda herself detached them, and, laying them carefully within the railings, she unhaltered the patient beast and, tying him only with a cord about his neck, left him a generous freedom of browsing upon the royal grass-plots and undergrowth.

The goats, however, perhaps alarmed by the trim daintiness of the place and the unwonted spectacle of unlimited leaves and forage, kept close together. One or two of them, indeed, smelt doubtfully at luxuriant tufts, but as they had only previously seen grass in single blades, and amid Saharas of gravel and sand, the experiment of eating an entire mouthful at a time appeared too hazardous and desperate. They were of a cautious turn of mind, in addition to which their udders had become so distended that little white beads were forcing themselves from the teats, and they expressed their desire for relief by plaintive whimperings and by laying their rough heads caressingly against La Giralda's short and primitive skirt and leather-cased legs.

In a few moments after they had reached the pavilion the Princess came shouting back. She was certainly a most jovial little person, Spanish at all points, with great dark eyes and cheeks apple-red with good health and the sharp airs of the Guadarrama. Doña Susana had walked a little in front of La Giralda and her flock, to show the superiority of her position, and also, it may be, to display the amplitude of her several chins, by holding them in the air in a manner as becoming as it was dignified.

"Milk them! Milk them quickly! Let me see!" the Princess shouted, clanging the pails joyously together. The walls of the pavilion in which La Giralda found herself were decorated with every kind of household utensil, but not such as had ever been used practically. Everything was of silver or silver-gilt. There was indeed a complete *batterie de cuisine*—saucepans, patty-pans, graters, a mincing machine with the proper screws and handles, shining rows of lids, and a complete graduated series of cooking spoons stuck in a bandolier. Salad dishes of sparkling crystal bound with silver ornamented the sideboard, while various earthen pots and pans of humbler make stood on a curiously designed stove under whose polished top no fire had ever burned. At least so it appeared to La Giralda, who, much impressed by the magnificence of the installation, would promptly have driven her goats out again.

But this the little Isabel would by no means permit.

"Here—here!" she commanded, "this is mine—my very own. My mother has a dairy—I have a kitchen. Milk the goats here, I command you, nowhere but here!"

And thrusting the bucket into the old woman's hand, she watched carefully and eagerly as La Giralda pressed the milk downwards in hissing streams. The she-goat operated upon expressed her gratitude by turning to lick the hand which relieved her.

At this the little girl danced with delight.

"It looks so easy—I could do it myself! I am sure of it. I tell you, Susana, I will do it. Stand still, *cabra!* Do you not know that I am Isabel the Second, Queen of all the Spains!"

But the she-goat, having no very strong monarchial sentiments, or perhaps being inclined to Carlist opinions, as soon as she felt the grip of un-accustomed fingers promptly kicked over in the dust the Queen of all the Spains.

The little girl had not time to gather herself up or even to emit the howl of disappointment and anger which hovered upon her lips, before her attendant rushed at her with pitiful cries :

"Oh, the wicked goat ! The devil-possessed emblem of Satan ! Let it be slain ! Did not your poor Susana warn you to have nothing to do with such evil things—thus to overturn in the dust the best, the sweetest, the noblest of Princesses !"

But the best and sweetest of Princesses, having violent objections to being gathered up into the capacious embrace of her nurse, especially before company, vigorously objected in much the same manner as the goat had done, and at last compelled Doña Susana to deposit her once more on the paved floor of the miniature kitchen. Having arrived in which place, her anger completely vanished, for a tankardful of rich warm goat's milk was handed to her by La Giralda, and in this flowing bowl she soon forgot her woes.

"You must come down to the palace and be paid," said the little girl ; "we are most of us very hungry there, and those who are not hungry are thirsty. The waggons from Madrid have been stopped on the way, and all the guards have gone to bring them back !"

At this Doña Susana looked quickly across to the old goatherdess and signalled that the little Princess was not to be informed of anything she might happen to know.

"You have not been in the town, I trust !" said Doña Susana.

Now La Giralda could conscientiously have declared that she had never been within the gates of San Ildefonso in her life, but thinking that in the

circumstances the statement might appear a suspicious one, she modified it to a solemn declaration
that she had come directly down from her farm on
the mountain-side, as, indeed, they themselves had
seen.

Satisfied of her veracity, Doña Susana took her
very independent and difficult charge by the hand
and led the way towards the palace of La Granja,
glimpses of which could be obtained through the
foliage which was still everywhere verdant and
abundant with the first freshness of spring—so high
did the castle lie on the hill-slopes, and so enlivening
were the waste waters downthrown from the rocky
crests of Peñalara, whose snows glimmered through
the trees, as it seemed, but a bowshot above their
heads.

The goats, each expecting their turn of milking,
followed at her heels as obediently as well-trained
dogs. Most of them were of the usual dark-red
colour, a trifle soiled with the grey dust on which
they had been lying. A few were white, and these
were the favourites of the little Queen, who, though
compelled to go on ahead, looked constantly back
over her shoulder and endeavoured to imitate the
shrill whistling call by which La Giralda kept her
flock in place.

When they arrived at the palace front the doors
stood wide open. At Doña Susana's call an ancient
major-domo appeared, his well-developed waistcoat
mating ill with the pair of shrunk and spindle shanks
which appeared beneath. The sentry boxes, striped
red and gold with the colours of Spain, were empty.
At the guard-houses there were no lounging sergeants
or smart privates eager to rise and salute as the little
Queen passed by.

There was already indeed about the palace an air of desolation. The great gates in front towards the town had been closed, as if to shut off infection, and the Court itself, dwindled to a few faithful old retainers of Fernando VII., surrounded his widow and her new husband with a devotion which was yet far more than their due.

It was not long before La Giralda had milked the remainder of the flock and sent the creaming white pitchers into the palace. Little Isabel danced with delight as one she-goat after another escaped with infinite tail-waggling and bleatings of pleasure. And in the dearth of other amusement she desired and even commanded the old woman to remain and pasture her herd within the precincts of the palace. But La Giralda had much yet to do. She must find out the state and dispositions of the town of San Ildefonso, and then rejoin her companions in the little corrie or cauldron-like *cirque* in which she and the sergeant had left Rollo and the other members of the expedition.

So after the small and imperious royal maid had been carried screaming and battling upstairs by Doña Susana and the globular major-domo, La Giralda, richly rewarded in golden coin of the realm, and with all the requisite information as to the palace, betook herself back to the gate by which she had left the ass. This she loaded again, and driving it before her she retraced her steps past the corner of the palace, and so to the porter's lodge by the great gate.

Here she was presently ushered out by a mumbling old woman who informed her that her husband and son had both gone to Madrid with the troops, but would undoubtedly return in an hour or two, a statement which with her superior information the old gipsy took leave to doubt.

The town of San Ildefonso lay beneath the chateau, and to her right as La Giralda issued from the gates. The houses were of an aspect at once grave and cheerful. They had been built mostly, not for permanent residence, but in order to accommodate the hordes of courtiers and their suites who, in the summer months, followed the royal personages over the mountains from Madrid.

As most of these had fled at the first invasion of the cholera, the windows, at this period of the year generally bright with flowers and shaded with emerald barred *jalousies*, were closely shut up, and upon several of the closed doors appeared the fatal black and white notices of the municipality, which indicated that there either was or had been a case of the plague within the infected walls.

La Giralda went down the streets uttering the long wailing cry which indicated that she had firewood to sell. But though she could have disposed of the milk from the goats over and over again, there appeared but little demand for her other commodity, even though she called, " *Leña-a-a-a !* *Ah, leña-a-a-a !* " from one end of San Ildefonso to the other.

A city watchman, with a pipe in his mouth, looked drowsily and frowsily out of the town-hall or *ayuntamiento*. He was retreating again to his settle when it suddenly struck him that this intruder had paid no duty upon her milk and firewood. True, he was not the functionary appointed by law to receive the tax ; but since he was on the spot, and for lack of other constituted the representative of civic state, he felt he must undertake the duty.

U

So, laying aside his pipe and seizing his halberd and cocked hat, he sallied grumblingly forth to intercept the bold contravener of municipal laws. But the active limbs of the old gipsy, the lightened udders of the she-goats, and the ass with his meek nose pointed homeward, took the party out of the village gate before the man in authority could overtake La Giralda.

Soon, therefore, the roofs of San Ildefonso and the white palace again lay beneath her as the gipsy reascended by her track of the morning. So long had she occupied in her various adventures that the evening shadows were already lengthening when she returned to the corrie where the party had spent in restful indolence the burden and heat of the day. The Sergeant had not yet arrived, and La Giralda delayed her story till he should give her leave to speak. For not even to the gipsies of the Guadarrama was José Maria a greater personage than Sergeant Cardono to La Giralda of Sevilla.

In the mean time she busied herself, with Concha's help, in preparing the evening meal, as quick upon her legs as if she had done nothing but lounge in the shade all day. It was almost sundown when the Sergeant came in, dropping unannounced over the precipice as if from the clouds.

"We must be in La Granja in two hours if we are to save a soul within its walls," he said, "but— we have an hour for dinner first ! Therefore let us dine. God knows when we shall taste food again !"

And with this dictum John Mortimer heartily agreed.

CHAPTER XXX

PALACE BURGLARS

THE startling announcement of the Sergeant at once set the whole party in motion. Their suspicions of the morning were cast to the winds, as the Sergeant and La Giralda in turn related their adventures. Concha, having formerly vouched so strongly for the old gipsy woman, now nodded triumphantly across to Rollo, who on his part listened intently. As Sergeant Cardono proceeded the young man leaned further and further forward, breathing deeply and regularly. The expression on his face was that of fierce and keen resolution.

The Sergeant told all the tale as it had happened, reserving only the identification of himself with the famous José Maria of Ronda, which the gipsies had made on the strength of the red mark about his neck, now once more concealed under his military stock. Cardono, however, made no secret that he was of the blood of Egypt, and set down to this fact all that he had been able to accomplish. In swift well-chosen words he told of the fierce little girl with the dark hair and blue eyes, who declared herself to be the daughter of Muñoz, sometime paramour and now reputed husband of the Queen-Regent—making it clear that she had indeed planned the wholesale slaughter, not only of those in the palace, but also of the inhabitants of the town of San Ildefonso.

Then in her turn La Giralda told of her visit to the pavilion, of the little Queen, passionate, joyous, kindly natured, absolutely Spanish, till the hearts of her hearers melted to the tale.

"Our orders are to capture her and her mother the Regent," said Rollo, thoughtfully. "It would therefore serve our purpose but ill if we permitted these two to be sacrificed to the bloodthirsty fury of a mob of plunderers!"

"Then the sooner we find ourselves within the gates, the more chance we shall have of saving them both!" said the Sergeant. "Serve out the *puchero*, La Giralda!"

Concha had taken no part in the discussion. But she had listened with all her ears, and now in the pause that followed she declared her unalterable intention of making one of the party.

"I also am of Andalucia," she said with calm determination, "there are two others of my country here who will answer for me. You cannot leave me alone, and La Giralda will be needed as guide when once you reach the palace precincts. I shall not be in the way, I promise you, and if it comes to gun and pistol, there I think you will not find me wanting!"

In his heart and though he made several objections, Rollo was glad enough to give way. For with all the unknown dangers of the night before them, and the certainty of bloodshed when the gipsies should attack, he relished still less the thought of leaving Concha alone in that pit on the chill side of Guadarrama.

"I promise you, Colonel, the maid will be worth

her billet," said the Sergeant, " or else she is no true
Andaluse. To such an one in old days I have often
trusted—— "

Thus far Cardono had proceeded when suddenly
he broke off his reminiscence, and with a paternal
gesture patted Concha's arm as she was bending over
to transfer a second helping of the *puchero* to his
dish.

The party was now in excellent marching order,
well-provisioned, well-fed, rested, and provided with
the best and most recent information. Even John
Mortimer's slow English blood developed some
latent Puritanic fire, and he said, " Hang me if I do
not fight for the little girl who was willing to pay
for the *whole* of the goat-milk ! "

To fight for a Queen, who at the early age of five
was prepared to give a wholesale order like that,
appeared to John Mortimer a worthy and laudable
deed of arms. He was free indeed to assist in
taking her captive, if by so doing he could further
the shipping of the Priorato he himself had paid for.
But to make over to a set of thieves and murderers
a girl who had about her the makings of a good
customer and a woman of business habits, stirred
every chivalric feeling within him.

The night was so dark that it was resolved that
the party should leave their horses behind them in
the stables of the deserted farm. They could then
proceed on foot more softly and with more safety to
themselves. To this La Giralda, knowing that they
must return that way, readily assented. For the
thought of the dead woman she had left in the first-
floor room haunted her, and even in the darkness of
the night she could see the stark outlines of the
sheet she had spread over the body.

So it came to pass that once more horseshoe iron clattered, and there was a flashing of lights and a noise of voices about the lonely and stricken farmhouse. But only La Giralda gave a thought to the little grave in the shady corner of the garden, and only she promised herself to revisit it when the stern work of the night should be over and the dawn of a calmer morning should have arisen.

Now, as soon as Sergeant Cardono returned, he placed himself as completely as formerly under the orders of Rollo. He was no more José Maria the famous gipsy, but Sergeant Cardono of the army of H.M. Carlos Quinto, and Señor Rollo was his colonel. Like a good scout he was ready to advise, but to the full as ready to hold his tongue and obey.

And Rollo, though new to his position, was not above benefiting continually by his wisdom, and as a matter of fact it was the Sergeant who, in conjunction with La Giralda, led the little expedition down the perilous goat-track by which the old gipsy had followed her flock in the morning. As usual Concha kept her place beside Rollo, with Mortimer and Etienne a little behind, while El Sarria, taciturn but alert as usual, brought up the rear.

It can hardly be said that they carried with them any extraordinary elements of success. Indeed, in one respect they were at a manifest disadvantage. For in an expedition of this kind there ought to be one leader of dignity, character, and military genius far beyond the others. But among this little band which stole so quietly along the mountain-paths of the Guadarrama, beneath the frowning snowclad brow of Peñalara, there was not one who upon occasion could not have led a similar forlorn hope.

Each member of the party possessed a character definite and easily to be distinguished from all the others. It was an army of officers without any privates.

Still, since our Firebrand, Rollo the Scot, held the nominal leadership, and his quick imperious character made that chieftainship a reality, there was at least a chance that they might bring to a successful conclusion the complex and difficult task which was before them.

* * * * *

They now drew near to the palace, which, as one descends the mountains, is approached first. The town of San Ildefonso lay further to the right, an indistinguishable mass of heaped roofs and turrets without a light or the vestige of a street apparent in the gloom. It seemed to Rollo a strange thing to think of this stricken town lying there with its dead and dying, its empty tawdry lodgings from which the rich and gay of the Court had fled so hastily, leaving all save their most precious belongings behind, the municipal notices on the door, white crosses chalked on a black ground, while nearer and always nearer approached the fell gipsy rabble intent on plunder and rapine.

Even more strange, however, seemed the case of the royal palace of La Granja. Erected at infinite cost after the pattern of Versailles and Marly, the smallness of its scale and the magnificence of its natural surroundings caused it infinitely to surpass either of its models in general effect. It had, however, never been intended for defence, nor had the least preparation been made in case of attack. It was doubtless presumed that whenever the Court sojourned there, the royal personages would arrive with such a guard and retinue as, in that lonely place, would make danger a thing to be laughed at.

But no such series of circumstances as this had ever been thought of; the plague which had fallen so heavily and as it seemed mysteriously and instantaneously upon the town; the precincts of the palace about to be invaded by a foe more fell than Frank or Moor; the guards disappeared like snow in the sun, and the only protection of the lives of the Queen-Regent and her daughter, a band of Carlists sent to capture their persons at all hazards.

Verily the whole situation was remarkably complex.

The briefest look around convinced Rollo that it would be impossible for so small a party to hold the long range of iron palisades which surrounded the palace. These were complete, indeed, but their extent was far too great to afford any hope of keeping out the gipsies without finding themselves taken in the rear. They must hold La Granja itself, that was clear. There remained, therefore, only the problem of finding entrance.

Between the porter's lodge and the great gates near the *Colegiata* they discovered a ladder left somewhat carelessly against a wall where whitewashing had been going on during the day, some ardent royal tradesman having ventured back, preferring the chance of the plague to the abandonment of his contract.

This they at once appropriated, and Rollo and the Sergeant, being the two most agile of the company, prepared to mount.

If the time had been less critical, and a disinterested observer had been available, it would at this moment have been interesting to observe the demeanour of Concha. Feeling that in a manner

she was present on sufferance, she could not of
course make any objection to the plan of escalade,
nor could she offer to accompany Rollo and the
Sergeant, but with clasped hands and tightly compressed lips she stood beneath, repeating under her
breath quick-succeeding prayers for the safety of
one (or both) of the adventurers.

So patent and eager was her anxiety even in
the gloom of the night that La Giralda, to whom
her agitation was manifest, laid her hand on the
girl's arm and whispered in her ear that she must be
brave, a true Andaluse, and not compromise the
expedition by any spoken word.

Concha turned indignantly upon her, shaking off
her restraining hand as she did so.

"Do you think I am a fool?" she whispered.
"I will do nothing to spoil their chances. But oh,
Giralda, at any moment he might be shot!"

"Trust José Maria. He hath taken risks far
greater than this," said La Giralda in a low voice,
wilfully mistaking her meaning. But Concha, quite
unconsoled, did nothing but clasp her hands and
quicken her supplications to the Virgin.

The ladder was reared against the gilded iron railing
and Rollo mounted, immediately dropping lightly
down on the further side. The Sergeant followed,
and presently both were on the ground. At a word
from Rollo, El Sarria pushed the ladder over and
the two received it and laid it along the parapet in
a place where it would remain completely hidden till
wanted.

The two moved off together in the direction
of the porter's lodge, at the door of which the
Sergeant knocked lightly, and then, obtaining no
answer, with more vehemence. A window was

lifted and a frightened voice asked who came there at that time of night.

The Sergeant answered with some sharpness that they wished for the key of the great gate.

Upon this the same old woman who had ushered out La Giralda appeared trembling at the lattice, and was but little relieved when the Sergeant, putting on his most serious air, informed her that her life was in the utmost danger, and that she must instantly come downstairs, open the gate, and accompany them to the palace.

" I knew it," quavered the old woman, " I knew it since ever my husband went away with the soldiers and left me here alone. I shall be murdered among you, but my blood will be on his hands. Indeed, sirs, he hath never treated me well, but spent his wages at the wine tavern, giving me but a beggarly pittance. Nay, how do I know but he had an intent in thus deserting me ? He hath, and I can prove it, cast eyes of desire on Maria of the pork-shop, only because she is younger and more comely than I, who had grown old and wrinkled bearing him children and cooking him *ollas!* Aye, and small thanks have I got for either. As indeed I have told him hundreds of times. Such a man ! A pretty fellow to be head porter at a Queen's gate ! I declare I will inform her Royal Majesty this very night, if I am to go to the palace, that will I ! "

" Come down immediately and let us in, my good woman," said the Sergeant, soothingly. For it appeared as if this torrent of accusation against the absent might continue to flow for an indefinite period.

" But how am I to know that you are not the very rogues and thieves of whom you tell ? " persisted the old lady with some show of reason.

"Well," said the Sergeant forbearingly, "as to that you must trust us, mother. It is the best you can do. But fear nothing, we will treat you gently as a cat her kitten, and you will come up to the palace with us to show us in what part of it dwell the Queen and her daughter."

"Nay, not if it be to do harm to my lady and the sweet little maid who this very day brought a pail of milk to poor old Rebeca the portress, whose husband hath forsaken her for a pork-shop trull. I would rather die!"

Rollo was about to speak, but the Sergeant whispered that the old lady was now in such good case to admit them, that she might be frighted by his foreign accent.

In a few moments the woman could be heard stiffly and grumblingly descending the stairs, the door was opened, and Rebeca appeared with the key in her hand.

"How many are there of your party?" she asked, her poor hand shaking so that she could scarcely fit the key in the lock, and her voice sunk to a quavering whisper.

"There are five men of us and two women," said the Sergeant, quickly. "Now we are all within, pray give me the key and show us the road to the Queen's apartments."

"Two women!" grumbled the poor old creature, whose mind appeared to be somewhat unhinged; "that will never suit her Royal Highness the Regent, especially if they are young and well-looking. She loves not such, any more than I love the hussy of the pork-shop. Though, indeed, my man hath not the roving eye in his head as her Señor Muñoz hath. Ah, the saints have mercy on all poor deserted women! But what am I saying? If the Lady Cristina heard me speak ill of him, she would set my poor old neck in the garrote. Then—crack—all would be over!"

The party now advanced towards the palace, which in the gloom of a starless night was still entirely hidden from their sight, save as a darker mass set square against the black vault of heaven.

By this time Concha and La Giralda had taken the trembling portress by the arms, and were bringing her along in the van, whispering comfort in her ears all the way. The sergeant and Rollo came next, with Mortimer and Etienne behind, a naked blade in the hand of each, for Rollo had whispered the word to draw swords. This, however, El Sarria interpreted to mean his faithful Manchegan knife, to which he trusted more than to any sword of Toledo that ever was forged.

At any other time they could not have advanced a score of yards without being brought to a standstill by the challenge of a sentry, the whistle of a rifle bullet, or the simultaneous turning out of the guard. But now no such danger was to be apprehended. All was still as a graveyard before cock-crow.

It is hard, in better and wiser days, when things are beginning to be traced to their causes, to give any idea of the effect of the first appearance of Black Cholera among a population at once so simple and so superstitious as that of rural Spain. The inhabitants of the great towns, the Cristino armies in the field, the country-folk of all opinions were universally persuaded that the dread disease was caused by the monks in revenge for the despites offered to them; especially by the hated Jesuits, who were supposed to have thrown black cats alive into rivers and wells in order to produce disease by means of witchcraft and diabolical agency.

So universal was this belief that so soon as the plague broke out in any city or town the neighbouring monasteries were immediately plundered, and the priors and brethren either put to death or compelled to flee for their lives.

Some such panic as this had stampeded the troops stationed in and about the little town of San Ildefonso, when the first cases of cholera proved fatal little more than a week before. A part of these had rushed away to plunder the rich monastery of El Parral a few miles off, lying in the hollow beneath Segovia. Others, breaking up into parties of from a dozen to a hundred, had betaken themselves over the mountains in the direction of Madrid.

So the Queen-Regent and the handsome Señor Muñoz remained perforce at La Granja, for the two-fold reason that the palace of Madrid was reported to be in the hands of a rebellious mob, and that the disbanding troops had removed with them every sort and kind of conveyance, robbed the stables of the horses, and plundered the military armoury of every useful weapon.

They had not, however, meddled with the treasures of the palace, nor offered any indignity to the Queen-Regent, or to any of the inmates of La Granja. But as the Sergeant well knew, not thus would these be treated by the roving bands of gipsies, who in a few hours would be storming about the defenceless walls. No resource of oriental torture, no refinement of barbarity would be omitted to compel the Queen and her consort to give up the treasures without which it was well known that they never travelled. Obviously, therefore, there was no time to be lost.

They went swiftly round the angle of the palace,

their feet making no sound on the clean delicious sward of those lawns which make the place such a marvel in the midst of tawny, dusty, burnt-up Spain. In a brief space the party arrived unnoted and unchecked under the wall of the northern part.

Lights still burnt in two or three windows on the second floor, though all was dark on the face which the palace turned towards the south and the town of San Ildefonso.

"These are the windows of the rooms occupied by my lady the Queen-Regent," whispered the portress, Rebeca, pointing upwards; "but promise me to commit no murder or do any hurt to the little maid."

"Be quiet, woman," muttered Rollo, more roughly than was his wont; "we are come to save both of them from worse than death. Sergeant Cardono, bring the ladder!"

The Sergeant disappeared, and it was not many seconds before he was back again adjusting its hooks to the side of an iron balcony in front of one of the lighted rooms. Almost before he had finished Rollo would have mounted, impetuously as was his custom, but the Sergeant held him back by the arm.

"I crave your forgiveness," he whispered, "but if you will pardon me saying so, I have much more experience in such matters than you. Permit me in this single case to precede you! We know not what or whom we may meet with above!"

Nevertheless, though the Sergeant mounted first, Rollo followed so closely that his hands upon the rounds of the ladder were more than once in danger of being trodden upon by the Sergeant's half-boots.

Presently they stood together on the iron balcony and peered within. A tall dark man leaned against

an elaborately carved mantelpiece indolently stroking
his glossy black whiskers. A lady arrayed in a
dressing-gown of pink silk reaching to her feet was
seated on a chair, and submitting restlessly enough
to the hands of her maid, who was arranging her
hair for the night, in the intervals of a violent but
somewhat one-sided quarrel which was proceeding
between the pair.

Every few moments the lady would start from
her seat and with her eyes flashing fire she would
advance towards the indolent dandy by the mantel-
piece as if with purpose of personal assault. At such
seasons the stout old Abigail instantly remitted her
attentions and stood perfectly well trained and motionless, with the brush and comb in her hand, till it pleased
her lady to sit down again.

All the while the gentleman said no word, but
watched the development of the scene with the
utmost composure, passing his beautiful white
fingers through his whiskers and moustache after
the fashion of a comb. The lady's anger waxed
higher and higher, and with it her voice also rose
in an equal ratio. What the end would have been
it is difficult to prophesy, for the Sergeant, realising
that time was passing quickly, produced an instrument with a broad flat blade bent at an acute angle
to the handle, and inserting it sharply into the crack
of the French window, opened it with a click which
must have been distinctly audible within, even in the
height of the lady's argument.

CHAPTER XXXI

OUT of the darkness Rollo and the Sergeant stepped quickly into the room. Whereupon, small wonder that the lady should scream and fall back into her chair, the waiting-maid drop upon the floor as if she had been struck by a Carlist bullet, or the gentleman with the long and glossy whiskers suspend his caresses and gaze upon the pair with dropped jaw and open mouth !

At his entrance Rollo had taken off his hat with a low bow. The Sergeant saluted and stood at attention. There was a moment's silence in the room, but before Rollo had time to speak the Queen-Regent recovered her self-possession. The daughter of the Bourbons stood erect. Her long hair streamed in dark glossy waves over her shoulders. Her bosom heaved visibly under the thin pink wrapper. Anger struggled with fear in her eyes. Verily Maria Cristina of Naples had plenty of courage.

" Who are you," she cried, " that dare thus to break in upon the privacy of the Regent Queen of Spain ? Duke, call the guard ! "

But her husband only shrugged his shoulders and continued to gaze upon the pair of intruders with a calm exterior.

" Your Majesty," said Rollo, courteously,

304

naturally resuming the leadership when anything requiring contact with gentlefolk came in the way, "I am here to inform you that you are in great danger—greater than I can for the moment make clear to you. The palace is, as I understand, absolutely without defence—the town is in the same position. It is within our knowledge that a band of two hundred gipsies are on the march to attack you this night in order to plunder the château, and put to death every soul within its walls. We have come, therefore, together with our companions outside, to offer our best services in your Majesty's defence!"

"But," cried the Queen-Regent, "all this may very well be, but you have not yet told me who you are and what you are doing here!"

"For myself," answered Rollo, "I am a Scottish gentleman, trained from my youth to the profession of arms. Those who wait without are for the present comrades and companions, whom, with your Majesty's permission, I shall bid to enter. For to be plain, every moment is of the utmost importance, that we may lose no time in putting the château into such a state of defence as is possible, since the attack of the gipsies may be expected at any moment!"

Rollo stepped to the window to summon his company, but found them already assembled on the balcony. It was no time for formal introductions, yet, as each entered, Rollo, like a true herald, delivered himself of a brief statement of the position of the individual in the company. But when La Giralda entered, the stout waiting-maid rose with a shriek from the floor where she had been sitting.

"Oh, my lady," she cried, "do not trust these wicked people. They have come to murder us all. That woman is the very old goatherdess with whom

the Princess Isabel was so bewitched this morning !
I knew some evil would come of such ongoings ! "

" Hush, Susana," said her mistress with severity ;
" when you are asked for any information, be ready
to give it.   Till then hold your peace."

Which having said she turned haughtily back
again to the strangers, without vouchsafing a glance
at her husband or the trembling handmaiden.

" I can well believe," she said, " that you have
come here to do us a service in our present temporary
difficulty, and for that, if I find you of approved
fidelity, you shall not fail to be rewarded.   Meantime, I accept your service, and I place you and the
whole of your men under the immediate command
of his Excellency the Duke of Rianzares ! "

She turned to the tall exquisite who still continued to comb his whiskers by the chimney-piece.
Up till now he had not spoken a word.

Rollo scarcely knew what to reply to this, and as
for the Sergeant, he had the hardest work to keep
from bursting into a loud laugh.

But they were presently delivered from their
difficulty by the newly nominated commander-in-
chief himself.

" This scene is painful to me," said Señor
Muñoz, placidly, " it irritates my nerves.   I have
a headache.   I think I shall retire and leave these
gentlemen to make such arrangements as may be
necessary till the return of our guards, which will
doubtless take place within an hour or so.   If you
need me you can call for me ! "

Having made this general declaration he turned
to Rollo and addressed himself particularly to him.

" My rooms, I would have you know, are in the
north wing," he continued ; " I beg that there shall

be no firing or other brutal noise on that side.
Anything of the kind would be most annoying.
So pray see to it."

Then he advanced to where his wife stood, her
eyes full of anger at this desertion.

"My angel," he said, calmly, "I advise you
sincerely to do the same. Retire to your chamber.
Take a little *tisane* for the cooling of the blood, and
leave all other matters to these new friends of ours.
I am sure they appear very honest gentlemen. But
as you have many little valuables lying about, do not
forget to lock your door, as I shall mine. Adieu,
my angel!"

And so from an inconceivable height of dandyism
his Excellency the Duke of Rianzares would have
stooped to bestow a good night salutation on his wife's
cheek, had not that lady, swiftly recovering from her
stupor, suddenly awarded him a resounding box on
the ear, which so far discomposed the calm of his
demeanour that he took from his pocket a handkerchief edged with lace, unfolded it, and with the most
ineffable gesture in the world wiped the place the
lady's hand had touched. Then, with the same
abiding calm, he restored the cambric to his pocket,
bowed low to the Queen, and lounged majestically
towards the door.

Maria Cristina watched him at first with a
haughty and unmoved countenance. Her hands
clenched themselves close to her side, as if she
wished the blow had been bestowed with the shut
rather than with the open digits.

But as her husband (for so he really was, though
the relationship was not acknowledged till many
years after, and at the feet of the Holy Father himself
in the Vatican) approached the door, opened it, and

was on the point of departing without once turning
round, Cristina suddenly broke into a half hysterical
cry, ran after him, threw her arms tenderly about his
neck, and burst out weeping on his broad bosom.

The gentleman, without betraying the least
emotion, patted her tolerantly on the shoulder, and
murmured some words in her ear, at the same time
looking over her head at the men of the company
with a sort of half-comic apology.

"Oh! Fernando, forgive me," she cried, "life
of my life—the devil must have possessed me! I
will cut off the wicked hand that did the deed.
Give me a knife, good people—to strike the best and
handsomest—oh, it was wicked—cruel, diabolical!"

Whatever may have been the moral qualities of
the royal blow, Rollo felt that in their present circumstances time enough had been given to its
consideration, so he interposed.

"Your Majesty, the gipsies may be upon us at
any moment. It would be as well if you would
summon all the servants of the palace together and
arm them with such weapons as may be available!"

Maria Cristina lifted her head from the shoulder
of her Ferdinand, as if she did not at first compre-
hend Rollo's speech, and was resolved to resent an
intrusion at such a moment. Whereupon the Scot
repeated his words to such good purpose that the
Queen-Regent threw up her hands and cried, "Alas!
this happens most unfortunately. We have only old
Eugenio and a couple of lads in the whole palace
since the departure of the guards!"

"Never mind," said Rollo; "let us make the best
of the matter. We will muster them; perhaps they will
be able to load and fire a musket apiece! If I mistake not, the fighting will be at very short range!"

It was upon this occasion that Señor Fernando Muñoz showed his first spark of interest.

"I will go and awake them," he said ; "I know where the servants are wont to sleep."

But on this occasion his fond wife would not permit him to stir.

"The wicked murderers may have already penetrated to that part of the castle," she palpitated, her arms still about his neck, "and you must not risk your precious life. Let Susana go and fetch them. She is old, and has doubtless made her peace with religion."

"Nay, it is not fitting," objected Susana with spirit. "I am a woman, and not so old as my lady says. I cannot go gadding about into the chambers of all and sundry. Besides, there has been purpose of marriage openly declared between me and the Señor Eugenio for upwards of thirty years. What then would be said if I——"

"Nay, then," cried Maria Cristina, "stay where you are, Susana. For me, I am none so nice. I will go myself. Do not follow me, Fernando!" And with that she ran to the door, and her feet were heard flitting up the stairway which led to the servants' wing of the palace. Muñoz made as if to accompany her, but remembering his wife's prohibition, he did not proceed farther than the door, where, with a curious smile upon his face, he stood listening to the voice of the Queen-Regent upraised in alternate appeal and rebuke.

During the interval, while the Sergeant and El Sarria were looking to their stores and munitions, Rollo approached the waiting-maid, Susana, and inquired of her the way to the armoury, where he expected to find store of arms and powder.

"If this young maid will go also, I will conduct you thither, young man!" said Susana, primly.

And holding Concha firmly by the hand, she took up a candle and led the way.

But to Rollo's surprise they found the armoury wholly sacked. All the valuable guns had been removed by the deserting guards. The gun racks were torn down. The floor of beaten earth was strewed with flints of ancient pieces of last century's manufacture. The barrels of bell-mouthed blunder-busses leaned against the wall, the stocks, knocked off in mere wantonness, were piled in corners; and in all the chests and wall-presses there was not an ounce of powder to be found.

While Rollo was searching, Señor Muñoz appeared at the door, languid and careless as ever. He watched the young Scot opening chests and rummaging in lockers for a while without speaking. Then he spoke slowly and deliberately.

"It strikes me that when I was an officer of the bodyguard, in the service of the late Fernando the Seventh, my right royal namesake (and in some sort predecessor), there was another room used for the private stores and pieces of the officers. If I mistake not it was entered by that door to the right, but the key appears to be wanting!"

He added the last clause, as he watched the frantic efforts of Rollo, who had immediately thrown himself upon the panels, while the Señor was in the act of rolling out his long-drawn Castilian elegances of utterance.

"Hither, Cardono," cried Rollo, "open me this door! Quick, Sergeant!"

"Have a care," said the Duke; "there is powder inside!"

But Rollo, now keen on the scent of weapons of defence, would not admit a moment's delay, and the Sergeant, inserting his curiously crooked blade, opened that door as easily as he had done the French window.

Muñoz stepped forward with some small show of eagerness and glanced within.

"Yes," he said, "the officers' arms are there, and a liberal allowance of powder."

"They are mostly sporting rifles," said Rollo, looking them over, "but there is certainly plenty of powder and ball."

"And what kills ibex and bouquetin on the sierras," drawled Muñoz, "will surely do as much for a mountain gipsy if, as you said just now, the range is likely to be a short one!"

Rollo began somewhat to change his opinion about the husband of the Queen. At first he had seemed both dandy and coward, a combination which Rollo held in the utmost contempt. But when Rollo had once seen him handle a gun, he began to have more respect for his recent Excellency the Duke of Rianzares.

"Can you tell us, from your military experience," Rollo asked, "which is the most easily vulnerable part of this palace."

"It is easily vulnerable in every part," answered Muñoz, carelessly snapping the lock of a rifle again and again.

"Nay, but be good enough to listen, sir," cried Rollo, with some heat. "There are women and children here. You do not know the gipsies. You do not know by whom they are led. You do not know the oaths of death and torture they have sworn——"

"By whom are they led?" said Muñoz, still playing carelessly with the rifle. "I thought such fellows were mere savages from the hills, and might be slaughtered like sheep."

"Perhaps—at any rate they are led by your own daughter!" said Rollo, briefly, growing nettled at the parvenu grandee's seeming indifference.

"*My daughter!*" cried Muñoz, losing in a moment his bright complexion, and becoming of a slaty pallor, "my daughter, that mad imp of hell—who thrice has tried to assassinate me!"

And as he spoke, he let the gun fall upon the floor at his feet. Then he rallied a little.

"Who has told you this lie?" he exclaimed, with a kind of indignation.

"A man who does not make mistakes—or tell lies—Sergeant Cardono!" said Rollo. "He has both seen and spoken to her! She has sworn to attack the palace to-night."

"Then I am as good as dead already. I must go directly to my wife!" answered Muñoz.

But Rollo stepped before him.

"Not without carrying an armful of these to where they will be of use," he said, pointing to the guns. And the Duke of Rianzares, without any further demur, did his will. Rollo in turn took as many as he could carry, and the Sergeant brought up the rear carrying a wooden box of cartridges, which had evidently been packed ready for transportation.

They returned to the large lighted room, where Mortimer, Etienne, and El Sarria had been left on guard. Concha and the waiting-maid seconded their efforts by bringing store of pistols and ammunition.

On their way they passed through a hall, which by day seemed to be lighted only from the roof.

Rollo bade them deposit the arms there, and bring the other candles and lamps to that place.

"Every moment that a light is to be seen at an outside window adds to our danger," he said, and Concha ran at his bidding.

Before she had time to return, however, the Queen-Regent came in with her usual dignity, the three serving-men following her. Rollo saw at once that nothing was to be expected of Eugenio, whose ancient and tottering limbs could hardly support the weight of his body. But there was more hope of the two others. They proved to be stout young fellows from the neighbourhood, and professed the utmost eagerness for a bout with the gipsies. From their youth they had been accustomed to the use of firearms—it is to be feared without due licence—in the royal hunting preserves of Peñalara and the Guadarrama.

But this made no difference to Rollo, who instantly set about equipping them with the necessary arms, and inquiring minutely about the fastenings of the lower doors and windows. These it appeared were strong. The doors themselves were covered without with sheet-iron, while all the windows were protected not only by shutters but by solid stanchions of iron sunk in the wall.

On the whole Rollo was satisfied, and next questioned the servants concerning the state of the town and whether any assistance was to be hoped for from that quarter. In this, however, he was disappointed. It appeared that the whole municipality of San Ildefonso was so utterly plague-stricken that scarce an able-bodied man remained, or so much as a halfling boy capable of shouldering a musket. Only the women stood still in the breach, true nursing mothers, not like her of Ramah, refusing to be comforted, but continuing rather to tend the sick and dying till they themselves also died—aye, even shrouding the dead and laying out the corpses. A faithful brother or two of the Hermitage abode to carry the last Sacraments of the Church through the deserted and grass-grown streets, though there were few or none now to fall on their knees at the passage of *Su Majestad*, or to uncover the head at the melancholy tolling of the funeral bell.

With characteristic swiftness of decision Rollo made up his mind that the best plan for the defence of the palace would be to place his scanty forces along the various jutting balconies of the second floor, carefully darkening all the rooms in their rear, so that, till the moment of the attack itself, the assailants would have no idea that they were expected. It was his idea that the small doors on the garden side of the house, which led right and left to the servants' quarters, would be attacked first. He was the more assured of this because the Sergeant had recognised, in the bivouac of the gipsies, a man who had formerly been one of the royal grooms both at La Granja and at Aranjuez. He would be sure to be familiar, therefore, with that part of the interior of the palace. Besides, being situated upon the side most completely removed from the town, the assailants would have the less fear of interruption.

While Rollo was thus cogitating, Concha came softly to his side, appearing out of the gloom with a suddenness that startled the young man.

"I have pulled up the ladder by which we ascended and laid it across the balcony," she said. "Was that right?"

"You—alone?" cried Rollo in astonishment.

She nodded brightly.

"Certainly," she answered ; "women are not all so great weaklings as you think them—nor yet such fools ! "

"Indeed, you have more sense than I," Rollo responded, gloomily ; "I ought to have remembered that before. But, as you know, I have had many things to think of."

"I am glad," she said, more quietly and submissively than ever in her life, "that even in so small a matter I am permitted to think a little for you ! "

Whereupon, though the connection of idea is not obvious, Rollo remembered the moment when he had faced the black muzzles of Cabrera's muskets in the chill of the morning, and the bitter regret which had then arisen to his mind. Out there in the dark of the palace-garden, death fronted him as really though not perhaps so immediately. He resolved quickly that he should not have the same regret again, if the worst came to the worst. There was no one in the alcove where Concha had found him. The Queen-Regent had disappeared to her suite of rooms, and thither after a time Señor Muñoz had followed her. The rest were at that moment being placed in their various posts by the Sergeant according to Rollo's directions.

So he stooped quickly and kissed Concha upon the mouth.

It was strange. The girl's inevitable instinct on such matters seemed to have deserted her. In a somewhat wide experience Concha could always tell to a second when an attempt of this kind was due. Most women can, and if they are kissed it is because they want to be. (In which, sayeth the Wise Man, is great wisdom!) A fire-alarm rings in their brain with absolute certainty, giving them time to evite the conflagration by a healthy douche of cold water. But Rollo the Firebrand again proved himself the Masterly Incalculable. Or else—but who could suspect Concha?

It is, again sayeth the Wise Man, the same with kicking a dog. The brute sees the kick coming before a muscle is in motion. He watches the eye of his opponent and is forearmed. He vanisheth into space. But when Rollo interviewed an animal in this fashion, he kicked first and thought afterwards. Hence no sign of his intention appeared in his eye, and the dog's yelp arrived almost as a surprise to himself.

So, with greatly altered circumstance, was it in the present instance. Rollo kissed first and made up his mind to it some time after. Consequently Concha was taken absolutely by surprise. She uttered a little cry and stepped back indignantly into the lighted room where the spare muskets were piled.

But again Rollo was before her. If he had attempted to make love, she would have scathed him with the soundest indignation, based on con- siderations of time, place, and personality.

But the young Scot gave her no opportunity. In a moment he had again become her superior officer.

"Take your piece," he said, with an air of assured command, "together with sufficient am- munition, and post yourself at the little staircase window over the great door looking towards the town. If you see any one approaching, do not hesitate to fire. Good-bye. God bless you! I will see you again on my rounds!"

And Rollo passed on his way.

Then with a curious constraint upon her tongue, and on her spirit a new and delightful feeling that she could do no other than as she was bidden, Concha found herself, with loaded musket and pistol, obediently taking her place in the general defence of the palace.

CHAPTER XXXII

LIKE A FALLING STAR

ROLLO judged aright. It was indeed no time for
love-making, and, to do the young man justice, he
did not connect any idea so concrete with the im-
pulsive kiss he had given to Concha.

She it was who had saved his life at Sarria. She
was perilling her own in order to accompany and
assist his expedition. She had drawn up the ladder
he had foolishly forgotten. Yet, in spite of the fact
that he was a young man and by no means averse
from love, Rollo was so clean-minded and so little
given to think himself desirable in the eyes of
women, that it never struck him that the presence of
La Giralda and Concha might be interpreted upon
other and more personal principles than he had
modestly represented to himself.

True, Rollo was vain as a peacock—but not of
his love-conquests. Punctilious as any Spaniard
upon the smallest point of honour, in a quarrel he
was as ready as a Parisian *maître d'armes* to pull out
sword or pistol. Nevertheless when a man boasted
in his presence of the favours of a woman, he thought
him a fool and a braggart—and was in general nowise
backward in telling him so.

Thus it happened that, though Concha had
received no honester or better intentioned kiss in
her life, the giver of it went about his military

duties with a sense of having said his prayers, or generally, having performed some action raising himself in his own estimation.

"God bless her," he said to himself, "I will be a better man for her sweet sake. And, by heavens, if I had had such a sister, I might have been a better fellow long ere this! God bless her, I say!"

But what wonder is it that little Concha, in her passionate Spanish fashion understanding but one way of love, and being little interested in brothers, felt the tears come to her eyes as Rollo's step waxed fainter in the distance, and said over and over to herself with smiling pleasure, "He loves me—he loves me! Oh, if only my mother had lived, I might have been worthier of him. Then I would not have played with men's hearts for amusement to myself, as alas, I have too often done. God forgive me, there was no harm, indeed. But—but—I am not worthy of him—I know I am not!"

So Rollo's hasty kiss on the dark balcony was provocative of a healthy self-reproach on both sides —which at least was so much to the good.

Concha peered out into the darkness towards the south where a few stars were blinking sleepily through the ground-mist. She could dimly discern the outline of the town lying piled beneath her, without a light, without a sound, without a sign of life. From beyond the hills came a weird booming as of a distant cannonade. But Concha, the careless maiden who had grown into a woman in an hour, did not think of these things. For to the Spanish girl, whose heart is touched to the core, there is but one subject worthy of thought. Wars, battles, sieges, the distresses of queens, the danger of royal princesses—all are as nothing, because her lips have been kissed.

"All the same," she muttered to herself, " he ought not have done it—and when I have a little recovered I will tell him so ! "

But at that moment, poised upon the topmost spike of the great gate in front of her, she saw the silhouette of a man. He was climbing upwards, with his hand on the cross-bar of the railing, and cautiously insinuating a leg over the barrier, feeling meanwhile gingerly for a foothold on the palace side.

" He is come to do evil to—to Rollo ! " she said to herself, with a slight hesitation even in thought when she came for the first time upon the Christian name.

But there was no hesitation in the swift assurance with which she set the rifle-stock to her shoulder, and no mistake as the keen and practised eye glanced along the barrel.

She fired, and with a groan of pain the man fell back outside the enclosure.

The sound of Concha's shot was the first tidings to the besieged that the gipsies had really arrived. Rollo, stealing lightfoot from post to post, pistol in hand, the Sergeant erect behind the vine-trellis on the balcony between the rearward doors, Etienne and John Mortimer a little farther along on the same side of the château, all redoubled their vigilance at the sound. But for the space of an hour or more nothing farther was seen or heard north, south, east, or west of the beleaguered palace of La Granja.

The gipsies had not had the least idea that their intention was known. They expected no obstacles till the discharge of Concha's piece put them on their guard, and set them to concerting other and more subtle modes of attack. It was too dark for those in the château to see whether the wounded man lay where he had fallen or whether he had been removed by his comrades.

Rollo hastened back to Concha and inquired in a low voice what it was she had fired at. Whereupon she told him the story of the man climbing the railings and how she had stayed his course so suddenly. Rollo made no remark, save that she had done entirely right. Then he inquired if she had recharged her piece, and hearing that she wanted nothing and was ready for all emergencies, he departed upon his rounds without the least leave-taking or approach to love-making. In her heart Concha respected him for this, but at the same time she could not help feeling that a Spaniard would have been somewhat warmer in his acknowledgments. Nevertheless she comforted herself with the thought that he had trusted her with one of the most important posts in the whole defence, and she prayed fervently to the Virgin that she might be able to do her duty there.

She thought also that, when the morning came, perhaps he would have more time. For her, she could wait—here she smiled a little. Yes, she acknowledged it. She who had caught so many, was now taken in her own net. She would go to the world's end for this young Scot. Nor in her heart of hearts was she ashamed of it. Above and beyond all courtesies and sugared phrases she loved his free-handed, careless, curt-spoken, hectoring way. After his one kiss, he had treated her exactly like any other of his company. He did not make love well, but—she liked him none the worse for that. In such matters (sayeth the Wise Man) excellence is apt to come with experience.

And he would learn. Yes, decidedly he might

Y

yet do credit to his teacher. To-morrow morning would arrive, and for the present, well—she would keep her finger upon the trigger and a pair of remarkably clear-sighted eyes upon the grey space of greensward crossed by black trellises of railing immediately before her. That in the mean time was her duty to her love and (she acknowledged it), her master.

Apart from these details of his feeling for Concha, however (which gave him little concern), Rollo was far from satisfied with the condition of affairs. He would rather (so he confided to the Sergeant) have defended a sheepfold or a simple cottage than this many-chambered, many-passaged, mongrel château. His force was scattered out of sight, though for the most part not out of hearing of each other. It was indeed true that, owing to his excellent dispositions, and the fortunate situation of the balconies, he was able to command every part of the castle enclosure, and especially the doors by which it was most likely that the chief attempt would be made.

So occupied had Rollo been with his affairs, both private and of a military character, that he had actually wholly forgotten the presence of the Queen-Regent, her daughter and husband, within the palace of La Granja. And this though he had come all that way across two of the wildest provinces of Spain for the sole purpose of securing their persons and transporting mother and daughter to the camp of Don Carlos. Nevertheless so instant was the danger which now overhung every one, that their intended captor had ceased to think of anything but how to preserve these royal lives and to keep them from the hands of the ruthless gipsies of the hills.

But circumstances quickly recalled the young

man to his primary purpose, and taught him that he must not trust too much to those whose interests were opposed to his own.

Rollo, as we have said, had reserved no station for himself, but constantly circulated round all the posts of his little army, ready at any time to add himself to the effective forces of the garrison at any threatened point. It was while he was thus passing from balcony to balcony on the second or defending storey that his quick ear caught the sound of a door opening and shutting on the floor beneath.

"Ah," thought Rollo to himself, suspiciously, "the Queen and her people are safe in their chambers on this floor. No person connected with the defence ought to be down there. This is either treachery or the enemy have gained admission by some secret passage!"

With Rollo Blair to think was to act. So in another moment he had slipped off his shoes, and treading noiselessly on his stocking soles and with a naked sword in his hand he made his way swiftly and carefully down towards the place whence he had heard the noise.

Descending by the grand *escalier* he found himself in one of the narrow corridors which communicated by private staircases with the left wing of the palace. Rollo stood still in the deepest shadow. He was sure that he could hear persons moving near him, and once he thought that he could distinguish the sound of a muttered word.

The Egyptian darkness about him grew more and more instinct with noises. There was a scuffling rustle, as of birds in a chimney, all over the basement of the house. A door creaked as if a slight wind had blown it. Then a latch clicked, and the wind, unaided, does not click latches. Rollo withdrew himself deeper into a niche at the foot of the narrow winding-stair which girdled a tower in the thickness of the wall.

The young man had almost resolved to summon his whole force from above, so convinced was he that the enemy had gained a footing within the tower and were creeping up to take them in the rear, when a sound altered his intention. There is nothing more unmistakable to the ear than the rebellious whimper of an angry child compelled to do something against its will.

Rollo instantly comprehended the whole chain of circumstances. The treachery touched him more nearly than he had imagined possible. Those for whom he and his party were imperilling their lives were in fact to leave them to perish as best they might in the empty shell of the palace. The royal birds were on the point of flying.

A door opened, and through it (though dimly) Rollo could see the great waterfall glimmering and above the stars, chill over the snowy shoulder of Peñalara. He could not make out who had opened the door, but there was enough light to discern that a lady wrapped in a mantilla went out first. Then followed another, stouter and of shorter stature, apparently carrying a burden. Then the whole doorway was obscured by the tall figure of a man.

"Muñoz himself, by Heaven!" thought Rollo.

And with a leap he was after him, in his headlong course dashing to the ground some other unseen person who confronted him in the hall.

In a moment more he had caught the tall man by the collar and swung him impetuously round back within the doorway.

"Move one sole inch and your blood be on your own head!" he muttered. And the captive feeling Rollo's steel cold at his throat, remained prudently silent. Not so the lady without. She uttered a cry which rang about the silent château.

"Muñoz! My husband! Fernando, where art thou? Oh, they have slain him, and I only am to blame!"

She turned about and rushed back to the door, which she was about to enter, when a cry far more sudden and terrible rang out behind her.

"*They have killed the Princess! Some one hath slain my darling!*"

At the word Rollo abandoned the man whom he was holding down, and with shouts of "Cardono!" "El Sarria!" "To me! They are upon us!" he flung himself outside.

There was little to be discerned clearly when he emerged into the cool damp darkness, only a dim heap of writhing bodies as in some combat of hounds or of the denizens of the midnight forest. But Rollo once and again saw a flash of steel and a hand uplifted to strike. Without waiting to think he gripped that which was topmost and therefore nearest to him, and finding it unexpectedly light, he swung the thing clear by the garment he had clutched. As he did so he felt a pain in his right shoulder, which at the time appeared no more than the bite of a squirrel or the sting of a bee. With one heave he threw the object, human or not he could not for the moment determine, behind him into the blackness of the hall.

"Take hold there, somebody!" he cried, for by this time he could hear the clattering of the feet of his followers on the stairs and flagged passages.

Outside under the stars something or some one larger and heavier lay on the ground and moaned. As Rollo bent over it there came a rush of men from all sides, and the young man had scarcely time to straighten himself up and draw his pistol before he found himself attacked by half a dozen men.

His pistol cracked and an assailant tumbled on his face, while the flash in the pan revealed that he had already an ally. The Sergeant was beside him, by what means did not then appear. For he had certainly not come through the door, and at this Rollo drew a long breath and applied himself to his sword-play with renewed vigour. The assailants, he soon found, were mostly armed with long knives, which, however, had little chance against the long and expert blades of the Sergeant and Rollo.

After proving on several occasions the deadly quality of these last, they broke and ran this way and that, while from the windows above (where the two royal servants were posted, with La Giralda on guard between them), a scattering fire broke out, which tumbled more than one of the fugitives upon the grass.

With great and grave tenderness Rollo and the Sergeant carried that which lay on the grass within. In a moment more they had the door shut and bolted, when from the rear of the hall came the voice of El Sarria.

"For God's sake," he cried, "bring a light! For I have that here which is in human form, yet bites and scratches and howls like a wild beast! I cannot hold it long. It is nothing less than a devil incarnate!"

*　　*　　*　　*　　*

Most strange and incomprehensible of all that

the light revealed, was the appearance of the giant
El Sarria, who, his hands and face bleeding with
scratches, and seated on the final steps of the cork-
screw staircase, held in his arms clear of the ground
the bent and contorted form of a young girl. So
desperate were her struggles that it was all he could
do to confine her feet by passing them under his
arm, while with one great palm he grasped two flat
and meagre wrists in a grip of steel. Yet in spite
of his best efforts the wild thing still struggled, and
indeed more than once came within a hair's-breadth
of fastening her teeth in his cheek.

As he had said, there was more of the wild beast
of the woods taken in a trap than of human creature
in these frantic struggles and inarticulate cries. The
girl foamed at the mouth. She threw herself backward into the shape of a bow till her head almost
touched her feet, and again momentarily twisting
herself like an eel half out of El Sarria's grasp, she
endeavoured, with a force that seemed impossible to
so frail a body, to reach the group by the door, where
Muñoz was still supporting the Queen Maria
Cristina.

Presently Cardono desisted from his examination
of the body of the waiting-woman. He shook his
head murmuring—"Dead! Dead! of a certainty
stone-dead!"

And the Sergeant was a good judge of life and
death. He had seen much of both.

Then he came over to where El Sarria was still
struggling awkwardly with the wild and maniacal
thing, as if he could not bring his great strength
to bear upon a creature so lithe and quick. At the
first glance he started back and turned his gaze on
the royal group.

For that which he now saw, distorted with the impotence of passion and madness, was no other than the little girl whom he had met in the camp of the gipsies on the side of Guadarrama—the daughter of Muñoz, the plan-maker and head-centre of the whole attack.

The Sergeant stood a moment or two fingering his chin, as a man does who considers with himself whether it is worth while shaving. Then with his usual deliberation he undid a leathern strap from his waist and with great consideration but equal effectiveness he buckled the girl's hands firmly behind her back. Then with a sash of silk he proceeded to do the like office with her feet.

Just as he was tying the final knots, the girl made one supreme effort. She actually succeeded in twisting her body out of the arms of El Sarria, and flung herself headlong in the direction of Muñoz and the Queen, spitting like a cat. But the Sergeant's extemporised shackles did their work, and the poor tortured creature would have fallen on her face upon the cold flags of the stone floor but that El Sarria caught her in his arms, and lifting her gently up, proceeded to convey her to another apartment where she might more safely be taken care of.

In order to do this, however, he had to pass close by the Queen-Regent and her consort. It happened that the latter, who till that moment had been wholly occupied by his cares for the recovery of his mistress, had scarcely glanced either at the motionless heap staining the floor with blood or at the wild thing scrambling and biting savagely in the arms of El Sarria.

But the girl's struggles were now over for that time. Her fit of demoniacal fury had apparently

completely exhausted her.   Her head lay back pale
and white, the livid lips drawn so as to show the
teeth in a ghastly smile, and her whole body drooped,
relaxed and flaccid, over her captor's arm.

The Queen-Regent was just able once more to
stand upon her feet when El Sarria passed with his
burden.   The eyes of Muñoz fell upon the girl's
pale distorted features.   He started back and almost
dropped the Queen in his horror.

"Whence came this she-devil?" he cried.
"What is she doing here?   Let her be locked in
a dungeon.   Eugene will show you where.   She
will cut all our throats else!"

"Has this child not the honour to be daughter
to his Excellency the Duke of Rianzares?" inquired
the Sergeant, grimly.

"She is a maniac, I tell you!   I put her in a
madhouse and she escaped!   She hath sworn my
death!" cried Muñoz, his supercilious calm for once
quite broken up.

"And what is this that she hath done?" he cried,
holding up his hands as his eyes fell on the body
of the nurse Susana.   In another moment, however,
he had partially recovered himself.

"My beloved lady," he said, turning to his wife,
"this is certainly no place for you.   Let me conduct
you to your own chamber!"

"Not without the added presence of one of my
people, sir," said Rollo, sternly; "this had not
happened but for your intention of secretly deserting
us, and leaving us to hold the castle alone against
the cruel enemy of whose approach we risked our
lives to warn you!"

Meanwhile the Queen-Regent had been casting
her eyes wildly and uncomprehendingly around.

Now she looked at the motionless form of the girl in the arms of El Sarria, now at the dead woman upon the floor, but all without the least token that she understood how the tragedy had come to pass.

But suddenly she threw her arms into the air and uttered a wild scream.

"Where is my Isabel—where is my daughter? She was in the arms of the nurse Susana who lies there before us. They have killed her also. This devil-born has killed her! Where shall I find her?—My darling—the protected of the Virgin, the future Queen of all the Spains?"

But it was a question no one could answer. None had seen the little Isabel, since the moment when she had passed forth through the portal of the palace into the night, clasped in the faithful arms of her nurse.

She had not cried. She had not returned. Apparently not a soul had thought of her, save only the woman whose life had been laid down for her sake, as a little common thing is set on a shelf and forgotten.

So, for this reason, the question of Maria Cristina remained unanswered. For, even as a star shoots athwart the midnight sky of winter, so the little Queen of Spain had passed and been lost in the darkness and terror without the beleaguered castle of La Granja.

CHAPTER XXXIII

CONCHA WAITS FOR THE MORNING

THE dead woman was carried into the mortuary attached to the smaller chapel of the *Colegiata*, and placed in one of the rude coffins which had been deposited there in readiness upon the first news of the plague. This being done, the mind of Rollo turned resolutely to the problem before him.

Every hour the situation seemed to grow more difficult. As far as Rollo was concerned, he owned himself frankly a mercenary, fighting in a cause for which he, as a free-born Scot, could have no great sympathy. But mercenary as he was, in his reckless, gallant, devil-take-the-hindmost philosophy of life there lurked at least no trace of treachery, nor any back-going from a pledged and plighted word. He had undertaken to capture the young Queen and her mother and to bring them within the lines of Don Carlos, and till utterly baffled by death or misadventure, this was what he was going to continue to attempt.

If therefore the little Princess were not in the castle, she must immediately be sought for outside it. The palace of La Granja was, as he well knew, surrounded by eager and bloody-minded foes, bent on the destruction of all within its walls. It was conceivable that Isabel might already be slain, though

331

in the absence of the daughter of Muñoz, he doubted
whether the gipses would go such lengths. To be
held to ransom was a much more probable fate. At
any rate it was clearly the duty of some one of the
party to make an attempt for her recovery.

At the first blush Sergeant Cardono appeared to
be the person designated by experience and qualifications for the task. But, on the other hand, how
could Rollo entrust to the most famous of ex-
brigands, a gipsy of the gipsies, of the blackest blood
of Egypt, the search for so great a prize as the little
Queen of Spain ? The difficult virtue of self-denial
in such a case could hardly be expected from a man
like José Maria of Ronda. Consider—a ransom, a
Queen put up to auction ! For both sides, Nationals
and Carlists alike, would certainly be eager to treat
for her possession. In short, Rollo concluded that
he had no right to put such a temptation in the way
of a man with the record of Sergeant Cardono.

His thoughts turned next to El Sarria. Concerning Ramon Garcia's loyalty there was no question—
still less as to his courage. But—he was hardly the
man to despatch alone on a mission which involved
so many delicate issues. Once outside the palace
there would in all probability be no chance of return,
and Rollo was persuaded that the best chance of
recovering the child lay in discovering her in some
of the hiding-places which would doubtless be
familiar to her about the grounds. To find the
little maid, to induce her to trust herself completely
to a stranger, and to guide her to a place of safety,
these would be tasks difficult enough for any combination of scout and diplomat. Now El Sarria, upon
meeting with opposition, was accustomed to storm
through it with the rush of a tiger's charge. No,

in spite of his assured fidelity and courage, it would be impossible to send El Sarria.

The others—well, they were good fellows, both of them, John Mortimer and Etienne. But it was obvious to his mind that the quest was not for them.

Rollo must go himself. That was all there was for it. After which remained the question as to who should command in the palace during his absence. Here the Sergeant was obviously the man, both from his natural talents for leadership, as well as from the confidence placed in him by General Cabrera. No such temptation would be presented to him within the walls as might confront him outside, in a position of authority among his blood-kin, and with a Queen of Spain in his power.

Whilst he was settling these questions in his mind, Rollo had been standing at one of the windows, where the two royal servants, young men of Castile, had been set to watch, with La Giralda between to perform the same office upon them. To these he did not think it necessary to say more than that they were to receive and obey the orders of Sergeant Cardono as his own. The old gipsy would of a certainty do so in any case.

Then the young man passed on to the balconies occupied severally by Etienne and Mortimer. These two volunteers he took occasion to commend for their constancy in holding fast their positions during the attack on the other side of the house. He also briefly communicated to them all that had taken place there, the attempt of the royal family to slip off in the darkness, the death of the old nurse, the capture of the daughter of Muñoz, and the fatal loss of the young Queen.

He further told them that he considered it his duty to venture out to seek for the missing girl. It came within the terms of his commission, he said, that he should leave no stone unturned to recover the Princess. Neither Etienne nor Mortimer offered any objection.

"The saints and the Holy Virgin bring you safely back," said Etienne, who was still in his pious mood; "I will not cease to pray for you."

"Good-bye, and good-luck, old fellow!" quoth John Mortimer. "But I say, if I should want more ammunition, where am I to get it?"

Such were the characteristic farewells of Rollo's two comrades in arms.

Equally simple was it to satisfy El Sarria, from whom our Firebrand parted on the great southward balcony which the outlaw guarded alone.

"Be of an easy mind. I will be responsible for all I can see from this balcony!" said the giant, calmly, "may your adventure be prosperous! I would I could both remain here and come with you!"

All that Rollo had now to do was to inform the Sergeant of his plans and to say good-bye to Concha. These tasks, however, promised something more of difficulty.

The Sergeant was immovable at his post behind the thick twisted vine-stems of the little balcony, over the twin doors, by one of which the royal party had attempted to escape into the garden. While Rollo was explaining his intentions, Cardono bit his lip and remained silent.

"Do you then not approve?" asked Rollo, gravely, when he had finished.

"Who is to command here in your absence?"

answered the Sergeant in the young Scot's own national manner.

"The command will naturally devolve on yourself," said Rollo, promptly; "you will have the entire responsibility within the palace!"

"Which includes complete discretion, of course?"

"Certainly!" answered Rollo.

"Then," said the Sergeant, firmly, "my first act will be to lay Señor Don Fernando Muñoz by the heels!"

"As to that, you can do as you like," said Rollo, "but remember that you may find yourself with another mad woman on your hands in the person of the Queen-Regent!"

"I know how to deal with her!" replied the Sergeant; "go your way, Colonel—depend upon it, the palace will be defended and justice done!"

Rollo nodded, and was turning on his heel without speaking, for the thought of his interview with Concha was beginning to lie heavy on his mind, when a whisper from the Sergeant called him back.

"When you are ready to go, return hither," he said; "I have the safest way out of the palace to show you without so much as the opening of a door or the unbarring of a window."

Rollo nodded again. He marvelled how it was that the Sergeant had appeared so opportunely at his elbow when he had called upon him for help. Now he was in the way of finding out.

The darkness was of the sort which might have been felt as Rollo stumbled along the passages to the opposite side of the palace where Concha, a loaded musket leaning against the wall on either side, was watching keenly the square of grey grass and green trees in front of her. Dark as the night was without, the girl had drawn the curtains behind her, so that she was entirely isolated upon the balcony on which she kneeled. In this, as usual, she had obeyed Rollo's commands to the letter, and made sure that no faintest gleam of light should escape by the window at which she kept her watch.

But spite of the intervening room and the thick curtains the girl had heard his footsteps, light and quick, heard them across the entire breadth of the palace, from the moment when he had quitted Sergeant Cardono, to that when, drawing aside the hangings with his hand, he stood behind her.

Nevertheless, Concha did not move immediately, and Rollo, standing thus close to her, was, for the first time in his life, conscious of the atmosphere, delicate yet vivid, of youth, beauty, and charm, with which a loving and gracious woman surrounds herself as with a garment.

But these were stern times. He had come to her balcony for a purpose and—there was no time to be lost.

"Concha," he began without ceremony—for after the kiss, regulated and conscientious as it had been and clearly justifiable to his sense of honour and duty, somehow the prefacing "Señorita" had come to be omitted between them. "Concha, the little Queen is lost! She may be wandering out there to meet her death among brigands and murderers! It is my duty to go and seek her. Listen!"

And then when at last she turned from the window and slowly faced him, Rollo told her all that had taken place below.

"I knew you were in danger when the shots went off," she said; "yet since you had not called for me, nor given me leave to quit my post——"

She did not finish her sentence. It was a kind of reproach that he had called for the Sergeant and not for her in his hour of need. She knew on whom *she* would have called.

"You did well—better than well—to stand by your post," said Rollo; "but now I must make over my authority to another. The Sergeant is to command here in my absence."

"Do you then make *my* allegiance over to the Sergeant?" asked Concha, in a quiet tone.

"God forbid!" cried Rollo, impetuously.

And little Concha, looking abroad over the darkling hills, thought within her heart that her morning was surely coming. It might be some time on the way, but all the same it was coming.

But yet when he told her of the desperate quest on which he was bound, that which had been glad became filled with foreboding, and the false dawn died out again utterly. The hills were both distant and dark.

But as Rollo continued to speak bravely, confidently, and took her hand to ask her bid him Godspeed, Concha smiled once more to herself in the darkness. And so, at the last, it came about that she even held up her lips to be kissed. For now (so strangely natural grows this quaint custom after one or two experiments) it seemed as if no other method of saying good-bye were possible between them. And to Rollo the necessity appeared even stronger.

But was this the reason of Concha's smile in the darkness? Or was it because she thought?—"He is indeed the prince of youths, and can lay his orders on whom he will, binding and loosing like Peter with the Keys. But there is that in the heart of a woman which even he cannot bind, for all his good opinion of himself!"

z

Yet stranger than all, she thought none the worse of Master Rollo for his confidence and heady self-conceit. And what is more, she let him go from her without a murmur, though she knew that her heart of hearts was his. And that above all carrying off of queens and honours military, more than many towns captured and battles won, she wished to hear from Rollo Blair's lips that his heart also was her own—her very own. Many men had told her that same thing in these very words, and she had only laughed back at them with a flash of brilliant teeth, a pair of the blackest Andalusian eyes shining meantime with contemptuous mirth.

But now, it seemed that if she did not hear Rollo say this thing, she would die—which shows the difference there may be between words which we desire to hear spoken and those that others wish to speak to us.

Yet in spite of all, or because of it, she let him go without a word or a murmur, because of the hope of morning that was in her heart.

CHAPTER XXXIV

OUR ROLLO TO THE RESCUE

And this was the manner of his going. He sought the Sergeant upon his balcony, outside which climbed and writhed a great old vine-stem as thick as a man's leg. He was for taking Killiecrankie by his side, against the Sergeant's advice.

"Killiecrankie and I," he urged, with the buckle in his hand, "have been in many frays together, and I have never known him fail me yet."

"A sword like a weaver's beam is monstrously unhandy dangling between the legs!" replied the Sergeant, "and that you will find before you are at the foot of yonder vine-stock. Take a pair of pistols and a good Albacete leech. That is my advice. I think I heard El Sarria say that you had some skill of knife-play in the Andalusian manner."

"So, so," returned Rollo, modestly. "I should not like to face you—your left hand to my right. But with most other men I might make bold to hold my own."

"Good!" said the Sergeant; "now listen. Let yourself down, hand-grip by hand-grip, clipping the vine-stem as best you may with your knees to make the less noise. You will be wholly hidden by the outer leaves. Move slowly, and remember I am here to keep watch and ward. Then stand a while in the shadow to

339

recover your breath, and when you hear me whistle thrice like a swallow's twitter underneath the eaves, duck down as low as you can and make straight for the thickest of the underbrush over there. I have watched it for an hour and have seen nothing move. Yet that signifies less than nothing. There may be a score, aye, or a hundred gipsies underneath the branches, and the frogs croaking undisturbed upon the twigs above all the while. Yet it is your only chance. If you find anything there in shape of man, strike and cry aloud, both with all your might, and in a moment I will be with you, even as I was before."

Rollo grasped the Sergeant's hand and thanked him silently as brave men thank one another at such times.

" Nay," said the Sergeant, "let us wait till we return for that. It is touch and go at the best. But I will stay here till you are safely among the bushes. And then—I shall have some certain words to speak to Señor Don Fernando Muñoz, Duke of Rianzares and grandee of Spain, Consort in ordinary to her Majesty the Queen-Regent !"

Even as he spoke, Rollo, whose ears were acute, turned quickly and dashed into the ante-chamber. He thought he had heard a footstep behind them as they talked. And at the name of Muñoz a suspicion crossed him that some further treachery was meditated. But the little upper hall was vague and empty, the scanty furniture scarce sufficient to stumble against. If any one had been there, he had melted like a ghost, for neither Rollo's swift decision nor the Sergeant's omniscient cunning could discover any trace of an intruder.

Rollo attempted no disguise upon his adventure.

He wore the same travel-stained suit, made to fit his slender figure by one of the most honest tailors in Madrid, in which he first appeared in this history. So with no more extent of preparation for his adventure than settling his sombrero a little more firmly upon his head and hitching his waist-belt a hole or two tighter, Rollo slipped over the edge of the iron balcony and began to descend by the great twisted vine-stem.

He did not find the task a difficult one. For he was light and agile, firmed by continuous exercise, and an adept at the climbing art. As he had been, indeed, ever since, on the east-windy braes of Fife, where swarming rookeries crown the great hog-back ridges, he had risen painfully through the clamour of anxious parents to possess himself of a hatful of speckled bluish-green eggs for the collection wherewith he was to win the tricksome and skittish heart of Mistress Peggy Ramsay, who (tell it not in the ducal house which her charms now adorn!) was herself no inexpert tree-climber in the days when Rollo Blair temporarily broke his boyish heart for her sake.

So in brief (and without a thought of Peggy) Rollo found himself upon the ground, his dress a little disordered and his hands somewhat scratched, but safe behind his screen of leaves. Remembering the advice of the Sergeant, Rollo waited for the appointed signal to fall upon his ear from above. He could see nothing indeed across the lawn but the branches of the pine trees waving low, and beneath them feathery syringa bushes, upland fern, and evergreens with leathery leaves.

What might be hidden there? In another moment he might rush upon the points of a hundred

knives. Another minute, and, like the good Messire
François, curé of Meudon, it might be his to set forth
in quest of the Great Perhaps.

At the thought he shrugged his shoulders and
repeated to himself those other last words of the
same learned doctor of Montpellier, " Ring down
the curtain—the farce is over ! "

But at that same moment he thought of little
Concha up aloft and the bitterness died out of his
heart as quickly as it had come.

No, the play was not yet played out, and it had
been no farce.   There was yet other work for him—
perhaps another life better than this cut-and-thrust
existence, ever at the mercy of bullet and sword's
point.   He stood up straight and listened, hearing
for the first five minutes nothing but the soft wind
of the night among the leaves, and from the town
the barking of the errant and homeless curs which,
in the streets and gutters, yelped, scrambled, and
tore at each other for scraps of offal and thrice-
gnawed bone.

From above came the contented twitter of a
swallow nestling under the leaves, yet with a curious
carrying quality in it too, at once low and far-
reaching.   It was the Sergeant's signal for his
attempt.

Rollo set his teeth hard, thought of Concha,
bent his head low, and, like a swift-drifting shadow,
sped silently across the smooth upland turf.   The
thick leaves of the laurel parted before him, the
sword-flower of Spain pricked him with its pointed
leaves, and then closed like a spiked barrier behind
him.   A blackbird fled noisily to quieter haunts.
The frogs ceased their croaking.   Panting, Rollo
lay still under the branches, crushing out the perfume

of the scrubby, scented geranium, which in the watered wildernesses of La Granja takes root everywhere.

But among the leaves nothing moved hand or foot against him. Nor gipsy nor mountaineer stirred in the thicket. So that when Rollo, after resting a little, explored quietly and patiently the little plantation, going upon all fours, not a twig of pine crackling under his palms, no hostile knife sheathed itself between his ribs.

For, as was now clear, the gipsies had not concealed themselves among the bushes. They had all night before them in which to carry out their projects. Doubtless (thought the young man) they had gone to possess themselves of the town. After that the palace would lie at their mercy, a nut to be cracked at their will.

From the first Rollo was resolved to find the little pavilion of which La Giralda had spoken. It was in his mind that the girl might, if free and unharmed, as he hoped, make her way thither. He had indeed only the most vague and general idea of its locality. The old gipsy had told him that it was near to the northern margin of the gardens, and that by following the mountain stream which supplied the great waterfall he could not fail to come upon it.

But ere he had ventured forth from his hiding-place, he heard again the swallow's twitter, louder than before, and evidently meant for his ear. Could it be a natural echo or his own disordered fancy which caused a whistle exactly similar to reach him from the exact locality he meant to search?

Rollo moved to that extremity of the thicket from whence the more regular gardens were visible. He concealed himself behind a pomegranate tree, and, while he stood and listened, mellow and clear the call came again from the vicinity of the waterfall.

But Rollo was not of those who turn back. Good-byes are difficult things to say twice within the same half-hour. No, he had burnt his boats and would rather go forward into the camp of a thousand gipsies than climb up the vine-stem and face the Sergeant and Concha with his task undone. Shame of this kind has often more to do with acts of desperate courage than certain other qualities more besung by poets.

It was obvious, therefore, that the gipsies were still within the enclosure of the palace, so Rollo gave up the idea of keeping straight up the little artificial rivulet, whose falls gleamed wanly before him, each square and symmetrical as a flag hung out of the window on a still day.

To the left, however, there were thickets of red geranium, the Prince's Flower of Old Castilian lore, five or six feet high. Among these Rollo lost himself, passing through them like a shadow, his head drooped a little, and his knife ready to his hand.

When he was halfway along the edge of the royal demesne he saw across the open glade a strange sight, yet one not unwelcome to him.

The palace storehouses had been broken into. Lights moved to and fro from door to door, and above from window to window. A train of mules and donkeys stood waiting to be loaded. Thieves' mules they were, without a single bell or bit jingling anywhere about their accoutrements.

Then Rollo understood in a moment why no further attack had been made upon the palace. To the ordinary gipsy of the roads and hills—half smuggler, half brigand, the stores of Estramenian hams, the granaries full of fine wheat of the Castiles, of maize and rice ready to be loaded upon their beasts, were more than all possible revenges upon queens and grandees of Spain.

In losing the daughter of Muñoz they had lost both inspiration and cohesion, and now the natural man craved only booty, and that as plentifully and as safely as possible. So there in the night torches were lighted, and barn and byre, storehouse and cellar were ransacked for those things which are most precious to men gaunt and lantern-jawed with the hunger of a plague-stricken land.

After this discovery the young Scot moved much more freely and fearlessly. For it explained what had been puzzling him, how it came about that so far no sustained or concerted attack had been made upon the palace.

And this same careless confidence of his, for a reason which will presently appear, had well-nigh wrecked his plans. All suddenly Rollo came upon the open door of a little low building, erected something after the model of a Greek temple. It was undoubtedly the pavilion which had been mentioned by La Giralda as the place where the goats had been milked.

Of this Rollo was further assured by the collection of shining silver utensils which were piled for removal before the door. A light burned dimly within. It was a dark lantern set on a shelf, among broken platters and useless crockery. The door was open and its light fell on half a dozen dusky figures gathered in a knot about some central object which the young man was not able to see.

Rollo recoiled into the reeds as if a serpent had

bitten him. Then parting the tall tasselled canes carefully, he gazed out upon the curious scene. A window stood open in the rear of the building, and the draught blew the flame of the open lantern about, threatening every moment to extinguish it.

One of the gipsies, observing this, moved to the bracket-shelf to close the glass bull's-eye of the lantern.

A couple of others looked after him to see what he was about, and through the gap thus made Rollo saw, with only a shawl thrown over her white night-gear, the little Queen herself, held fast in a gipsy's bare and swarthy arms.

"I have told you before," he heard her say in her clear childish treble, "I know nothing—I will tell nothing. I have nothing to give you, and if I had a whole world I would not give a *maravedi's* worth to you. You are bad men, and I hate you!"

Rollo could not hear what the men said in reply, but presently as one dusky ruffian bent over the girl, a thin cord in his hand, high and bitter rose a child's cry of pain.

It went straight to Rollo's heart. He had heard nothing like it since Peggy Ramsay got a thorn in her foot the day he had wickedly persuaded her to strip and run barefoot over the meadows of Castle Blair. He compressed his lips, and moved his knife to see that the haft came rightly to his hand. Then as calmly as if practising at a mark he examined his pistols and with the utmost deliberation drew a bead upon the burly ruffian with the cord. The first pistol cracked, and the man dropped silently. Instantly there ensued a great commotion within. The most part of the gipsies rushed to the door, standing for a moment clear against the lighted interior.

Rollo, all on fire with the idea that the villains had been torturing a child, fired his second pistol into the thick of them, upon which arose a sudden sharp shriek and a furious rushing this way and that. The lamp was blown out or knocked over in the darkness, and Rollo, hesitating not a moment, snapped back the great Albacetan blade into its catch and rushed like a charging tiger at the door. Twice on his way was he run against and almost overturned by fugitives from the pavilion. On each occasion his opponents' fear of the mysterious fusillade, aided by a sharp application of the point of the *Albacete*, cleared Rollo's front. He stumbled over a body prone on the ground, caught his hand on the cold stone lintel, and in a moment was within.

He said aloud, "Princess Isabel, I am your friend! Trust me! I have come to deliver you from these wicked people!"

But there was no answer, nor did he discover the little Queen's hiding-place till an uncontrollable sobbing guided him to the spot.

The child was crouching underneath the polished stove with which in happier days she had so often played. Rollo took the little maid in his arms.

"Do not be afraid," he whispered, "I, Rollo Blair, am your friend; I will either take you to your friends or lay down my life for you. Trust me!—Do what I tell you and all will be well!"

"Your voice sounds kind, though I cannot see your face," she whispered; "yes, I will go with you!"

He lifted her up on his left arm, while in his

right hand he held the knife ready to be plunged to the hilt into any breast that withstood him.

One swift rush and they were without among the reeds.

"I will take you to your mother—I promise it," he said, "but first you must come through the town with me to the Hermitage of the good friars. The palace is surrounded with wicked men to-night. We cannot go back there, but to-morrow I will surely take you to your mother!"

"I do not want to go to my mother," whispered the little Queen, "only take me to my dear, *dearest* Doña Susana!"

And then it was that Rollo first realised that he had undertaken something beyond his power.

CHAPTER XXXV

THE EXECUTIONER OF SALAMANCA

But, indeed, the problem before Rollo was one difficult enough to cause him to postpone indefinitely all less immediate and pressing evils. As they lay hid among the reeds, and while Rollo endeavoured more completely to gain the good-will of the little Queen, they heard the bell of the Hermitage of San Ildefonso strike the hour sonorously.

Rollo could hardly believe his ears as the number lengthened itself out till he had counted twelve. He had supposed that it must be three or four in the morning at the least. But the night had worn slowly. Many things which take long to tell had happened in brief space, and, what to Rollo appeared worst of all, it would be yet some five hours till daylight.

As they crouched among the canes, the effect of his sudden discomfiture of the captors of the child Isabel became apparent. The whole palace was ringed with a sudden leaping fire of musketry. The angry fusillade was promptly answered from the balconies, and Rollo had the satisfaction of knowing, from the shouts and yells of pain and fury beneath, that not only were his folk on the alert, but that he had reason to be satisfied with the excellence of their marksmanship.

More than one rambling party of gipsies passed

their hiding-place. But these for the most part searched in a perfunctory manner, their heads over their shoulders to listen to the progress of their comrades who were attacking the palace, and perhaps also no little afraid lest death should again leap out upon them from the darkness of the cane-brake. Rollo, immediately upon his return to the thicket, had recovered and recharged his pistols by touch, and presently, having made all ready, he caught up the little girl in his arms, urging her to be silent whatever happened, and to trust everything to him.

Isabel, who was of an affectionate and easy disposition, though ever quick to anger, put her arm readily about the young man's neck. He had a winsome and gracious manner with all children, which perhaps was the same quality that won him his way with women.

Rollo had an idea which had come to him with the chime of the Hermitage bell as it tolled the hour of midnight. There, if anywhere, he would find good men, interested in the welfare of the Princess, and with hearts large enough to remain calmly at the post of duty even in a deserted and plague-ruined town. For one of the chief glories of the Roman Church is this, that her clergy do not desert their people in the hour of any danger, however terrible. Nothing else, indeed, is thought of. As a military man would say, " It is the tradition of the service ! "

Now if Rollo had been in his own Scottish land during the visitation of this first cholera, he would have had good grounds for *hoping* that he would find the ministers of his faith in the thick of the fight with death, undismayed, never weary. There were many, very many such—many, but very far from all. The difference was that here in ignorant Spain Rollo knew without deduction that of a certainty the monks and parish priests of the ancient creed would be faithful.

It might indeed in some cases be otherwise with some selfish and pampered Jesuits or the benefice-seeking rabble of clerics who hang about the purlieus of a court. A father-confessor or two might flee overseas, an abbot go on timely pilgrimage to Rome, but here in San Ildefonso, Rollo knew that he would either find the priests and holy brothers of the Church manfully doing their noble work, or dead and in their sainted graves—in any case, again in military phrase, "all present or all accounted for !"

To the Hermitage of San Ildefonso, therefore, recently enlarged and erected into a monastery, Rollo directed his steps. It was no easy task at such a time. There was the great railing to negotiate, and a passage to force through a town by this time alive with enemies. In spite of the darkness the gipsies at any point might stop his way, and he was burdened with a child whom he must protect at all hazards.

But this young man loved to be driven into a corner. Danger excited him, as drinking might another man. Indeed, so quick were his parts, so ready his invention, that before he had left the reed-bed he had turned over and rejected half a dozen plans of escape. Yet another suggested itself, to which for the moment he could see no objection.

He spoke to the little Isabel, who now nestled closely and confidently to him.

"Did they not tell me," he said, "that there was somewhere about the palace a dairy of cows ?"

"Yes—it is true," answered the little Queen;

"at least, there is a place where they are brought in to be milked. It belongs to my mother. She loves them all, and often used to take me there to enjoy the sight and to drink the milk warm with the froth upon it because it is good for the breathing !"

"Can you show me the way, little Princess Isabel ?" said Rollo.

"Yes, that can I, indeed," she made answer; "but you must not take away my mother's milk-pails, nor let the wicked gipsies know of them. Old Piebald Pedro drives the cows in and out every day, riding upon his donkey. They live at my mother's farm in the valley that is called in French ' Sans Souci !' Is it not a pretty name ?"

"His donkey ?" said Rollo, quickly, catching at the idea ; "where does he keep it ?"

"In a little shed not far from the dairy," she answered, " the stable is covered all over with yellow canes, and it stands near a pool where the green frogs croak !"

It had been Rollo's intention to drive some of the royal cows out before him as a booty, passing himself off as one of the gipsy gang. But upon this information he decided that Pedro the cowherd's ass would suit his purpose much better, if he should be fortunate enough to find it. He was sure that among so many gipsies and ill-conditioned folk who had joined the tribes of Egypt for the sake of adventure and booty, there must be many who were personally unknown to each other. And though he could not speak deep Romany like La Giralda and the Sergeant, Rollo was yet more expert at the " crabbed Gitano " than nine out of ten of the northern gipsies, who, indeed, for the most part use a mere thieves' slang, or as it is called, *Tramper's Dutch.*

The little girl directed him as well as she could, nevertheless it was some time before he could find the place he was in quest of. For Isabel had never been out at night before, and naturally the forms of all things appeared strangely altered to an imaginative child. Indeed, it may be admitted that Rollo stumbled upon the place more by good luck than because he was guided thither by the advice of Isabel. For the utmost the child could tell him was only that Piebald Pedro's hut was near the dairy, and that the dairy was near Pedro's hut.

The donkey itself, however, perhaps excited by the proximity of so many of its kind (though no one of the thieves' beasts had made the least actual noise), presently gave vent to a series of brays which guided them easily to the spot.

Rollo set the Princess on the ground, bidding her watch by the door and tell him if any one came in sight. But the little girl, not yet recovered from her fright, clung to his coat and pled so piteously to be allowed to stay with him, that he could not insist. First of all he groped all around the light cane-wattled walls of Pedro's hut for any garment which might serve to disguise him. For though Rollo's garments were by no means gay, they were at least of somewhat more fashionable cut than was usual among the gipsies and their congeners.

After a little Rollo found the old cowherd's milking-blouse stuffed in an empty corn-chest among scraps of harness, bits of rope, nails, broken gardening-tools, and other collections made by the Piebald One in the honest exercise of his vocation. He pulled the crumpled old garment out and donned it without scruple. His own *sombrero*, much the worse for wear and weather, served well enough, with the brim turned down, to give the young man the appearance of a peasant turned brigand for the nonce.

His next business was to conceal the little girl in order that they might have a chance of passing the gipsy picket at the gates, and of escaping chance questionings by the way.

Rollo therefore continued to search in the darkness till he had collected two large bundles, one of chopped straw, and the other of hay, which he stuffed into the panniers, in the larger of which he meant to find room also for the Princess. Once settled, a sheet was thrown over her shoulders, and the hay lightly scattered over all. Then she was ordered to lie down and to keep especially still if she should hear any one speak to her companion. And so naturally did the little girl take to secrecy and adventure that after having assured herself of Rollo's kindness, not a murmur passed her lips.

On the contrary, she promised all careful obedience, and it was no great while before they set out, making so bold as to pass once more by her own private kitchen. For Rollo had resolved to take possession of some of the silver utensils, that he might have somewhat wherewith to satisfy plunderers if they should chance to be stopped, and the ass's burdens in danger of being too closely examined.

They found the silver vessels and pans lying where they had been piled outside the door. Apparently no one had been near them. One of the gipsies, however, who had been wounded, still lay groaning without, cursing the cravens who had left him and fled at a couple of pistol shots. But the other, he who had first been dealt with by Rollo's bullet out of the cane-brake, gave no sign. He lay still, shot through the heart, the torture-cord still in his hand.

Without taking the least notice of the wounded man, Rollo coolly loaded the silver dishes upon his own shoulders, placing one or two of the largest copper pans upon the donkey in such a manner as to shelter the Princess from observation should any one turn a lantern upon them on their way to the Hermitage of San Ildefonso.

They kept wide of the palace itself, however, for though the fire had slackened, and the besieged only replied when one of their assailants incautiously showed himself, yet the place was evidently still completely beset, and the loaded trains of mules and donkeys departing from the storehouses had released many of the younger and more adventurous gipsies, who had brought no beast with them on which to carry off their plunder.

At about the same time, a red glow began to wax and wane uncertainly above the granaries most distant from Rollo and his charge. A ruddy volume of smoke slowly disengaged itself from the roofs. Windows winked red, glowed, and then spouted flame. It was evident that the gipsies had fired the plundered storehouses.

In their own interests the act was one of the worst policy. For their movements, which had hitherto been masked in darkness, now became clear as day, while the advantages of the besieged within the palace were greatly increased.

But (what principally concerns us) the matter happened ill enough for Rollo and the little Queen. They had to pass under the full glare of the fire, through groups of gipsies assembled about the great gate, chaffering and disputing. But there appeared to Rollo at least a chance of getting past unobserved, for all seemed to be thoroughly occupied with their own business. Rollo accordingly settled the little Queen deeper in the great pannier, and readjusted the hay over her. He then hung an additional pair of copper vessels across the crupper, chirruped to the beast, and went forward to face his fate with as good a heart as might be within his breast.

"Whither goest thou, brother?" cried a voice from behind him, just when Rollo was full between the portals of the great gate.

"Brother, I go into the town to complete my plunder," answered Rollo in Romany, "and to help my kinsfolk of the Gitano!"

"Strangely enough thou speakest, brother," was the reply; "thy tongue is not such as we wanderers of the Castiles speak one to the other!"

Rollo laughed heartily at this, his hand all the while gripping the pistol on his thigh.

"Indeed," said he, "it were great marvel an it were. For I am of Lorca, which is near to Granada; and what is more, I am known there as a very pretty fellow with my hands!"

"I doubt it not," said the Castilian gipsy, turning away; "and not to speak of the pistol, that is a pretty enough plaything of a tooth-pick which hangs at thy girdle, brother!"

As he turned carelessly away he pointed to the long knife the Sergeant had given Rollo, and which, owing to some mysterious marks upon its handle, proved on more than one occasion of service to him.

Presently, as he was urging his donkey to the

left out of the silent town, he came upon a knot of
gipsies who stood with heads all bent together as if
in consultation. They were deep within the shadow
of an archway a little raised above the level of the
street, and Rollo could not see them before he was,
as it were, under their noses. One of them, a great
brawny hulk of a man, sun-blackened to the hue
of an Arab of the Rif, struck his knuckles with
a clang on the brazen vessel which sheltered the
little Queen.

Rollo caught his breath, for it seemed certain
that the child must cry out with fear.

But the little maid abode silent, her Spanish heart
taking naturally to concealments and subterfuges—
then, as in after years.

"Ha, brother," said this great hulk in deep
tones, and in better Romany than the former had
used, "thou art strangely modest in thy plundering.
Hay and straw, brass kettles and tin skillets, my
friend, are like that neatherd's cloak of thine, they
cover a multitude of things better worth having.
What hast thou there under thy pots and pans?"

The young man's often tried fate stood again on
tiptoe. He knew well that he was within a pin-
prick of getting his throat cut from ear to ear. But
nevertheless the cool head and fiery heart which were
the birthright of Rollo Blair once more brought
him through. He instantly laid his hand upon
his knife-handle and half drew it from its leathern
sheath.

"I would have you know, sir," he cried in an
incensed tone, "that I am Ruiz Elicroca of Lorca,
own sister's son to José Maria of Ronda, who gave me
this knife, as you may see by the handle. I am not
to be imposed upon by cut-purses and bullies—no,

not though they were as big as a church, and as black-angry as the devil on a saint's day!"

The huge fellow fell back a step, with a sort of mockery of alarm, before Rollo's vehemence. For he had advanced into the middle of the highway, so as to bar the path by the mere bulk of his body. He appeared better satisfied, however, though by no means intimidated.

"Well," he growled, "you are a cockerel off a good dung-hill, if things be as you say. At all events you crow not unhandsomely. But whither go you in that direction? You are well laden as to your shoulders, my young friend. That plate looks as if it might be silver. I warrant it would melt down into a hundred good *duros* with the double pillar upon each of them. You need not want for more. But turn and go another way. The Hermitage is yet to be tapped, and I warrant that monk's roost hath good store of such-like—gold and silver both. That we claim as ours, remember!"

"And, sir, what do you expect one man to do?" cried Rollo. "Can I take and rob the armed and defended retreat of the friars? I warrant they have either buried their plate in a safe place or have kept a sufficient guard there to protect it—even as they have up yonder. Hark to them!"

The sound of a brisk interchange of shots came to their ears from the direction of the palace.

"These be young fools who run their heads against stone walls," said the huge gipsy; "we are wiser men. They seek gold, and are in danger of getting lead. Like you, we will be content with silver. Altar furniture is by no means to be despised. It fits the melting-pot as egg-meat fits egg-shell! But whither do you fare?"

"I am passing in this direction solely that I may reach a place known to my uncle and myself, where the pair of us have a rendezvous," answered Rollo; "mine uncle Don José hath no wish to meddle in other men's matters, as indeed he told some of you yesterday morning. But as for me, seeing that I was young of my years and desired to make my mark, he permitted me to come. But I would rather give up all my booty, though honestly taken with the strong hand, than keep José Maria waiting!"

The Moorish gipsy now laughed in his turn.

"Nay, that I doubt not," he said, "but here we are all good fellows, right Roms, true to each other, and would rob no honest comrade of that for which he hath risked his life. Pass on, brother, and give to José Maria of Ronda the respects of Ezquerra, the executioner, who on the Plaza Mayor of Salamanca removed the spike from the iron cravat that so deftly marked him for life!"

With a burst of gratitude quick and sincere, Rollo seized the huge hand and wrung it heartily.

"You saved José Maria's life," he cried, "then mine is at your service!"

"Pass on, boy," smiled Ezquerra, grimly; "it is not the first time, since I became usher to the Nether World, that I have been able to do a friend and brave comrade a good turn. Only warn him that now they have a new operator at Salamanca in whose veins circulates no drop of the right black blood of Egypt. He must not try the collar twice!"

Rollo passed on with his donkey, and he was into the second street before he dared to lift the covering of hay which hid the child. He expected to find her in a swoon with fright or half dead with fear and anxiety. Isabel the Second was neither.

" Take off that platter of metal," she whispered;
" what funny talk you speak. It sounded like cats
spitting. You must teach it to me afterwards when
Doña Susana is out of the way. For she is very
strict with me and will only let me learn French and
Castilian, saying that all other languages are only
barbarian and useless, which indeed may well be ! "

" Hush," said Rollo ; " we are not yet in safety.
Here is the way to the Hermitage ! "

" But will you teach me the cat language ? "

" Yes, yes, that I will and gladly," quoth Rollo
to the little Queen, anxious to buy her silence on
any terms, " as soon, that is, as there is time ! "

After passing the gate and the group collected
there, Rollo had turned rapidly to the right, and
soon the ancient walls of the Ermita of San Ildefonso
rose before him, gleaming dimly through the dense
greenery of the trees. If any of the fathers, who
made their home at that sacred place, still remained,
the outside of the building gave no sign of their
presence.

But it was not a time for Rollo to stand on any
ceremony. With a rough tug at the rein he compelled the donkey to follow a narrow winding path
which, entering at an angle, made its way finally to
the main door of the Hermitage. The young man
thundered at the knocker, but, receiving no answer,
he selected a flattish stone of a size suitable for passing between the iron *grille* of the window-bars, and
threw it up at them with all his force. The jingling
of glass followed, upon which presently a white face
was seen behind the bars, and a mild voice inquired
his business.

" The brethren are either asleep or gone about
the affairs of their order in the town," the monk

said; "there is no general hospitality here in time of plague!"

"I have not come to claim any," said Rollo; "I am here to warn you that San Ildefonso is in the hands of wicked and cruel men—gipsies of the mountains! Call your Superior and admit me at once!"

"Alas," answered the man, "our Prior is dead! I am only almoner here, and there are but three of us left. All the others are dead among the sick folk of the town. They laboured till they died. I have laboured also to provide them food when they could crawl back for it—setting it in the guest-chamber and going out again upon their arrival—God knows, not from any fear of the infection, but because if I chanced to be taken our work would be at an end. For none of the others can so much as cook an omelette or dish up a spoonful of *gazpacho* fit for any son of man to eat."

"Well," said Rollo, "at any rate let me in. I carry no infection and the time is short. I will help you to hold your Hermitage against the malefactors!"

"But how," answered the monk, shrewdly, "can I be certain that you are not of the gang, and that if I open the door a hundred of you will not rush in and slay me and us all out of hand?"

Rollo put his hand into the pannier of his ass and raised the Princess upon his arm.

"Turn a light upon this little lady," he said, "and see whether she will not convince you of my good intent!"

It was a moment or two before the man returned with a lantern, and directed the stream of light downwards.

"The young Queen!" he cried aghast; "what is she doing here at this hour of the night?"

"Let me in, and I will tell you," cried the lady herself, "quick—do you hear? I will complain to Father Ignacio, my mother's confessor, if you do not, and you will be deprived of your office. You will be put on bread and water, and very like have your head cut off as well!"

In a minute more they heard the noise of the pulling of bolts and bars, and were presently admitted into the little whitewashed hall of the Ermita de San Ildefonso. There they found themselves face to face with four monks in white habits, their faces pale and grave in the candle-light. They gave Rollo no sign of welcome, but each of them bowed his head low to the little Queen and then glanced inquiringly at her protector.

"Let the *burro* enter also," commanded Rollo. "Thrice I have been stopped on the way, and if our enemies find the ass without they will be the readier to believe that I have hidden my treasure with you!"

Then in the little whitewashed refectory, before the simple table on which the fathers, now sadly reduced in numbers, took their repasts, Rollo told his story. And, sinking on her knees devoutly before the great crucifix that hung over the mantelpiece, the little Queen repeated her childish prayers as placidly as if she had been at her nurse's knees in the royal palace at Madrid, with the sentries posted duly, and the tramp of the guard continually passing without.

CHAPTER XXXVI

THE DEATH-CART

THUS came the little Isabel of Spain into sanctuary.
That the respite could only be temporary, Rollo
knew too well. The monks were stout and willing
men, but such arms as they had belonged to almost
primitive times, chiefly old blunderbusses of various
patterns from the middle of the sixteenth century to
the end of the eighteenth, together with a halberd or
two which had been used from time immemorial in
the Hermitage kitchen for breaking bones to get out
the marrow, chopping firewood, and such like humble
and peaceful occupations.

Two of the remaining brothers of the Ermita were
as other men, plain, simple and devout, ready to give
up their lives, either by dying of disease at their
post of duty, or by the steel of cruel and ignorant
men, as the martyrs and confessors of whom they
read in their breviaries had done in times past.

The cook-almoner on the other hand proved to
be a shrewd little man, with much ready conversation,
a great humorist at most times, yet not without a due
regard for his own safety. Him the little Princess
knew well, having often stolen off through the gardens
and down the long " Mall " to taste his confectioned
cakes, made in the Austrian manner after a receipt
which dated from the time of the founder of blessed

363

memory, Henry the Fourth of that name, and often partaken of by Catholic sovereigns when they drove out to the lofty grange and Hermitage of the Segovian monks of El Parral.

The fourth and principal friar proved upon acquaintance to be a man of another mould. He was a tall square-shouldered man, now a little bent with age, but with the fires of loyalty burning deep within eyes of the clearest and most translucent blue. His hair was now quickly frosting over with premature infirmity, for not only was his constitution feeble but he was just recovering from a dangerous attack of pneumonia. Altogether Brother Teodoro was a·northern-looking rather than a Spanish man. It was not till afterwards that Rollo discovered that he belonged to the ancient race of the Basques, and that in his day he had fought as a bold soldier in the *partidas*, which rose in the rear of Napoleon's marshals when he sent his legions across the Pyrenees. Indeed, he had even followed *El Gran' Lor* to Toulouse when the battered remnants of that great army skulked back home again beaten by the iron discipline of England and the gad-fly persistence of the Spanish *guerrilleros*.

It was with Brother Teodoro then, as with a man already walking in the shadow of death, that Rollo in quick low-spoken sentences discussed the possibilities of the Hermitage as a place of defence. It was clear that no ordinary military precautions and preparations would serve them now. The four brethren were willing, if need were, to lay down their lives for the young Queen. But saving the pistols and the limited ammunition which Rollo had brought with him in his belt, and the bell-mouthed blunderbusses aforesaid, rusted and useless, there was not a single weapon of offence within the Hermitage of San Ildefonso of greater weight than the kitchen poker.

The Basque friar laid his hand on his brow and leaned against the wall for a minute or two in silent meditation.

"I have it," he said, suddenly turning upon Rollo, "it is our only chance, a ghastly one it is true, but we are in no case for fine distinctions. *We will get out the death-cart and gather us an army !*"

Rollo gazed at the monk Teodoro as if he had suddenly lost his wits.

"The death-cart! What is that?" he cried, "and how will that help us to gather an army ?"

The Basque smiled, and Rollo noticed when he did so that his eyebrows twitched spasmodically. There was a broad scar slashed across one of them. This man had not been in the army of the *Gran' Lor* for nothing. For in addition to the sabre cut, he had great ideas under that blue-veined, broad, sick man's forehead of his.

"Yes," answered Teodoro, calmly, "our brother, whose duty it was to collect the bodies of the plague-stricken, died two days ago, and the oxen have not been in the town since. As for me, I too have been sick—a mere *calentura*, though for a time the brethren feared that the plague had laid its hand on me also; and as for those other two, they have enough to do to keep up their ministrations among the living. To give the last sacrament to the dying is, after all, more important than to cover up the dead. At such times one has to remember how that once on a time the Virgin's Son said, 'Let the dead bury their dead !'"

He was silent a little, as if composing a homily on this text.

" But all things work good to the chosen of God,"
he said. " To-night we will make of these very
dead an army to defend our little Queen—the Lord's
anointed. For in this matter I do not think as do
the most of my brothers of the Church. I am no
Carlist, God be my witness ! "

Rollo was still in a maze of wonder and doubt
when they arrived at the little stables attached to the
long low building of the Hermitage and began to
harness the oxen to the cart. He prided himself
on his quickness of resource, but this was clean
beyond him.

" One of us must abide here," continued the
monk. " I am still sick unto death, so that I greatly
fear I can give you no help. Bleeding and this
calentura together have left me without power in my
old arms. But lend me your pistols, of which you
will have no need. I am an old soldier of the wars
of the Independence, and have not forgotten mine
ancient skill with the weapons of the flesh. Do not
fear for the little Princess. Only make such speed
as you can."

And with the utmost haste the Basque instructed
Rollo as to his behaviour when he should reach the
town, whilst at the same time he was helping him
into the dress of a Brother of Pity and arranging
the hood across his face.

" Hold your head well down," so ran the monk's
rubric for the dread office, "repeat in a loud voice
' *Bring out your dead ! Bring out your dead !* ' No
more than that and no less. With the butt of your
ox-staff strike the doors whereon you see painted
the red cross, and those that remain will bring
out whom the plague hath smitten."

The young man listened as in a dream. The

oxen started at the friar's gentle chirrup. The ox-staff was placed in Rollo's hand, and lo, he was guiding the meek bent heads softly towards the town before he even realised that he was now to encounter a foe far more terrible than any he had ever faced in battle or at the rapier's point upon the field of honour.

The trees were as solidly dark as black velvet above him. The oxen padded softly over the well-trodden path. In the gloom he dropped his goad, and only became conscious when he tried to pick it up that the Basque had drawn over his hands a pair of huge gloves which reached down almost to his wrists. These had been carefully tarred outside, and doubtless furnished at least some protection against infection.

The great well-fed beasts, white oxen of the finest Castilian breed, a gift of the Queen-Regent to the brethren, were under perfect control; and though Rollo had only once or twice before handled the guiding staff, he had not the least difficulty in conducting the cart towards the town.

Indeed, so often had the animals taken the same road of late, that they seemed to know their destination by instinct, and gave the tall young monk in the hood no trouble whatever. The wheels, however, being of solid wood of a style ancient as the Roman occupation, creaked with truly Spanish *crescendo* to the agony point. For in all countries flowing with oil and wine no man affords so much as a farthing's worth of grease for his waggon-wheels. But upon this occasion the lack was no loss—nay, rather a gain. For even before Rollo's shout gained assurance and sonorousness, the creaking of the wheels of the cart far-heard scattered various groups of marauders

about the streets of the town as if it had been the
wings of the angel of death himself.

"*Bring out your dead! Bring out your dead!*"

Certainly it was a solemn and awful cry heard
echoing through the streets in the chilly hours of
the night. Here and there at the sound a lattice
opened, and some bereaved one cried down to the
monk to stop.

Then staggering down the staircase, lighted (it
may be) by some haggard crone with a guttering
candle, or only stumbling blindly in the dark with
their load, the bearers would come. In a very few
cases these were two men, more frequently a man
and a woman, and most frequently of all two
women.

"*Bring out your dead! Bring out your dead!*"

"Brother, we cannot!" a shrill voice came from
high above; "come up hither and help us, for God's
sake and the Holy Virgin's! She is our mother, and
we are two young maids, children without strength."

Rollo looked up and saw the child that called
down to him. Another at her shoulder held a
lighted candle with a trembling hand.

"She is so little and light, brother," she pleaded,
"and went so regularly to confession. Brother
Jeronimo gave her the sacrament but an hour before
she parted from us. Come up and help us, for dear
Mary's sake!"

It went to Rollo's heart to refuse, but he could
not well leave his oxen. He was a stranger to them
and they to him; and his work, though well begun,
was yet to finish.

While he stood in doubt, his mind swaying this
way and that, a figure darted across to him from the
opposite side of the street, a boy dressed in a suit of

the royal liveries, but with a cloak thrown about his shoulders and a sailor's red cap upon his head.

"Give me the stick," he said in a muffled voice ; "go up and bring down the woman. If need be, I will help you."

Without pausing to consider the meaning of this curious circumstance, where all circumstances were curious, Rollo darted up the staircase, his military boots clattering on the stone steps, strangely out of harmony with his priestly vocation.

He found the little maiden with the candle waiting at the door for him. She appeared to be about eight years old, but struck him as very small-bodied for her age. Her sister had remained within. She was older—perhaps ten or twelve. She it was who had pleaded the cause of the dead.

"Indeed, good brother," she began, "we did our best. We tried to carry her, and moved her as far as the chair. Then, being weak, we could get no farther. But do you help, and it will be easy !"

Rollo, growing accustomed to death and its sad victims, lifted the shrouded burden over his shoulder without a shudder. He was in the mood to take things as they came. The two little girls sank on their knees on the floor, wailing for their lost mother, and imploring his blessing in alternate breaths.

"Our mother—our dear mother !" they cried, "pray for us and her, most holy father !"

"God in heaven bless you," Rollo said aloud in English, and strode down the stairs. A knot of straggling gipsies furtively expectant stood about the door. The cart was still in the middle of the street with its attendant boy, in the exact place where Rollo had left it.

"Here, lend me a hand," he cried in a voice of

2 B

command, as he emerged into their midst with his white-wrapped burden.

But at the mere sight of the monk's habit and of the thing he carried on his shoulder, the gipsies dispersed, running in every direction as if the very plague-spectre were on their track. The boy in the red cap, however, crossed the road towards him, and at the same moment the elder of the little girls sobbingly opened the lattice, holding the candle in her hand to take a last look at her mother.

The feeble rays fell directly on the boy's upturned face. At the sight Rollo stumbled and almost fell with his burden. The youth put out his hand to stay him. His fingers almost touched the dead.

"Hands off!" thundered Rollo, in fierce anger. "Concha Cabezos, how dare you come hither?"

The boy looked up at the man and answered simply and clearly—

"Rollo, I came because *you* dared!"

CHAPTER XXXVII

THE DEAD STAND SENTINEL

They walked on for a while in silence, Rollo too much thunderstruck and confounded to speak a word. His whole being was rent with the most opposite feelings. He was certainly angry with Concha. So much was clear to him. It was rash, it was unmaidenly to follow him at such a time and in such a guise. Yet, after all the girl had come. She was risking a terrible death for his sake. Well, what of that? It was right and natural that he should hold his life in his hands. All his life he had loved adventure as men their daily bread—not passionately, but as a necessity of existence.

But this—it was too great for him, too mighty, too surprising. For his sake! Because he dared! All the girls to whom he had made love—ay, even Peggy Ramsay herself, running barefoot in the braes of Falkland—instantly vanished. Life or death became no great matter—almost, as it seemed to him then, the same thing. For here was one who held all the world as well lost for him.

Meanwhile Concha walked silently alongside, the ox-staff still in her hands, but dimly understanding what was passing in his mind. Love to her was exceedingly simple. Her creed contained but two articles, or rather the same truth, brief, pregnant, uncontrovertible, stated in different ways : "*If he live, I will live with him ! If he die, I will die with him !*"

So with her eyes on the oxen and her goad laid gently on this side and that of the meek heads, Concha guided them along the silent streets. Nevertheless, she was keenly aware of Rollo also, and observed him closely. She did not understand what he was doing in the garb of a friar, collecting the dead of the plague on the streets of San Ildefonso. But it did not matter, it was sufficient that he was doing it, and that (thank God !) she had escaped from the beleaguered palace in time to help him. She even reminded him of his duty, without asking a single question as to why he did it—self-abnegation passing wonderful in a woman !

"You have forgotten to cry," she whispered, dropping back from the ox's head. "We have passed two alleys without a warning !"

And so once more there rang down the streets of the town of San Ildefonso that dolorous and terrible cry which was to be heard in the dread plague-years, not only in the Iberian peninsula but also in England and Rollo's own Scotland, "*Bring out your dead ! Bring out your dead !*"

It chanced that in the next street, the last of the little town, they made up their full complement. The heads of the oxen were directed once more towards the Hermitage. They turned this corner and that slowly and decorously till, with a quickening of pace and a forward inclination of the meek, moist nostrils, the pair struck into the woodland path towards their stable at the Hermitage.

Not one word either of love or of reproach had Rollo spoken since those into which he had been startled by the fear lest the girl should set her hand upon the dead of the plague. Nor did they speak even now. Rollo only put out his gloved hand to steady the cart here and there in the deeper ruts, motioning Concha to remain at the head of the oxen, where no breath of the dead might blow upon her.

Thus, no man saying them nay, they arrived at the Hermitage of San Ildefonso. It was quiet even as they had left it.

As they came round to the front of the building, the Basque at the door was before them. He met them on the steps, a lantern in his hand.

"Who is this?" he asked, with a significant gesture towards Concha.

"Carlos—a lad of our company, an Andalucian," said Rollo, in answer. "I met him by chance in the town, and he has helped me with the oxen."

The friar nodded and, letting down the rear flap of the cart, he surveyed the melancholy harvest.

"Twelve!" he said. "Not many, but enough. The dead will guard us well from the evil men! Ay, better than an army of twelve thousand living!"

And attiring himself in an apron of tarred stuff similar to the gloves, he fastened another of the same material upon Rollo.

"We will now proceed to set our sentries!" he said, grimly.

As Rollo put on the gauntlets and approached to help Brother Teodoro to draw out the corpses, Concha hovered near, half timid, and yet with a certain decision of manner. The timidity was lest she should be refused in that which it was upon her tongue to ask.

"Let me help the brother," she said at last; "I have nursed many—no plague will touch me!"

The monk stared at the lad in wonder as he proffered his request. But Rollo roughly and angrily ordered Concha back to the heads of the oxen, which, with true Spanish fortitude, stood chewing the cud till they should be set free and returned to their stalls.

"Is this boy by any chance your brother?" said the monk, as between them they settled the first sheeted dead in his niche by the side of the great door.

"Nay," said Rollo, "not my brother."

"Then of a surety he hath a great affection for you," continued the monk. "It is a thing unusual in one of his age!"

To this Rollo did not reply, and in silence the cart was led about the house till every door and practicable entrance was guarded by one of these solemn warders. Then, the dead-cart being pushed within its shed and the oxen restored to their stalls, the three went within and the doors were locked, the bolts drawn, and everything about the Hermitage made as secure as possible.

It was yet a good two hours from daylight, and if the gipsies were coming that night their appearance would not be long delayed. It was Rollo's opinion that they would attack with the first glimmer of light from the east. For the Ermita de San Ildefonso was not like La Granja, a place set amongst open *parterres*. It was closely guarded by tall trees, and in the absence of a moon the darkness was intense, a faint star-glimmer alone being reflected from the whitewashed walls of the Hermitage.

Within, the two stout brothers and the little

humorously featured almoner had already seen to the safety of every window and door. Above stairs in a retired chamber the little Queen had been sequestered from any breath of the plague-stricken sentries keeping their last vigil without, and also that she might be safe from every random bullet if the place should be attacked.

Rollo followed the Basque upwards to the roof, and Concha, with her *capa* still about her shoulders, followed Rollo into the light of the hall, nervously dragging the folds as low as possible about her knees.

The little Queen had two candles before her, and under her fingers was a great book of maps, upon which dragons and tritons, whales and sea monsters, writhed across uncharted seas, while an equal wealth of unicorns and fire-breathing gryphons freely perambulated the unexplored continental spaces. As it chanced Isabel was not at all sleepy, and to quiet her the Basque had set out some of the illuminating materials belonging to the order on slabs of porcelain, and with these she was employed in making gay the tall pages with the national yellow and red, and (as her great namesake had done before her) planting the flag of Spain over considerably more than half the world.

But as soon as the girl's eyes fell on Concha, she sprang up and let paint-brush and china-slab fall together to the ground.

"Oh, I know you," she cried (here Rollo trembled); "you are the new page-boy from Aranjuez! He was to arrive to-day. What is your name?"

"Carlos," said the new page-boy from Aranjuez, from whose cheek also the rose had momentarily fled.

"And why do you wear that curious red cap?"
cried the little Queen. "I know Doña Susana
would be very angry if she saw you. Pages must
show their own hair and wear it in curls too. Have
you pretty hair?"

"It is the cap of liberty the boy wears, Princess!"
said the Basque friar, breaking in quickly, and with
some irony. "Do you not know that since Señor
Mendizabel came to Madrid from England we are
all to have as much liberty as we want?"

"Well," replied the Princess, tartly, "all I know
is that I wish *I* had more of it. Doña Susana will
not let me do a single thing I want to do. But
when I grow up I mean to do just what I like."

Which truly royal and Bourbon sentiment had a
better fate than most prophecies, for Isabel the
Second afterwards lived to fulfil it to the uttermost,
both in the spirit and in the letter.

But the girl had not yet finished her inspection
of Concha.

"Do you know," she went on, "I think you are
the very prettiest boy I have ever seen. You may
come and kiss me. When I am grown up, I will
make you an officer of my bodyguard!"

*　　　*　　　*　　　*　　　*

Leaving little Isabel Segunda to make friends
according to her heart with the page-boy from Aranjuez (to whom she immediately proceeded to swear
an unalterable fidelity), Rollo and Brother Teodoro
retired, to await with what patience they might the
long-delayed approach of the gipsies.

"Twice during your absence did I believe them
on their way," said the friar. "On the first occasion
I heard in the wood wild cries, mixed with oaths,
cursings, and revilings, unfit for any Christian ears.

God help this land that holdeth such heathens within it ! But something must have affrighted the factious, for little by little the noises died away. I saw the red gleam in the sky wax and wane. And once there was a scream, strange and terrible, like that of a demon unchained. But, lo ! when you came again with the oxen and the dead, all grew still. It was passing strange ! "

"Not, as I think, more strange than that ! " said Rollo, looking out over the parapet and pointing to the grim line of sentries which guarded the Hermitage of San Ildefonso. The ruddy light of approaching day scarce tinged the tree-tops, but the highest fleecy clouds had caught the glow long before the horizon was touched. Yet the darkness down among the trees was less absolute than before. There was also a weird, far-away crying, and then the cheerful clatter of hoofs upon a road nearer at hand. A slight stirring among the higher foliage advertised the coming of a breeze. Involuntarily the two men shivered, as with a soughing murmur a blast of icy wind swept down from the peaks of Peñalara, and the Basque gripped his companion by the arm. Priest as he was, the superstitions of his ancient race were not dead in his heart, nor had he forgotten his early military association with camps and sentinels.

"*Grand rounds !* " he cried ; "*it is the Angel of Death visiting his outposts !* "

But Rollo had other and more practical thoughts. He was aware that after the fatigues of the night and the proximity of so many victims of the plague, a chill would most likely be fatal. So he carefully drew a silken handkerchief from his pocket and fastened it calmly about his throat, advising the monk to cover his head with his hood.

Then suddenly another sound caught his ear. It was the identical signal he had heard from Sergeant Cardono, the same that had been repeated in the garden of the royal palace as he stood among the reeds of the cane brake. Beginning with the low morning twitter of the swallow, it increased in volume till it carried far over the woodlands, wild and shrill as he remembered the winter cry of the whaups sweeping down from the Fife Lomonds to follow the ebb tide as it sullenly recedes from Eden Mouth towards Tents Muir.

"They are here," he whispered hoarsely to his companion. "It is the gipsies' battle signal!"

The Basque spread abroad his hands, raising them first to heaven and anon pointing in the direction of the approaching foe.

"The scourge of God!" he cried, "let the scourge of God descend upon those that do wickedly! The prayer of a dying man availeth! Let the doom fall!"

He was silent a moment, and then added with an air of majestic prophecy—"Oaths and cursings are in their mouths, but, like the dead in the camp of Sennacherib, they shall be dead and dumb."

Again he spread his hands abroad, as if he pronounced a benediction upon the sentries posted below.

"Blessed souls," he cried, "for whom we of this Holy House have died that you might live, cause that your poor vile bodies may fight for us this night! Let the dead meet the living and the living be overthrown! Hear, Almighty Lord of both quick and dead—hear and answer!"

CHAPTER XXXVIII

CONCHA SAYS AMEN

LOOKING down from their station on the roof, Rollo
and the friar could see what appeared to be the main
force of the gipsies drawing near through the alleys
of the wood. They approached in no order or
military formation, which indeed it was never their
nature to adopt. But they came with a sufficiency
of confused noise, signalling and crying one to
another through the aisles of the forest.

"They are telling each other to spread out on
the wings and encircle the house on the north,"
whispered Rollo in a low voice to the Basque friar
by his side.

The monk laughed a low chuckling laugh.

"They will find the holy Hermitage equally well
guarded on that side!" he said. And as they stood
silent the rose of dawn began slowly to unfold itself
over the tree-tops with that awful windless stillness
which characterises the daybreaks of the south. The
glades of the wood were filled with a glimmering
filmy light, in which it was easy to imagine the
spirits of the dead hovering over their earthly
tenements.

The gipsies came on as usual, freely and easily,
land pirates on their own ground, none able to make
them afraid. They had been checked, it is true, at

the palace. The royal guard (so they imagined) seemed to have returned unexpectedly thither, contrary to their information, but on the other hand they had successfully plundered all the storehouses, cellars, and *despachos* of the great square.

Some of them still carried *botas* of wine (the true "leather bottel") in their hands or swung across their shoulders, and ever and anon took a swig to keep their courage up as they came near. Some sang and shouted, for were they not going to rout the lazy monks, always rich in money and plate, out of their lurking places? Was it not they who had first tried to make Christians of the Romany, and by so doing had shown the government how to entrap them into their armies, subjecting the free blood of Egypt to their cursed drafts and conscriptions?

"To the knives' point with them, then!" they shouted. "They who prate so much of paradise, let them go thither, and that with speed!" This would be a rare jest to tell for forty years by many a swinging kettle, and while footing it in company over many a lonely and dispeopled heath.

Thus with laughter and shouting they came on, and to Rollo, peering eagerly over the battlements, the white-wrapped corpses along the walls seemed to turn slowly blood-red before his eyes—the flaunting crimson of the sky above contrasting with the green of the woods, and tinging even the white shrouds with its ominous hue. But still the gipsies came on.

First of all strode the man who had called himself the Executioner of Salamanca, Ezquerra, he who had saved the life of José Maria upon the scaffold. He came forward boldly enough, intending to thunder with his knife-handle upon the great door. But at the foot of the steps he stopped.

Looking to either hand, he saw, almost erect within their niches, a strange pair of figures, apparently wrapped in bloody raiment from head to foot. He staggered back nerveless and shaken.

"What are these faceless things?" he cried; "surely the evil spirits are here!" And in deadly fear he put his hand before his eyes lest his vision should be blasted by a portent.

And from the other side of the Hermitage came an answering cry of fear.

"Be brave, Ezquerra!" called out one behind him; "'tis nothing—only some monk's trick!"

Ezquerra over his shoulder cast a fierce glance at the speaker.

"Brother," he cried, "you who are so full of courage that you can supply others, go up these steps and find out the trick for yourself!"

Nevertheless through very pride of place as their temporary leader, Ezquerra set his feet once more to the steps and mounted. The shrouded figures grew less red as he approached.

"After all it *is* some trick!" he shouted angrily. "We will make the fools pay for this! Did they think to practise the black art upon those whose fathers have used all magic, black and white, for ten thousand years?"

So saying he set his hand to the face-cloth of the nearest figure and plucked it away. Then was revealed to his affrighted and revolted gaze the features swollen and bloated of one who had died of the Black Plague.

At the same moment, and before his followers could set their hands to their mouths or retreat a step, round both corners of the building there came a double swarm of gipsies, running at random

through the tangle of the wood and streaming frantically along the paths.

The Executioner of Salamanca also turned and
ran down the steps.

"Touch the thing who will!" he cried; "I have
done with it!"

And the entire attacking party with their knives
and sledge-hammers would in like manner have fled,
but for a strange and unlooked-for event which
happened at that moment.

As Rollo peered over the low parapet, he saw
a slight form rush suddenly across the front of the
fleeing gipsies, shouting at and striking the fugitives.
And even at that distance he was sure that it must
be the daughter of Muñoz, whom he had left captive
in La Granja. She had been safely enough locked in
the castle—how then had she escaped? He remembered the Sergeant's last threat that he would
have some conversation with Señor Muñoz. He
wondered if the girl's escape had anything to do
with that. That it was not impossible to escape
from the palace, the presence of Concha Cabezos
upstairs informed him.

But all theorising of this kind was stopped at
sight of the vehement anger of the girl, and of the
evident power she had over these wild and savage
men. She did not even hesitate to strike a fugitive
with her clenched fist if he attempted to evade her.
Nay, in her fury she drew a knife from Ezquerra's
belt and struck at the throat of the Executioner of
Salamanca.

So vehement was her anger and so potent her
influence, that the girl actually succeeded in arrest-
ing more than half the fleeing gipsies. Some,
however, evaded her, and she would stay her head-

long course a moment to send a fierce curse after them.

"She is crazed!" thought Rollo; "her wrongs have driven her mad!"

But the sight of that glimmering array of plague-stricken sentinels waiting for them still and silent in the red dawn, was more than the fortitude of the rallied forces could stand. Upon approaching the Hermitage the gipsies again showed symptoms of renewed flight.

Whereupon the girl, shrilly screaming the vilest names at them and in especial designating Ezquerra as the craven-hearted spawn of an obscene canine ancestry, mounted the steps herself with the utmost boldness and confidence.

"I will teach you," she screamed; "I, a girl and alone, will show you what sacks of straw ye are frighted of. Do ye not know that the great prize is here, within this very house, behind these defenceless windows and cardboard doors? The Queen of Spain, whose ransom is worth twice ten thousand *duros*, even if your coward hearts dared not shed her black Bourbon blood. Behold!"

It was only by craning far out over the parapet (so far indeed that he might easily have been discovered from below had there been any to look) that Rollo was able to see what followed. But every eye was fixed on the girl. No one among all that company had even a glance to waste upon the sky-line of the Ermita de San Ildefonso.

This was the thing Rollo saw as he looked.

The girl spurned the fallen face-cloth with her bare foot, and catching the body of the dead man in her arms, she dragged it out of its niche and cast it down the steps upon which it lay all abroad, half revealed and hideous in the morning light. This done, rushing back as swiftly and with the same volcanic energy to the occupant of the other niche, she hurled him by main force after his companion. Then, panting and wan, with her single tattered garment half rent from her flat ill-nourished body, she lifted one arm aloft in triumph and cried, " There, you dogs, that is what you were afraid of ! "

But even as she stood thus revealed in the morning light, a low murmur of terror and astonishment ran round all who saw her. For in the struggle the girl had uncovered her shoulder and breast, and there, upon her young and girlish skin, appeared the dread irregular blotches which betrayed the worst and most deadly form of the disease.

" The Black Plague ! The Black Plague ! " shrieked the throng of besiegers, surging this way and that like a flock of sheep which strange dogs drive, as with wild and shrill cries they turned and fled headlong towards the mountains.

The girl, speechless with wrath, and perhaps also with the death-sickness far advanced within her, took a step forward as if to follow them. But forgetful of where she stood, she missed her footing, fell headlong, and lay across the dead sentinel whom she had first dragged from his post.

The Basque priest looked over Rollo's shoulder and pointed downwards with a certain dread solemnity.

" What did I tell you ? " he said. " The finger of God ! The finger of God hath touched her ! Let us go down. The sun will be above the horizon in twenty minutes."

" Had we not better wait ? " urged Rollo. " They may return. Think of our responsibility, of our feeble defences, of—— "

"Of Concha," he was about to say, but checked himself, and added quietly, "of the little Queen!"

The monk crossed himself with infinite calm.

"They will not return," he said; "it is our duty to lay these in the quiet earth ere the sun rises. There is no infection to be feared till an hour after sunrise."

"But the girl, the daughter of Muñoz?" said Rollo, "did not she take the disease from the dead?"

"Nay," said the Basque. "I have often beheld the smitten of the plague like that. It works so upon very many. For a time they are as it were possessed with seven devils, and the strength of man is vain against them. They snap strong cords even as Samson did the Philistine withes. Then—puff! Comes a breath of morning air chill from the Sierra, and they are gone. They were—and they are not. The finger of God hath touched them. So it was with this girl."

"I will follow you!" said Rollo, awe-stricken in spite of himself. "Tell me what I am to do!"

The monk pressed his hand again to his brow a little wearily. "I fear," he said, "that it will fall to you to perform the greater part of the work. For Brother Domingo, our good almoner, he of the merry countenance, died of his fatigues early this morning, and the other two, my brethren, are once more in the town bringing God to the dying!"

Instinctively Rollo removed his hat from his head.

"But," added the monk, "they dug the graves in holy ground before they went!"

In silence Rollo permitted himself to be covered with an armour of freshly tarred cloth, which was

2 C

considered in Spain at that time to be a complete
protection against plague infection. The monk
Teodoro was proceeding to array himself in like
manner, when Concha appeared beside them and
held out her hands for the gauntlets.

"The little Princess is asleep," she said eagerly;
"I am strong. I have as good a right to serve God
as either of you—and as great is my need!"

The Basque gazed at her curiously. Her hair
was still wholly covered by the sailor's red cap. To
the eye she appeared a mere boy in her page's dress,
but there was at all times something irresistibly
attractive about Concha's face. Now her lips
quivered sensitively, but her eyes were steady. She
continued to hold out her hands.

"I demand that you permit me to serve God!"
she cried to Brother Teodoro.

The monk shrugged his shoulders with a pitying
gesture and looked from one to the other.

"I am an old dragoon," he said, "and under the
guidons of *El Gran' Lor'* I have seen the like. It is
none of my business, of course, but all the same it
is a pity. I should be happier to leave you watching
the slumbers of the Princess!"

"Ah!" cried Concha, earnestly, "if you are
indeed an old soldier, and a good one under guidon
or holy cross—for this time let me be one also!"

"You are young—I pray you, think!" urged
the Basque. "There is great danger! Look at that
maid yonder, and what she hath brought on herself."

"Ah," said Concha, softly—so softly indeed as
to be almost inaudible, "but the difference is that
she did this thing for hate—while—I—I———"

She did not finish her sentence, but raising her
eyes, wet with seldom-coming tears, to those of the

stern-faced brother, she said instead, "Give me the dress and let us be gone. The sun is rising!"

"If you are indeed determined, you shall have that of Brother Domingo," said Teodoro; "he was of little more than your height, and died, not of the plague, but simply from doing his duty."

"Then let me die in no other way!" said Concha, putting it on as happily as another maiden might dress for a ball.

These three went out to their terrible task, and as they were harnessing the bullock cart once more and spreading a clean cloth over it, Rollo, moved in his heart of hearts, came near. Never did two such lovers as they meet more strangely arrayed. Yet he laid his black gauntlet across her arm and whispered a word which Brother Teodoro did not hear, being, as he took good care to be, much busied about the straps and harnessings.

"I do not think that Love will let us die—yet!" he said.

"That is a prayer. Amen!" said Concha, in a whisper, lifting her eyes to his.

It was a strange betrothing, and little said. But when at last he put the ox-goad in her hands, Concha knew that the night had indeed passed away and that the morning was come.

CHAPTER XXXIX

A HANDFUL OF ROSES

PATIENTLY and softly went the oxen about the little pottage garden of the friars, till, where the soil was sandiest and the ground most open, under a south-looking wall on which the roses were still clustering (for they grow roses late at La Granja), lo! a trench was dug. It was not so deep as a rich man's grave in other countries, but in Spain as elsewhere a little earth covers a multitude of sorrows.

The long shallow trench had been the last work of the two remaining monks ere they departed to their duty in the stricken village. Savage men, heathen of heart and cruel of hand, might await them there. Black plague would certainly lurk in every doorway. Yet these two brothers, simple in the greatness of their faith—not of the wise of the land, not of the apparent salt of the earth, but only plain devout men, ignorant of all beyond their breviaries and their duty to their fellows—had gone forth as quietly and unostentatiously as a labouring man shoulders his mattock and trudges to his daily toil.

Of the three that remained, Brother Teodoro did his best ; but in spite of his endeavours the bulk of the work fell to Rollo and Concha. Yet under the page's dress and the rude outer slough of tarred canvas the girl's heart sang. There was nothing

388

terrible in death when he and she together lifted the
spent stuff of mortality and laid it in its last resting-
place. Without a shudder she replaced a fallen face-
cloth. With Rollo opposite to her she took the feet
of the dead that had guarded them so well in the red
morning light, and when all were laid a-row in the
rest which lasts till the Judgment Day, and before
the first spadeful of earth had fallen, Concha, with a
sudden impulse, took a kerchief from her neck, and
plucked a double handful of the roses that clustered
along the wall. They were white roses, small, but of
a sweet perfume, having grown in that high mountain
air. Then without a word, and while the monk was
still busy with his prayers for the dead, she sprang
down to where at the corner opposite to Brother
Domingo the daughter of Muñoz had been laid, the
pinched fierceness of her countenance relaxed into a
strange far-away smile.

Concha spread the kerchief tenderly over the face
of the girl, dropping tears the while. And she
crossed the little hands which pain and madness had
driven to deeds of darkness and blood, upon the
breast in which the angry young heart had beaten so
hotly, and scattered the white roses over all.

Then while the Basque Teodoro did his office
over his dead brother, Concha kneeled at the foot of
the trench, a little crucifix in her hand. Her lips
moved as she held the rude image of the Crucified
over that fierce little head and sorely tortured body.
He who had cast out so many devils, would surely
pardon and understand. So at least she thought.
Rollo watched her, and though brought up to be a
good Presbyterian by his father, he knew that this
little foolish Concha must yet teach him how to
pray.

"God may hear her before the other, who knows!" he murmured. "One is a man praying for men—she, a maiden praying for a maid!"

Then Rollo made the girl, whom the scene had somewhat overwrought, go off to a secluded part of the garden and wash in the clean cool water of a fountain, while he remained to shovel in the soil and pack it well down upon the bodies of the dead who had served his purpose so faithfully. Last of all he unyoked and fed the oxen, leaving them solemnly munching their fodder, blinking their meek eyes and ruminating upon the eternal sameness of things in their serene bovine world. He came out, stripped himself to the skin, and washed in one of the deserted kitchens from which Brother Domingo, sometime almoner and cook to the Ermita of San Ildefonso, had for ever departed.

This being completed to his satisfaction, he went out to find Concha, who, her face radiant with the water of the Guadarrama (and other things which the young morning had brought her), met him as he came to her through the wood.

She held up her face to be kissed as simply and naturally as a child. Death was all about them, but of a truth these two lived. Yea, and though they should die ere nightfall, still throughout the eternities they might comfort themselves, in whatsoever glades of whatsoever afterworlds they might wander, that on earth they had lived, and not in vain.

For if it be true that God is Love, equally true is it that love is life. And this is the secret of all things new and old, of Adam and Eva his wife, of Alpha and Omega, of the mystic OM, of the joined serpent, of the Somewhat which links us to the Someone.

*   *   *   *   *

It was now Rollo's chiefest desire to get back to the palace and find out what had happened there during his absence. He had heard the rattle of musketry fire again and again during the night, and he feared, as much from the ensuing silence as from the escape of the daughter of Muñoz, that some disaster must have occurred there. He would have started at once to reconnoitre, but Brother Teodoro, hearing of his intention, volunteered to find out whether the gipsies had wholly evacuated the neighbourhood.

There was a private path from the grounds of the Hermitage which led into those of the palace. By this the Basque hastened off, and it was no long time before he returned, carrying the news that not only was the town clear and the gardens of the palace free from marauders, but that Rollo's people were still in full possession of La Granja. He had even been able to speak with one of the royal servants for an instant, a man with whom he had some acquaintance. But this conference, the Basque added, had been hastily interrupted by a certain old woman of a fierce aspect, who had ordered the young man off. Nevertheless he had gained enough information to assure him that there would now be no danger in the whole party returning openly to the Palace of La Granja.

Accordingly Rollo set out, with Concha still wrapt in the cloak which covered her page's dress. Rollo would gladly have carried the little Princess, but Isabel had taken so overwhelming a fancy to Concha that she could not be induced to quit her side for a moment. Indeed, she declared her intention of leaving her mother and Doña Susana and returning to Aranjuez with Concha so soon as her message should be delivered.

Rollo whispered that the pretended page should

not discourage this sudden devotion, since in the
journey that still lay before them the willingness of
the little Princess to accompany them might make all
the difference between success and failure.

The Sergeant received them at the garden door,
which he had so carefully watched all night.   There
was a kindlier look than usual upon his leathern and
saturnine features.

"I judge, Señor," he said, as he saluted Rollo,
"that you have more to tell me than I have to tell
you."

"In any case, let me hear your story first," said
Rollo ; "mine can keep !"

"In brief, then, having your authority," began
the Sergeant, "I permitted his Excellency the Duke
of Rianzares to have an interview with his daughter,
at which, for safety's sake, I was present, and gained
a great deal of information that may be exceedingly
useful to us in the future.   But in one thing I
confess that I was not sufficiently careful.   The girl,
being left to herself for a moment, escaped—by what
means I know not.   Nor " (this with a quaint glance
at Concha) "was she the only lady who left the
palace that night without asking my leave ! "

But without answering, the cloaked page passed
him rapidly, and with the Princess still clinging to
her hand, she passed upstairs.   The Sergeant looked
after her and her young charge.

"You are sure of this lady's discretion ? " he
said.

"I have proved it to the death," answered the
young man briefly and a little haughtily.

The Sergeant shrugged his shoulders as if he
would have said with the Basque friar, "It is none
of my business."   But instead he took up his report

to his superior and continued, " We buried the body of the poor woman Doña Susana within the precincts of the *Colegiata*———"

"And an hour ago I buried the body of her slayer," said Rollo, calmly.

For an instant the Sergeant looked astonished, as indeed well he might, but he restrained whatever curiosity he felt, and only said :

"You will let me hear what happened in your own time, and also how you discovered and regained the little Princess ? "

Rollo nodded.

"And speaking of the Princess, if she asks questions," continued Cardono, " had she not better be told that Doña Susana has gone to visit her relations—which, as she was the last of her family, is, I believe, strictly true ! "

"But the Queen-Regent and the Duke—Señor Muñoz, I mean ? " queried Rollo. " What of them ? " For the young man had even yet no high opinion of that nobleman or of his vocation in life.

"Oh, as to the Duke," answered the Sergeant, " I do not think that we shall have much trouble with him. The Queen is our Badajoz. She is so set on returning to Madrid that she will not move a step towards Aragon, and we have not enough force to carry her thither against her will with any possibility of secrecy."

"We might take the little Princess alone," mused Rollo ; "she would go with Concha anywhere. Of that I am certain."

The Sergeant shook his head.

"The Queen-Regent, and she alone, is the fountain of authority. If you kidnap and sequester her within the Carlist lines, you will certainly paralyse

the government of Madrid. Especially you may
prevent the sweeping away of the monasteries—
which, I take it, is at the bottom of all this pother,
though for the life of me I cannot see what concern
the matter is of yours. But to carry off the Princess
would profit you nothing. Isabel Segunda is but a
child, and will not come of age for many years.
Your friend the Abbot would gain nothing by her
captivity. But the Queen-Regent were a prize
indeed ! "

After he had spoken thus freely, Rollo continued
to muse, and the Sergeant to watch him. The latter had
a great opinion of this young man's practical ability.

" If he had had but the fortune to be born poor—
and in Andalucia, he might have been one day as
great as I ! " was the opinion of this modest Sergeant.
And indeed he spoke but the words of truth and sober-
ness. For it was the opinion of nine out of ten of
his countrymen that he, José Maria of Ronda, was
the greatest man of all time.

" Well," said Rollo at last, " let us go up and
talk a little to my friends and El Sarria. I think
I see a way of inducing her Royal Highness to
accompany us. But it will require some firmness,
and even a certain amount of severity."

The Sergeant nodded with grim appreciation.

" It is a pity with women," he said philosophically, " but sometimes, I know, it is the only
way."

" The severity I speak of," continued Rollo, not
regarding his words, " will mostly fall to the lot of
the Señor Muñoz. But we may chance to work on
the lady's feelings through him."

The Sergeant gave Rollo a quick glance, in which
was discernible a certain alertness of joy. The

Sergeant also did not love his grandeeship, the Duke of Rianzares.

So these two went abreast up the great staircase, and found the Princess Isabel already playing joyously with Etienne, John Mortimer joining clumsily in as best he could. Concha had vanished, and La Giralda was nowhere to be seen.

"The rogue is in no haste to visit her mother after her night adventure!" said the Sergeant in a low tone, as Rollo and he stood watching the scene from the doorway.

"Nor I," admitted Rollo with a smile, "yet see the lady we must!"

"And shall!" said the Sergeant.

Yet in spite of the unpleasant interview which lay before him, Rollo could not help smiling at the game that was going forward in the upper hall.

> "Sur le pont d'Avignon,
> Tout le monde y passe,"

chanted Etienne.

"Tout le monde y passe!" chorused the little Princess, holding out her hands.

John Mortimer made a confused noise in his throat and presently was compelled to join the circle and dance slowly round, his countenance meantime suggestive of the mental reserve that such undignified proceedings could only be excused as being remotely connected with the safe shipment of a hundred hogsheads of Priorato.

> "The children walk like this,
> And the ladies walk like that——"

There was no help for it. Etienne and the Princess first mimicked the careless trip of the children, and then, with chin in the air and lift of

imaginary furbelow, the haughty tread of the good
dames of Avignon as they took their way homeward
over that ancient bridge.

But suddenly arrested with both hands in the
air and his mouth open, John Mortimer looked on
in confusion and a kind of mental stupor. He was
glad that no one of his nation was present to see
him making a fool of himself. The next moment
Isabel had seized his hand, and he found himself
again whirling lumpishly round to the ancient
refrain :—

> " *Sur le pont d'Avignon,*
> *Tout le monde y passe !* "

The little Queen's merry laugh rang out at his
awkwardness, and then seeing Rollo she ran impetuously to him.

"Come you and play," she cried, "the red
foreigner plays like a wooden puppet. And where
is that darling little page-boy from Aranjuez ?"

"That I cannot tell," quoth Rollo, smiling, "but
here comes his sister !"

A moment after Concha entered the room talking confidentially to La Giralda. She was now
dressed in her own girlish costume of belted blouse,
black *basquiña* pleated small after the Andalucian
manner, and the quaint and pretty *rebozo* thrown
coquettishly back from the finest and most bewitch-
ing hair in Spain.

The little Isabel went up to Concha, took her
by the hand, perused her from head to foot, and
then remarked with deep feeling—

"You are very well, Señorita, but—I liked your
brother better !"

CHAPTER XL

ALL DANDIES ARE NOT COWARDS

IT was not, however, so simple a matter as Rollo supposed to obtain an audience with the Queen-Regent of Spain. Her daughter, willing, but by no means eager to see her mother, had at last been taken up to her room by one of the serving-men, whose faithfulness during the night had been so greatly stimulated by La Giralda's declared intention of shooting either of them who should fail from his post for an instant.

To the same gold-laced functionary, upon his return, Rollo made his request.

"Tell her Majesty that those gentlemen who last night defended the palace, wish to be admitted into her presence in order that they may represent to her the danger of remaining longer in a house exposed alike to the attacks of bloodthirsty villains and to the ravages of the plague."

"Her Majesty, being otherwise engaged, is not at present able to receive the gentlemen," was the civil but unsatisfactory answer brought back.

Rollo stood a moment fuming, biting his thumb-nail as he had a fashion of doing when thinking deeply. Then he asked a sudden question—

"Where is El Sarria?"

"Without on the terrace—doing a little sentry

397

duty on his own account," said the Sergeant. " I
told him that the gipsies, being walkers in darkness,
had gone off for at least twelve hours, and that there
was no use in any further vigilance till nightfall,
should it be our ill-fortune to spend another night
in this place. But " (here the Sergeant shrugged his
shoulders very slightly, as only an Andalucian or
a Frenchman can), " well—our excellent Don Ramon
is the best and bravest of men. But it is a pity that
he has not room here for more than one idea at
a time ! "

And Sergeant Cardono tapped his brow with his
forefinger.

" I do not know," said Rollo, smiling, " if the
one idea is a good one, it may carry a man far ! But
that matters nothing now. Let these two friends of
mine, Don Juan and M. de Saint Pierre, take his
place on the terrace. We have a difficult part to
play upstairs, and we want only men of your nation
or mine—men neither easily excited nor yet too over-
scrupulous ! "

He added the last words under his breath.

And so, on pretext that it was time El Sarria
should be relieved, a few minutes thereafter John
Mortimer and Etienne found themselves pleasantly
situated on the broad terrace looking out on the dry
fountains and the glittering waterfalls of La Granja,
while El Sarria solemnly mounted the stairs to hold
audience with his young leader.

No great talker was El Sarria at any time, and
now he had nothing to say till Rollo informed him
why he wanted his help. Then he was ready to do
everything but talk—go to the world's end, fight to
the death, give up all except Dolóres (and risk even
her !) that he might do the will of his chief. El

Sarria was not good at fine ethical distinctions, but he understood obedience prompt and unquestioning, through and through and up and down.

Rollo did not directly reveal his intentions to his followers, nor did he take Concha into his confidence. He had not even spoken another word to her, but a glance had passed between them, and Concha was satisfied. It had told her much—that he loved her, that his heart held her to be the best-beloved thing the sun shone on—that there were dangers and difficulties before them, but that whatever happened neither would look back nor take their hands from the plough. Yes, oh too wise sceptic, it was indeed a comprehensive glance, yet it passed as swiftly as when in a placid lake a swallow dips his wing in full flight and is off again with the drops pearling from his feathers.

"I wish you to follow me, gentlemen," he said slowly. "Bring your arms. If her Majesty the Queen-Regent of Spain will not see us, perhaps we may fare better with the Queen's Consort! I for one intend that we shall!"

Without offering any further explanation, Rollo turned and marched steadily but not hastily to the chamber door of Señor Muñoz, Duke of Rianzares. The liveried servant who was approaching with a jug of hot water (the younger of La Giralda's charges on the previous night), called out to them that they could not at that moment see his Excellency. He was, it appeared, in the act of dressing. With the coming of the morning light these two gentlemen of the bed-chamber had resumed the entire etiquette of the Spanish court, or at least such modified forms of it as, a little disarranged by altitude and the portent of an informal and (as yet) unauthorised Prince Consort, prevailed at La Granja.

But Rollo would have nothing of all this. Enough time had been wasted. He merely moved his head a hair's-breadth to the side, and the young man in gold lace, a most deserving *valet-de-chambre*, found himself looking down at the curved edge of El Sarria's sword-bayonet, whose point touched his Adam's apple in a suggestive manner. He promptly dropped the silver pipkin, whereupon the shaving-water of the Duke slowly decanted itself over the *parqueterie* floor. A portion scalded the valet's finely shaped leg, yet he dared not complain, being in mortal fear of the sword-bayonet. But in spite of the danger, his mind ran on the question whether the skin would accompany the hose when he had an opportunity to remove the latter in order to examine his injuries.

Rollo knocked on the Duke's door with loud confident knuckles, not at all as the gentleman with the shaving-water would have performed that feat.

Whereupon, inclining his ear, he heard hasty footsteps crossing the floor, and, suspecting that if he stood on any sort of ceremony he might find the door bolted and barred in his face, Rollo turned the handle and quietly intruded a good half of a bountifully designed military riding-boot within the apartment of the Duke.

So correctly had he judged the occupant's intentions that an iron bolt was actually pushed before Don Fernando discovered that his door would not close, owing to an unwonted obstruction.

"Your Excellency," cried Rollo, in a stern voice, "we desire to speak with you on a question which concerns the lives of all within this castle. Being unable to obtain an interview with her Majesty the Queen-Regent, we make bold to request you to convey our wishes and—our intentions to her!"

"I am dressing—I cannot see you, not at present!" cried a voice from within.

"But, Señor, see you we must and shall," said Rollo, firmly; "in half a minute we shall enter your apartment, so that you have due notice of our intention."

For this Rollo of ours had an etiquette of his own applicable even to circumstances so unique as obtained at the Castle of La Granja—which, had the occurrences we describe not been the severest history, might justly have been called the chiefest of all "Chateaux en Espagne."

Watch in hand Rollo stood, absorbed in the passage of the thirty seconds of which he had given notice, and had not the Sergeant suddenly dashed the chamber door open, the young Scot's foot would certainly have been crushed to a jelly. For by this act the excellent Duke of Rianzares was disclosed in the very act of dropping a ponderous marble bust of his wife's grandfather upon the young man's toes.

After that, of course, there was no more ceremony with Señor Muñoz. He was immediately relieved of his weapons, ordered to the farther side of the room away from all possible avenues of escape, and further guarded by the Sergeant, who bent upon him a stern and threatening brow.

Then Rollo began to develop his intentions in a loud clear voice. For if, as he suspected, Maria Cristina chanced to be within earshot, it might save an explanation in duplicate if she should hear at first hand what he was now about to communicate to her consort.

On either side of the young man were his two aides, the Sergeant and Ramon Garcia, the first gaunt, tough, and athletic, of any age between thirty and sixty, courage and invincible determination written plainly on his brow, and in his eyes when as now he was angered, the Angel of Death himself standing like a threat. On the other side stood Don Ramon Garcia, gigantic in stature, deep-chested and solemn, driven by fate to actions of blood, but all the same with the innocent heart of a little child within his breast.

"Señor Muñoz," said Rollo, speaking sharp and sudden, "let me introduce these gentlemen to your notice. They are two of the most famous men in all Spain and worthy of your acquaintance. This on my left is Señor Don José Maria, late of the town of Ronda, and this on my right is Don Ramon Garcia, better known as El Sarria of Aragon !"

For the first time the colour slowly forsook the handsome but somewhat florid countenance of the Duke of Rianzares. He was, as his valet had truly said, engaged at his toilet, and it is certainly difficult to look impressive in a flowered dressing-gown. Being Spaniards and therefore gentlemen, El Sarria and the Sergeant bowed slightly at Rollo's introduction, and stood waiting. Rollo, noways loth, continued his speech.

"Your Excellency is now aware of the names of two of those whom you may thank for your safety. I myself, to whom the Queen-Regent owes the recovery of her daughter, am a Scottish gentleman of good birth. My companions below are severally the Count de Saint Pierre, a French nobleman of ancient family, and Don Juan Mortimer, an English merchant of unchallenged probity.

"Here therefore are five men who have defended the Queen-Regent with their lives, and who now judge it to be necessary for her and the Princess that they should put themselves immediately under our protection and leave this place of instant and terrible danger !"

"The Queen will not be dictated to by any combination of men whatsoever," the Duke answered; "she has resolved to remain at La Granja, and therefore nothing can move her !"

Rollo bowed gracefully, but there was a dangerous glitter in his eye which might have warned his opponent.

"Your Excellency," he went on, with great calmness, "we look confidently for your voice and interest in this matter. You will have the goodness to introduce us into the presence of the Queen-Regent. You are at liberty to announce our intentions and prepare her Majesty for a visit !"

A quick light flashed over the indifferent and dogged countenance of Señor Muñoz. The hope of escape was written there as plainly as if printed in Roman characters across his brow. But for this also Rollo had made provision.

"Guard that inner door," he cried to El Sarria; and the giant moved swiftly to his post, motioning away the gentleman-in-waiting as one might displace a dog from a cushion. Then Rollo stepped briskly into the corridor, set his hand to his mouth and called a single word aloud.

"Concha !"

And the girl stood before him almost ere his voice had ceased to echo along the corridors. Silent she waited his pleasure. For this time it was not Rollo, upon whose love for her the new sun had risen, who called her, but Colonel Rollo Blair, the chief of the expedition of which she was no insignificant part.

"You are armed ?" he queried, as she followed

him within the door and her quick eyes took in the scene.

The girl nodded a little resentfully. Surely it was a superfluous question. An Andalucian maiden, whose lover's life is in danger every hour, always goes armed. But of course it was Rollo's duty as an officer to make certain. All the same he might have known. *She* would.

"Then," said Rollo, firmly, "you will accompany this gentleman to the apartments of the Queen-Regent. You will permit him ten minutes' private conversation with her Majesty in your presence. You will then accompany him back. During his absence he is not to lay his hand upon any weapon, have any personal contact with the Queen, or open any drawer, cabinet, or case-of-arms. Also he is to return with you as soon as you inform him that the time allotted is at an end. Here is my watch!"

"And if the *Señor* should refuse to comply with any of these demands?" suggested Concha.

"He will not refuse," answered Rollo; "but if the thing should happen, why, you have full discretion! You understand?"

Concha nodded, and her lips, ordinarily so sweet and yielding, grew firm with determination. She understood. So also did Muñoz.

"You do not need to say more," she said clearly; "I am an Andalucian."

Rollo turned to Muñoz. Not being a Spaniard, he thought it necessary to make the matter yet more clear.

"You have heard," he said; "treachery will do you no good, and may indeed suddenly deprive her reigning Majesty of the inestimable consolations of your companionship. Be good enough to accompany

this young lady, sir. In ten minutes I shall expect
your return with a favourable answer. Permit them
to pass, Don Ramon!"

But the consort of the Queen-Regent Maria
Cristina fingered his chin uncertainly without
moving, and Rollo's brow darkened ominously, while
the Sergeant began to look hopeful. Neither were
in the mood to put up calmly with any further refusal
or hesitation.

"I am quite willing—nay, even anxious to oblige
you," said Muñoz; "I would gladly undertake the
commission, but—but—— !"

He stopped as if searching for words, still, however, rubbing his chin.

"But what?" thundered Rollo. The blood of
all the Blairs was rising.

"Well, to put the matter plainly, I have never
appeared before her Majesty in this condition before.
You would not have me go as I am?"

"In what condition?" cried the Scot in great
astonishment.

"Unshaven, and with my hair undressed. That
idiot there"—pointing to the trembling valet—"spilt
the water just when you came in."

"Nay," laughed Rollo, much relieved that there
was to be no shedding of blood, "indeed you must
forgive him for that. El Sarria there is entirely to
blame. And on this occasion I trust that her Most
Catholic Majesty will pardon the informality of your
appearance. You can point out to her that you
come, not on your own part, but as the ambassador
of others who were somewhat over-earnest in persuading you. I am sure that my two friends here
will share with me the very serious responsibility of
your unshaven chin."

"That I shall not fail to represent to her Majesty," said the Duke, bowing imperturbably.

And without any further objections he went out, followed by Concha. And that young lady with all the dignity of responsibility swelling in pride under the crossed folds of her *rebozo*, did not vouchsafe even so much as one glance to Rollo, but passed her commanding officer with eyes like those of a rear-rank man on parade, fixed immovably on the broad back of Señor Muñoz. As soon as they were alone, however, she moved up alongside, fingering her pistol-butt significantly. For this little Concha was quite resolved to use her discretion to the uttermost should any treachery be intended—aye, or even the appearance of it.

During their absence the remaining quartette in the chamber of Don Fernando Muñoz held their ground without a word of mutual converse. Rollo stared out of the window and listened eagerly to the slamming of doors and the far-away murmur of voices in the direction of the royal apartments. Ramon, like the natural fine gentleman he was, fixed his eyes on the Persian rugs which strewed the polished floor and awaited orders. But Sergeant Cardono, unconditioned by any such fine scruples, regarded with undisguised contempt mingled with pity the gold and ivory fittings of the ducal dressing-table, the plated lamps, the gilt candelabra, the Dresden china shepherdesses holding out ash-trays, and all the varied elegancies which the affection and gratitude of a Queen had provided for the tobacco-seller of Torrejon de Ardoz, who, like our own Shakespeare, was said to have held many a steed outside his father's door for a meagre dole of pence. For thus by merit, diverse in kind it is true, do the really great soar above the insignificance of their birth.

Thus in a straining silence, acute almost to breaking point, they waited. Yet something of the epic's argument came to them even at that distance—a shrill woman's voice vehemently debating, then a bass mutter of masculine argument, a quick stamp, distinctly feminine, upon the floor, then the slamming of a door, and on the back of that the sound of returning footsteps.

"The Queen refuses to receive you, I am sorry to inform you, gentlemen," said the Duke. "That I did my best this lady will bear me witness. But having had no opportunity of private conference with her Majesty, I was unable (as indeed I anticipated) to effect anything."

Rollo turned to Concha without wasting words on his former ambassador.

"Return to the Queen's chamber," he said, "and inform her Majesty that we will wait her pleasure here for other ten minutes. And if by the end of that time we are not honoured with a visit from her Majesty, we shall (most reluctantly and with all respect) be compelled to shoot Señor Fernando Muñoz, whose person we hold as a hostage for her Majesty's complaisance in the affair we have undertaken. We can waste no more time."

Concha's lips became more rigid than ever. They looked as if they never would, should, or could be kissed. Juno herself, passing sentence upon the object of great Jove's latest admiration, could not have appeared more inflexibly stern.

But she only saluted, turned on her heel like a drill-sergeant, and marched out by the side door.

In these trying circumstances the Duke of

Rianzares displayed an unexpected and wholly admirable calm. He leaned against the mantel-piece, glanced once at the ormolu timepiece with the address of a Paris maker below the winding-holes, and fell again to fingering his unshaven chin. He then turned quickly toward the trembling valet, who regarded him with eyes which seemed to apologise for such unprecedented circumstances.

"There would have been time to shave me even yet," he said, "only that you were fool enough to spill the shaving-water."

Then, as if relinquishing hope, he sighed again and fell listlessly to regarding himself in the mirror. He was a handsome man, even with an unshaven chin that showed over a dressing-gown with yellow flowers on a purple ground. Also the pulses of the tobacco-seller's son of the Ardoz *estanco* must have been urged by a pretty equal-beating heart, to enable him to take matters so calmly.

The Sergeant muttered to himself once or twice as if making mental note of an important fact which he desired to remember.

"All dandies are not cowards," was what he was saying.

CHAPTER XLI

FIVE, six, seven, eight of the ten slow minutes passed away, and beyond a glance at the clock and a more absorbing interest in the furze on his chin, Señor Muñoz had not moved. The seconds hand upon the clock on the mantelshelf was crawling round its miniature dial for the ninth time with vast apparent deliberation, when a noise was heard from the direction of the Queen's apartments.

There was a rapid gabble of tongues, a scurry of footsteps, the hissing rustle of stiff silken skirts along narrow passages, and a voice which exclaimed more and more shrilly, " The murderers ! The cowards ! Surely they will never dare ! Have they forgotten that I am a Queen ? "

And with these words Maria Cristina of Naples burst like a whirlwind into the room. Her long black hair streamed down her back. Her little daughter followed, a comb still in the hand with which she had been struggling to take the place of the lost Doña Susana, who, as before related, had gone to visit her relations.

After these two Concha followed, in appearance calm and placid as the windless Mediterranean on a day of winter.

Upon his mistress's entrance the Duke threw himself upon one knee. The rest of the company

bowed with grace or awkwardness according to
their several abilities, but the Queen-Regent did not
heed them. She flew instantly to her husband and
raised him in her arms.

"Fernando," she cried, "what is this I hear? Did
they threaten to kill you if I would not grant them
an interview? Well, here I am. Let them slay me
instead. What have you to say to me, gentlemen
and cowards? What I have to say to you is that I
hope you may not live to repent having used such
compulsion with a woman and a Queen."

Again Rollo bowed very low, and was about to
speak when the Queen interrupted.

"And as for this hussy," she cried, turning upon
Concha, "if I had my way she should be indicted
for witchcraft and burnt alive at the stake as in the
good times of the Holy Office. Yet you, Fernando,
for whom I daily risk my life, you defended her—
yes, defended her to my very face!"

"Beloved and most honoured," said the Duke,
soothingly, "I did but suggest that it would be
better to convert the girl—to make a good Christian
of her——"

"Yes—yes," cried the Queen, stamping her
foot, "but did you not add that in that case you
would like to be her Father-Confessor?"

"Certainly I did not, most gracious one,"
answered her husband, soothingly, "you wholly
mistook my meaning. All that I said was no more
than that many might be anxious to obtain the office
of Father-Confessor, being, as it were, eager to
take the credit for the restoration of so notable a
penitent."

But Rollo had small patience with the bickerings
of royal lovers at such a time.

"I must crave your Majesty's strict and instant attention," he said, suddenly dropping all ceremony. "I will only detain you for a moment if, as I anticipate, I receive your consent to what I have the honour of proposing to you."

At once the easily jealous woman froze into a Queen and fronted the young man with a haughty stare.

"Your Majesty," he began, "I do not dwell upon our services of the past night. They are known to you. Had it not been for my friends it is probable that no one of your party would at this moment have been left alive. Now the day is passing and you are no safer than you were last night. It is necessary, therefore, that you put yourselves unreservedly under the escort and protection of myself and my friends. We must leave La Granja at once."

"Never!" cried Maria Cristina, fiercely. "Am I, the Queen-Regent of Spain, to be thus badgered and commandeered? I have never suffered it since I left my father's house in Naples. A boy and a foreigner shall not be the first. My royal guards will assuredly be here in an hour at the latest. The roads will be cleared, and as for you, you shall be safe in prison cells, where, for your insolences, you ought to be lying at this moment."

"Then," said Rollo, gravely, "I deeply regret that I am obliged to use the only means that are open to me to fulfil my orders, and to induce your Highness to place yourself in safety."

"And pray," cried Maria Cristina, indignantly, "from whom can you have orders to place a Queen of Spain in restraint?"

In a moment Rollo realised that it was impossible for him to reveal his position as an officer of the Carlist armies, but a fortunate remembrance of some words dropped by the Abbot of Montblanch instantly gave him his cue.

"I act," he said calmly, "under the immediate direction of the Holy Father himself, at whose feet, in the Vatican of Rome, you shall one day kneel to ask pardon of your sins."

This unexpected reply seemed to agitate the Queen-Regent, who, though forced to create herself a party out of the men of liberal opinions in her realm, was at heart, like all the Bourbons, a convinced and even bigoted religionist. But Muñoz, who had hitherto been silent, stooped and whispered something in her ear.

"How am I to be convinced of that?" she cried, turning on him fiercely. "I will not believe it even from you!"

"I regret," said Rollo, "that your Highness must be compelled to believe it. Pray do me the honour of following my argument. The Holy Father judges it necessary for the peace of this realm, and your own soul's profit, that you should be placed in a situation where you may be able to act more in accordance with what he knows to be your secret desires for the welfare of the Church of which he is God's vicegerent on earth."

Rollo was glad to reflect that, in uttering these words, he was only repeating the sonorous phrases of Don Baltazar Varela when the Abbot delivered him his commission in his own chamber at Montblanch. He added of his own accord a little prayer to the recording angel that he might be guilty of no blasphemy in thus acting at second hand as an emissary of Holy Church. After all, it was entirely the Abbot's affair, and Rollo was anxious that it should so be understood above.

But the lady chiefly concerned continued obdurate. She would not budge an inch. She professed an absolute certainty that her guard would appear in a few hours, and with them her Father-Confessor, who would inform her how to reply to any genuine and authentic message from his Holiness Gregory the Sixteenth. Further than that she could not be moved.

"In that case," said the young man, "I will not conceal it from your Highness that considerable discretion has been granted to me. Your company and that of your daughter we must have upon our journey. It is our intention to place you and her in a place of safety——"

"To steal us—to kidnap us, you mean!" cried the Queen, with the utmost indignation.

"Your Majesty," continued Rollo, "I am not disputing about words. Our actions of last night will best explain our intentions of this morning. But with respect to this gentleman "—he turned to Señor Muñoz as he spoke—" I have no directions either to permit or compel him to accompany us. Yet since we must act with the greatest speed and secrecy, it is clearly impossible to leave him behind. I am compelled, therefore, to put an alternative before you, which, having had an opportunity to remark the Señor's courage, I am pained to declare. If your Majesty will consent to accompany us at once and without parley, Don Fernando may do so also. But if not, since we have not force sufficient to deal with additional prisoners on such a journey, it will be my unhappy duty to order the gentleman's instant execution."

A shriek from the Queen punctuated the close of this speech—one of the longest that Rollo had ever made. But the Queen, hardly yet believing in the reality of their threats, still held out. As for Muñoz, he said no word until Rollo abruptly ordered him to kneel and prepare for death.

"In that case," said the ex-guardsman, "permit me to put on a decent coat. A man ought not to die in a dressing-gown. It is not soldierly!"

Rollo bade the valet bring his master what he wanted, and presently the Duke of Rianzares, in his best uniform coat, found himself in a position to die with credit and self-respect.

But so unexpected was the nerve and resolution of the Queen that it was only when the Duke had been bidden kneel down between the halves of a French window which opened out upon a balcony that Cristina, flinging dignity finally to the winds, fell upon his neck and cried to her captors, "Take me where you wish. Do with me what you will. Only preserve to me my beloved Fernando."

Rollo turned away with a sudden easing of his heart and no little admiration. He was glad that the strain was over, and besides, he would rather have led the forlornest of hopes than have played twice upon a woman's fears for her lover. But at his back he heard the Sergeant whisper across to El Sarria, who, entirely unmoved, was uncocking his piece with much deliberation, "'Tis a deal more than she would have done for her *first* well-beloved Fernando!"

＊　　　＊　　　＊　　　＊　　　＊

In less than an hour the whole party was well on its way. The Queen-Regent was mounted on a white mule, which had been brought in from the hill pastures above El Mar. Behind came Piebald Pedro's donkey, with a basket-chair strapped upon its back for the little Princess, who was in high glee, holding Concha's hand and singing for gladness to be done with La Granja. The Sergeant and El Sarria walked one on either side of Señor Muñoz, who, by suggestion of Rollo, had assumed a coat less decorative than that in which he had proposed to make his exit from life.

In addition to the Queen's mule and the donkey, the Sergeant led a horse which was presently to be mounted by Muñoz, so soon, that is, as the rest of the party should regain the steeds they had left behind at the deserted farmhouse on the hill. But till that time it was judged most safe that the Queen's consort should walk between Ramon Garcia and the Sergeant. Rollo, with a wandering eye towards Concha and the Queen, walked and talked with Etienne and John Mortimer, whom of late the joint compulsions of love and war had compelled him somewhat to neglect.

But these good fellows bore no malice, though certainly Etienne grew a little red when Rollo, with the frankness that distinguished his every word and action, launched into enthusiastic praise of the nobility, courage, fidelity, and every other virtue characteristic of La Señorita Concha.

"In addition to which she is very pretty!" added Etienne, significantly.

Rollo stopped with the semi-indignant air of a horse pulled up short in full career. But in a moment he had recovered himself.

"Yes," he said doggedly, "she *is* very pretty!"

"Not that you are a man to care for beauty. You never were!" persisted Etienne, with a side look at Mortimer. "You have always said so yourself, you know!"

"No! I never did care!" Rollo agreed a little hastily. "But yonder is the farmhouse. I wonder if we shall find our horses as we left them."

Here Etienne laughed sardonically for no reason at all.

"I am in hopes that they will be fed and refreshed," continued Rollo, imperturbably; "we must let them have a feed of corn, too, before they start."

La Giralda, who had been leading the Queen's white mule, at that moment gave up her post to Concha, and fell back in order to whisper something to the Sergeant.

"Ah," said he aloud, as soon as he had listened to her, "that is well thought on. La Giralda and I have a little business of our own to attend to which may occupy us a few minutes. With your leave, Colonel, we will go on ahead and arrange matters for the Queen's reception. From what La Giralda tells me, it may be as well to avoid entering the house."

So when the Queen-Regent, with Concha in attendance and the little Isabel riding demurely alongside on her diminutive donkey, delighting in the unexpected excursion, arrived at the farm, they found that a large barn and granary, cool, airy, and with a roof of stone arched like the vaults of a fortress, had been prepared for them. The horses of the party had been fed and watered. Cloaks had been unstrapped and laid on piles of straw for the ladies to rest upon—that is, for her Majesty the Queen Maria Cristina—Concha being one of the comity, and little Isabel dancing everywhere after her as her inseparable tyrant and slave. For with the easy and fortunate memory of childhood, Isabel had ceased even to mention the nurse who had been with her ever since her birth, or at most remembered her only when she happened to be tired or hurt or sleepy. Indeed, she learned in a wondrously short space to run to Concha with all her troubles. So constant was the companionship of these two that it was with the utmost difficulty, and after several failures, that Rollo managed to exchange even a word with his sweetheart.

"You have been very brave," he whispered. "I should have failed but for you!"

Concha blushed hot with swift pleasure, but on this occasion her usual readiness of speech seemed to have deserted her, and she stood silent like a tongue-tied maid, greedy for the first time in her life of her own praise.

Before either could speak again, the Sergeant was back to report that La Giralda and he had dinner ready for the party.

"You must not expect much," he said; "there is little available for the pot which may with safety be cooked."

But indeed in such weather there was need for nothing better than the *arroz con pollo*—the chicken with rice, together with the abundant *gazpacho*, for the first of which he had found the materials in the store-chamber and barn-yard of the deserted farm-house.

"Also there is an abundance of vegetables in the garden—when you get them separated from the weeds, that is," he explained; "the clear air of these heights has enabled them to keep their flavour to perfection."

He did not add that he had also seen in that same garden a mound of newly-dug earth, under

2 E

which lay, beside her little daughter, a mother as loving and more faithful than that Queen-Mother for whose sake they were risking their lives.

The Sergeant's hurriedly prepared lunch was a prodigious success.

The great folk partook as heartily as any, and (perhaps owing to their extreme youth) the *pollos* tasted much more tender than could have been expected, considering the fact that the Sergeant had found them industriously pecking and scratching in the dust of the farmyard upon his arrival, and that, while he dug the grave, he had sent La Giralda to drive them into a wood-shed, where presently they were captured *en masse*.

Rollo ate but little, for he was intensely excited. He had succeeded beyond expectation so far, and now he was beginning to see his way past all entanglements to the successful accomplishment of his mission. His plan was to proceed by unfrequented paths, such as were, however, perfectly familiar to his adjutant Sergeant Cardono, along the northern slopes of the Guadarrama till he should be able to look out across the fertile plain of the Duero towards the mural front of the Sierra de Moncayo.

Thence by forced marches across the valley, undertaken at night, he might hope in two stages at most to put his charges under the care of General Elio, the immediate representative of Don Carlos, who had established his headquarters there. Small wonder that Rollo grew excited. The worst seemed over—the myriad adventures, the perilous passes, the thousand enemies. Now the plains lay before him, and—Concha loved him.

If only this weight of responsibility were once off his mind—ah, then!

Poor Rollo! And indeed poor humankind in general! How often the wind falls to a breeze, heat-tempering, grateful, which comes in fits and starts, not severe enough to chill, yet long enough to cool the body weary of the summer heats, with a sense of grateful relief.

And it is precisely in the teeth of such a gentle-breathing, cheek-fanning earth-wind that the thunder-storm comes riding up overhead, its flanks black and ragged with rain and fierce spurts of hail, and in the midst of all the white desolating lightnings zigzag-ging to the ground.

CHAPTER XLII

A SNARE NOT SPREAD IN VAIN

THE town of Aranda lay to the left, perched high
above them on the slopes of the Sierra de Moncayo.
Rollo looked past the crumbling grey turrets of the
little fortalice and over the juniper-and-thyme covered
foothills to the red peaks of the Sierra. From the
point at which they stood Moncayo fronted them
like a lion surprised at the mouth of his lair, that
raises his head haughtily to view the rash trespassers
on his domain.

The lower slopes of the mountain were tawny-
yellow, like the lion's fell, but from the line at
which the scant mane of rock-plants ceased, Moncayo
shone red as blood in the level rays of the setting
sun.

"There, there!" thought Rollo, "I have it
almost in hand now. Beyond that flank lie Vera
and the headquarters of General Elio!"

They were riding easily, debouching slowly and
in single file out of one of the many defiles with which
the country was cut up. The Sergeant and Rollo
were leading, when, as they issued out upon the
opener country, suddenly they heard themselves
called upon peremptorily to halt, at the peril of
their lives.

420

"Whom have we here? Ah, our highly certificated Englishman! And in his company—whom?"

The speaker was a dark-haired man of active figure and low stature, whose eyes twinkled in his head. He was dressed in the full uniform of a Carlist general. About him rode a brilliant staff, and from behind every rock and out of every deep gully-cleft protruded the muzzle of a rifle, with just one black eye peering along it from under the white Basque *boina* or the red one of Navarre.

And for the third time Rollo Blair, out upon his adventures, had come face to face with General Don Ramon Cabrera of Tortosa.

Yet it was with glad relief in his heart that Rollo instantly rode up to Cabrera, and having saluted, thus began his report, "I have the honour, General, to report that I have been fortunate enough to induce her Majesty the Queen-Regent of Spain and her daughter the young Queen Isabel to place themselves under my protection. I am proceeding with them to the headquarters of General Elio according to my instructions; and if it be at all convenient, I should be glad of an additional escort, that I may be able to bring my charges safely within the lines of Vera!"

The brow of General Cabrera had been darkening during this speech, and at the close he burst out with an oath.

"I know no such person as the Queen-Regent of Spain. I have heard of a certain light-o'-love calling herself Maria Cristina, widow of the late King Fernando the Seventh. And if this be indeed the lady and her brat, we of the true opinion owe you, Don Rollo, a debt of gratitude which shall not be easily repaid. For she and hers have troubled the peace of this country much and long. Of which now, by San Nicolas, there shall be a quick end!"

As he spoke he ran his eyes along the line to where Muñoz rode behind his mistress.

"And the tall gentleman with the polished whiskers? Who may he be?" he cried, a yet more venomous fire glittering in his eyes.

"That, General Cabrera," said Rollo, quietly, "is his Excellency the Duke of Rianzares."

"At last, *estanco*-keeper!" cried Cabrera, riding forward as if to strike Muñoz on the face. "I, Ramon Cabrera of Tortosa, have waited a long time for this pleasure."

Muñoz did not answer in words, but, as before, preserved his imperturbable demeanour. His half contemptuous dignity of bearing, which had irritated even Rollo, seemed to have the power of exciting Cabrera to the point of fury.

"Colonel," he cried, "I relieve you of your charge. You have done well. I am the equal in rank of General Elio, and there is no need that you should convoy this party to his camp. I will assume the full charge—yes, and responsibility. By the Holy St. Vincent, I promised them twenty for one when they slew my mother in the Square of the Barbican. But I knew not from how evil a vine-stock I should gather my second vintage. A poor commandant's wife from a petty Valentian fort was the best I could do for them at the time. But now —the mother of Ramon Cabrera shall be atoned for in such a fashion as shall make the world sit dumb!"

While Cabrera was speaking Rollo grew slowly chill, and then ice-cold with horror.

"Sir," he said, his voice suddenly hoarse and broken, "surely you do not realise what you are

saying. These ladies are under my protection.
They have committed themselves to my care under
the most sacred and absolute pledges that their lives
shall be respected. The same is the case with
regard to Señor Muñoz. It is absolutely necessary
that I should place them all under the care of General
Elio as the personal representative of the King!"

"I have already told you, sir," cried Cabrera,
furiously, "that I am of equal rank with any Elio
or other general in the armies of Don Carlos. Have
not I done more than any other? Was it not I who
carried my command to the gates of Madrid? Aye,
and had I been left to myself, I should have succeeded
in cutting off that fox Mendizabal. Now, however,
I am absolutely independent, owing authority to no
man, save to the King alone. It is mine to give or
to withhold, to punish or to pardon. Therefore
I, General Ramon Cabrera, having sworn publicly to
avenge my mother, when, where, and how I can,
solemnly declare that, as a retaliation, I will shoot
these three prisoners to-morrow at sunrise, even
as Nogueras, the representative of this woman who
calls herself Queen-Regent of Spain, shot down my
innocent mother for the sole crime of giving birth
to an unworthy son! Take them away! I will
hear no more!"

* * * * *

Thus in a moment was Rollo toppled from the
highest pinnacle of happiness, for such to a young
man is the hope of immediate success. He cursed
the hour he had entered the bloodthirsty land
of Spain. He cursed his visit to the Abbey of
Montblanch, and the day on which he accepted a
commission from men without honour or humanity.
He was indeed almost in case to do himself a hurt,

and both Concha and the Sergeant watched him with anxious solicitude during the remainder of the afternoon as he wandered disconsolately about the little camp, twirling his moustache and clanking Killie-crankie at his heels with so fierce an air, that even Cabrera's officers, no laggards on the field of honour, kept prudently out of his way.

The royal party had been disposed in a small house, a mere summer residence of some of the *bourgeois* folk of Aranda, and there, by an unexpected act of grace and at the special supplication of the Sergeant, La Giralda had been permitted to wait upon them.

The beauty of Concha was not long in producing its usual effect upon the impressionable sons of Navarre and Guipuzcoa. But the Sergeant, whose *prestige* was unbounded, soon gave them to understand that the girl had better be left to go her own way, having two such protectors as Rollo and El Sarria to fight her battles for her.

To the secret satisfaction of all the Sergeant did not resume his duties in the camp of Cabrera. The troop to which he belonged had been left behind to watch the movements of the enemy. For Cabrera had barely escaped from a strong force under Espartero near the walls of Madrid itself, by showing the cleanest of heels possible. Cardono, therefore, still attached himself unreproved to the party of Rollo, which camped a little apart. A guard of picked men was, however, placed over the quarters of the royal family. This Cabrera saw to himself, and then sullenly withdrew into his tent for the night to drink *aguardiente* by himself, in gloomy converse with a heart into whose dark secrets at no time could any man enter. It is, indeed, the most charitable supposition that at this period of his life Ramon Cabrera's love for a mother most cruelly murdered had rendered him temporarily insane.

Deprived of La Giralda, and judging that Rollo was in no mood to be spoken with, Concha Cabezos took refuge in the society of El Sarria. That stalwart man of few words, though in the days of her light-heartedness quite careless of her wiles, and, indeed, unconscious of them, was in his way strongly attached to her. He loved the girl for the sake of her devotion to Dolóres, as well as because of the secret preference which all grave and silent men have for the winsome and gay.

"This Butcher of Tortosa," she said in a low voice to Ramon Garcia, "will surely never do the thing he threatens. Not even a devil out of hell could slay in cold blood not the Queen-Regent only, but also the innocent little maid who never did any man a wrong."

El Sarria looked keenly about him for possible listeners. Concha and he sat at some distance above the camp, and El Sarria was idly employed in breaking off pieces of shaly rock and trying to hit a certain pinnacle of white quartz which made a prominent target a few yards beneath them.

"I think he will," said Ramon Garcia, slowly. "Cabrera is a sullen dog at all times, and the very devil in his cups. Besides, who am I to blame him —is there not the matter of his mother? Had it been Dolóres—well. For her sake I would have shot half a dozen royal families."

"The thing will break our Rollo's heart if it cannot be prevented," sighed Concha, "for he hath taken it in his head that the Queen and her husband trusted themselves to his word of honour."

Ramon Garcia shook his head sadly.

"Ah, 'tis his sacred thing, that honour of his—his image of the Virgin which he carries about with him," he said. "And, indeed, El Sarria has little cause to complain, for had it not been for that same honour of Don Rollo's, Dolóres Garcia might at this moment have been in the hands of Luis Fernandez!"

"Aye, or dead, more like," said Concha; "she would never have lived in the clutches of the evil-hearted! I know her better. But, Don Ramon, what can we, who owe him so much, do for our Don Rollo?"

"Why—what is there to do?" said Ramon, with a lift of his eyebrows. "Here in the camp of Cabrera we are watched, followed, suspected. Do you see that fellow yonder with the smartly set *boina*? He is a miller's son from near Vitoria in Alava. Well, he hath been set to watch that none of us leave the camp unattended. I will wager that if you and I were to wander out fifty yards farther, yonder lad would be after us in a trice!"

"Ah!" said Concha, in a brown study. "Yes—he is not at all a bad-looking boy, and thinks excessively well of himself—like some others I could mention. Now, El Sarria, can you tell me in which direction lies Vera, the headquarters of General Elio?"

"That can I!" said El Sarria, forgetting his caution. And he was about to turn him about and point it out with his hand, when Concha stopped him.

"The miller's son is craning his neck to look," she whispered: "do not point. Turn about slowly, and the third stone you throw, let it be in the direction of Vera!"

El Sarria did as he was bid, and after the third he continued to project stones Vera-wards, explaining as he did so—"Up yonder reddish cleft the road goes, a hound's path, a mere goat's slide, but it is the directest road. There is open ground to the very foot of the ascent. Many is the time I have ridden thither, God forgive me, on another man's beast! Then cast him loose and left him to find his way home as best he could. There are good hiding-places on the Sierra de Moncayo, up among the red sandstone where the caves are deep and dry, and with mouths so narrow and secret that they may be held by one man against fifty."

Concha did not appear to be greatly interested in El Sarria's reminiscences. Even guileless Ramon could not but notice her wandering glances. Her eyes, surveying the landscape, lighted continually upon the handsome young Vitorian in the red *boina*, lifted again sharply, and sought the ground.

At this El Sarria sighed, and decided mentally that, with the exception of his Dolóres, no woman was to be trusted. If not at heart a rake, she was by nature a flirt. And so he was about to leave Concha to her own devices and seek Rollo, when Concha suddenly spoke.

"Don Ramon," she said, "shall we walk a few hundred yards up the mountain away from the camp and see if we are really being watched?"

El Sarria smiled grimly to himself and rose. The stratagem was really, he thought, too transparent, and his impression was strengthened when Concha presently added, "I will not ask you to remain if you would rather go back. Then we will see whom they are most suspicious of, you or I. A girl may often steal a horse when a man dares not look over the wall."

In the abstract this was incontestable, but El Sarria only smiled the more grimly. After all Dolóres was the only woman upon whose fidelity one would be justified in wagering the last whiff of a good *cigarillo*. And as if reminded of a duty El Sarria rolled a beauty as he dragged one huge foot after another slowly up the hill in the rear of Concha, who, her love-locks straying on the breeze, her *basquiña* held coquettishly in one hand, and the prettiest toss of the head for the benefit of any whom it might concern, went leaping upwards like a young roe.

All the while Rollo was sitting below quite unconscious of this treachery. His head was sunk on his hand. Deep melancholy brooded in his heart. He rocked to and fro as if in pain. Looking down from the mountain-side Ramon Garcia pitied him.

" Ah, poor innocent young man," he thought, "doubtless he believes that the heart of this girl is all his own. But all men are fools—a butterfly is always a butterfly and an Andaluse an Andaluse to the day of her death ! "

Then turning his thoughts backward, he remembered the many who had taken their turn with mandolin and guitar at the *rejas* of Concha's window when he and Dolóres lived outside the village of Sarria ; and he (ah, thrice fool !) had taken it into his thick head to be jealous.

Well, after all this was none of his business, he thanked the saints. He was not responsible for the vagaries of pretty young women. He wondered vaguely whether he ought to tell Rollo. But after turning the matter this way and that, he decided

against it, remembering the dire consequences of
jealousy in his own case, and concluding with the
sage reflection that there were plenty of mosquitoes
in the world already without beating the bushes for
more.

But with the corner of an eye more accustomed to
the sun glinting on rifle barrels than to the flashing eyes
of beauty, El Sarria could make out that the Vitorian
in the red *boina* was following them, his gun over
his shoulder, trying, not with conspicuous success
to assume the sauntering air of a man who, having
nothing better to do, goes for a stroll in the summer
evening.

" 'Tis the first time that ever I saw a soldier off
duty take his musket for a walk!" growled El
Sarria, "and why on the Sierra de Moncayo does
the fellow stop to trick himself out as for a *festa*?"

Concha looked over her shoulder, presumably at
El Sarria, though why the maiden's glances were so
sprightly and her lips so provokingly pouted is a
question hard enough to be propounded for the
doctorial thesis at Salamanca. For Ramon Garcia
was stolid as an ox of his native Aragon, and arch
glances and pretty gestures were as much wasted
on him as if he chewed the cud. Still he was not
even in these matters so dull and unobservant as
he looked, that is, when he had any reason for
observing.

"Here comes that young ass of Alava," he
murmured. "Well, he is at least getting his money's
worth. By the saints favourable to my native
parish, the holy Narcissus and Justus, but the *burro*
is tightening his girths!"

And El Sarria laughed out suddenly and sardonically. For he could see the lad pulling his

leathern belt a few holes tighter, in order that he might present his most symmetrical figure to the eyes of this dazzling Andalucian witch who had dropped so suddenly into the Carlist camp from the place whence all witches come.

CHAPTER XLIII

CONCHA and El Sarria sat down on an outcrop of
red sandstone rock, and gazed back at the prospect.
There below them lay the camp and the house in
which was imprisoned the reigning branch of the
royal family of Spain. A couple of sentries paced
to and fro in front. A picket had established itself
for the night in the back courtyard. Beyond that
again stood the tent in which the General was at
present engaged in drinking himself from his usual
sullen ferocity into unconsciousness.

A little nearer, and not far from their own camp-
fire, at which the Sergeant was busily preparing the
evening meal, sat Rollo, sunk in misery, revolving a
thousand plans and ready for any desperate venture
so soon as night should fall. Concha gave a quick
little sigh whenever her eye fell on him. Perhaps
her conscience pricked her—perhaps not! With
the heart of such a woman doth neither stranger nor
friend intermeddle with any profit.

The sauntering Vitorian halted within speaking
distance of the pair.

"A fine evening," he said affably. "Can you give
me a light for my cigarette?"

It was on the tip of El Sarria's tongue to inquire
whether there were not plenty of lights for his

431

cigarette back at the camp-fires where he had rolled it. But that most excellent habit, which Don Ramon had used from boyhood, of never interfering in the business of another, kept him silent.

"Why should I," he thought, "burn my fingers with stirring this young foreigner's *olla* ? Time was when I made a pretty mess enough of my own ! "

So without speech he blew the end off his *cigarillo* and handed it courteously to the Carlist soldier.

But Concha had no qualms about breaking the silence. The presence of a duenna was nowise necessary to the opening of her lips, which last had also sometimes been silenced without the intervention of a chaperon.

"A fine evening, indeed," she said, smiling down at the youth. " I presume that you are a foot soldier from the musket you carry. It must be a fine one from the care you take of it ! But as for me, I like cavaliers best."

" The piece is as veritable a cross-eyed old shrew as ever threw a bullet ten yards wide of the mark," cried the Alavan, tossing his musket down upon the short elastic covering of hill-plants on which he stood, and taking his cigarette luxuriously from his lips. "Nor am I an infantry-man, as you suppose. Doubtless the *Señorita* did not observe my spurs as I came. Of the best Potosi silver they are made. I am a horseman of the Estella regiment. Our good Carlos the Fifth (whom God bring to his own !) is not yet rich enough to provide us with much in the way of a uniform, but a pair of spurs and a *boina* are within reach of every man's purse. Or if he has not the money to buy them, they are to be had at the first tailor's we may chance to pass ! "

"And very becoming they are ! " said Concha,

glancing wickedly at the youth, who sat staring at her and letting his cigarette go out. " 'Tis small wonder you are a conquering corps ! I have often heard tell of the Red Boinas of Navarre ! "

" I think I will betake me down to the camp—I smell supper ! " broke in El Sarria, curtly. He began to think that Mistress Concha had no further use for him, and, being assured on this point, he set about finding other business for himself. For, with all his simplicity, Ramon Garcia was an exceedingly practical man.

" The air is sweet up here ; I prefer it to supper," said Concha. " I will follow you down in a moment. Perhaps this gentleman desires to keep you company to the camp and canteen."

But it soon appeared that the Vitorian was also impressed by the marvellous sweetness of the mountain air, and equally desirous of observing the changeful lights and lengthening shadows which the sun of evening cast, sapphire and indigo, Venetian red and violet-grey, among the peaks of the Sierra de Moncayo. When two young people are thus simultaneously stricken with an admiration for scenery, their conversation is seldom worth repeating. But the Señorita Concha is so unusual a young lady that in this case an exception must be made.

Awhile she gazed pensively up at the highest summits of the mountain, now crimson against a saffron sky, for at eventide Spain flaunts her national colours in the very heavens. Then she heaved a deep sigh.

" You are doubtless a fine horseman ? " she cried, clasping her hands—" oh, I adore all horses ! I love to see a man ride as a man should ! "

The young man coloured. This was, in truth,

2 F

the most open joint in his armour. Above all things
he prided himself upon his horsemanship. Concha
had judged as much from his care of his spurs. And
then to be mistaken for an infantry tramper !

"Ah," he said, "if the *Señorita* could only see my
mare La Perla ! I got her three months ago from
the stable of a black-blooded National whose house
we burnt near Zaragoza. She has carried me ever
since without a day's lameness. There is not the
like of her in the regiment. Our mounts are for
the most part mere *garrons* of Cataluña or Aragonese
ponies with legs like the pillars of a cellar, surmounted
by barrels as round as the wine-tuns themselves."

At this Concha looked still more pensive. Presently she heaved another sigh and tapped her
slender shoe with a chance spray of heath.

"Oh, I wish——" she began, and then stopped
hastily as if ashamed.

"If it be anything that I can do for you," cried
the young man, enthusiastically, "you shall not have
to wish it long !"

As he spoke he forsook the stone on which he
had been sitting for another nearer to the pretty
cross-tied shoes of Andalucian pattern that showed
beneath the skirts of Concha's *basquiña*.

"Ah, how I love horses !" murmured Concha ;
"doubtless, too, yours is of my country—of the
beautiful sunny Andalucia which I may never see
again !"

"The mare is indeed believed by all who have
knowledge to have Andalucian blood in her veins,"
answered the Alavan.

Concha rose to her feet impulsively.

"Then," she said, "I must see her. Also I am
devoured with eagerness to see you ride."

She permitted her eyes to take in the trim figure of the Vitorian, who had also risen to his feet.

"Do go and bring her," she murmured; "I will take care of your musket. You need not be a moment, and—I will wait for you!"

A little spark kindles a great fire in a Spanish heart, and the young man, counting the cost, rapidly decided that the risk was worth running. The horses of the Estella regiment were picketed in a little hollow a few hundred yards behind the main camp. It was his duty to watch these two strangers, of whom one had already gone back to the camp, while as to the other—well, Adrian Zumaya of the province of Alava felt at that moment that he could cheerfully devote the rest of his life to watching that other.

In a moment more he had laid down his musket at Concha's feet, and set off as fast as he could in the direction of the horses, keeping well out of sight in the trough of a long roller of foot-hill until he was close to the cavalry lines, and could smell the honest stable-smell which in the open air mingled curiously with those of aromatic thyme and resinous juniper.

In five minutes he was back, riding his best and sitting like a Centaur.

Concha's eyes glistened with pleasure, and she ran impulsively forward to pat the cream-coloured mare, a clean-built, well-gathered, workmanlike steed.

Now the young man was very proud of the interest this pretty Andalucian girl was showing in his equipment and belongings to the exclusion of those of his comrades. Perhaps he might have been less pleased had he known that the young lady's interest extended even to the gun he had left behind him, the charge of which she had already managed to extract with deft and competent fingers.

" La Perla she is called," he cried with enthusiasm,
" and sure none other ever better deserved the name !
I wish we of the camp possessed a side-saddle that
the *Señorita* might try her paces. She has the easiest
motion in the world. It is like riding in a great
lady's coach with springs or being carried in a Sedan-
chair. But she is of a delicate mouth. Ah, yes—if
the *Señorita* mounted, it would be necessary to
remember that she must not bear hard upon the
reins. Then would La Perla of a certainty take the
bit between her teeth and run like the devil when
Father Mateo is after him with a holy water
syringe ! "

Concha smiled as the young fellow dismounted,
flinging himself off with the lithe grace of youth and
constant practice.

" You forget," she said, " I also am of the
Province of Flowers. Do not be afraid. La Perla
and I will not fall out. A side-saddle—any saddle !
What needs Concha Cabezos with side-saddle when
she hath ridden unbroken Andalucian jennets wild
over the meadows of Mairena, with no better bridle
than their manes of silk and no other saddle than
their glossy hides, brown as toasted bread ! "

As she made this boast Concha patted La Perla's
pretty head, who, recognising a lover of her kind,
muzzled an affectionate nose under the girl's arm.

" Oh, how I wish I could try you," she cried,
" were it but for a moment—darling among steeds,
Pearl of Andalucia ! "

" La Perla is very gentle," suggested the young
cavalier of Alava, as he thought most subtly.
" With me at the mare's head the *Señorita* might
safely enough ride. But for fear of interruption let
us first proceed a little way out of sight of the camp."

They descended behind the long ridge till the camp was entirely hidden, and as they did so the heart of the young Vitorian beat fast. They think plentifully well of themselves, these young men of Alava and Navarre. And this one felt that he would not disgrace the name of his parent city.

"Only for a moment, *Señorita*, permit me—there! The *Señorita* goes up like a bird! Now wait till I take her head, and beware of jerking the rein hastily on account of the delicacy of the little lady's mouth. So, La Perla,—gently and daintily! Consider, jewel of mares, what a precious burden is now on thy back!"

"A moment, only a moment!" cried Concha, her hands apparently busy about her hair, "this *rebozo* is no headgear to ride in. What shall I do? A handkerchief is not large enough. Ah, *Cavallero*, add to your kindness by lending me your *boina*! I thank you a thousand times! There! Is that so greatly amiss?"

And she set the red *boina* daintily upon her hair, pulling the brim sideways to shade her eyes from the level evening sun, and smiled down at the young man who stood at her side.

"Perfect! Beautiful!" cried the young Vitorian, clasping his hands. "The sight would set on fire the heart of Don Carlos himself. Ah, take care! Bear easily on that rein. Stop, La Perla! Stop! I beseech you!"

And he started running with all his might. Alas, in vain! For the wicked Concha, the moment that he had stepped back to take in the effect of the red *boina*, dropped a heel (into which she had privately inserted half an inch of pin, taken from her own headgear), upon the flank of La Perla. The mare

sprang forward, with nostrils distended and a fierce
jerk of the head.   Concha pulled hard as if in terror,
and presently was flying over the plain towards the
cleft on the shoulder of Moncayo beyond which lay
the camp of General Elio.

The young Carlist stood a moment aghast. Then
slowly he realised the situation.   Whereupon, crying
aloud the national oath, he ground his heel into the
grass, snatched at his gun, kneeled upon one knee,
took careful aim, and clicked down the trigger.   No
report followed, however, and a slight inspection satisfied him that he had been tricked, duped, made a fool
of by a slip of a girl, a girl with eyes—yes, and eyelashes. He leaped in the air and shouted aloud great
words in Basque which have no direct equivalents in
any polite European language, but which were well
enough understood in the stone age.

However, he wasted no time foolishly.   Well he
knew that for such mistakes there was in Cabrera's
code neither forgiveness nor, indeed, any penalty save
one.   Adrian Zumaya of the province of Alava was
young. He desired much to live, if only that he might
meet that girl again at whose retreating figure he had
a moment before pointed an empty gun barrel.   Ah,
he would be even with her yet ! So, wasting no time
on leave-taking, he bent low behind the ridge, and
keeping well in the shelter of boulder and underbrush, made a bee-line for the cliffs of Moncayo,
where presently, in one of the caves of which El
Sarria had spoken, he counted his cartridges and
reloaded his rifle, with little regret, except when he
wished that the incident had happened after, instead
of before supper.

However, he had in reserve a hand's-breadth of
sausage in his pocket, together with a fragment of

most ancient and rock-like cheese. These, since no better might be, he made the best of, and as the sun sank and the camp below him grew but a blur in the gloom, he washed them down with the water which percolated through the roof of the cave and fell in great drops, as regularly as a pendulum swings, upon the floor below. These he caught in his palms and drank with much satisfaction. And in the intervals he execrated the Señorita Concha Cabezos, late of Andalucia, with polysyllabic vehemence.

But ere he curled himself up to sleep in the dryest corner of the cave, he burst into a laugh.

"In truth," he said, "she deserves La Perla. For a cleverer wench or a prettier saw I never one!"

The young man's last act before he laid himself down in his new quarters had been to take from his coat the circular disc with the letters "C. V.," the badge of the only Catholic, absolute, and legitimate king. Then, approaching the precipice as nearly as in the uncertain light he dared, he cast it from him in the direction of the Carlist lines.

"Shoot whom you will at sunrise, queen or camp-wench, king or knave," he muttered, "you shall not have Adrian Zumaya of Vitoria to put a bullet through!"

So easily was allegiance laid down or taken up in these civil wars of Spain. And that night it was noised abroad through all the camp that young Zumaya of the Estella regiment of cavalry had taken his horse and gone off with the pretty *Señorita* whom he had been set to watch.

Upon which half his comrades envied him, and the other half hoped he would be captured, saying, "It will be bad for Adrian Zumaya of the Estella regiment if he comes again within the clutches of our excellent Don Ramon Cabrera."

And this was a fact of which the aforesaid Adrian himself was exceedingly well aware. But the most curious point about the whole matter is that when he awoke late next morning he found the sun shining brilliantly into the mouth of the cave. The camp had vanished. There was a haze of sulphur in the air which bit his nostrils, and lo! beneath him, on a little plot of coarse green grass and hill-plants, a cream-coloured horse was quietly feeding.

"It is my own Perla!" he cried, as, careless of danger, he hastened down. There was a red object attached to the mare's bridle. He went round and detached a red *boina*, to which was pinned a scrap of paper. Upon it was written these words:

"*I hope you have not missed either of the objects herewith returned. They served me nobly. I send my best thanks for the loan.—C. C.*"

"That is very well," said the young man, smiling as he mounted his horse, "but all the same, had my heels not served me better than my head, your best thanks, pretty mistress, had come too late. They would not have kept me from biting the dust at sunrise with half a dozen bullets in my gizzard, instead of waking here comfortably on an empty stomach. Well, I suppose I must don the cap of liberty now and be a *chapelgorri*. It is a pity. 'Tis not one half so becoming as the *boina* to one of my complexion."

Then Adrian Zumaya, late of the Estella regiment of Carlist horse, meditated a little longer upon the mutability of all earthly affairs.

"Yet perhaps that is just as well!" he added.

"It is ever my hard fate to lose my head where a woman is concerned."

For he thought how the last admirer of his red *boina* had served him. So with a little sigh of regret he tossed it into the first juniper bush, and tying a kerchief about his head in the manner of the Cristinos, rode forth light-heartedly to seek his fate, like a true soldier of *fortune*.

CHAPTER XLIV

"FOR ROLLO'S SAKE"

YET for all this brave adventure Concha was as far as ever from meeting with General Elio. She had not even reached Vera, where it sits proudly on the northern slopes of the Moncayo—not though El Sarria had quite correctly pointed out the path, and though La Perla had served her like the very pearl and pride of all Andalucian steeds.

For once more, as so often in this history and in all men's lives, the cup had slipped on its way to the lip, the expected unexpected had happened—and Concha found herself in the wrong camp.

She rode at full speed (as we have seen) out of sight—that is, the sight of La Perla's owner. And owing to the red *boina*—which Master Adrian considered to become her so well, she came very near to riding out of this history. For, through the higher *arroyo* of Aranda de Moncayo, which (like a slice cut clean out of a bride's cake) divides the shoulder of the mountain, she rode directly into the camp of a field force operating against Cabrera under the personal command of General Espartero, the future dictator and present Commander-in-Chief of all the armies of the Queen-Regent.

At first she was nowise startled, thinking only that Vera and General Elio were nearer than had been represented. "Well," she thought, "so much the better!"

But as she came near she saw the measured tread of sentries to and fro. She observed the spick-and-span tents, the uniforms and the shining barrels of the muskets, which in another moment would have arrested her headlong course.

Concha at once perceived, even without looking at the standard which drooped at the tent door of the officer in command, that this could be no mere headquarters of Carlist *partidas*.

As women are said by the Wise Man to be of their lover's religion if he have one, and if he have none, never to miss it; so Concha was quite ready to be of the politics which were most likely to deliver Rollo from his present difficulties. Therefore, taking the red *boina* from her head, an act which disturbed still more the severe precision of her locks, she dashed at full speed into the camp, crying, "*Viva la Reina! Viva Maria Cristina! Vive Isabel Segunda!*"

Checking her steed before the standard, Concha first saluted the surprised group. Then giving a hand to the nearest (and best-looking) officer, she dismounted with a spring light as the falling of a leaf from a tree. With great solemnity she advanced to the staff from which the heavy standard hung low, and taking the embroidered fringe between finger and thumb, touched it with her lips.

Yet if you had called our little Concha a humbug —which in certain aspects of her character would have been a perfectly proper description—she would have replied in the utmost simplicity, and with a completely disarming smile, "But I only did it for Rollo's sake!"

Which was true in its way, but (strangely enough)

the thought of an audience always stirred Mistress
Concha to do her best—"for Rollo's sake!"

"Take me to the General," she said, with a
glance round the circle; "I have ridden from the
camp of the enemy to bring him tidings of the
utmost importance. Every moment is precious!"

"But the General is asleep," a staff-officer objected;
"he gave orders that he was not to be called on
any account."

"Tell him that upon his hearing my news depend
the lives of the Queen-Regent and her daughter, the
young Queen. The Cause itself hangs in the
balance!"

And to hear Concha pronounce the last words
was enough to have made a convert of Don Carlos
himself. Who could have supposed that till within
a few hours she had been heart and soul with the
enemies of "The Cause"? Certainly not the
smart Madrid officers who stood round, wishing that
they had shaved more recently, and that their
"other" uniforms had not been hanging, camphor-
scented on account of the moths, in the close-
shuttered lodgings about the Puerta del Sol.

The Commander-in-Chief solved the difficulty,
however, at that very moment, by appearing opportunely at the door of his tent.

General Espartero at this time was a man of forty-
five. His services in South America had touched his
hair with grey. In figure he was heavily built, but,
in spite of fever-swamps and battle-wounds, still erect
and soldierly.

"What news does the *Señorita* bring?" he asked
with a pleasant smile.

"That I can only tell to yourself, General," the
girl answered; "my name is Concha Cabezos of

Seville. My father had the honour to serve with you in the War of the Independence!"

"And a good soldier he was, *Señorita*," said Espartero, courteously. "I remember him well at Salamanca. He fought by my side like a brother!"

Now since Concha was well aware that her father had not even been present at that crowning mercy, she smiled, and was comforted to know that even the great General Baldomero Espartero was an Andalucian —and a humbug.

For which the Commander-in-Chief had the less excuse, since *he* could not urge that it was done " for Rollo's sake!"

Concha knew better than to blurt out her news concerning the presence of the Queen and her daughter so near the camp. That wise little woman had her terms to make, and for so much was prepared to give so much.

Therefore from the first word she kept Rollo in the foreground of her narrative. He it was who, single-handed, had saved the little Queen. He it was who had defended La Granja against the gipsies. It was, indeed, somewhat unfortunate that the Queen-Regent should have conceived a certain prejudice against him, but then (here Concha smiled) the General knew well what these great ladies were —on mountain-heights one day, in deep sea-abysses the next. Rollo had compelled the party to leave the infected district of La Granja for the healthy one of the Sierra de Moncayo. What else, indeed, could he do? The road to Madrid was in the hands of roving *partidas* of the malignant, as his Excellency knew, and it was only in this direction that there was any chance of safety. That was Master Rollo's whole offence.

Most unfortunately, however, when on the very

threshold of safety, his party had been ambushed and taken by Cabrera. But the captor's force was a small one, and with boldness and caution the whole band of the malignants, together with their prisoners, might be secured. The Carlist General had threatened to murder the two Queens and the Duke of Rianzares at sunrise, as was his butcherly wont. And if Espartero would deliver the royal party, not only was his own future assured, but the fortunes of all who had taken any part in the affair.

The General listened carefully, looking all the while, not at Concha, but down at the little folding table of iron which held a map of Northern Spain. He continued to draw figures of eight upon it with his forefinger till Concha's eyes wearied of watching him, as she nervously waited his decision.

"How came you here?" he asked at last.

"I borrowed a mare and a Carlist *boina*, and rode hither as fast as horseflesh could carry me. I heard from a friend of the Cause that your command was in the neighbourhood!"

"And from whom did you receive that intelligence? I thought the fact was pretty well concealed? Indeed, we only arrived an hour ago!"

Concha cast about for a name. The necessary fiction was also, of course, "for Rollo's sake." A thought struck her. She would serve another comrade, as it were, *en passant*.

"From a good friend in the Carlist ranks," she said, "one Sergeant Cardono!"

The General looked a little nonplussed, for, like many generals of all nationalities, he had no slight *penchant* for omniscience.

"I never heard of him," he said sharply. "Who may he be?"

Concha leaned yet closer and laid a small, soft, brown hand gently upon the General's gold-embroidered cuff. The General, not being so simple as he looked, drew back his arm a little so that the hand rested a moment on his wrist ("for Rollo's sake") before it was gently withdrawn.

"You have heard of José Maria of Ronda?" she whispered.

The General's face lighted up, and as swiftly dulled down.

"Certainly; what Andalucian has not?" he said. "But José Maria is dead. He was executed at Salamanca!"

"Ah," said Concha, "that tale was for the consumption of Don Carlos and his friends! In fact, he is the best spy we Nationals ever had—aye, or ever will have!"

"Ah!" said Espartero, lost in thought. There were some matters which seemed to need clearing up, but on the whole the thing looked probable.

Espartero had but recently been appointed to the district, and, being an Andalucian, he was naturally still imperfectly acquainted with much that had been done by his many incapable predecessors. Now, it is true that on this occasion our Concha was inventing, or rather (for the word is a hard one to use of so charming a personality) restating as facts certain hints which had fallen from the lips of La Giralda. But she was also speaking from a profound knowledge of gipsy nature, which, as in the case of Ezquerra and La Giralda herself, never attaches itself permanently or from conviction to any cause, but uses all equally according to whim, liking, or self-interest.

Concha, in a whirlwind of excitement, would have

liked the General to attack the Carlist camp immediately, but the more cautious Don Baldomero only
shook his head.

"That is all very well when a small force is to
be rushed at any cost," he said, "or a strong position
taken along lines previously studied by daylight or
opened up by artillery. But when our object is to
preserve the lives of persons so important to the
world as the royal family of Spain, lying at the
mercy of ruffians who would not hesitate to murder
every one of them in cold blood—it is best to wait
for the attack till the morning. So I will push
forward my forces on all sides, and, if all goes well,
surprise Cabrera at the earliest glimmering of dawn."

"And my friends who have suffered so much
to bring this about?" urged Concha, anxiously.
"What of them?"

"I promise you, on my honour, that they shall
be protected and rewarded!" said Espartero.

"And Don Rollo, the brave Scot—even if the
Queen continues to dislike him?" persisted Concha.

"*Señorita*," smiled the General, "it will be a
vastly greater peril to the young man, I fear, if *you*
like him! He will have so many jealous rivals on
his hand!"

For Baldomero Espartero also was an Andalucian, and the men of that province, high and low,
never permit themselves to get out of practice when
there is opportunity for a compliment.

Concha looked the General full in the face with
her deep, magnificent eyes, which were aquamarine,
violet, or dark-grey, according to the light upon them.
They were (as she would sometimes own) fallacious
eyes, and upon occasion were wont to express far more
than their owner meant to stand by. But, the latent

love power behind them once fixed, these same eyes could convince the most sceptical of the unalterable nature of the affection which they professed. So it was in the present instance. Concha merely looked at the General squarely for a moment, and said, without flinching, "*I love him !*"

Espartero stooped and touched her brow lightly with his lips, graciously and tenderly as a father might upon a solemn occasion. Then he gathered up her little brown hands in his. They were trembling now, not rock-steady as when they held the musket on the balcony at La Granja.

"My daughter," he said, "do not fear for your young Scot. Queens and consorts and premiers are not the most powerful folk in Spain—not, at least, so long as Baldomero Espartero, the Andalucian, commands those good lads out there !"

Then the future Dictator stepped to his tent door, summoned a staff officer, and ordered him to put a tent at the disposal of the young *Señorita*. "And request the commandants of the several columns to come immediately to me at headquarters, as also the gipsy-spy Ezquerra, our late headsman of Salamanca !"

Thus did Mistress Concha, "for Rollo's sake !"

CHAPTER XLV

FORLORNEST HOPES

BUT Rollo himself, our firebrand from the slopes of
the Fife Lothians—what of him ? The foxes that
Samson sent among the cornfields of Philistia, with
the fire at their tails, ran not more swiftly than his
burning thoughts.

We have followed his career long enough to
know that he is not of those who sit long with his
head upon his hands. Even as we look we feel
assured that while he grasps it between his palms,
plans, ideas, possibilities, are passing and repassing
within that brain, coming up for judgment, being set
aside for reconsideration, kicked into the limbo of
the finally rejected, jerked sharply back by the collar
for another look over, or brayed in a mortar and
mixed into new compounds—all finally settling down
within him into a series of determinations and alter-
natives as definite as Euclid and more certain
of being carried into practice than most Acts of
Parliament.

After a long time Rollo raised his head. With
supremest indifference he heard about him the first
hubbub of the hue-and-cry after Concha. So heavy
was his heart within him that (to his shame be it
writ !) he had never even missed her as she went up
the mountain. Yet she would have missed him had

fifty queens and princesses been in danger of their lives—aye, and her own honour and that of her race at stake throughout all their generations.

Rollo, however, gave no heed, but following his intent, stalked slowly and steadily to the General's quarters.

"No one is allowed to enter," called out an officer, whose only mark of rank was a small golden badge with "C. V." upon it, pinned upon the collar of his blue shirt. He was sitting cross-legged on the grass, mending the hood of his cloak with a packing needle.

"I am Colonel Rollo Blair," said the young man ; "I brought hither the royal party, and I must see General Cabrera ! "

"Young man," said the other, in good English, "I am a countryman of yours—in so far, that is, as a poor Southern may be, whose ancestors fought on the wrong side at Bannockburn. But for your own sake I advise you not to disturb the General at this hour. The occupation cannot be recommended on the score of health."

"I thank you, sir," said Rollo, "but I have my duty to do and my risks to run as well as you. And if you, an Englishman, desire to be art and part in the shooting of a Queen-Mother and her little royal daughter, well—I wish you joy of your conscience and your birthright of Englishman ! "

The other shrugged his shoulders as he answered.

"I have nothing to do with the matter. Colonel Rollo Blair brings the party hither, and General Cabrera shoots them. You two can divide the responsibility between you as you please ! "

"That is just what I mean to do," quoth Rollo, and lifted the flap of the tent door.

"General Cabrera," he said, "I would speak
to you!"

An inarticulate growl alone replied, and though
there was more of wild beast wrath than permission to
enter in the tone, Rollo put aside the flap and entered.

Cabrera was lying on a camp bed, his face a
deathly white, from which a pair of small bloodshot
eyes peered out with startling effect. He had bound
a red handkerchief about his black hair, and
altogether his appearance was more that of an
engorged tiger roused from the enjoyment of his
kill, than that of a leading General in the service of
the most Christian and Catholic of Pretenders.

"Your Excellency," said Rollo, "I have come
to urge you to reconsider your intentions with
regard to Queen Maria Cristina, widow of the late
King, and the child her daughter, and that for
several reasons."

"Let me hear them—and as briefly as may be,
señor," thundered Cabrera. "I shall then make up
my mind whether it would not make for the King's
peace that such a firebrand adventurer as you should
not be shot along with them. And, I can tell you
this, that if all the pretty girls in the peninsula were
to come with a whole herd of Papal Bulls, they
would not save you a second time!"

As he spoke Cabrera reared himself on his elbow
and glared at Rollo, who stood still holding the
tent flap in his hand.

"These are my reasons for this request, General,"
said Rollo, without taking the least notice of the
threat. "First, such an act would alienate the
sympathy of the whole civilised world from the cause
of Don Carlos."

"For that I do not give the snap of my finger,"

cried Cabrera. "I bite my thumb at the civilised world. What has it done for us or for Don Carlos either? Next!"

"Secondly, I appeal to your pity, as a man with the heart of a man within his breast. This lady hath never done you any wrong. Her daughter is little more than a babe. Spare them, and if an example must be made, be satisfied with executing Señor Muñoz and myself. I shall right willingly stand up by his side, if the shedding of my blood will save the Queen and the little Princess!"

"And the fair maid Doña Concha?" said Cabrera, mockingly. "What would she say to such an act of self-sacrifice?"

"She would rejoice to see me do my duty, General!" said Rollo, with confidence.

Cabrera laughed long, loud, and scornfully.

"Not by a thousand leagues!" he cried, "not if I know a maiden of Spain—to save another woman! No, no; go out of this tent in safety, Don Rollo. I like a man who has no fear. And indeed great need have you of the fear of God, for, when a man dares thus to beard Ramon Cabrera, the fear of man is not in him. Go out, I say, and give thanks to any god you heathen Scots may worship. But do not come hither a second time to prate of mercy and innocence, and 'those who never did me any harm.' See here, *hombre*——"

Rollo was about to speak, but Cabrera suddenly rose to his feet, steadied himself a moment upon the tent pole, and lifted from a stool a small tin case like a much battered despatch box. Opening it, he revealed another casket within. He unlocked that, and drawing out a long grey tress of woman's hair he put it to his lips.

"The hatred of men has been mine," he cried fiercely, "aye, ever since I was twelve years old has my knife kept my head. But through all one woman has loved me—and only one. See that! 'Tis my mother's hair, which the butcher officers of the woman Cristina sent me in mockery, warm and clotted from the shambles of the Barbican. Touch it, cold man of the north! Aye, let it stream through your fingers like a love token, and say—what would you do to those who sent you that?"

Again he kissed the long grey tresses passionately, ere he laid them in Rollo's hand.

"Your mother's hair, wet with your mother's blood!" he cried, "a pretty talisman to make a man merciful! 'Never harmed me,' did I hear you say? Answer me now! What harm had my poor mother done them? Answer me! Answer me, I say. You Scots know the law. They say you read the Bible. 'An eye for an eye, and a tooth for a tooth!' So I have heard the clerics yelp. Is it not true? Well, for each hair you hold in your hand will I exact a life, queen or consort, maid or babe, what care I? Have you any more to say? No? Then give it back to me!"

With these final words he raised his voice to a shout, and threw himself on the bed in a passion of tears, with the tress of long grey hair pressed to his face.

And Rollo went out, having indeed no words wherewith to reply.

*   *   *   *   *

But though worsted at the General's tent, the young adventurer was by no means defeated. None knew better how to fall back that he might the further leap. He had failed utterly with Cabrera, and as he came out the camp was still humming with the scandal concerning Concha. The Englishman, having finished repairing the cape of his military cloak, had been awaiting events within the tent with the greatest interest. In fact, he had been undisguisedly listening.

As Rollo came out he congratulated him in a low tone.

"Every moment since you entered," he said, "I have been expecting to hear the guard summoned and orders given to have you shot forthwith. Ramon Cabrera does not wait a second time to assure himself of his prisoners, I can tell you. You have come off very well. Only take my advice and don't try it again!"

"I will not!" said Rollo, whose thoughts were elsewhere. "I am obliged to you, sir!"

"By the way," continued the other, with a pertinacity which offended Rollo in his present state of mind, "there is great news in the camp. That girl who came with you proved to be a spark among our tinder. These Spaniards can resist nothing in the shape of a petticoat, you know. And gad, sir, I don't know why in this case they should. For I will say that a handsomer girl I never set eyes upon, and demmy, sir, Colonel Frank Merry has seen some high steppers in his time, I can tell you!"

"If you refer to the Señorita Concha Cabezos," said Rollo, haughtily, "she is betrothed in marriage to me, and such remarks are highly offensive!"

"No offence—no offence—deuced sorry, I'm sure," said Colonel Frank, whose name as well as his jolly proportions indicated the utmost good-humour. "But the fact is, I heard—mind, I only say I *heard*—

that the young lady has gone off with a good-looking young Vitorian trooper of the Estella regiment, one Adrian Zumaya. He removed his horse from the lines on pretext of grooming it, and the pair have gone off together ! "

" If you will favour me with the name of your informant," answered Rollo, " I shall have the pleasure of running him through the body ! "

The Falstaffian Colonel Don Francisco Merry waved his hand and smiled blandly.

" In that case, I fear, you must decimate the entire command," he said ; " the boys down there are all on the shout on account of Master Adrian's good fortune. But I should advise that ingenious young gentleman to make the best of his time, for if he comes across his old comrades and their General, he will get singularly short shrift ! "

" You are at liberty to contradict the story," said Rollo, serenely, passing, as his nature was, instantly from anger to indifference. " Listen—the Señorita Concha may have left the camp. Your Vitorian friend may have left the camp. Only, these two did not go together—note that well. If any man affirm otherwise, let him come to me. I will convince him of his error ! "

And having spoken these words, Master Rollo dismissed the matter from his mind and marched off towards his companions' camp-fire, revolving his new alternative plan for the saving of the royal party.

The bivouac of the little group of friends and allies was close beside the white house where were bestowed the Queen, her husband, and her little daughter. But sentinels paced vigilantly to and fro before it, and besides the soldiers in the courtyard, there was a Carlist post upon a rocky eminence equipped with a field-gun, which commanded the whole position. So that for the present at least there was no hope of doing anything to deliver the prisoners.

Rollo called his council together cautiously. They could talk without suspicion during supper, which in old friendly Spanish (and Scottish) fashion was served up in the pot in which it had been cooked. Thus they clustered round and discussed both plans and pottage as they dipped their spoons into the steaming *olla*.

One of the leader's most serious difficulties had been to decide whether or not he could afford to trust the Sergeant; a little thought, however, soon assured Rollo that he could not do without José Maria, so that there remained no choice. The Sergeant had openly attached himself to their party. They could discuss nothing and undertake nothing without exciting his suspicion. Certainly he had been in Cabrera's command. He had joined them thence, but—Concha vouched for him, and La Giralda swore by him. He was a gipsy, and therefore his own interests were his only politics.

So to the company about the steaming *olla*-pot on the hillside, as the twilight deepened, Rollo related the story of his interview with Cabrera. There was no hope in that quarter. So much was certain. If the Queen-Regent and her little daughter could not be delivered before the morning, they would assuredly be murdered.

"You have a plan, I can see that," said the Sergeant, shrewdly, polishing upon a piece of wash-leather the silver spoon which he habitually carried.

"You will aid me in carrying it out if I have?" Thus with equal swiftness came Rollo's cross-question.

A curious smile slowly overspread the gipsy's leathern visage.

"I think," he said slowly, "that all of us here have most to gain by keeping the two queens alive. But I confess I would not be sorry to make the General a present of my gentleman of the dressing-gown!"

Then Rollo, reassured by the Sergeant's words, went on to develop his plans.

"We must obtain sufficient horses to mount the royal party, and one of us must guide the Queen and the others on their way to General Elio's camp. For the horses we will look to you, Sergeant."

"I have done as much under the eyes of an army in broad daylight, let alone at night and on a mountain-side," replied the man of Ronda, calmly, lighting another of his eternal cigarettes.

"Then," continued the young leader, "next we must secure some means of communicating with the prisoners within the house. La Giralda will afford us that. The sentries must first be drawn off, then secured, and with one of us to accompany and guide the party, we must start off the great folk for the camp of General Elio at Vera, where, at least, their persons will be safe, and they will be treated honourably as prisoners of war."

"And who is to accompany them?" inquired the Sergeant, his face like a mask. For he hated the thought that Muñoz should escape a half-dozen Carlist bullets. José Maria the brigand, El Sarria the outlaw—even Cabrera the butcher of Tortosa were in the scheme of things, but this Muñoz —pah!

"This is what I propose," said Rollo. "Let no more than three horses be brought. So many can easily be hidden in the side gullies of the *barranco*. That will allow one for the Queen, one for Muñoz, and whichever of us is chosen to accompany them can carry the little Princess before him as a guarantee for the good behaviour of the other two."

"But which may that be?" persisted the Sergeant, with his usual determination to have his question answered.

Rollo made a little sign with his hand as if he would say, "All in good time, my friend!"

"Those of us who stay behind," he went on, "will take up such a position that we may stay the pursuit till the fugitives are out of reach. One thing is in our favour. You have heard the silly cackle of the camp about the escape of Concha. If I know her, she is on her way to warn Elio of the disgrace to the cause intended by Cabrera. In that case, we may, if we can hold out so long, hope to be rescued by an expeditionary party. Moreover, Elio will come himself, knowing full well that nothing but his presence as representative of Don Carlos will have power to move Cabrera from his purpose—that, or the menace of a superior force."

"And who is to go with the Queen?" asked the Sergeant, for the third time.

Rollo waited a moment, his glance slowly travelling round the group about the little camp-fire.

"Let us see first who cannot go—that is the logical method," he answered, weighing his words with unaccustomed gravity. "For myself obviously I cannot. The post of danger is here, and I alone am responsible. Don Juan there and the Count are also barred. Etienne does not know the way, nor Mortimer the language. La Giralda is an old woman and weak. Sergeant Cardono and El Sarria —you two alone remain. What say you ? It lies between you."

"Go or stay—it is the same to me," said the Sergeant. "Only let me know."

"I say the same !" echoed El Sarria.

"Then we will settle it this way," said the young man. "Sergeant, whom have you in the world depending solely on you for love or daily bread ?"

A gleam, like lightning seaming a black cloud irregularly, for a moment transfigured the face of the ex-brigand of Ronda.

"Thank God," he said, "there is now no one !"

"Then," said Rollo, with a mightily relieved brow, "it is yours to go, El Sarria ! For not one alone, but two, await you—two who depend upon you for very life."

Ramon Garcia did not reply, but an expression, grim and sardonic, overspread the features of the Sergeant.

"For other reasons also it is perhaps as well," he said ; "for had I been chosen, an accident might have happened to a grandee of Spain !"

CHAPTER XLVI

THE SERGEANT'S LAST SALUTE

IT was almost time for starting. The two sentries lay on their faces, trussed and helpless, with gags in their mouths. El Sarria and Rollo had dropped down upon them as if from the clouds a few minutes after the officer had made his two-hourly visitation. The Sergeant was ready with the horses in the hollow, keeping them quiet with cunning gipsy caresses and making soft whistling *chalan* noises in their ears.

So far all had gone well, and Rollo, standing with his knife in suggestive proximity to the tied-up sentries, silently congratulated himself. The dawn was doubtless coming up behind the hills to the east, but the darkness was still absolute as ever about the camp, save indeed for the lambent brilliancies of the stars.

They were now waiting only for the royal party, and the time seemed long to impatient Rollo. Were all his plans, so carefully laid, to be made naught because, forsooth, a queen in danger of her life must still keep up the punctilios of a court and cherish the pettishnesses and caprices of a spoilt child? Was his reputation to go down to posterity as that of a man who, being trusted with the lives of a woman and a child, had brought them straight to the shambles?

At last—there! They were coming. But why,
for God's sake, could not they make less noise?

With a motion of his hand which directed El
Sarria to keep an eye upon the gagged sentries,
Rollo went forward to receive the Queen and conduct
her to her horse. Muñoz, however, came out first,
carrying in his arms the little Princess, who, so soon
as she heard Rollo's voice, whispered her desire to
be transferred to him. But Rollo had already
offered the Queen his arm, and whispering her to
tread carefully, led the way to the little hollow where
Sergeant Cardono kept the three bridles in his hand,
cursing meanwhile the slow movements of crowned
heads and ennobled *estanco*-keepers in Romany of the
deepest and blackest.

He had cause to curse another peculiarity of
monarchs and spoilt children before many minutes
had gone by. Till now the success of the plot had
been complete. There remained indeed only to
mount and ride. El Sarria brought up the rear,
assuring himself for the hundredth time that his
weapons were in good order and ready to his hand.
No great general, Ramon Garcia was a matchless
legionary.

But the Queen-Regent would by no means submit to be assisted to her seat (it was a man's saddle)
by Rollo. She called to her husband in a voice
clearly audible all about.

"Fernando—my love! Come to me—I want
you!"

As Rollo said afterwards—no queen born under
the lilies of Bourbon ever ran a nearer chance of
having the rude hand of a commoner set over her
august mouth than did Maria Cristina of Naples on
this occasion.

Nor was the appeal without effect.

Señor Muñoz instantly put the little Princess down upon the ground and hastened to his wife. What happened *after* that is not very clear, even when the subject has been repeatedly and exhaustively threshed out by the persons most immediately concerned.

Perhaps the little Princess, deposited thus suddenly upon the ground, caught instinctively at one of the long tails of the horses which (in common with those of almost all Spanish horses) almost swept the ground. Perhaps the animals themselves grew suddenly panic-stricken. At all events one of the three lashed out suddenly. The Sergeant bent sideways to snatch Isabel from among their hoofs. In so doing he dropped a rein, and in another moment one of the steeds went clattering up the dry *arroyo*, scattering the gravel every way with a wild flourishing of heels, and making, as the Sergeant growled, " enough noise to arouse twenty camps."

For a hundred heart-beats all the party held their breath. Then Rollo whispered to Señor Muñoz to mount and take the little Princess before him.

"As for you, you must run for it, Ramon !" he said to El Sarria. " The fat is in the fire now, and all we can do is to hold them back as long as we can. Make straight for the gorge towards Vera. You know the way. May God help you to reach it before they can turn our flank ! "

Then it was that the Sergeant received a definite shock of surprise. That queens would be foolish, arbitrary, even absolutely idiotic, was no marvel to him. That they should choose their favourites from *estanco*-keepers and guardsmen, and elevate them at a day's notice to grandeeships, dukedoms of Spain, and privileges even higher, did not in the least astonish him. But that the person so elevated should after all, in his less corporeal attributes, prove to be a man, was a first-rate surprise to José Maria.

Muñoz was now to furnish the Sergeant with an absolutely new sensation.

"*Señor*," he said, quietly addressing El Sarria, "be good enough to mount and conduct the Queen to a place of safety. I intend to remain here with these gentlemen!"

Then he went up to Maria Cristina and spoke a few sentences to her in a tone so low that only the last words were audible.

"If not, by the Immaculate Virgin, I swear that you shall never see my face again!"

"Fernando! Fernando! Fernando! You are cruel!" was the answer uttered through choking sobs.

But El Sarria was by this time in the saddle. The little Princess was set in her place in front of him.

"Off with you!" whispered Rollo.

And in this manner the cavalcade began its momentous march.

The Sergeant stood gazing at Muñoz, who rubbed the backs of his hands alternately as if there had been a chill in the night air. Muñoz on his part turned to Rollo.

"Let me have the use of that gentleman's piece," he said; "I do not like this silence. I think we shall have a hot time of it within the next five minutes."

At that moment the escaped charger came cantering back, neighing and alarming all the picketed horses for miles, which snorted back an answer. Sentries meditating in quiet corners became upon a sudden exceedingly awake. One of the two whom Rollo and El Sarria had left triced up at the door of the royal prison at last got the extemporised gag out of his mouth, and found his breath in a lusty shout of warning.

The ex-guardsman was right. Within less than five minutes the entire camp was awake. The escape of the prisoners had been discovered. The recovered sentry pointed out the direction of the *barranco* as that in which the fugitives had taken their departure.

Whereupon there ensued a hurried rush thither. Indeed, scarcely had the dark forms of the two horses with their riders ceased to break the skyline upon one verge of the ravine, before Cabrera's men were clambering and shouting along the other. Luckily the precipice was sheer immediately opposite, and the pursuers had to try a furlong or two farther down, at a place where a landslide had enabled them on the previous evening to lead their horses to and from the few stagnant pools which now represented those full-fed torrents the spring rains send down from the Sierra de Moncayo.

"Let them have it!" whispered Rollo, as the first straggling groups stood up dark between them and the stars.

Accordingly, out of the darkness of the *barranco*, a volley flamed irregularly enough, the rattle of musketry running down the whole front of the line. Six pieces in all spoke out their message to Cabrera's men to halt. For La Giralda, having taken possession of Concha's armament, drew a bead upon her man with probably as much success as any of the others. It was still too dark for accurate shooting, and the worst shot was not much inferior to the best.

But these six bullets sent across the valley from unseen foes, spattering the stones about their feet, checked that first fierce rush of angry men. Some enemy was in force on their front—so much was evident. It would be well to discover of what sort.

"We are holding them," said Rollo, triumphantly, "that is all we can hope for. Pass down the word to fire only when they advance. Time is what El Sarria and his party need. And so far as I can see, unless Concha hurries, a dead Carlist or so more or less will not make much difference to us!"

But Rollo soon found that the men who were opposed to him knew all there was to know about *guerrilla* warfare. They pushed forward steadily from rock to rock, and as they came on in overwhelming numbers the dauntless six were compelled to retire upwards till they gained the rugged brink of the *barranco*, from which the uplands swell away in broad unclothed downs in the direction of the gorge of Vera.

Here they took up their several posts in a position of great natural strength, if only they had had a sufficiency of men to defend it.

Already the morning was growing manifestly lighter. The red peaks of Moncayo above their heads began to emerge out of the grey uncoloured night. They could see each other now, and Rollo looked down his line with some pride.

There they were, each behind his shelter, loading and firing according to his liking and the bowels that were in him. The Sergeant was sternly winging each shot with intent to slay, Muñoz firing as if he had been practising at a target for sport and feeling bored for the want of a cigarette, Etienne with swift and contagious gaiety of mood, while John Mortimer did his work with a plain and businesslike devotion to the matter in hand that argued well for his father's spinning mills at Chorley if ever he should return thither—a chance which at present seemed somewhat remote.

La Giralda, like the Sergeant, fired to kill her man, and as for Rollo himself, he did not fire at all unless he could plant a bullet where it would induce a Carlist to alter his mind about advancing further.

The end, however, was clearly only a matter of time. The light came faster up out of the east. Rollo stood on his feet, and heedless of the bullets that buzzed like bees about him looked eagerly towards the gorge of Vera. He could see nothing of Ramon Garcia or of the Queen, and his heart gave a bound of thankful joy.

But there were ups and downs on the rolling moorland country that stretched away to the right. El Sarria and his companions might only be temporarily hidden in the trough of one of these waves.

"We can hold on a while yet, lads!" he cried, and dropped down behind his rock, shaking his rifle into its nook beside his ear to be ready for the next spot of red or white crawling towards them through the dusty *arroyo*.

But at that moment there came from far away the sound of cheering. A mounted man dashed at full gallop up to the edge of the ravine opposite to them.

"Do not fire," said the Sergeant; "that is Cabrera—he is a brave man!"

But John Mortimer, not caring or not understanding the language, fired promptly, and his rifle bullet threw up a cloud of dust between the horse's feet. The animal reared and almost threw his rider. But in a moment he was erect as ever in the saddle, and Rollo could see him shouting furious commands to his men—apparently ordering them to bear round to the left so as to take the defending party on their least protected side.

For the next few minutes, as Muñoz had foretold, it was hot work enough, and Rollo had no time to look behind him, or he might have seen a sight that would have astonished him—a single horsewoman, riding swiftly towards the *barranco*, followed at the distance of half a mile by a cloud of mounted men.

Suddenly the General on the opposite bank, who all the while had been darting about hither and thither like a gadfly, held up his arm, and with astonishing pride of horsemanship (and faith in the soundness of his girths) rode his charger straight down the shelving sides of the ravine, the slaty fragments crumbling and slipping under the iron-shod hoofs.

With a cheer the red *boinas* of the Estella regiment followed, and then straight up the opposite slopes of shale they dashed towards Rollo and his poor defences.

"Hold your fire!" he cried, first in English, and then in Spanish. "Wait till you are sure of them. We are only half a dozen, and we must wing a man apiece!"

It chanced, however, just as the horseman (who,

as the Sergeant had supposed, was Cabrera himself, almost out of his mind with disappointed fury) surmounted the ridge a little to the right of Rollo's position, but close to where the Sergeant lay behind his rock, that Concha threw herself off her charger (or rather one of General Espartero's), and with a joyous shout informed them that the Queen was safe and that twelve hundred Cristino regulars were following close behind her!

Thus these two, the disappointed murderer and the triumphant deliverer, met almost face to face. Cabrera heard Concha's glad proclamation. He saw the plumes of Espartero's troopers already topping the rise, strong well-knit men of the best farming stock in Old Castile mounted on Gallegan horses.

Quite breathless with her headlong course, Concha stood panting, her hand pressed on her breast. Her eyes were wandering every way in search of Rollo, and in her haste and happiness she had left her weapons behind in the camp of Espartero.

"At any rate I will make sure of you!" cried the Butcher of Tortosa, bitterly, and drawing a pistol he covered Concha at point-blank distance. But from behind his rock (as it were out of the ground) arose the tall gaunt form and leathern visage of Sergeant Cardono.

With a sweep of the arm he set Concha behind him, and as the General's pistol went off he received the shot in his own bosom.

The next moment the Castilian horsemen crashed full on the front of Cabrera's advance and hurled it down the side of the ravine, the General himself being borne away in the thickest of the surge.

Meantime another part of Espartero's command had bent round to the east and was by this time taking the Carlists on the flank. In thirty seconds the ridge of the *barranco*, which the six had defended so well, was deserted ; even slow-going John Mortimer had been swept into the tide of pursuit.

But the Sergeant lay still, with the breast of his jacket opened, and his head on Concha's shoulder. She dropped warm tears over his face. Rollo, too, was there, and held the dying man's hand. He beckoned La Giralda to him and whispered a word in Romany. She nodded, and presently returned with the same great bulk of a man, brown as a Moor of Barbary, whom Rollo had encountered on the night of the plunder of San Ildefonso.

"Ezquerra," the Sergeant whispered, "I am spent. There is a spike in the neck-band this time. All that is honestly come by, I want you to give to this young lady. You will find it by itself under the hearthstone in my house at Ronda. The rest you will take no objections to, I know, on the ground of morals. Keep it for yourself!"

Concha glanced once up at Rollo and then, receiving his nod of approval, bent down and kissed the Sergeant.

The Andalucian looked up with that wondrous flavour of gay humour which distinguishes those born in the joyous province. His saturnine visage brightened into the sweetest smile. Very feebly he raised his hand to his brow in a last salute in acknowledgment of Concha's favour. His head fell back on her breast.

"A thousand grateful thanks, *Señorita !*" he said. And then noting the executioner he added, "Ah, Ezquerra, this is better than dying on the

Plaza Mayor of Salamanca with the iron collar about one's neck!"

They were his last words. And so passed José Maria of Ronda, whom to this day every Spanish peasant holds to have been the greatest man Spain has seen since the dead Cid rode forth on Babieca for the last time to outface the Moors.

CHAPTER XLVII

MENDIZÁBAL

ROLLO and his companions rode into Madrid amid
the clamour and rejoicing of thousands, as indeed he
might have done behind Don Carlos had he been
successful in his first intention. Madrid was healthy
and hungry. The plague had been stayed by the
belt of barren country which cinctures the capital
village of Spain. And as for fear, do not the
inhabitants say that what happens not in Madrid,
happens not at all !

Rollo, so long accustomed to the high clear
silences of the *sierra* or the scarcely less restful valleys
where the birds sing all day in the spring, felt himself closed in and deafened by the clamour, blinded
by the brilliant colours, and in ill-humour with all
things—chiefly, it must be confessed, because Concha,
attired by the Queen's own waiting-maid from Aranjuez, sat in a carriage with the aplomb of a duchess.

They were all in high favour. For Muñoz
(now more than ever the Power behind the Throne,
and perhaps secretly proud of having played the
man at the defence of the *barranco* of Moncayo) had
quickly turned the tide of the Queen-Regent's
displeasure. And at this period there was scarcely
any honour that she would not have bestowed upon
her preservers.

For in distracted hither-and-thither Spain of the early Carlist wars, it seemed nothing extraordinary to any one that Rollo should have saved their Majesties' lives with a Carlist commission in his pocket, or that Sergeant Cardono of the command of General Cabrera should have been shot dead by his superior officer while fighting vehemently for the opposite party. For these are incidents common to most civil wars and specially common in Spain, that land of adventurous spirits with little to do and plenty of time in which to do it. Indeed a feather or a favour, the colour of a riband or the shape of a cap, often made young men Carlist or Cristino, National or Red Republican, as the case might be.

On the third day after their arrival the privilege of a royal interview was granted to the young Scot. Rollo smiled as he thought of the first he had been favoured with, and of that other when he had started off a cavalcade consisting of two Queens and an outlaw under sentence of death with the loud "*Arré!*" of a muleteer.

But Rollo had learned to be calm-eyed before royalties. He was a Scottish gentleman, and had grown accustomed to Queens during these latter days. Court lords and the ruck of Madrid politicians stared at him in the corridors, but, affrayed by something in his eye, meekly or reluctantly according to their mood took the wall from him as he strode on, careless, hard-bitten, a little insolent, perhaps, in bearing. At last he stood in the great hall of audience, his plain well-worn coat and knee-breeches the secret scorn of every courtier. But a glance at Killiecrankie, once more a-swing by his side, was sufficient to sober too impertinent male interest, while the reputation of his exploits and the keen soldierlike face which he turned so pensively towards the window, awakened the liveliest interest in many a pair of dark eyes.

Somewhat after this fashion ran the prattle.

"Look! there goes the man who delivered the Regent and the young Queen! They say that both José Maria, whom every one thought dead, and El Sarria the outlaw were of his band. More than that, it is certain that one very near to the Queen-Regent's person was content to take service with him as a common soldier. How great and famous then must he be! And, above all, how certain of preferment! It were indeed well to cultivate his acquaintance. For what shall be done to the man whom two Queens and a Consort unite in delighting to honour? His threadbare coat? A mere eccentricity of genius, my love. His huge battered sword a-dangle at his side? It is said that he has slain over twenty men with that same blade! Decidedly not a man to be despised; speaks all languages, even the crabbed Gitano—Castilian like a native of Valladolid. He will marry a Spanish wife and become one of *nosotros*, as did O'Donnel, Duke of Tetuan, Sarsfield, Blake, and a score of others—all once poor and neglected, now thrice-hatted and set among the finest clay of the court potter."

Thus in the ante-chambers of Queens spake the wily, the wise, the far-seeing. And from such Rollo had many offers of service. But with a delicate politeness at which none could take offence he declined all these, making (as his father had advised him) his words at once "firm and mannerly."

Thank you, but he was content to wait. He had been sent for by the Queen-Regent. Till then—but at that moment, after a preliminary peep from behind a curtain, the Princess herself ran skipping across the hall, and, catching Rollo by the hand, bewildered him with a chatter of joyous questionings.

Where was Concha ? Would her brother never come back ? Why had he not been at Aranjuez ? She sent him a kiss. (The which Rollo promised without fail to deliver, and what is more, meant to keep his word.)

Yes (he answered with amusement), perhaps one day the Princess would see Concha's brother again. It was certainly very dull in Madrid. Royal palaces were as little to his liking as to that of the Princess.

Then the little lady had her turn. Did he remember when he had hidden her underneath the great brass pot among the hay ? Did he know that once a straw had tickled her beneath the chin so funnily that she came near to bursting out laughing ? Rollo did not know, but the very thought turned him cold even among that throng of courtiers, all casting sidelong glances and trying to get near enough to listen politely to the conversation without appearing to do so. He seemed to be once more threading his way through the scattered groups of gipsies, the dark brows of Egypt bending suspiciously upon him and the royal storehouses flaring up like torches.

"Ah, there he comes—just like him ! " cried the little girl, stamping her foot after the pattern of her mother ; " now you and I will have no more good talk. But I shall wait for you at the gate when you come out. There—now bend down. I want to give you another kiss for that pretty boy, the brother of that Concha of yours ! "

As she ran off Rollo found a friendly hand on his arm, and lo ! there at his elbow was Don Fernando Muñoz, Duke of Rianzares, come in person to convey him into the presence. His manner was characterised by the utmost cordiality, together with a certain humanity altogether new, which made Rollo think that a few more *barrancos* to defend would do . this favoured grandeeship a great deal of good.

Rollo had expected to be ushered into the presence of her Majesty in person, but instead, a plain English-looking man stood alone in a little room, the window of which commanded a vast and desolate prospect. There was a tall chair with a golden crown over it at the top of a table covered with red cloth, while several others, all uncushioned and severely plain, were ranged regularly about it.

The English-looking man came forward bluffly, and put out his hand to Rollo. He looked more like a healthy fox-hunting squire, just intelligent enough to sit in Parliament and make speeches against reform and the corn laws, than the political confidant of a Queen of Spain.

Then in a moment it flashed through Rollo's mind that this hearty Anglo-Iberian could be none other than Mendizábal himself, the Prime Minister of Spain, the scourge of monks and monasteries, the promised regenerator of the finances of Spain. Another thought crossed his mind also. He had actually not so very long ago practically accepted a commission to kill this man if he should chance to cross his path.

Yet the remembrance did not dim the brightness of the young man's smile as he took the other's hand.

"Ten to one he will talk to me about the weather," said Rollo to himself, "to me who ought at this moment to be inserting a twelve-inch Manchegan knife between his ribs."

And it fell out even as he had anticipated.

"You have been favoured with fine weather for your many adventures," said the Prime Minister of the Queen-Regent; "it is almost like an English June, clear, but with a touch of cold in the mornings and after sunset."

Rollo modestly supplied the appropriate conversational counter.

"Your name strikes me as in some way familiar," said Mendizábal; "was not your father Alistair Blair of Blair Castle, a client of mine when I was a banker in London and operating on the Stock Exchange?"

"He was, sir," quoth candid Rollo, "not greatly to his advantage—or mine!"

The Premier coloured a little but did not alter his friendly tone.

"Well, perhaps not," he said; "I myself lost every penny I possessed in the world at the same time. Our Spanish stocks were not so favourable an investment as they have become since we obtained recognition and a guarantee from England. But when I have been turned out of my present occupation, I wish you would permit me to look into your affairs. Your father's old vouchers should be worth something now. You have not, I hope, had to sell the old place of your ancestors?"

"No," said Rollo, carelessly; "an ancient retainer of the family lives in the castle with his wife. There is a dovecote in the yard, so they eat the pigeons which eat the farmers' crops, who in turn forget to pay their rents. Thus the ball rolls. And indeed the years have been so bad of late that I have not asked them!"

"You prefer a life of adventure abroad?" asked

the Premier, who had not ceased to look at Rollo with the most earnest attention.

Rollo shrugged his shoulders slightly at the question.

"I do not know," he said simply, "I have not tried. The most ordinary affairs turn out adventurous with me. But then, I would rather undergo any conceivable hardship than live on in one place like a beetle pinned to a card, able only to waggle my feet, till a merciful death put a limit to my sufferings."

Further conversation was cut short by the entrance of the Queen-Regent. Her husband conducted her to the door or rather *portière* curtain of the council-room, and immediately withdrew—a slight waving of the tapestry, however, affording some reasons for suspecting that his Excellency the Duke of Rianzares had not removed himself the entire distance required by etiquette from the councils of his Sovereign.

Maria Cristina extended first to Mendizábal and then to Rollo a plump hand to kiss.

"I have to thank you," she said to the latter, not ungraciously, "for the many and great services you have rendered to me, my daughter—and—to other friends also. The result has certainly been most fortunate, though the manner of service at times left something to be desired!"

Then as Rollo kept his head modestly lowered, the Queen-Regent relented a little, thinking him covered with confusion at her severity, which indeed was far from being his real state of mind.

"But after all you are a brave man, of excellent parts, and personable to a degree——"

"Which in this age and country goes for no

little ! " said Mendizábal, bowing to the Queen as if he intended a compliment. " You have heard how our soldiers chant as they go into battle :

> " ' Old Carlos is a crusty churl,
> But Isabel's a sweet young girl ! ' "

The Queen bowed, with however a little frown upon her face. She was never quite sure whether her Prime Minister was laughing at her or not. Then she returned to the subject of Rollo.

" You have some employment of a sort suited to the taste of this adventurous young man ? " she went on. " I understand and sympathise with his desire not to return to the wars in the North."

" There is the little matter of the suppression of the monasteries," returned Mendizábal, " to take effect (as your Majesty doubtless remembers) on the twentieth of the month. It is already the sixth. There may be some slight trouble where the orders are strong. I propose that we send this distinguished young Scottish soldier (whose noble father I had the honour of knowing somewhat intimately) to Valencia or the Baleares with vice-regal powers. We have great need of such men at such a time."

Rollo gasped and bowed his head. The crimson rose to his cheek. To be a Governor with almost regal powers and soldiers at his beck, to hold a turbulent province quiet under his hand ! How he wished there were no such thing as " honour " anywhere, keeping him by mere iteration and irritancy to the resolution his conscience had extorted from him.

Mendizábal thought the young man only doubtful of his capacity, and patted him on the shoulder with fatherly tolerance and encouragement.

"You will do very well," he said kindly, "we will give you a free hand, full powers, and as many soldiers as you want. Besides, the Carlists have been some while in these regions, and we have not been able to get our own men. Now you can look them up!"

Then Rollo, suddenly finding words, spoke his mind fully and freely.

"I cannot go," he said; "at least, not till I have fulfilled a sacred duty which lies heavily upon me. I took up a charge. I have not fulfilled it. I cannot serve the Queen-Regent till I have laid down that which I undertook, and to the person who charged me with the mission!"

The Queen stared at the bold young man, but the Prime Minister understood better.

"It is his point of honour," he explained to Maria Cristina; "those of his nation cannot help it. It is in the blood and in the gloomy creed which they profess—a sour and inconvenient religion in which there is no confession."

"No confession!" cried the Queen, casting up her hands in horror, "no absolution! How then can they go on living from day to day?"

"Much like other people," said the Premier, smiling; "they repent, and then—repent of their repentances!"

"And is this young man not a Christian?" cried the Queen. "Is he also of this dark and gloomy superstition—what was it that you called the heresy?"

"I am indeed a Presbyterian," said Rollo, smiling; "at least, my father was, and I also when any one contradicts me. For the rest I am, I fear, but an indifferent Christian!"

"Ah," murmured the Queen with a reflective sigh, "then even heretics may have their uses. In that case it will be easier for you to oppress—I mean to argue with and convince the holy friars of the righteous intentions of the government with regard to them!"

"Well," said Mendizábal, quickly, desirous of diverting the conversation from a dangerous subject, "off with you, sirrah! Go satisfy that Calvinistic conscience of yours! But first kiss her Majesty's royal hand. Let no one spoil your beauty, and return betimes to the post which we will keep open for you!"

Rollo did as he was bidden. He kissed the hand of the Queen, who was graciously pleased to give his fingers a slight pressure as hers rested a moment in his. For the handsome face and high bearing of Rollo Blair had been working their usual way with Maria Cristina.

The Prime Minister, noting a slight movement of the *portière* curtains, bustled Rollo off lest he should lose his favour with the Power Behind the Throne. But, pausing a moment at the door, he whispered in his ear—"Have you any objection to telling me the name of the person from whom you had this commission? I promise you upon my sacred honour that you shall have no cause to repent your frankness. Neither you nor he shall suffer on account of my knowledge—no, not if it were Don Carlos himself."

"His name is Don Baltasar Varela, Prior of the Abbey of Montblanch!" said Rollo, after a moment's hesitation.

"I understand," said Mendizábal, with an inscrutable expression. "Nevertheless, I will keep my word."

CHAPTER XLVIII

A POINT OF HONOUR

THERE remained Concha to be dealt with. Ah, yes, and also his companions El Sarria, Mortimer, and Etienne. Only—they did not count. What man does count when the one woman is in the question? Friends of a lifetime are skipped like the historical introduction of an exciting romance, through whose pages battle, murder, and sudden death play gaily at leap-frog and devil-take-the-hindmost.

Yes, Rollo owned it, Concha mattered. There was no blinking the fact. It would be bitter almost as death for him to tell her that he must once more leave her to take his life in his hand, upon a mere point of honour. She might not understand. Like his friends she might denounce his purpose as arrant quixotry and folly. Well, that would certainly make it harder—but even then he would carry it through.

He found them seated in the lodgings which Rollo had secured for Concha and La Giralda in a house that looked upon the Puerta del Sol. Opposite, but upon the same staircase and landing, lodged El Sarria, who, if it would have given any pleasure to Rollo, would have slept all night outside his sweetheart's door.

Etienne, Mortimer, and Rollo himself had rooms

482

on the other side of the great square. But upon
Rollo's return all were now assembled in Concha's
sitting-room, as had grown to be their easy custom.
Concha needed no chaperon, and if the straiter
convenances required one, was there not La Giralda
with her myriad wrinkles busied about the pots in
the little adjacent kitchen or seated with her knitting
in the window-seat like a favoured guest? For it
was in this simple fashion that these six people had
come to dwell together. And as he entered, the
heart of the young man smote him sore.

Alas! that he, Rollo Blair, whom these had
followed loyally, questionless, as clansmen follow
their chief through mirk midnight and the brazen
glare of noon, should now come among these faithful
hearts like a mute with the bowstring, to put an end
to all this comradeship and true comity!

All knew in a moment that there was something
in the air, for though Concha offered to prepare
a cigarette with her own fingers, Rollo declined it
and sat down among them heavy and sad. It was
some time before he could bring himself to speak.

"You who are all my friends," he said, "my best
and only friends—listen to me. I will hide nothing
from you. I have come directly from the Queen.
She and Mendizábal have offered me a high position,
and one in which we might all have kept together
in great content, if such had been your desire. Yet
for the present I cannot accept it. I am not a free
man. For it lies on my soul that the Abbot of
Montblanch trusted us three when we had neither
aim nor end in life. He gave us both of these.
He fitted us out for our mission. For me he did
much more. He made me an officer in the army
of Don Carlos, though Heaven knows Don Carlos

was no more to me than any other stupid fool—I
crave your pardon, Etienne ! I forgot your relationship."

"Say on," cried Etienne, gaily, flipping his
cigarette ash with his little finger, "do not consider
my feelings. All my cousins are stupid fools! I
have always said so."

"Well, then," said Rollo, "to this man, who
among other things gave us each other's friendship,
and " (here he reached out his hand to take Concha's)
"who gave me this——"

He was silent for some moments, still holding
the girl's hand, while her eyes were doubtless lovely
as moonlit waters, could any man have seen them.
But no man did, for the fringed lashes remained
resolutely, if somewhat tremulously, downcast.

"Well, then, I cannot leave this man to think
me a mere common traitor. No, not if it loses me
life and—all. I have failed in my mission. Not
only so, but by the irony of fate I have fought
against his friends and been saved by his enemies."

"We were saved by Concha Cabezos there, I
tell you," said John Mortimer, who thought all this
mere rant. "Let the old priest alone, Rollo.
Marry the girl you want to marry, and take a good
job when it is offered to you. You may not get
a second chance of either. And that is a plain man's
mind upon the matter, whether you want it or not !"

Sadly but determinedly Rollo shook his head.

"No, John," he said, "that I cannot do. I were
bankrupt for life in my own esteem if I did not go
straight to the Prior, frankly explain our failure,
resign my commission into his hands, and offer him
any other service in my power. I think I see my
way to one even now !"

"My advice," said Etienne, suddenly striking in, "is to let my good uncle continue in his mistake a little longer, if indeed any mistake there be. You use a delicacy he would have been the last to use with you. I do not believe the old fox would have cared a straw if all our throats had been cut, so that we had served his turn. Depend upon it, we three were the poorest kind of pawns in his game. If I am not greatly mistaken Cabrera and Elio were only his prancing knights, and Don Carlos, my dear cousin, the stupid old king who is of no use except to get himself checkmated."

"And who," said Rollo, smiling for the first time, "may the Queen be upon this little family chessboard?"

"There is indeed rather a superabundance of Queens, as we have seen," said Etienne, "but he who pushes about all the pieces is doubtless the petticoated old rogue himself. Baltasar Varela has been at the bottom of every plot these thirty years, and if anything goes wrong, he will be the first to skip over the mountains! Take a friend's advice, Rollo"—here the honest fellow grasped his friend's hand hard—"send your explanations and unused commissions to my respected relative by post. For me, I would not go within fifty miles of him for all the revenues of Montblanch twice told!"

"Well, El Sarria, what say you? They are all against me, you see!" said Rollo, mournfully, adding after a moment, "as indeed I knew they would be!"

As usual the ex-outlaw had little to say, and was deplorably shy as to saying it.

"Señor," he said after a long pause, "you have doubtless your own point of honour. I had one once which very nearly cost myself and another a lifetime of misery. Let the señor weigh the matter well and often before he runs a like risk!"

"That also is against me!" said Rollo, smiling; "Concha, you have heard all the others—what do you say?"

Concha rose and stood beside him. She put her arm gently on his shoulder so that her hand touched his cheek.

"I understand, if they do not!" she said. "*I* understand all. You are right. Go!"

*   *   *   *   *

So Rollo set forth, and with him there also journeyed to the north Etienne—first, because he was tired of Madrid, second, because he was returning to France, thirdly (and privately), because the village of Sarria and a certain green garden lattice were to be found on the route thither; John Mortimer, because if Rollo were bound to see the Prior, perhaps after all something might be done about the *Priorato*; El Sarria, because night and morning, noon and midnight, he prayed with his face towards that Convent of the Holy Innocents where Dolóres and her babe waited for him; La Giralda, because she might as well go northward as in any other direction; and Concha—but it is superfluous to say why Concha was going.

Nevertheless Rollo insisted that since he was solely responsible, he alone should adventure the anger of the Prior, though indeed any or all of the others would readily have accompanied him to Montblanch.

But the young Scot felt acutely how perversely, and like a cross-grained jade, Fate had treated him. He knew also that appearances were against him and in what fashion his actions might have been misrepresented to the Prior. Being singularly little given to suspicion, Rollo was not greatly affected by Étienne's estimate of his uncle. Besides, there was the information concerning the approaching suppression of the convents to be communicated, in such a form that it might be of use to the Abbot and brethren of Montblanch, and yet do no injury to those through whom he had come into possession of the secret.

In due time, therefore, after leaving Madrid the party arrived at the village of Sarria. For, being possessed of all manner of governmental passes and recommendations, they travelled rapidly and luxuriously considering the difficult and troublous times. At Sarria, Rollo, looking out eagerly northward to where above the horizon the peaks of Montblanch pushed themselves up blue and soft like a row of ragged and battered ninepins, paused only to assure himself of the well-doing of Dolóres Garcia and her son under the roof of the good Sisters in the Convent of the Holy Innocents. There were also a few arrangements to be made—and his will. Which last did not take long time. It contained only one clause : " I leave all of which I die possessed to my betrothed wife Concha Cabezos of Seville.— ROLLO BLAIR."

The arrangements were these—Concha remained to assist Don Ramon, who had once more assumed the position of a property-holder and. man of authority among his townsfolk, to open out and prepare his house for the reception of Dolóres. That little wife and mother, in spite of her new joy, continued delicate in health, though (needless to say) the nuns had given her the very best possible nursing. But those who saw the meeting of

husband and wife knew that now she would have
a better chance of recovery than all the bitter tisanes
and laborious simples of the Sisters' store-cupboard
had afforded her.

Etienne and John Mortimer decided to await
events at the hostelry of Gaspar Perico. The former
took the first opportunity of converting the silent
serving-maid as far as possible to his interests by
a judicious gift of some half a dozen gold pieces. Immediately thereafter, having thus protected his rear,
he sought the green lattice. It had been taken
down and a seven-foot wall had been built. Indeed
a mason, who was at that moment engaged in laying
the coping, informed him that the family had left
for South America. Whereupon Etienne went back
in haste and found the barefooted Abigail.

"Why did you not tell me that they were gone
—before—— ?" he demanded angrily.

"Before what?" asked the Abigail, putting the
corner of her apron to her mouth and biting it with
the utmost simplicity.

"Before I gave you that money ?"

"Because—why, because your Excellency never
asked me !"

"And pray, *Señorita*," growled Etienne, waxing
grimly satirical, "what did you suppose that I gave
you the money for ?"

The maid-servant let go the apron, put one finger
to her mouth instead, and, looking down with
infinite modesty, sketched with her bare toe upon
the ground.

"Well ?" queried Etienne, impatiently, and with
a sharp rising inflection.

"Because," fluttered the little maid-of-all-work,
"because I—*I thought you liked me !*"

Etienne turned away in a dumb rage, and the small sharp-featured Abigail got behind the back-kitchen door to dance three steps and a double shuffle all to herself.

When he had recovered his powers of speech Etienne called her the several kinds of fiend which can be defined by the French language, but this broke no bones.

" Well, dear *Señorita*," she remarked very sagely, when tasked by Concha with duplicity (after the manner of Satan reproving sin), " he never asked me, and besides, *then* he would not have given me the six Napoleons ! "

Which last proposition of the Abigail of Sarria would not have gained in credibility had it been supported by a Papal Bull.

CHAPTER XLIX

LIKE FIRE THROUGH SUMMER GRASS

On the whole Rollo could not complain of his reception at the Abbey of Montblanch. His heart had indeed been at war within him as he took his way up the long zigzags of the hill road. There was the very thorn branch which had brushed off his hat as he set forth so gladsomely with his new commission in his pocket, his comrades riding staunchly by his side, and the Abbot's good horse between his knees.

Well, he had done his best. Things, after their manner, had turned out cross-grained—that was all. He had, thank Heaven, enough of Mendizábal's generous draft left in his pocket to repay the Abbot for what he had spent upon their outfit. After returning the commission, it only remained as delicately as possible to impart the disastrous news of the coming dissolution of monasteries and the date of the assumption of all conventual property by the State.

Then he would depart. Sarria and Concha were not so far off. He began to take heart even before he reached the great gate of the Abbey.

No one could have been more cordially moved to see a long-lost brother than Don Baltasar Varela, the Abbot of Montblanch, to welcome his dear, his well-beloved Don Rollo.

And his noble nephew Saint Pierre—how fared he? Then that stolid solemn Englishman—did he know that his *Priorato* had long been shipped from Barcelona, an arrangement having been made with the Cristino custom-house?

"But the price? He has not paid it. I warrant that Mortimer knows nothing of the matter," said Rollo, excited for his friend's credit and good name.

The Abbot smiled as he answered.

"Our agent in France," he said blandly, "has received and cashed a draft from some one of the same name in England—ah, there are none like the English for business the world over! But here is a letter which has long been waiting for that young gentleman here."

"I will deliver it to him immediately, and with great pleasure," quoth Rollo.

The Abbot did not pursue the subject, but rising, said courteously, "You will excuse me for the present. You know the library. You will find my Father-Confessor there, whom I think you have met. There are also works on travel and lives of the saints in various languages, exceedingly improving to the mind. And above all you must dine with me to-night."

Thus the Abbot, with a kindness which Rollo felt deeply, put off hearing the full story of his adventures till the evening. Dinner was served in the Prior's own chamber as before, but on this occasion much more simply—indeed rather as two gentlemen might have dined at a good inn where their arrival had been expected and prepared for.

Rollo's simple heart was opened by the hospitality shown him. The beaming and paternal graciousness of Don Baltasar, the difference between what he had expected and what he found, wrung his soul with remorse for the message he had to deliver.

At last he was permitted to tell his tale, which he did from the beginning, slurring only such matters as concerned his relations with Concha. And at the end of each portion of his story the Abbot raised a finger and said smilingly to his Father-Confessor, who stood gloomily silent in the arch of the doorway, "A marvel—a wonder! You hear, Father Anselmo?"

And without stirring a muscle of his immovable countenance the ex-inquisitor answered, "I have heard, my Lord Abbot."

Then Rollo told of the plague and the strange things that had happened at La Granja, their setting out thence with the Queen-Regent and the little Princess, their safe arrival upon the spurs of Moncayo, almost indeed at the camp of General Elio. Then, with his head for the first time hanging down, he narrated the meeting with Cabrera, and that General's determination to murder the Queen-Regent and her little daughter.

"Abominations such as that no man could endure," said Rollo more than once as he proceeded to tell the tale of their delivery, of how he had despatched mother and daughter to the camp of General Elio, of their subsequent capture by Espartero, and how he, Rollo Blair, had hastened all the way from Madrid to lay the whole matter before the Prior.

"'Tis a marvellous tale, indeed, that our young friend tells—have you missed nothing?" inquired the Abbot of the Father-Confessor.

"Nothing!" said the Confessor, glaring down

upon Rollo as a vulture might upon a weakly lamb on the meadows of Estramadura, "not one single word hath escaped me!"

Then Rollo delivered to the Abbot (who handed them forthwith to his reverend conscience-keeper) all his commissions and letters of recommendation. With a drooping head and a tear in his eye, he gave them up. For though he had enlisted in the Carlist cause purely as a mercenary, he had yet meant to carry out his undertakings to the letter.

When at last Rollo looked up, he found the grey eyes of the Abbot regarding him with a quiet persistence of scrutiny which perturbed him slightly.

"Have you anything more to tell me?" inquired the ecclesiastic, laying his hand affectionately on Rollo's shoulder, "you have done all that was possible for you. No man could have done more. May a continual peace abide in your heart, my son!"

"My Father," said Rollo, laying a strong constraint upon himself, "I have indeed a thing to tell that is hard and painful. The monasteries throughout all Spain are to be suppressed on the twentieth day of this month by order of the Madrid Government."

As the words passed his lips, the bland expression on Don Baltasar's face changed into one of fierce hatred and excitement. There was forced from his lips that sharp hiss of indrawn breath which a man instinctively makes as he winces under the surgeon's knife.

Then almost instantly he recovered himself.

"Well," he said, "we cannot save the Abbey, we cannot save the Holy Church from this desecration. I have cried 'Pater mi, si possibile est, transeat a me calix iste!' But now I say 'Verumtamen non sicut ego volo, sed sicut tu!'"

Then with a curious change of countenance (the difference between a priest's expression at the altar and in the sacristy when things have gone crossly) he turned to Rollo.

"Nevertheless," he said, "I do not deny that to you we owe all thanks and gratitude. Perhaps some day you shall be repaid!"

When Rollo looked round the saturnine priest had disappeared. His host and he were alone. The Abbot poured out the coffee.

"You will take some of our famous *liqueur*," he said, calmly and graciously as ever. "The receipt has been in the possession of the Abbey for well-nigh a thousand years."

It seemed a pity that so many things which had lasted a thousand years should come to an end on the twentieth day of the month. Meantime, however, he imitated the nonchalance of the Abbot. The *liqueur* was not to be despised.

Rollo held out his glass scarcely knowing what he did. The Abbot poured into it a generous portion of the precious fluid. It was of the keen cold green known to painters as viridian—the colour of turnip leaves with the dew on them.

Don Baltasar drew a glass towards him across the table.

"I am no winebibber," he said, "my vows do not allow of it. But I will give you a toast, which, if you permit me, I will drink with you in the pure wine of the flint."

Rollo rose to his feet, and stood looking at the Prior out of his steadfast blue eyes. They touched their glasses ceremoniously, the elder, however, avoiding the gaze of the younger.

"May you be rewarded, not according to your

successes, but according to your deserts!" said Don Baltasar.

They drank, and Rollo, astonished by the strange bitter-sweet taste of the *liqueur*, could only stammer, "I thank you, Prior. Indeed, you are over kind to me. I only wish I had had—better news—better news to bring you!"

And then, somehow, it appeared to the young man that a kind of waving blackness in wreaths and coils like thick smoke began to invade the room, bellying upwards from the floor and descending from the roof. He seemed to be sinking back into the arms of the Father-Confessor Anselmo, who grimaced at him through the empty eye-sockets and toothless jaws of a skull. There were at least fifty abbots in the room, and a certain hue of dusky red in the shadows of the window curtains first made him shudder to the soul and then affected him with terror unutterable. Finally chaos whirled down darkling and multitudinous, and Rollo knew no more.

*   *   *   *   *

When the young man came to himself he was in altogether another place. He lay flat on his back, with something hard under his head. His face seemed cold and wet. The place, as his eyes wandered upward, was full of shifting shadows and uncertain revealings of cobwebby roof-spaces filled with machinery, huge wheels and pulleys, ropes and rings and hooks, on all of which the blown light of candles flickered fitfully.

To one side he could dimly perceive the outlines of what seemed like a great washerwoman's mangle. He remembered in Falkland town turning old Betty Drouthy's for hours and hours, every moment expecting that Peggy Ramsay would come in, basket

on arm, the sweetest of Lady Bountifuls, to visit that
venerable humbug, who had all her life lived on too
much charity and who died at last of too much
whiskey. Strange, was it not, that he should think
of those far-off days now?

His head, too, was singing and thumping even
as poor Betty's must have done many a morning after
Rollo had paid her for the privilege of turning the
mangle, and Peggy Ramsay secretly bestowed half-a-
crown out of her scanty pocket-money upon her,
because—well, because she was a widow and every-
body spoke ill of her.

After a while Rollo began to see his surroundings
more clearly. Some one was sitting at a great table
covered with black cloth. A huge crucifix swung
over his head—upon it a figure of the Safety of the
World, startlingly realistic.

"Who has brought me here?" he said aloud,
uncertain whether or not he still dreamed. His
voice sounded in his own ears harsh and mechanical.

Then Rollo tried to lift a hand in order to wipe his
brow. He could move neither the right nor the left.
Both appeared to be fastened firmly to some band
or ring let into a framework of wood.

Then he heard a voice from the figure seated
under the black crucifix.

"Bring forward the traitor! He shall learn the
great mystery!"

Rollo felt himself slowly lifted on to his feet, or
rather the entire wooden oblong to which his limbs
were lashed was erected by unseen forces. He could
discern the breathing of men very close to his ear.

"Listen," said the voice from the tribunal.
"You, Rollo Blair, have not only betrayed the
sacred cause of the blessed King Carlos, but, what is

ten thousand times worse, you have been a traitor to
Holy Church, in her battle against much wickedness
in high places."

"Who charges me with these things?" cried
Rollo, giving up a vain struggle for freedom.

"Out of your own mouth are you condemned,"
came the answer. "I who speak have heard your
confession."

Then Rollo knew that Anselmo, the dark confessor, was his accuser and judge. His executioners
he had yet to make acquaintance with. The voice
from the tribunal went on, level and menacing.

"The Abbot of Montblanch may forgive a traitor
an he will. He may make and unmake pacts with a
heretic if it please him. As for me, my conscience
shall be clean as were those of blessed San
Fernando, of Gimenez, of holy Torquemada, and
of the most religious San Vicente Ferrar. Die you
shall, as every traitor ought. But since I would not
send an immortal soul quick to hell, I offer you this
opportunity to be reconciled to Holy Church. I bid
you disavow and utterly abhor all your treacheries
and heretic opinions!"

"I am sorry enough for my sins, God knows, if
so be I must die," said Rollo, making a virtue of
necessity; "but I have done no treacheries. And as
for heresy—I have none too much religion of any
sort. If you can help me to more and better, I shall
be grateful, without being too particular as to creed.
But my father lived and died a good Presbyterian,
and so, Heaven helping me, shall I!"

The gloomy monk rose at these words, made the
gesture of washing the hands, and then, turning
about, kissed the wood of the black crucifix.

"Lay the young man on the rack," he said;

" when he is ready to recant and be reconciled, you know where to find me ! "

The two executioners of Anselmo's will were clad in black robes from head to foot, even their hands being hidden. A tall pointed mask with eye-holes alone revealed anything human underneath, as, panting with the exertion, the men raised Rollo to the level of the huge table with the double rollers beneath. Then he felt his hands and feet one by one deftly loosened and refastened. The frame was slipped from underneath him, and Rollo found himself stretched on the rack.

Then calmly seating themselves on a raised shelf close to his head, his two executioners removed their tall black hoods, apparently in order that they might wipe their beaded brows. But that they had a further purpose was immediately apparent.

With infinite surprise Rollo recognised Luis Fernandez and his brother Tomas. Luis smiled evilly as his ancient enemy rolled his head in his direction.

" Yes," he said, " I told you my turn would come. I only wish that we had also the pleasure of the company of your friend the outlaw, Ramon Garcia. But after all, that great maundering oaf would never have spoilt my plans but for your cursed interference. Twice, thrice, I had him trapped as surely as a sheep in a slaughter-pen with the butcher's knife at his throat. And then you must needs come in my way. Well, every dog has his day, and now this day I shall square all reckonings."

Fernandez waited for Rollo to reply, but though his Scots instinct was to give back defiance for defiance, he held his peace. After a pause the ex-miller of Sarria rolled a cigarette and continued serenely between the puffs.

"Now listen," he said, "this is my revenge. I have had to pay blood for it, but now it is mine. For this I sold myself to the monks, truckled to them, fetched and carried for them. To poor mad Anselmo, with his antiquated inquisition and holy office, I became a bond-slave. I knew you would come back hither, and now I can do with you as I will. How much the Prior knows or suspects of this pleasant subterranean retreat I am unable to determine. At any rate you cannot expect that he will be very much delighted with your performances. But, mark you, it is I, and not he, who will rack your body till you weep and howl for mercy. I have studied these dainty instruments. I alone put them in order—I, Luis Fernandez, whose home you broke up, whose house you burnt down to the bare blackened walls, whom you made desolate of the love of woman——"

"Nay," cried Rollo, hot on a sudden as El Sarria himself—"the love of Dolóres Garcia never was yours—no, nor ever would have been in a thousand years!"

"It would—I tell you!" responded Fernandez, as fiercely. "I know these soft, still, easy-tempered women. They cannot do without a shoulder to lean upon. In time she would have loved me—aye, and better than ever she did that hulking man-mountain of a Garcia! Do you hear that?"

Rollo heard but did not reply.

"So this is my sweet revenge," Fernandez continued. "The good Father-Confessor prates of heretics and times for repentance. But he is mad—mad—mad as Don Quixote, do you understand? I, Luis Fernandez, am not mad. But if you have any reason for desiring to live—live you shall—*on my terms.* All I ask is that you answer me one question, or rather two—as the price of your life."

Only Rollo's eyes looked an interrogation. For the rest he held his peace and waited.

" Tell me where you have hidden Dolóres Garcia —and at what hour, and in what place Ramon, her husband, lays him down to sleep ! If you declare truthfully these two things, I promise to leave you with three days' water and provisions, and to provide for your liberation at the end of that time. If not, I bid you prepare to die, as the men died who have lain where you lie now ! "

Rollo's answer came like the return of a ball at tennis.

" Señor Don Luis," he said, " if I had ten Paradises from which to choose my eternal pleasures, I would not tell you ! If I had as many hells from which to select for you the tortures of the damned, I would not speak a word which might aid such a villain in his villany ! Let it suffice for you to know that Dolóres Garcia is now where you will never reach her, and as for her husband—why, you cowardly dog, asleep or awake, sick or well, you dare not venture within a mile of him ! Nay, I doubt greatly if you dare even face him dead ! "

Fernandez rose and motioned his brother to the handle which turned the great wooden wheel at Rollo's feet. Then the young man lay very still, listening to the dismal groaning of the ungreased bearings and wondering almost idly what was about to happen to him.

*   *   *   *   *

" God in Heaven, he is here ! I tell you I heard him cry ! Do you think I do not know his voice ?

I will tear up the floor with my fingers, if you do not make haste !''

It was Concha who spoke or rather shouted these words along the rabbit-warren of passages which ran this way and that under the Abbey of Montblanch.

But it had been through Ezquerra and La Giralda that the dread rumour of danger to Rollo had first come to Sarria. The gipsies have strange ways of knowledge—mole-runs and rat-holes beneath, birds of the air to carry the matter above. Some servitor in the Monastery, with a drop of black blood in him, had heard a word let fall by Don Tomas Fernandez in his cups. The brothers, so he boasted, would not now have long to wait. The cherry had dropped into their mouths of its own accord—thus Don Tomas, half-seas-over, averred — or at least his confessorship would shake the bough and the fruit would come down with a run. This silly Tomas also knew who was to have Rollo's horse when all was over—a *tostado* not met with every day.

It was enough—more than enough. From Sarria to Espluga in Francoli Concha raged through the villages like fire through summer grass. The Abbey —the Friars, the accumulated treasure of centuries, the power of pit and gallows, of servitude and Holy Office—all these were to end on the twentieth of the month. Meantime a man was being tortured, done to death by ghouls—a friend of El Sarria, a friend of José Maria—nay, the saviour of two Queens and the beloved of generals and Prime Ministers ! Would they help to save him ? Ah, would they not !

Other rumours came up, thick and rank as toadstools on dead wood. There was such-an-one of the village of Esplena, such-an-other of Campillo in

the nether Francoli—they refused the Friars this,
that, and the other! Well, did not they enter the
Monastery walls, never to be heard of more?

Given the ignorant prejudices of villagers, the
hopes of plunder awakened by a lawless time and an
uncertain government, Concha a prophetess volleying
threats and promises—and what wonder is it that in
an hour or two a band of a thousand men was pouring through the gates of the great Abbey, clambering
over the tiles, and with fierce outcries diving down
to the deepest cellars! But from gateway to gateway
not a brother was found. All had been warned in
time. All had departed—whither no man knew.

El Sarria, by his reputation for desperate courage,
for a while kept the mob from deeds of violence and
spoliation. But still Rollo was not found.

Concha, pale of face and with deep circles under
her eyes, ran this way and that, her fingers bleeding
and bruised. In her despair she flung herself upon
one obstacle after another, calling for this door and
that to be forced. And strong men followed and
did her will without halt or question.

But of all others it was the cool practical John
Mortimer who hit upon the trail. He remembered
how, on their first visit to Montblanch, Rollo himself,
at a certain place near the door of the strong-room
in which the relics were kept, had declared that he
heard a sound like a groan. And there in that very
place Concha was driven wild by hearing, she knew
not whence, the voice of her lover. It seemed to her
that he called her by name.

Men ran for crowbars and forehammers. The
floor was forced up by mere strength of arm. The
dislodging of a heavy stone gave access to an underground passage, and men swarmed down one after

the other, El Sarria leading the way, a bar of iron
like a weaver's beam in his hand.

The searchers found themselves in a strange
place. The vaulting which they had broken through
so rudely, enabled them to scramble downward
amongst great beams and wheels to a raised platform
covered with moth-eaten black. The groaning
which Concha had heard was stilled, but as El Sarria
held up his hand for silence they could hear something scuffling away along the dark passages like rats
behind a wainscot.

Without regarding for the moment something
vague and indefinite which lay stretched out on
a strange mechanism of wood, El Sarria darted like
a sleuth-hound on the trail up one of the passages
into which he had seen a fugitive disappear. It was
no long chase. The pursued doubled to the right
under a low archway. The dim passage opened
suddenly upon a kind of gallery, one side of which
was supported on pillars and looked out upon the
great gulf of air and space on the verge of which the
Monastery was built.

The quarry came into view as they reached the
sunlight, dazzled and blinking—a smallish lithe man,
running and dodging with terror in his eyes. But
he was no match for his pursuer, and before he had
gained the end of the gallery, the giant's hand closed
upon the neck of his enemy.

Then Luis Fernandez, knowing his hour,
screamed like a rabbit taken in a snare.

And through the manifold corridors of the
Abbey, and up from underground, rang the dread
cry "Torture!" "They have been torturing
him to death in their accursed dungeons! Kill!
Kill! Death to the Friars wherever found!"

For the blind mouths of down-trodden villages, long dumb, had at last found a universal tongue.

Ramon Garcia looked once only into the face which glared up at him. In that glance Luis Fernandez read his fate. Without a word of anger or any sound save his own footsteps, El Sarria walked to the nearest open arcade of the gallery and threw his enemy over with one hand, with the contemptuous gesture of a man who flings carrion to the dogs.

Luis Fernandez fell six hundred feet clear and scarce knew that he had been hurt.

"God grant us all as merciful a death!" cried Concha; "little did he deserve it!"

They untied Rollo from the trestle work of the rack which the miller of Sarria had used to gratify his revenge. At first he could not stand on his feet. His hands trembled like aspen leaves, and he had perforce to sit down and lean his head against Concha's shoulder.

"Nay, do not weep, little one," he said, "I am not hurt. You came in time! But" (here he smiled) "another turn of that wheel and I would have told them all!"

Meanwhile the hammers were clanging multitudinous. At the sight of Rollo's pale drawn face the populace went wild. Their mad clamour rose to heaven. All that night the great Abbey of Montblanch, with its garniture of stall and chapel, carven reredos and painted picture, went blazing up to the skies.

At such times men knew no half measures, drew no fine distinctions. For, especially in Spain, revolutions are never yet effected with a spray of rose-water. The great Order of our Lady of Montblanch which had endured a thousand years, perished in one day because of the vengeance of Luis Fernandez and the madness of the priest Anselmo.

Meanwhile, in the sacristy of a little chapel by the gate, safe from the spoilers' hand, but lit irregularly by the bursting flames, and to which the wild cries of the iconoclasts penetrated, Concha sat nursing Rollo.

From time to time he would doze off, awaking with a start to find his hand clasped in that of his betrothed. Her ear was very near his lips, and when he wandered a little she soothed him with the tender croonings of a mother over a sick child, moaning and cooing over him with inarticulate love, her hands a hundred times lifted to caress him, but ever fluttering aside lest they should awake the beloved from his repose.

"Who is it?" he said once, more clearly than usual, yet with remains of fear in his eyes very pitiful to see.

"It is I—Concha!"

Ah, how soft, how tender at such times a woman's voice can be! The wind in the barley, the dove calling her mate, the distant murmur of a sheltered sea—these are not one-half so sweet. The angels' voices about the throne—they are not so human. Children's voices at play—they have known no sorrow, no sin. They are not so divine.

"*It is I—Concha!*"

"Ah, beloved, do not leave me—they may come again!"

"*They cannot. They are dead!*"

Keen as the clash of rapiers, triumphant as trumpets sounding the charge, rang the voice that was erstwhile so soft, so tender.

"All the same, do not leave me! I need you, Concha!"

Who would have believed that this swift and

resolute Rollo, this firebrand adventurer of ours, would have been brought so low—or so high. But his words were better than all sweet singing in the ears of Concha Cabezos. She clasped his hand tightly and smiled. She would have spoken but could not.

"Ah—I knew you would not leave me!" he murmured, turning a little towards her. "It was foolish to ask!"

Then he was silent for a moment, and as she settled his head more easily on an extemporised pillow, he glanced towards the closed shutters of the little sacristy.

"When will the morning come?" he asked wearily.

For answer Concha threw open the outer door and the new-risen sun shone full upon his pale face.

"*The morning is here!*" she said, with all the glory of it in her eyes.

CHAPTER L

THUS ended the princely Abbey and its inmates. And so it stands unto this day, a desolation of charred beams, desecrated altars, fire-scarred walls roofless and weed o'ergrown, to witness if I lie. Time hath scarcely yet set its least finger-mark upon it. Under the white-hot southern sun and in that dry upland air, Montblanch may remain with scarce a change for many a hundred years. Ezquerra's hammer strokes are plain on the stones. The crowbar holes wherewith El Sarria drove out the flagstones over the torture chamber—once called the Place of the Holy Office—these any man may see who chooses to journey thither on mule-back, jolting *tartana*, or by the plain-song office of heel-and-toe.

As to the brethren, they had had, thanks to Rollo Blair, due and sufficient warning. They mounted their white mules and rode over the mountains into France, by a secret way long settled upon and laid with friendly relays of food and equipage.

Only the Father-Confessor, the gloomy and fanatic Anselmo, was found dead in his bed, whether from the excitement of reviving his ancient functions of Inquisitor-in-Chief, or from poison self-administered

507

was never rightly known or indeed inquired into. Men had other things to think of in those days.

His body was hastily huddled into a grave in the cloister, where, equally with those of mitred priors and nobles of twenty descents, you may see the wild roses clambering about it in the spring.

On the day which followed the great spoliation, a man limped painfully and slowly along the ravine beneath the still smouldering turrets and gables of Montblanch. From the despoiled Abbey a thin blue reek disengaged itself lazily into the air far above him. The man was following a path which passed along the side of the deep cleft. His method of advance was at once skulking and arrogant.

Thirty yards or so beneath him he saw a congregation of vultures, the national and authorised scavengers of Spain. So thickly did these unholy fowls cluster that the man, being evidently curious, was compelled to throw several stones among them, before he could induce them to move that he might catch a glimpse of their quarry.

Then having made his observation, he said, " Ah, brother Luis, you that were so clever and despised poor Tomas, giving him ever the rough word and the bitter jest, hath not that same poor Tomas somewhat the best of it now ? He at least shall not be meat for vultures yet awhile. No, he will drink many good draughts yet—that is, when he hath sold the freehold of the mill and disposed of any outlying properties that are left. Luis liked red wine, I liked white—and *aguardiente*. Ha, ha, Luis will never again taste the flavour of the *Val-de-peñas* he was so fond of, and so the more will be left for Tomas ! "

He stood and meditated awhile. Then he struck his pockets lugubriously. " I wish I had a cup of good *aguardiente* now," he muttered. Anon his face brightened, as he looked at the dark object among the vulture folk.

"*Caramba!* I have it. It will help me over a difficulty. Brother Luis's pockets were always well lined. The birds have no need of golden ounces nor do they carry off silver *duros*. Besides, there is the key of the strong box hidden in the ravine! Ah, I remember that he carried it about his neck. These can do no good now to Luis, or indeed, for the matter of that, to any vulture alive. It were only kind and fraternal to take such things for a keepsake. I ever loved Luis. He was my favourite brother!"

So saying, Don Tomas descended slowly and painfully to the body—for indeed he had been roughly used by the mob before they brought him to El Sarria, that the outlaw might do with him as with his brother. For they wanted to see the sight.

The vultures slowly and reluctantly withdrew on heavily flapping pinions.

"Ah," meditated Tomas, as he went placidly about his gruesome business, "what a fine thing it is to be known for a man quiet and harmless. For Ramon Garcia said to me with a wave of his hand, 'There is the door! Get through it hastily and let me see your face no more!' Then to the robber crew he said, 'Without his brother, señors, this fellow is as a serpent without the fangs, harmless as a blade of grass among the stones which the goats nibble as they wag their beards.'"

So after a pause this most respectable man finished his task and went his way, jingling full pockets and pleasing himself with meditations upon the abiding usefulness of a good character and of being in all things blameless, humble, and a man of peace.

*   *   *   *   *

There dwells an old peasant now at Montblanch who will act as your guide for a *real*, and points you out the place before the great altar where Ramon Garcia, sometime called El Sarria, cast himself down. Then he shows you where the Abbot stood when he stopped the pursuit of the outlaw to his own ultimate undoing.

"Yes, Excellency," he says, in a voice like green frogs croaking in the spring, "true it is as the sermon preached last Easter Day. For these dim old eyes saw it—also the chamber of the relics I will show you, and the cloisters with the grave of the Father-Confessor Anselmo.

"And truly the devil's own work I have to keep that same reverend and undefiled, for Anselmo was a man much hated. Yet as I think, unjustly, being mad and at the last not rightly responsible for his acts. But only a stout stick will convince these young demons of the village that thrice-blessed ground is not a draught-house wherein to play their evil cantrips! I declare to the Virgin I have worn out an entire plantation of saplings chasing them forth of the holy place."

Last of all (but this will cost another *real* and is worth the money) the peasant-guide shows you the Place of the Holy Office. That black stain against the wall is where they burnt the last rack in Spain. One or two great wooden wheels with scarce a spoke remaining, loom up, imagined rather than seen, in the dusky shadows above.

"This way along a passage (take care of your honourable head!) and I will show you the window from which Luis Fernandez was cast forth like the evil spawn he was."

"And was anything ever heard thereafter of the Prior or the Brethren?" you ask, looking around on all the wasted splendour.

The old man shakes his head, but there is something in his eye which, if you are wise, causes you to slip him a piece of silver.

"Nothing more," he says, "nothing!"

Then looking about him cautiously, he adds, "But upon a certain evening near the time of sundown there came one all clad in poor garments of leather, worn and frayed. He wore a broad hat and the names of many holy places were cut on his staff—altogether such a wandering pilgrim the man was, as you may see at any fair in Spain. And very humbly the penitent asked permission of me to view the ruins. So knowing him for a pilgrim and thinking that perchance he desired to say a prayer in peace before the great altar (and also because I had no expectations of a gift), I let him go his way unattended, and so forgat about him. But when I came up out of my vegetable garden a little after sunset to close the great gate, such being the order of the Governor of the Province who pays me a yearly stipend (four *duros* it is, and very little, but I depend upon the generous charity of those who like your Excellency come hither!)—well, as I say, coming out of my pottage garden I remembered of this pilgrim. I went in search of him, and lo! he stood weeping in the place where the Abbot's great chair had been.

"Then looked I full in his face and all at once I knew him. It was Don Baltasar Varela—of a surety the last Abbot of Montblanch. There was no mistake. For many years I had known him as well as I knew my old dame. And through his tears he also knew that I knew him. So he said presently, 'Reveal not that I came hither, and I will give thee—this—together with my blessing!' And with one hand he gave me a golden ounce worth sixty *pesetas* and more in these bad times. And with the other, as I kneeled down (for I am a good Christian), he bestowed upon me his episcopal blessing with two fingers outstretched, being as you remember a bishop as well as an Abbot! Then after he had stood awhile and the sun was quite gone down, Baltasar Varela, Abbot of Montblanch—the last they say of eighty-four, went out into the darkness, weeping very bitterly."

* * * * *

With the after history of the Queens Maria Cristina and Isabel the Second, this historian is not concerned. Nor is it his to tell how, greatly wronged and greatly tempted, the daughter followed all too closely in the footsteps of her mother. Such things belong to history, and especially to Spanish history— which, because of its contradictions and pitiful humanities, is the most puzzling in the world. His business is other and simpler.

For a moment only he must lift the curtain, or rather a corner of it—like one who from the stage desires to see how the house is filling, or perchance to give the carpet a final tug for the characters to pair off upon and make their farewell bows.

* * * * *

In another southern province far enough from the village of Sarria, there is a white house with sentinels before it. They do not slouch as they walk nor lean bent-backed against a pillar when nobody is looking, as is the wont of Spanish sentries elsewhere. It is the house of the Governor of the once turbulent province of Valencia. The Governor is one General Blair, Duke of Castellon del Mar, and twice-hatted grandee of Spain, but he is still known from Murcia even to Tarragona as "Don Rollo." For he has cleared the southern countries of Carlists, put down the Red Republicans of Valencia and Cartagena with jovial good humour, breaking their heads affectionately with his stout oak staff when they rioted. They had grown accustomed to being shot in batches, and rather resented the change at first, as reflecting on their seriousness. However, they have since come to understand the firebrand General and to like him. Usually they favour him with a private message a day or two before they intend to make a revolution. Whereupon Rollo goes himself into the woods and cuts himself a new stick of satisfactory proportions.

In this manner he has survived an abdication, two dictatorships, and a restoration with undiminished credit, chiefly by holding his province easily and asking from Madrid neither reinforcements of soldiers nor of money.

His wife is not receiving to-day, but in English fashion there are a few friends who drop in for dinner, *habitués* of the house, beloved comrades of Don Rollo's with whom (for the Señora is the old Concha still) his wife flirts a little, chats a great deal, and gives the best advice in return for boundless admiration and delight in her beauty and wit.

"Dolóres," she says to a friend who has arrived and sits patiently folding her little hands on a sofa, "it was pretty of you to come in such a lovely gown—just to please those poor old bachelors. Here, Étienne, hold the baby, and be sure not to drop him, sir. There—what did I tell you? You

2 L

have made him cry! Monster! Well, he shall be
sent away, sweetest pet, that he shall! He is a
buffalo of the *marisma*, a tiger of the jungle, an ogre
out of a story book—that he is, sweetest! There,
La Giralda, take the darling away! Oh, and give
him—but stay—I too will come, else the little
villain may howl till midnight."

She continues to talk quickly as she goes toward
the door.

"What a voice—just like his father's when he
is in the place of arms and the men do not please
him! There—sweetest" (she goes behind the
curtain), "there——!"

And, contented, the young man stills that parade
voice of his into gentle murmurings like those of a
bee within the bell of a flower.

Presently a tall young man comes striding in, in
a plain uniform with the starred shoulder-straps of
the highest rank. Behind him is a broad-chested,
deep-bearded veteran, his chest blazing with decora-
tions.

The younger man, whose hair gives promise of
early threads of grey, enters with swift impetuosity,
dashing a chance servitor out of the way and opening
the inner door as if a gust of wind had come rioting
through the corridors.

"Where is Concha?" he cries as soon as he
enters.

"Here!" replies a voice, a little muffled, it is
true, from a neighbouring room; "no, stay where
you are! I shall be back in a moment."

"Ah, Etienne—John, how are you? Have
they given you any breakfast? Etienne, any more
loves? There are four pretty girls in the Plaza
Villarasa. I saw them on the balcony as I rode

through with the Sagunto regiment the other day——"

"Trust him for that!" comes the voice from behind the curtain.

"My Lord Duke," says Etienne in a master-of-ceremonies' voice, "so long as I am permitted daily to gaze upon the beauty of your incomparable wife, how can this heart turn from that to the admiration of any meaner object?"

"What nonsense is he talking now?" asks Concha, returning demurely. "I know at least three girls of this city of Valencia who have the best reasons for expecting M. de Saint Pierre to make proposals for the honour of their hands. But what can you expect of such a wretch?"

"Well, Master Etienne," says Rollo, "you will now have a chance to forget Mistress Concha and make some fair Castilian happy. For I must send you immediately with these despatches to Madrid. You will stay a week and return with the answers. That will give such a lady-killer ample time to bring matters to a head with the most hard-hearted of the *señoritas* of the capital."

"Ah," sighs Etienne, kissing a hand to Concha, as he prepares to take his leave, "your husband wrongs me. He who hath so much, misjudges me who have so little! Truly, I shall be soon able to say, turning about the old catch :

> "'My soul is in Valencia,
> My body is in Madrid!'"

"Well, John, this is great seeing," said Rollo, when Etienne had departed to busy himself about horses and an escort; "what in the world has brought you hither? Surely your father cannot want you to make another thousand pounds in order that you may have the right to attend his twirling spindles from 8.30 every morning to 5.30 every night?"

"Oh, I am a partner now," Mortimer answered, "even though the old boy insisted upon pocketing every penny of the profit on the Abbot's *Priorato*. Strict man of business, my father! He said it would teach me in the future to be spry about getting my goods shipped. And when I explained, he only said that what had been possible for him there in England, sitting at ease in his arm-chair, ought to have been possible for me on the spot and with money in my pocket!"

"And what did you do?" asked Rollo, smiling.

"Well, at any rate, I struck him for a commission on my having secured the order, and the Convent onions were good for the rest. So now I am a partner in the firm with a good quarter interest."

"And what are you doing here? More onions?" laughed his friend.

John blushed and looked down at the carpet. They had a carpet at the Governor's house—though in her heart Concha always wants to have it up when any one comes in lest they should tread upon it.

"No," he said slowly, "the fact is I think you spoiled me a bit for staying at home, mill hours —and that sort of thing. So now I am to be foreign agent and buyer. I've been taking lessons in the language, and if you can put any business in my way, I shall be glad."

Rollo took him to the window by the arm.

"Do you see those fellows?" he demanded.

As he spoke he pointed to a detail of the wiry

little Valencian soldiers in their white undress blouses and *bragas*.

"Now, John," he went on, "I can't get stuff here that won't tear the first time they do the goose-step or even sneeze extra hard. The contractors are thieves every man Jack. What can you do for me? I have twenty thousand of these fellows and lots more coming on, down in the *huertas* and rice fields!"

"Heavens!" cried John Mortimer, "this is an order indeed. Wait! I will let you know my best possible in a moment!"

And he pulled out a notebook crammed with figures.

"I can give you very good terms indeed," he said after a moment.

Concha jumped to her feet and clapped her hands.

"Oh," she cried joyously, "and I know Señor de Mendia, the head of the Customs. And oh, Rollo, you and he can arrange about getting it through, and all my dress materials as well. It will be quite an addition to our income, if Don Juan sells you the stuff cheap!"

For an instant Rollo looked a little indignant and then went up to his wife and kissed her.

"My dear," he said, "you can never under-stand! We don't do these things in our country!"

At which John grinned incredulously.

"I have done business in Glasgow," he said suggestively.

"At any rate," said Rollo, nettled, "*I* don't do them."

Here Concha pouted adorably, and with her slippered toe kicked a footstool which certainly was not doing her any harm.

" I am sure we are very poor ! " she cried. " I wish that wretch Ezquerra, whom they have made a General of, had given us much more than he did. I think you should write to him, Rollo ! "

" Better keep friends with Ezquerra," laughed the Governor ; " you and I are rich enough, Concha, and baby shall have an ivory ring to cut his teeth upon. You shall have one new dress a year, and there are always enough vegetables in the garden with which to toss you up a salad. Oh, we shall live, spoilt one, we shall live ! "

And he kissed her, not heeding the others.

" But why must we keep in with Ezquerra ? " said Concha, still unsatisfied ; " he was an executioner once."

" Well," said Rollo, " the fellow has been at his old trade again, it seems. He may be Dictator any day now. They say he has ended the war in the north—murdered fourteen of his own brother Generals and bought fourteen of the other side. Bravo, Ezquerra, I always knew he would do something in the fine old style one of these days ! But fourteen at a time is epic, even for Spain ! "

" And so the war is ended—well, that is always one good thing anyway ! " said Concha, careless of the means ; " come, Dolóres, let us go and look at the babes ! These people ache to talk politics. They don't want us. It is easy to see that ! "

So taking the arm of Dolóres Garcia (who had glanced once at her husband when he came in and never looked at him again), little Concha walked to the door sedately as became a matron and the wife of a grandee. Then in her old flashing manner she turned about swiftly and from her finger-tips blew the company a dainty collective kiss.

The curtain closed, leaving the three men all staring after her.

But in another moment it was put aside and Concha's pretty head peeped out.

"Rollo," she said, softly, "you can come up when you like—when you have quite finished your politics—just to look at baby. He has not seen you since morning."

THE END

PRINTED BY WILLIAM CLOWES AND SONS, LIMITED, LONDON AND BECCLES.

MACMILLAN'S
NEW AND NOTABLE
SIX-SHILLING NOVELS

BY

RUDYARD KIPLING

F. MARION CRAWFORD

THE AUTHOR OF "ELIZABETH AND
HER GERMAN GARDEN"

S. R. CROCKETT

EGERTON CASTLE

ROSA N. CAREY

UNA L. SILBERRAD

STEPHEN GWYNN

ERIC PARKER

EVELYN SHARP

B. K. BENSON

A. C. FARQUHARSON

DR. S. WEIR MITCHELL

S. MERWIN and H. K. WEBSTER

MACMILLAN AND CO., Ltd., LONDON

MARION CRAWFORD

*A story of
Venice in
the 15th
Century . .*

Crown 8vo.   Gilt top

Price 6s.

Marietta: a Maid of Venice

In his new story, *Marietta: a Maid of Venice,* just published by Messrs. Macmillan, Mr. Marion Crawford draws on fifteenth century records of a Dalmatian Zorzi Ballarin, who, being taken into the office of Angelo Beroviero, a great craftsman in the art of glass-blowing, so wins upon his master, and shows such aptitude for the art, that he is admitted to the practice of it, in defiance of the law which forbids any foreigner to learn and practise the art in Venice. Angelo's son, a mere manufacturer by spirit, regards with jealousy the intruder, who knows more and is taught more than his father will let him know, and he puts the law in operation against him. But Marietta, his sister, loves Zorzi, and vindicates him to her father, and finally he wins permission from the Council of Ten to work in Venice for the glory of Venice. The intrigue of the book concerns itself with the future of a young noble to whom Marietta was betrothed against her will, and of the Georgian slave whom he loved, and of the Georgian's formidable lover, a Greek pirate captain. But the main interest for most readers will consist in the mass of curious and picturesque knowledge about the Venetian glass-blowing which Mr. Crawford utilises with his customary skill.

S. R. CROCKETT

*An exciting
story of the
Carlist
Wars . .*

Crown 8vo.   Gilt top

Price 6s.

The Firebrand
By S. R. Crockett

The Firebrand, by S. R. Crockett, is a stirring tale of the Carlist wars, full of cheerfully related intrigue, bloodshed, and conspiracy. It links the fortunes of El Sarria, outlawed for stabbing one whom he supposed his wife's lover, to those of three adventurers—a Scot, a Frenchman, and an Englishman—in the service of Don Carlos. The three, led by the Scot, set out on the enterprise of capturing Queen Cristina and her son; they take into their train, besides El Sarria, a sergeant of the Carlist army, who is no other than the chief of the gipsies, also an old gipsy woman, and a charming young lady for the Scot to fall in love with. The perils that the expedition undergoes from Cabrera the insurgent leader, from domestic treachery, from plague, and other exciting circumstances, are manifold; but it all comes to a satisfactory conclusion.

EGERTON CASTLE	STEPHEN GWYNN
"A Novel of signal dis-tinction." — Daily Mail .	*Author of "Highways & Byways in Donegal"* . .
Crown 8vo. Gilt top	Crown 8vo. Gilt top
Price 6s.	**Price 6s.**

The Secret Orchard

By

Egerton Castle

Some Press Opinions

DAILY CHRONICLE. — " We expected much. . . . *The Secret Orchard* does more than rise to our expectations. . . . We follow the rapid development of the tragedy with a sympathetic interest which never flags."

DAILY MAIL. — "A novel of signal distinction and beauty."

GLOBE. — "The story, as a whole, is eminently effective, eminently readable, and can be recommended cordially to all and sundry."

ACADEMY. — " The style and manner of telling the story is of the easy luminous character that we associate with the authors of *The Bath Comedy*."

MORNING POST. — "There can be no doubt of the dramatic force with which it is told or of the interest it inspires."

THE TIMES. — " A finished piece of work."

The Old Knowledge

By

Stephen Gwynn

The Old Knowledge, by Mr. Stephen Gwynn, is a story of Donegal in the present day. It relates the experiences of an English girl who goes to lodge alone in an Irish cottage to fish and paint. She is brought into close and friendly relations with both peasants and gentlefolk. Two men fall in love with her, of whom one, the central figure in the book, is a peasant, but a man of rare gifts, a visionary who paints his own visions. " The old knowledge " of which the title speaks may be described as the folk-beliefs of the peasants, interpreted by him in the light of modern mysticism; and it covers the unusual adaptation of an old magical rite by which he endeavours to win the girl. The book attempts to suggest the character and charm of scenery and life in the north-west of Ireland, and the beliefs, passions, and prejudices of the people.

THE SPECTATOR. — "It is admirably written; it has an interesting theme, and its development in plot and characterisation . . . is in faithful correspondence with the facts of life. In a word, the book is both charming and convincing."

UNA L. SILBERRAD

Author of .

" The Enchanter "

Crown 8vo. Gilt top

Price 6s.

Princess Puck

By

Una L. Silberrad

Miss Silberrad's New Novel, which is running as a serial through the pages of *Macmillan's Magazine*, will be published simultaneously in England and the United States of America on the 22nd of January, 1902.

ROSA N. CAREY

" The story is well conceived and well sustained." — The World . . . .

Crown 8vo. Gilt top

Price 6s.

Herb of Grace

By

Rosa N. Carey

Some Press Opinions

WESTMINSTER GAZETTE. — " A clever delineator of character, possessed of a reserve of strength in a quiet, easy, flowing style, Miss Carey never fails to please a large class of readers. *Herb of Grace* is no exception to the rule. . . . Run on the even keel of quiet romance that is most refreshing after tumblings on the seas of sensational plots and problem novels."

WORLD. — " The story is well conceived and well sustained."

GLOBE. — " The story, as a whole, is eminently effective, eminently readable, and can be recommended cordially to all and sundry."

MANCHESTER GUARDIAN. — "On the picture of the two sisters living so happily together, Miss Carey has expended some of her most careful and successful work."

DAILY CHRONICLE. — " In every respect a worthy successor to *Rue with a Difference.*"

ERIC PARKER

New Novel

by a New

Writer . .

Crown 8vo. Gilt top

Price 6s.

The Sinner and the Problem

By

Eric Parker

The Sinner and the Problem are two small schoolboys who attach themselves by sympathy to an artist staying as a guest at a private school in a pretty country place. One of the boys is a cousin of the beautiful young lady who owns a neighbouring place with a lake and swans, and through the boys the artist becomes acquainted with the Lady of the Lake. There is little plot : the book is really concerned with presenting the ways and works of two picturesque and rather pathetic youngsters, and an artist's enjoyment of nature as a background to his own idyll.

Some Press Opinions

DAILY TELEGRAPH.—"This quaint and refreshing romance. . . . The charm of the matter is reinforced by the author's graceful and ingenious style."

THE ACADEMY.—"Bright, well written."

LITERATURE.—"A delicate, sympathetic study of a handful of people as they appear to a sensitive artist with a keen sense of humour."

SPECTATOR.—"Refreshingly original . . . this quaint and refreshing romance."

A. C. FARQUHARSON

New Novel

by a New

Writer . .

Crown 8vo. Gilt top

Price 6s.

St. Nazarius

By

A. C. Farquharson

St. Nazarius, by A. C. Farquharson, is the idyllic story of two cousins, joint inheritors of a castle in a forest, brought up together at a monastery in the forest and sent to the university together. Each presents a type in its ideal development, one the artist, the other the priest, and in their different ways they love one woman. The action of the story passes at no particular time, in no particular country, and the distinctive character of the book—which may fairly be called an idyll—is that all the actions in it are prompted by love of a noble kind, but by many kinds of love.

S. WEIR MITCHELL

*A study of
life in Phila-
delphia . .*

Crown 8vo. Gilt top

Price 6s.

Circumstance

By

Dr. S. Weir Mitchell

*Author of " The Adventures of Francois,"
Dr. North and His Friends," etc.*

Circumstance is a study of life in Phila-
delphia, rather curious as showing the
exclusiveness of American Society. It
is also a study of an adventuress. The
point of the title lies in the varying
resistance of character to external events,
and the striking influence on inferior
character of accidents, such as that
which almost made Mrs. Hunter a mur-
deress, or that which enabled her to
attain her end without resorting to so
disagreeable a step or sacrificing any of
her complacency.

B. K. BENSON

*A sequel to
"Who Goes
There?"*

Crown 8vo. Gilt top

Price 6s.

A Friend with
the Countersign

By

B. K. Benson

*Author of
" Who Goes There ? "*

In *A Friend with the Countersign* Mr. B.
K. Benson continues the story related in
his book *Who Goes There?* The hero of
the earlier book who, owing to a lapse of
memory following on a wound, served on
both sides in the American Civil War, is
in this story represented as profiting by
the position thus established, and gain-
ing information for the Federals by
retaining his footing among the Confed-
erates. Another chief character is an
agent of Napoleon III., working to offer
the Southerners an alliance with the
French on condition of their recognising
Maximilian in Mexico.

Press Notice

GLASGOW HERALD.—"Will well
repay perusal, being full of stirring incidents, while the atmosphere is realistic
to a degree."

EVELYN SHARP

With Illus-

trations by

Charles E.

Brock . .

Crown 8vo.   Gilt top

Price 6s.

The Youngest Girl in the School

By

Evelyn Sharp

Author of "The Making of a Schoolgirl," " Wymps," etc.

Miss Sharp treats her girls' school in very much the same spirit of frank realism as the author of *Tom Brown* treated Rugby, and conveys in the same way her ideal of what the head of a school should be like.

Some Press Opinions

SPECTATOR.—"The story shows a wholesome and humorous grasp of life, and the book, which is in its primary intention a book for girls, may be read with amusement by older people."

PALL MALL GAZETTE.—"The book is an unusual one, bringing humour and sympathy to bear on a part of life which has not often been so treated. It is unusual and unusually nice, and may be very heartily commended to the reading of girls."

ST. JAMES'S GAZETTE.—"Interesting and amusing. . . . 'Babs' is delightful, and withal a very clever and sympathetic piece of drawing. . . . Would make an excellent Christmas present for young ladies of from ten to sixteen or so."

MERWIN & WEBSTER

The Authors

of "The Short-

Line War" .

Crown 8vo.   Gilt top

Price 6s.

"Calumet 'K'"

By

S. Merwin & H. K. Webster

Authors of "The Short-Line War"

"Calumet 'K'" is a two-million-bushel grain-elevator, and this story tells how Charlie Bannon built it "against time." Bannon says of himself, "I've been working like an all-the-year-round blast-furnace ever since I could creep." He has looked for a chance to be quiet, "since I was twelve years old." But when this chance finally comes, Bannon, with the girl who has consented to share his restless life, yields to habit, and the dream of a cosy farm is forgotten in the stress of new work. The elevator must be done by December 31. There are persons that are interested in delaying the work, and it is these, as well as the "walking delegates," that Bannon has to fight. The story of how they tried to "tie up" the lumber two hundred miles away, and of how he outwitted them and "just carried it off," shows the kind of thing that Bannon can do best. In spite of his temptation to brag—he was for two years a "chief wrecker" on the Grand Trunk, and has many stories to tell—Bannon is one of the men without whom American commerce could not get on.

Mr. Henry Kitchell Webster and Mr. Samuel Merwin have discovered in the exciting movements of trade and finance a field of fiction hitherto overlooked by American writers, but containing a great wealth of romance.

MAURICE HEWLETT

"A fine and original romance."

—Frederic Harrison . . . .

Crown 8vo. Gilt top

Price 6s.

Richard Yea-and-Nay

By

Maurice Hewlett

Some Press Opinions

MR. FREDERIC HARRISON in *THE FORTNIGHTLY REVIEW* for January :—"Such historic imagination, such glowing colour, such crashing speed, set forth in such pregnant form carry me away spell-bound. . . . *Richard Yea-and-Nay* is a fine and original romance."

DAILY TELEGRAPH.—" The story carries us along as though throughout we were galloping on strong horses. There is a rush and fervour about it all which sweeps us off our feet till the end is reached and the tale is done. It is very clever, very spirited."

DAILY NEWS.—"A memorable book, over-long, over-charged with scenes of violence, yet so informed with the atmosphere of a tumultuous time, written with a pen so vital and picturesque, that it is the reader's loss to skip a page."

DAILY CHRONICLE.—"We have to thank Mr. Hewlett for a most beautiful and fascinating picture of a glorious time. . . We know of no other writer to-day who could have done it."

MAURICE HEWLETT

Fifty-third Thousand in England and America

Crown 8vo. Gilt top

Price 6s.

The Forest Lovers

A Romance

Some Press Opinions

SPECTATOR.—" *The Forest Lovers* is no mere literary *tour de force*, but an uncommonly attractive romance, the charm of which is greatly enhanced by the author's excellent style."

DAILY TELEGRAPH.—"Mr. Maurice Hewlett's *Forest Lovers* stands out with conspicuous success. . . . He has compassed a very remarkable achievement . . . . For nearly four hundred pages he carries us along with him with unfailing resource and artistic skill, while he unrolls for us the course of thrilling adventures, ending, after many tribulations, in that ideal happiness towards which every romancer ought to wend his tortuous way. . . . There are few books of this season which achieve their aim so simply and whole-heartedly as Mr. Hewlett's ingenious and enthralling romance."

BERTHA RUNKLE

First American Edition

100,000

Copies . . .

Crown 8vo. Gilt top

Price 6s.

The Helmet of Navarre

By

Bertha Runkle

Some Press Opinions

THE SPEAKER.—"Among the three or four really good novels of romantic adventure that have been published this season."

LITERARY WORLD.—"The book will be the pleasure of countless readers this summer."

THE QUEEN.—"The story moves with unflagging spirit."

OXFORD CHRONICLE.—"A cordial welcome must be extended to a novelist whose brilliant work is at least new to readers on this side of the Atlantic. To have produced a story which at once takes rank with the best work of Stanley Weyman, Marion Crawford, Egerton Castle, Henry Seton Merriman, and Anthony Hope, is a literary *tour de force*, on which we may well congratulate the author."

THE OUTLOOK.—"A taking romance, briskly written."

BEULAH MARIE DIX

"A fine picture of Colonial America".

Crown 8vo. Gilt top

Price 6s.

The Making of Christopher Ferringham

Some Press Opinions

ST. JAMES'S GAZETTE.—"A brave tale and stirring."

PALL MALL GAZETTE.—"A most excellent and stirring tale. . . . The character-drawing of Christopher is a masterpiece of literary workmanship."

DAILY GRAPHIC.—"An admirable book, well constructed, and written in a strain of bold realism."

DAILY EXPRESS.—"Miss Dix brings action before the mind's eye most vividly. We hear the smacking blows, the sibilant curses, the thuds of defeat; there is hearty goodwill in the writing, it is virile, unaffected, true."

LITERATURE.—"A fine picture of colonial America. . . . The book is clever and conscientious."

THE SCOTSMAN.—"In his unmade state, Christopher Ferringham is a delightful person. . . . The book is thoroughly good reading from the first page to the last."

DATE DUE

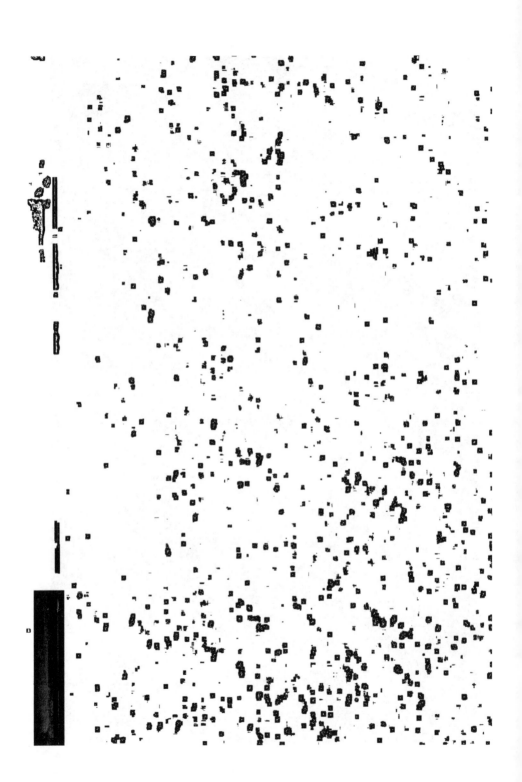

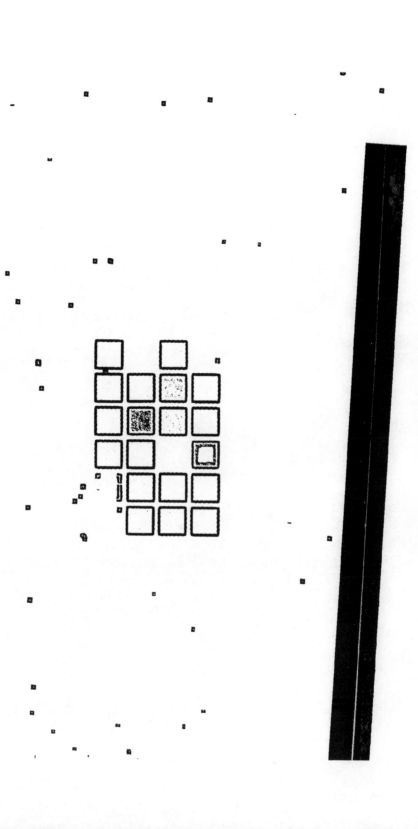

Lightning Source UK Ltd.
Milton Keynes UK
UKHW020817091222
413648UK00007B/975